Linguistic Linked Data

Philipp Cimiano • Christian Chiarcos •
John P. McCrae • Jorge Gracia

Linguistic Linked Data

Representation, Generation and Applications

 Springer

Philipp Cimiano
Semantic Computing Group
Bielefeld University
Bielefeld
Germany

Christian Chiarcos
Angewandte Computerlinguistik
Goethe-University
Frankfurt am Main
Germany

John P. McCrae (iD)
Insight Centre for Data Analytics
National University of Ireland
Galway, Ireland

Jorge Gracia
Aragon Institute of Engineering
Research (I3A)
University of Zaragoza
Zaragoza, Spain

ISBN 978-3-030-30227-6   ISBN 978-3-030-30225-2   (eBook)
https://doi.org/10.1007/978-3-030-30225-2

This Springer imprint is published by the registered company Springer Nature Switzerland AG.
The registered company address is: Gewerbestrasse 11, 6330 Cham, Switzerland

Preface

The four authors of this book have a long-standing collaboration that goes back to the year 2009 at least, when the project Monnet funded by the European Commission started. This was one of the first EC-funded projects concerned with investigating the relationship between language and ontologies and linked data in particular. Within this project, in which Jorge Gracia, John McCrae and Philipp Cimiano were direct collaborators, crucial foundations for the work described in this book were laid. On the one hand, the lemon model was developed as a direct result of the Monnet project. Further, seminal work on how to localize ontologies into multiple languages was carried out as part of the Monnet project. Within the LIDER project, also funded by the European Commission subsequently to Monnet, Jorge Gracia, John McCrae and Philipp Cimiano collaborated on developing guidelines for the modelling, generation and publication of linguistic linked data. Since January 2019, these activities are being continued in the context of the H2020 project 'Prêt-à-LLOD[1]: Ready-to-use Multilingual Linked Language Data for Knowledge Services across Sectors', now involving all authors of this book and with a focus on the practical application of linguistic linked data technologies.

Independently of the line of work pursued within Monnet and LIDER, applications of linked data and semantic technologies to language resources and language technology have been developed in various other projects around this time. Most notably, this includes large-scale coordinated research actions, e.g. a project on 'Sustainability of Linguistic Data' funded by the German Research Foundation as a collaborative effort between three Collaborative Research Centres situated in Tübingen, Hamburg and Berlin/Potsdam, respectively. Out of this context, Christian Chiarcos began to apply semantic technologies, and in particular the ontology web language (OWL), to model linguistic annotations since 2005, and annotated corpora since 2009.

---

[1]The authors acknowledge funding by the European Commission under H2020 project Prêt-à-LLOD under grant agreement 825182.

These and related efforts by interested scholars and applicants of language resources and semantic technologies increasingly converged with the foundation of the Open Linguistics Working Group (OWLG), founded in October 2010, with Christian Chiarcos as one of its founding members, and the development of the Linguistic Linked Open Data (LLOD) cloud that grew out of this working group since early 2011. Around the same time, in July 2011, the Working Group on the Ontology-Lexicon Interface (Ontolex) was founded, with the Ontolex-lemon model as its output, and remarkable impact on the digital edition of lexical resources since then. With increasing interest in linked data beyond open resources, the term 'linguistic linked data' emerged as a generalization over 'linguistic linked open data'. Throughout this book, both terms are used interchangeably, and albeit the technology not being restricted to open resources, many prominent data sets are indeed available under open licenses.

The following four publications can be regarded as the seminal publications that defined the linguistic linked data paradigm:

- Christian Chiarcos, Sebastian Nordhoff, and Sebastian Hellmann. Linked Data in Linguistics. Representing and Connecting Language Data and Language Metadata. Springer, Heidelberg, 2012.
- Christian Chiarcos, Steven Moran, Pablo N. Mendes, Sebastian Nordhoff, and Richard Littauer. Building a Linked Open Data cloud of linguistic resources: Motivations and developments. In Iryna Gurevych and Jungi Kim (eds.), The People's Web Meets NLP. Collaboratively Constructed Language Resources. Springer, Heidelberg, 2013.
- Christian Chiarcos, John McCrae, Philipp Cimiano, and Christiane Fellbaum. Towards open data for linguistics: Lexical Linked Data. In Alessandro Oltramari, Piek Vossen, Lu Qin, and Eduard Hovy (eds.), New Trends of Research in Ontologies and Lexical Resources. Springer, Heidelberg, 2013.
- Jorge Gracia, Elena Montiel-Ponsoda, Philipp Cimiano, Asunción Gómez-Pérez, Paul Buitelaar, and John McCrae. Challenges for the multilingual Web of Data. Journal of Web Semantics, vol. 11, pp. 63–71. Elsevier B.V., 2012.

Since these seminal publications, a number of workshops have been organized on the topic including the well-known series of workshops on *Linked Data in Linguistics*, the series of workshops on the *Multilingual Semantic Web* as well as the *Summer Datathon on Linguistic Linked Open Data* series of summer schools, and the conference series on *Language, Data and Knowledge* (LDK). The authors of this book have all been key players in the organization of all these events.

The ideas developed in the above-mentioned initial collaborations roughly 10 years ago have been spreading at an initially unimagined way. What started as a rather naive and idealistic effort of improving the state of affairs concerning data reuse and interoperability, has turned into a standard approach for data sharing in computational linguistics, lexicography, typology, language research and digital humanities. The vocabularies that have emerged as part of the working groups related to the linguistic linked data paradigm, such as lemon, are widely used for the publication of language and linguistic resources.

The authors of this book deeply enjoy the uptake that their ideas have received. For all of us, it has been a big honour to be able to work together with so many people on the foundations of linguistic linked data.

This book is thus a result of the efforts of a whole community that has firmly pushed the ideas of sharing and reusing linguistic resources further and has worked out many details of the linked data approach in linguistics. This book would not have been possible without all these community efforts. The authors thus would like to dedicate this book to this passionate community that has vigorously believed in the ideas of open science and reused open standards and formats to improve the affairs of data sharing, publishing and reuse in linguistics by adopting the linked data principles put forth by Tim Berners-Lee. The linguistic linked data program is showing clear fruits by now, in that in using linked data principles to publish linguistic datasets and language resources, it is demonstrably easier to find and reuse datasets.

We hope you like this book!

Bielefeld, Germany   Philipp Cimiano
Frankfurt, Germany   Christian Chiarcos
Galway, Ireland   John P. McCrae
Zaragoza, Spain   Jorge Gracia
June 2019

Contents

Part V   Conclusions

Acronyms and Abbreviations

This section lists the set of acronyms and abbreviations used in this book.

BioNLP	Biomedical Natural Language Processing
CC(-BY)(-NC)(-SA)(-ND)	Creative Commons (Attribution) (NonCommercial) (ShareAlike) (NonDerivative)
CCR	CLARIN Concept Registry
CIDOC	(French) *Comité International pour la Documentation*
CIDOC CRM	CIDOC Conceptual Reference Model
CL	Computational Linguistics
CLARIN	Common Language Resources and Technology Infrastructure
CoNLL	Conference on Computational Natural Language Learning
CSV	Comma-Separated Values
CTS	Canonical Text Service
cURL	Client for URLs/Curl URL Request Library
DC	Dublin Core
DCAT	Data Catalogue Vocabulary
DC-Terms	Dublin Core Terms
DH	Digital Humanities
DTD	Document Type Definition
DTS	Distributed Text Services
ELRA	European Language Resource Association
FAIR	Findable, Accessible, Interoperable and Re-usable
HTML	Hypertext Markup Language
HTTP	Hypertext Transfer Protocol
HTTPS	Hypertext Transfer Protocol Secure
ID	Identifier
IOB(ES)	Inside-outside-beginning-end-start format
IRI	Internationalized Resource Identifier

ISO	International Standards Organization
JSON	JavaScript Object Notation
JSON-LD	JavaScript Object Notation for Linked Data
KOS	Knowledge organization system
LAF	Linguistic Annotation Framework
LD	Linked data
LDC	Linguistic Data Consortium
lemon	Lexicon model for ontologies
LLD	Linguistic linked data
LLOD	Linguistic linked open data
LMF	Lexical Markup Framework
LOD	Linked Open Data
LOV	Linked Open Vocabularies
LR	Language resource
NER	Named entity recognition
NLP	Natural language processing
NIF	NLP Interchange Format
OLAC	Open Language Archives Community
OWL	Web Ontology Language
OWL (2) DL	Web Ontology Language (version 2), Description Logics
OWLG	Open Linguistics Working Group
POS	Part of speech
RDF	Resource Description Framework
RDFa	RDF in attributes
RDFS	RDF Schema
RST	Rhetorical Structure Theory
SGML	Standard Generalized Markup Language
SKOS	Simple Knowledge Organization System
SKOS-XL	Simple Knowledge Organization System eXtension for Labels
SPARQL	SPARQL Protocol and RDF Query Language
SRL	Semantic role labelling
SW	Semantic Web
TBX	TermBase eXchange format
TEI	Text Encoding Initiative
TSV	Tab-separated values
Turtle	Terse RDF Triple Language
UD	Universal Dependencies
URI	Uniform Resource Identifier
URL	Uniform Resource Locator
URN	Uniform Resource Name
W3C	World Wide Web Consortium
XML	eXtensible Markup Language
XSD	XML Schema Definition

Part I
Preliminaries

Chapter 1
Introduction

Digital language resources, comprising spoken and written material, are key to many fields, including linguistics research, lexicography, typology, the study of minority or extinct languages, but also to the development of machine-learned models for automated natural language processing (NLP).

Thus, many groups and institutions worldwide are active in the creation of language resources, comprising activities such as data collection, transcription of recordings, corpus creation, data annotation, quality control, etc.

The digital language resources that have been created so far and that will be created in the future represent an important cultural asset and treasure that not only allows us to develop NLP solutions or perform linguistic research today, but also to document the status of development of languages worldwide and preserve our way of thinking, our cultural identity, etc.

Language resources are thus an important cultural asset that need not only to be preserved, we need to also make sure that these resources can be reused as much as possible. In particular, a crucial issue is to maximize secondary reuse of language resources, that is ensuring that the data can be used by others for a different purpose than it was originally collected for. However, secondary reuse is in many cases hindered by a number of proprietary choices made by the data collector. Such choices include, for instance, the use of proprietary formats (either because no standard formats are available or because some formats require paying licenses for proprietary software, etc.). Other obstacles for secondary reuse are of a more conceptual nature including choices in data collection or annotation that limit the scope and applicability of the data in other contexts as well as mismatching conceptualizations of phenomena as reflected in annotation schemas. To maximize reuse, as a community we need guiding principles that can be followed when documenting, publishing and processing data.

© Springer Nature Switzerland AG 2020
P. Cimiano et al., *Linguistic Linked Data*,
https://doi.org/10.1007/978-3-030-30225-2_1

1.1   FAIR Principles

Secondary reuse of data is not only a concern within linguistics research. It is an issue that is relevant for any scientific discipline. In fact, the degree to which agreed-upon principles and standards for data management and reuse are available and followed on can be regarded as an indicator of maturity of a scientific discipline.

As a step towards increasing transparency and reproducibility in science, in 2016 a group of researchers around M.D. Wilkinson postulated the so-called FAIR Guiding Principles [1]. The acronym FAIR stands for Findable, Accessible, Interoperable and Re-usable:

- *Findability* implies that data and metadata are assigned globally unique and eternally persistent identifiers, and that the data is accompanied by rich metadata and that data is registered or indexed somewhere where it can be found.
- *Accessibility* implies that (1) data is retrievable by their identifier using an (2) open, free and universally implemented protocol, and (3) the protocol supports authentication and authorization if necessary.
- *Interoperability* implies that the data is described using a formal, accessible, shared and a standard data model to support sharing.
- Finally, *re-usability* implies accurate and relevant attributes, clear licensing and data usage terms and conditions, linking to provenance of data and the adherence to community standards.

The FAIR principles are clearly also relevant for linguistics research and there should be a broad interest in ensuring the FAIR principles for digital language resources to maximize their reuse. However, most of the solutions proposed so far fail on a number of FAIR principles.

1.2   Linked Data as an Opportunity to Realize the FAIR Principles

Language resources (dictionaries, terminologies, corpora, etc.) developed in the fields of corpus linguistics, computational linguistics and natural language processing (NLP) are often encoded in heterogeneous formats and developed in isolation from one another. This makes their discovery, reuse and integration for both the development of NLP tools and daily linguistic research a difficult and cumbersome task. In order to alleviate such an issue and to enhance interoperability of language resources on the Web, a community of language technology experts and practitioners has started adopting techniques coming from the field of linked data (LD). The LD paradigm emerged as a series of best practices and principles for exposing, sharing and connecting data on the Web [2].

The LD principles state that unique resource identifiers (URIs) should be used to name things in a way that allows people to look them up, to get useful information for each of these resources and to discover related resources or entities. The four linked data principles are the following:

1. Use URIs as (unique) names for things.
2. Use HTTP URIs so that people can look up those names.
3. When someone looks up a URI, provide useful information, using Web standards such as the Resource Description Framework (RDF) and SPARQL.
4. Include links to other URIs, so that they can discover more things.

The first principle means that we assign a unique identifier (URI, [3]) to every element of a resource, i.e. each entry in a lexicon, each document in a corpus, every token in a corpus and to each data category that we use for annotation purposes. The benefit is that this makes elements, categories and annotations uniquely and globally identifiable in an unambiguous fashion. The second principle entails that any agent wishing to obtain information about the resource can contact the corresponding web server and retrieve this information using a well-established protocol (HTTP) that also supports different 'views' on the same resource. That is, computer agents might request a machine-readable format, while web browsers might request a human-readable and browsable view of this information as HTML. The third principle requires the use of standardized, and thus inter-operable data models for representing data (RDF, [4]) and querying linked data (SPARQL, [5]). The fourth principle fosters the creation of a network of language resources where objects of linguistic interest (words, senses, annotations) are connected to each other via links that express equivalence, relatedness, etc. and are linked to data categories defined in data category repositories such as ISOCat.

LD emerged in the context of the Semantic Web, an extension of the Web in which information is given *'well-defined' meaning, 'better enabling computers and people to work in cooperation'* [6]. The LD principles have been applied to transform the current human-readable Web into a 'Web of Data' in which resources are linked across datasets and sites, and where facts and related knowledge are available for consumption by advanced, knowledge-based software agents as well as by humans through suitable interfaces.

The Semantic Web builds on so-called ontology languages, the Web Ontology Language (OWL)[1] in particular, to formally and axiomatically define the vocabulary used to describe data. The data model used to describe data is the Resource Description Framework (RDF),[2] which models data through the central notion of triples (s, p, o) consisting of a subject, a predicate and an object.

We mention below how the LD principles can support the realization of the FAIR principles for language data:

- Findability: First of all, by relying on URIs as globally unique identifiers, LD allows to unambiguously identify a particular data source as well as data element

---

[1]https://www.w3.org/OWL/.
[2]https://www.w3.org/RDF/.

contained in that resource. By relying on standard languages for description of content and metadata used for LD as well as by following the LD principles, language resources can be published in such a way that they can be indexed by semantic search engines and repositories that themselves can expose them in an appropriate fashion for their community members. LD provides mechanisms and vocabulary to describe information about a resource (metadata). This ensures that data can be searched and found more effectively.

- Accessibility: By following standard data models such as RDF and publishing data following the LD principles, homogeneity in data publication and thus data access can be achieved. By dereferencing URIs, people can get direct access to the content described in standard data formats and languages, being able to use standard tools for processing, querying and visualizing the data.
- Interoperability: LD fosters the reuse of existing ontologies and vocabularies and thus creates the basis for interoperability by encouraging the reuse of vocabulary elements existing already. As these vocabulary elements are formally described using ontology languages, this allows one to review and assess whether the meaning is appropriate when reusing the corresponding vocabulary elements, thus reducing ambiguity and making semantic choices transparent. Publishing and describing resources in a semantically non-ambiguous way creates the foundations for interoperability.
- Re-usability: By fostering reuse of semantically well-defined vocabularies and by adherence to standard data formats, LD has the potential to facilitate the reuse of data beyond its primary purpose. LD provides vocabularies for describing provenance information, terms of use and licensing conditions associated with data, a crucial aspect for data reuse.

As a consequence of the above advantages, imagine that for some linguistic study, all relevant datasets can be queried in the same manner for data describing a particular phenomenon under investigation. Such an integrated view over very different datasets is not possible given the current best practices in the management and sharing of language resources.

Given the advantages and the potential of LD for improving the usability and reusability of language and linguistic resources, since 10 years a research community has emerged that is studying how the LD principles can be applied to the modelling of linguistic data and language resources, taking into account the peculiarities of this domain of application. The community has been very active in developing vocabularies, best practices, tools, but also in understanding the benefits of the LD approach as well as systematizing the field.

As one aspect of this systematization effort, the community has developed early on the so-called *Linguistic Linked Open Data (LLOD) cloud*,[3] which is a depiction of the growing ecosystem of semantically connected linguistic datasets on the Web. The LLOD cloud is a community effort launched by The Open Knowledge Foun-

---

[3]http://linguistic-lod.org/llod-cloud.

dation's Working Group on Open Data in Linguistics (OWLG)[4] [7, 8] as a first step
to bridge the gap between the advances in language technologies, and linguistics
in general, and those taking place in the Semantic Web and artificial intelligence
communities. Its main goal is to promote and track the use of LD in linguistics
and facilitate the access to available language resources. Some recent advancements
in LLD have also been driven by the activities developed within the framework of
international projects such as LIDER,[5] FREME[6] and, more recently, Prêt-à-LLOD,[7]
among others. Workshops, datathons and conferences such as the Multilingual
Semantic Web Workshop,[8] the linked data in Linguistics Workshop (LDL),[9] the
Workshop on Knowledge Extraction and Knowledge Integration (KEKI),[10] the
Summer Datathon on Linguistic Linked Open Data,[11] the Conference on Language,
Data and Knowledge (LDK),[12] the NLP&DBpedia Workshop Series,[13] among
other initiatives, have encouraged interdisciplinary contributions and community
gathering, and provide a perfect scenario to establish new collaborations along these
lines of work.

As the interest of the Semantic Web and computational linguistics communities
in LLD keeps increasing, and successive initiatives and workshops encourage and
discuss their use and their potential benefits, the number of contributions that dwell
on LLD grows rapidly. LD is increasingly being adopted by the computational
linguistics and the digital humanities communities [7, 9–17], and an extensive
number of efforts are now devoted towards the conversion of language resources
to RDF.

This book describes how the LD principles can be applied to modelling language
resources. The first part of this book until Chap. 3 provides foundations for
understanding the remainder of the book. Chapter 2 in particular introduces the data
models, ontology and query languages used as the basis of the Semantic Web and
linked data. Chapter 3 provides a more detailed overview of the Linguistic Linked
Data (LLD) Cloud as mentioned above.

The second part of the book focuses on modelling language resources using
LD principles. Chapter 4 describes how to model lexical resources using Ontolex-
lemon, the lexicon model for ontologies. Chapter 5 describes how to annotate and
address elements of text represented in RDF. While Chap. 6 shows how to model

---

[4]http://linguistics.okfn.org/.

[5]http://lider-project.eu/.

[6]http://www.freme-project.eu/.

[7]http://www.pret-a-llod.eu/.

[8]http://msw4.insight-centre.org/.

[9]http://ldl2018.linguistic-lod.org/.

[10]http://keki2016.linguistic-lod.org/.

[11]http://datathon2017.retele.linkeddata.es/.

[12]http://ldk2017.org/.

[13]http://nlpdbpedia2015.wordpress.com/, http://nlpdbpedia2016.wordpress.com/.

annotations, Chap. 7 describes how to capture metadata of language resources. Chapter 8 shows how to represent linguistic categories and concludes Part II.

In the third part of the book, we describe how language resources can be transformed into LD in Chap. 9. Chapter 10 describes how links can be inferred and added to the data to increase connectivity and linking between different datasets. Chapter 11 discusses how to use LD resources for natural language processing.

The last part of the book, part IV, describes concrete applications of the technologies introduced in this book: that is representing and linking multilingual wordnets (Chap. 12), applications in digital humanities (Chap. 13) and discovery of language resources (Chap. 14).

References

1. M.D. Wilkinson, M. Dumontier, I.J. Aalbersberg, G. Appleton, M. Axton, A. Baak, N. Blomberg, J.W. Boiten, L.B. da Silva Santos, P.E. Bourne et al., The FAIR guiding principles for scientific data management and stewardship. Sci. Data **3**, 160018 (2016)
2. C. Bizer, T. Heath, T. Berners-Lee, Linked data-the story so far. Int. J. Semant. Web Inf. Syst. **14**, 205 (2009)
3. T. Berners-Lee, R. Fielding, L. Masinter, Uniform Resource Identifier (URI): Generic Syntax (RFC 3986). Technical Report W3C (2005), http://www.ietf.org/rfc/rfc3986.txt
4. G. Klyne, J. Carroll, B. McBride, Resource Description Framework (RDF): Concepts and Abstract Syntax. Technical Report W3C Recommendation (2004), http://www.w3.org/TR/2004/REC-rdf-concepts-20040210/
5. S. Harris, A. Seaborne, SPARQL 1.1 query language. W3C recommendation, World Wide Web Consortium (2013)
6. T. Berners-Lee, J. Hendler, O. Lassila et al., The Semantic Web. Sci. Am. **284**(5), 28 (2001)
7. C. Chiarcos, S. Hellmann, S. Nordhoff, The Open Linguistics Working Group of the Open Knowledge Foundation, in *Linked Data in Linguistics* (Springer, Heidelberg, 2012), pp. 153–160
8. J. McCrae, C. Chiarcos, F. Bond, P. Cimiano, T. Declerck, The Open Linguistics Working Group: developing the Linguistic Linked Open Data cloud, in *Proceedings of the 10th Language Resources and Evaluation Conference (LREC)*, Portoroz, 2016, pp. 2435–2441
9. T. Declerck, P. Lendvai, K. Mörth, G. Budin, T. Váradi, Towards linked language data for digital humanities, in *Linked Data in Linguistics* (Springer, Berlin, 2012), pp. 109–116
10. C. Chiarcos, J. McCrae, P. Cimiano, Towards open data for linguistics: linguistic linked data, in *New Trends of Research in Ontologies and Lexical Resources* (Springer, Berlin, 2013), pp. 7–25
11. S. Hellmann, J. Lehmann, S. Auer, M. Brümmer, Integrating NLP using linked data, in *Proceedings of the International Semantic Web Conference (ISWC)* (Springer, Berlin, 2013), pp. 98–113
12. P. Cimiano, J.P. McCrae, T. Gornostay, B. Siemoneit, A. Lagzdins, Linked terminology: applying linked data principles to terminological resources, in *Proceedings of the 4th Biennial Conference on Electronic Lexicography (eLex)* (2015), pp. 1–11
13. J. McCrae, C. Fellbaum, P. Cimiano, Publishing and linking WordNet using lemon and RDF, in *Proceedings of the 3rd Workshop on Linked Data in Linguistics* (2014)
14. T. Flati, R. Navigli, Three birds (in the LLOD cloud) with one stone: BabelNet, Babelfy and the Wikipedia Bitaxonomy, in *Proceedings of SEMANTiCS* (2014)
15. I. El Maarouf, E. Alferov, D. Cooper, Z. Fang, H. Mousselly-Sergieh, H. Wang, The GuanXi network: a new multilingual LLOD for language learning applications, in *Proceedings of the*

2nd Workshop on Natural Language Processing and Linked Open Data (NLP&LOD2) (2015), p. 42

16. M. Villegas, M. Melero, N. Bel, J. Gracia, Leveraging RDF graphs for crossing multiple bilingual dictionaries, in *Proceedings of the 10th Language Resources and Evaluation Conference (LREC)*, Portoroz (2016)

17. E. González-Blanco, G. Del Río, C.I. Martínez Cantón, Linked open data to represent multilingual poetry collections. A proposal to solve interoperability issues between poetic repertoires, in *Proceedings of the 5th Workshop on Linked Data in Linguistics (LDL 2016): Managing, Building and Using Linked Language Resources*, Portoroz (May 2016)

Chapter 2
Preliminaries

Abstract This chapter introduces preliminaries that are essential to follow the content in the remainder of this book. First of all, we introduce the core data model of the Semantic Web and linked data, that is the Resource Description Framework, RDF. This format was designed in the 1990s and its core purpose is to represent data and knowledge in a Web-compatible fashion, taking into account that the Web can be regarded as a network of linked sites. RDF allows one to define networks of connected 'things' rather than a network of connected documents. We briefly introduce the semantics of RDF and also introduce the most popular serialization formats for RDF, that is N-Triples, Turtle, XML and JSON-LD. Glossing over many details, we briefly introduce the Web Ontology Language (OWL) as a vocabulary to describe ontological and terminological knowledge and SPARQL, the query language for RDF and linked data. Finally, we briefly discuss aspects of publishing linked data.

2.1 Introduction

Linked data is the term used to refer to *interlinked* collections of datasets published on the Web. To support publication of datasets and their linking, a number of standards have been developed, in particular by the World Wide Web Consortium (W3C) as part of the effort to provide standards and representation languages for a machine-readable Web in which information is given *'well-defined' meaning*, to *'better enable computers and people to work in cooperation'* (see [1]). Inspired by the fact that the Web is a network/linked graph of documents, the goal of the Semantic Web was not only to talk about 'documents' but also about the 'things' that exist in the world, elevating the latter to objects than one can actually talk about and describe in terms of their relations/connections to other objects that exist as well.

The basic data model behind the Semantic Web and linked data is the *Resource Description Framework* (RDF). As the name suggests, it is a data model that allows to describe resources, mainly via attributes and their relations to other resources. The data model relies on triples (s, p, o) connecting a so-called subject s to an

© Springer Nature Switzerland AG 2020
P. Cimiano et al., *Linguistic Linked Data*,
https://doi.org/10.1007/978-3-030-30225-2_2

object o via predicate (called property in RDF) p. An RDF document is a set of such triples. Alternatively, an RDF document can also be viewed as a directed, labelled graph where s and o correspond to vertices (nodes) and p is the label of an edge connecting node s to node o.

A number of tools and further models have been developed allowing to access, query and manipulate RDF data. For example, the *RDF Schema Language* (RDFS) allows to define further rules to infer additional triples from the data that are not explicitly mentioned in the data. The *Web Ontology Language* (OWL) further extends this reasoning capability allowing for a subset of First-Order Logic statements to be made, following the family of so-called *Description Logics* [2]. For example, one could define rules such as that "The *gender* property of any *Noun*, whose *language* value is *French*, has the value of either *masculine* or *feminine*."

The need to store and query RDF data is of course paramount to its usability. SPARQL, the *SPARQL Protocol and RDF Query Language*, was developed for this purpose in order to provide ways for querying RDF datasets, analogously to the use of SQL in traditional relational databases. Further, as most of the data on the Web is not in RDF, an important task consists in transforming it into RDF. In particular, we will look at the *JSON-LD* data model, which allows JSON documents to be interpreted as RDF documents.

2.2   Resource Description Framework

The Resource Description Framework (RDF) is a standard that was created for the representation of data on the Semantic Web. As mentioned above, an RDF document essentially consists of a set of triples $\langle s, p, o \rangle$, with s being the so-called subject and o being the object of the triple and p being the property relating the subject to the object. Subject and object are so-called *resources* that are typically represented using Uniform Resource Identifiers (URIs), resp. Internationalized Resource Identifiers (IRIs) as standardized by the World Wide Web Consortium.[1]
By using URIs to identify resources, one can uniquely identify the entity denoted by these URIs. It is important to note that URIs as identifiers are global and thus shared across all Web documents existing worldwide. As an exception to using URIs at subject, predicate and object position (predicates are represented by URIs too!), we can use so-called blank nodes at subject and object position. While not totally accurate, for the sake of this book it is sufficient to understand blank nodes as existentially quantified variables, the scope of which is limited to a given RDF document. In contrast, URIs are logically speaking constants that are globally defined. We note that the use of blank nodes is often discouraged for a number of technical reasons (see [3], for instance).

---

[1]The original RDF specification required the use of URIs. RDF 1.1 requires IRIs, instead, that is the internationalized form of URIs with non-ASCII characters are supported.

A URI is a string of the following form [4]:

```
scheme:[//authority]path[?query][#fragment]
```

These are defined as follows

- **Scheme**: The scheme defines the protocol by which the resource may be located; it is usually one of the standard web protocols, e.g. http, https or ftp.
- **Authority:** This typically identifies the server where the resource is available normally of the form user:password@host:port where

  - **User and Password:** These are log-in details for the host. This is generally omitted as most URLs do not require a log-in to access.
  - **Host:** The name of the server that holds the resource either as an IP address or more frequently as a DNS name such as www.example.org.
  - **Port:** The port of the server to use. If omitted it is assumed that this will be the default port for the protocol, e.g. 80 for HTTP.

- **Path:** The scheme-specific locator for the resource. In the case of HTTP URLs, this is the path of the file on the server.
- **Query:** An optional extra path used for the dynamic generation of resources. URIs in RDF should generally not have a query string as resources represent fixed data.
- **Fragment** An identifier for locating the resource within a single file. The fragment is not normally passed to the server, but instead should be resolved by the client as a fragment normally refers to a resource that is a part of a larger document.

In RDF, predicates have a dual role. On the one hand they can be used to describe a subject (resource) by its relation to some other resource (object). The type of relation is then specified by the predicate. In this case the object is another resource denoted by a URI. Predicates can also be used to describe intrinsic properties of subject resources, thus playing the role of attributes. In this case the object can be a (typed) literal, which can be one of the following:

- A **plain literal** is just a (Unicode) string and should be used in limited contexts, i.e. for representing codes and identifiers.
- A **typed literal** has a type, typically from the XML Schema Types [5], although custom values may be defined (see [6]). This can be used for typical data values such as numeric, date and time values. Note that a plain literal is considered to have the XML Schema string type but is not equivalent to a typed literal with this type. This type must be a URI.
- A **Language-tagged literal** allows to add a specification of language by way of a so-called language tag, which is typically a two-letter code from ISO-639-1 [7, 8], but may be any IETF language tag (Sect. 8.2.2).

2.3   Serializing RDF

There are different formats for serializing RDF data so that it can be published on the Web. In this section we briefly present the most important RDF serializations, including N-Triples, Turtle, RDF/XML, RDFa and JSON-LD.

2.3.1   The N-Triples Language

An RDF graph consists of a set of triples that are contained in a single document. There are different possible serializations for RDF data. One of them is the N-Triples syntax, which lists all of the triples in their full form separated by the period symbol ".". URIs are typically given in their full form surrounded by angular brackets, e.g. <http://www.example.org/resource#identifier> and must be absolute (i.e. specify the scheme and path). Blank nodes start with _: and then a label that is an alphanumeric string. Literals are enclosed in double quotes, e.g. ", and may be followed by either a language tag with the @ sign or a datatype with the ^^ symbol followed by a URI (in angular brackets).

An example of RDF data serialized in N-Triples format is given in Fig. 2.1. The example describes an English WordNet synset *06422547-n* that represents the concept book.

This refers to a particular document at a given URI:

```
http://wordnet-rdf.princeton.edu/rdf/id/06422547-n
```

Typing this URI into a browser will allow direct access to the data contained in Princeton WordNet. In the example, we see that the following facts are given

- There is a resource identified by 06422547-n that is denoted by the URL above.
- It has the label "book" in English (en).

```
1   <http://wordnet-rdf.princeton.edu/rdf/id/06422547-n>
2     <http://www.w3.org/2000/01/rdf-schema#label>
3       "book"@en .
4   <http://wordnet-rdf.princeton.edu/rdf/id/06422547-n>
5     <http://wordnet-rdf.princeton.edu/ontology#partOfSpeech>
6       <http://wordnet-rdf.princeton.edu/ontology#noun> .
7   <http://wordnet-rdf.princeton.edu/rdf/id/06422547-n>
8     <http://wordnet-rdf.princeton.edu/ontology#hyponym>
9       <http://wordnet-rdf.princeton.edu/rdf/id/06423235-n> .
10  <http://wordnet-rdf.princeton.edu/rdf/id/06422547-n>
11    <http://wordnet-rdf.princeton.edu/ontology#hypernym>
12      <http://wordnet-rdf.princeton.edu/rdf/id/06423396-n> .
```

Fig. 2.1 A RDF document in N-triples format describing a synset from English WordNet

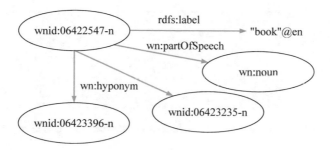

Fig. 2.2 A graphical depiction of the RDF data in Fig. 2.1 document

- Its part-of-speech value is noun.
- It is a hyponym of two resources identified as 06423235-n and 06423396-n. More information about this resource can be discovered by dereferencing the URIs given.

This information is also depicted graphically in Fig. 2.2.

2.3.2   Turtle

While N-Triples is easy to parse, it can be excessively verbose. For this reason, a format called *Turtle* (*Terse RDF format*) was developed. Every document in N-Triples is also a Turtle document, but Turtle is more compact in that it allows for a number of abbreviations to avoid repetitive elements in the triple listing. Firstly, an abbreviation of URIs may be given to avoid repetition of long URIs, e.g.

```
1   @prefix wn: <http://wordnet-rdf.princeton.edu/ontology#> .
```

Then a URI can be given with a prefix followed by a colon and the suffix term without angular brackets, e.g. wn:Synset. In this case the URI is constructed by appending the target of the prefix to the value after the colon, so that the full URI, e.g. http://wordnet-rdf.princeton.edu/ontology#Synset is constructed. Secondly, triples may be separated by colon (;) or comma (,). In the case of separation with a colon, the subject is assumed to be fixed for the next triple and only the predicate and object need to be stated. In the case of a separation with a comma, both the subject and predict are fixed so that only the new object of the next triples needs to be stated. Thirdly, there are some further simplifications; for example, URIs may be given relatively and integers and decimals may be given as literals without quotes. Thus, the data in N-Triples format in Fig. 2.1 could be represented as the data Fig. 2.3 in Turtle.

```
1  @prefix wnid: <http://wordnet-rdf.princeton.edu/rdf/id/> .
2  @prefix wn: <http://wordnet-rdf.princeton.edu/ontology#> .
3  @prefix rdfs: <http://www.w3.org/2000/01/rdf-schema#> .
4
5  wnid:06422547-n rdfs:label "book"@en ;
6     wn:partOfSpeech wn:noun;
7     wn:hyponym wnid:06423235-n , wnid:06423396-n .
```

Fig. 2.3   A simple RDF document in Turtle format for our WordNet synset example

2.3.3   RDF/XML

RDF is also frequently serialized in XML, and this format has been considered the default format for representing RDF. However, the RDF/XML serialization is generally very verbose and difficult for humans to understand. We will resort to the Turtle syntax for the remainder of this book as it is the most readable and concise syntax and thus suitable for a book format. For more details on the RDF/XML serialization, we refer the reader to [9].

2.3.4   RDFa

In addition, it is also possible to embed RDF markup within an HTML page, in an ePub document or in other types of XML documents. This is done with the *RDF in Attributes* (RDFa) specification [10]. In this case the URL for elements on a page may be specified with a special about attribute and the value of properties with the property attribute. In addition, links to URLs may be given with the href property as is usual in HTML. For example, we may give some metadata about WordNet as a resource, including Title, Author and Right as in Fig. 2.4. This generates the triples given in Turtle in Fig. 2.5.

2.3.5   JSON-LD

A recent development has been the recommendation of JSON-LD [11] as a new standard model for the representation of RDF data as JSON (JavaScript Object Notation). This model has a number of advantages:

1. JSON is a widely supported data model for which there exist a large number of libraries that support the interaction, including flexible object mapping libraries such as Jackson, Lift-JSON, etc.
2. JSON is easy for clients to access and has fewer security restrictions than other formats (e.g. XML).

```
1   <div about="http://www.example.com/resource">
2     <ul>
3       <li>Title: <span
4       property="http://purl.org/dc/terms/title">WordNet</span>
5       </li>
6       <li>Author: <span
7       property="http://purl.org/dc/terms/author">Christiane
8       Fellbaum</span>
9       </li>
10      <li>Rights: <a property="http://purl.org/dc/terms/rights"
11      href="https://wordnet.princeton.edu/license-and-commercial-
        use"
12      >WordNet License</a></li>
13    </ul>
14  </div>
```

Fig. 2.4 Using RDFa to include metadata properties about Wordnet as a resource into an HTML document

```
1   @prefix dct: <http://purl.org/dc/terms/> .
2   <http://www.example.com/resource>
3     dct:title "WordNet" ;
4     dct:author "Christiane Fellbaum" ;
5     dct:rights
6        <https://wordnet.princeton.edu/license-and-commercial-use> .
```

Fig. 2.5 The equivalent Turtle RDF code for the RDFa code included in the HTML snippet in Fig. 2.4

```
1   {
2       "label": "book"
3       "hyponym": ["wnid:06423235-n", "wnid:06423396-n"],
4       "definition": {
5           "value": "a written work or composition"
6       }
7   }
```

Fig. 2.6 A simple example of a JSON document describing the synset for book

3. There are robust databases that can easily process, store and query JSON data such as MongoDB.[2]

JSON was designed as a strict subset of JavaScript for use in data exchange. It allows to describe objects in terms of a key/value dictionary whose keys must be string literals and whose values can be any JSON value. The object is denoted with curly braces and a colon between the key and the value. A WordNet synset can be described in JSON as shown in Fig. 2.6.

---

[2]https://www.mongodb.com/.

An *array* is a list of values, each of which is another JSON value. The array is marked with square brackets and items are separated with a comma. The values in an array do not have to be of the same type.

A *literal* is a single value. The most frequent of these values is a string literal, enclosed in double quotes. A numeric literal is given without quotes and must be a valid number in decimal or scientific notation. Finally, the key words `true`, `false` and `null` may be used as literal values.

A JSON document per se does not assign any semantics to the keys used. To solve this problem, JSON-LD was introduced as a way to make the semantics of keys explicit by adding a so-called *context* object to documents that describes how the keys are to be interpreted. Technically, this is achieved by adding a new property to a JSON document named `@context` that specifies the semantics by mapping each key to a URI or to a datatype. Figure 2.7 shows an example of a JSON document with an inline `@context`. The data corresponds to the data in Turtle RDF in Fig. 2.8.

In the context document we see the prefixes `wnid`, `wn` and `rdfs` being defined. A URI is defined for each of the keys of the JSON object. Each of these is associated

```
1   {
2       "@context": {
3           "rdfs": "http://www.w3.org/2000/01/rdf-schema#",
4           "wnid": "http://wordnet-rdf.princeton.edu/rdf/id/",
5           "wn": "http://wordnet-rdf.princeton.edu/ontology#",
6           "label": {
7               "@id": "rdfs:label",
8               "@language": "en"
9           },
10          "hyponym": {
11              "@id": "wn:hyponym",
12              "@type": "@id"
13          },
14          "definition": {
15              "@id": "wn:definition",
16              "@type": "@id"
17          },
18          "value": {
19              "@id": "http://www.w3.org/1999/02/22-rdf-syntax-ns#
                    value",
20              "@language": "en"
21          },
22      },
23      "label": "book"
24      "hyponym": ["wnid:06423235-n", "wnid:06423396-n"],
25      "definition": {
26          "value": "a written work or composition"
27      }
28  }
```

Fig. 2.7 A JSON-LD document with an embedded context

```
1  @prefix wnid: <http://wordnet-rdf.princeton.edu/rdf/id/> .
2  @prefix wn: <http://wordnet-rdf.princeton.edu/ontology#> .
3  @prefix rdfs: <http://www.w3.org/2000/01/rdf-schema#> .
4
5  <> rdfs:label "book"@en ;
6    wn:hyponym wnid:06423235-n, wnid:06423396-n
7    wn:definition [
8        rdf:value "a written work or composition"@en
9    ] .
```

Fig. 2.8 The translation of the JSON-LD document in Fig. 2.7 into Turtle

with a URI by means of the @id property and additionally is associated with a @type or a @language. This determines whether the value associated with this key is a URI or a literal. The datatype properties are assigned a language tag so that the language of the data can be made explicit.

The context document does not need to be provided in full with every document. Instead, the URI of the context can be given as the value of the @context key or alternatively can be provided by the header of the JSON request by means of the Link header.

2.4 RDF Semantics, RDFS and OWL

In this section we briefly describe how the semantics of RDF is defined. We also introduce RDF Schema as well as the Web Ontology Language (OWL).

2.4.1 RDF Semantics

RDF has a model-theoretic semantics that allows to interpret the vocabulary with respect to a model. An interpretation I of a vocabulary V consists of:

- IR, a non-empty set of resources
- IP, a subset of IR, corresponding to the properties
- LV, a subset of IR, corresponding to the literal values

Further, the interpretation is defined by a number of functions:

- I_S, a function mapping URIs from V into IR
- I_L, a function mapping typed literals from V into IR
- I_{EXT}, a function mapping properties from IP into $2^{(IR \times IR)}$ (i.e. to a set of pairs of resources)

The interpretation of the vocabulary is now defined as follows.

- A URI is interpreted via the function I_S: $I(u) = I_S(u)$
- A literal is interpreted as its own value: $I("s") = s$,
- A language-tagged literal is interpreted formally as the pair of value and language tag: $I("s"@l) = (s, l)$
- A typed literal is interpreted by the mapping I_L into the subset of literal values: $I("s"\char`^\char`^t) = I_L(s)$

This allows to formulate a notion of truth of a triple under an interpretation I as follows: a triple (s,p,o) is true under an interpretation I if and only if s, p, and o are in the vocabulary V and the pair of the interpretation of s and o is in the extension of p, i.e.

$$I((s,p,o)) = \text{true} \quad \text{iff} \quad (I(s), I(o)) \in I_{EXT}(I(p))$$

An RDF graph G is true if and only if every triple contained in the graph is true, i.e.

$$I(G) = \text{true} \quad \text{iff} \quad \text{for all } t \in G : I(t) = \text{true}$$

On this basis one can define an entailment relation between RDF graphs as follows: An RDF graph G_1 entails an RDF graph G_2 if and only if for every interpretation I for which $I(G_1) = \text{true}$, it is also the case that $I(G_2) = \text{true}$.

The RDF semantics defines a calculus that allows to infer new triples from existing triples by using entailment rules of the following form:

> Existing RDF triples
>
> ─────────────────────
>
> Entailed RDF Triples

We give two examples for RDF entailment rules:

- Every p in a triple (s,p,o) is an RDF Property:

```
s p o .
```
─────────────────────────
```
p rdf:type rdf:Property .
```

- rdf:type is a special type of Property:

─────────────────────────
```
rdf:type rdf:type rdf:Property .
```

2.4.2 RDF Schema

RDF Schema formally provides a data-modelling vocabulary for RDF data. Most importantly, RDF Schema introduces the notion of classes, subclasses and subproperties on top of RDF. Classes in RDFS are organized into hierarchies by means of the `rdfs:subClassOf` property and a URI in RDF may be said to be a member of a class using the `rdf:type` property. Classes can also be used to indicate the so-called *domain* and *range* of a property, that is constraints on the types of entities that can occur at subject and object position of a predicate. For instance, we might specify that the `author` property is defined for artworks as subject and persons as objects. The property `hyponym` is defined for synsets both at subject and object position. In RDFS, the domain and range are inferred but do not act as restriction on the values that a property can have as its subject or object. That is, we do not require that every object of the `author` property is explicitly typed as a `Person`. Instead, the RDFS semantics would infer that every object of the `author` property is of type `Person`. RDFS also provides some support for building collections of data of a fixed length by supporting linked lists, bags and sets.

Consequently, the interpretation function is extended to accommodate classes by defining a function I_{CEXT} which assigns resources to sets of resources: I_{CEXT} : $IR \to 2^{(IR)}$.

The set of elements of a class, that is its **extension**, can be defined as follows:

$$I_{CEXT}(c) = \{x \mid (x, c) \in I_{EXT}(I(\texttt{rdf:type}))\}$$

Here are some examples for RDFS entailment rules:

- If predicate p has domain c, then from (x,p,y) it follows that x is of type c:

      p rdfs:domain c .
      x p y .
      ───────────────────
      x rdf:type c .

- If predicate p has range c, then from (x,p,y) it follows that y is of type c:

      p rdfs:range c .
      x p y .
      ───────────────────
      y rdf:type c .

- If c is a subclass of c', then every x that is of type c is also of type c':

      c rdfs:subClassOf c' .
      x rdf:type c .
      ───────────────────
      x rdf:type c' .

- If (x, p, y) holds and p is a subproperty of p' then (x,p',y) also holds:

```
x p y
p rdfs:subPropertyOf p' .
```

```
x p' y .
```

- The subProperty predicate is transitive:

```
p1 rdfs:subPropertyOf p2 .
p2 rdfs:subPropertyOf p3 .
```

```
p1 rdfs:subPropertyOf p3 .
```

Giving the above rules, on the basis of the following triples:

```
wnid:06422547-n wn:mero_part wnid:06356501-n .

wn:mero_part rdfs:subPropertyOf wn:mero .
wn:mero rdfs:domain ontolex:LexicalConcept ;
  rdfs:range ontolex:LexicalConcept .

ontolex:LexicalConcept rdfs:subClassOf skos:Concept
```

we could among others infer the additional triples:

```
wnid:06422547-n rdf:type rdfs:Resource .
wnid:06422547-n wn:mero wnid:06356501-n .
wnid:06422547-n rdf:type ontolex:LexicalConcept .
wnid:06422547-n rdf:type skos:Concept .
```

For a more complete and accurate description of RDF and RDFS semantics, the reader is referred to the official document by Hayes describing the semantics of RDF [12].

2.4.3   Web Ontology Language (OWL)

From a logical point of view, RDF has a limited expressibility, so that the domain knowledge that can be axiomatized is limited. For this purpose, the Web Ontology language (OWL) has been developed as a more expressive language to encode ontological/world knowledge by way of logical axioms. OWL builds on a family of logics representing fragments of first order-logic known as description logics (DLs) [2]). In this section we provide a brief description of OWL; readers interested in more details should consult Allemang et al. [13].

OWL provides a logical vocabulary allowing to specify composite classes that are defined compositionally on the basis of given primitive or atomic classes and allows to specify logical/subsumption relationships between classes. A summary of the most important language constructions for defining complex/compositive classes is

Table 2.1 The syntax and key constructs of OWL

RDF property	DL syntax	Manchester syntax	Example
subClassOf	$C \sqsubseteq D$	C SubClassOf D	Cat SubClassOf Animal
equivalentClass	$C \equiv D$	C EquivalentTo D	Cat EquivalentTo FelisCatus
disjointWith	$C \sqcap D = \perp$	C DisjointWith D	Cat DisjointWith Dog
intersectionOf	$C \sqcap D$	C AND D	Cat AND Pet
unionOf	$C \sqcup D$	C OR D	Cat OR Human
complementOf	$\neg C$	NOT C	NOT Cat
oneOf	$\{a\} \sqcup \{b\}$	{a, b}	{Smoky, Tiddles}
someValuesFrom	$\exists R.C$	R SOME C	eats SOME Food
allValuesFrom	$\forall R.C$	R ONLY C	eats ONLY CatFood
minCardinality	$\geq N R$	R MIN N	whiskers MIN 6
maxCardinality	$\leq N R$	R MAX N	legs MAX 4
cardinality	$= N R$	R EXACTLY 1	heads EXACTLY 1
hasValue	$\exists R\{a\}$	R VALUE a	scientificName VALUE "Felis Catus"

given in Table 2.1, where the name of the RDF property, the standard logical symbol as well as the so-called Manchester syntax is given [14]. Firstly it is possible to define classes as being the intersection, union or complement of given classes. For instance, we can describe the class of FrenchNouns as being the intersection of those things that are French words and that are either masculine or feminine:

$$\text{FrenchNoun} \equiv \text{FrenchWord} \sqcap (\text{MasculineNoun} \sqcup \text{FeminineNoun})$$

The equivalent to this axiom in first-order logic would be:

$$\forall x \; FrenchNoun(x) \leftrightarrow FrenchWord(x) \wedge (MasculineNoun(x) \vee FeminineNoun(x))$$

Or alternatively in Manchester Syntax "FrenchNoun EquivalentTo FrenchWord AND (MasculineNoun OR FeminineNoun)". We can also define classes via the relationships they have with other classes. For instance, we might define that a word occurring in a French sentence is a necessarily a French word, or in OWL:

$$\text{FrenchSentence} \sqsubseteq \forall \; inSentence.FrenchWord$$

The equivalent to this axiom in first-order logic would be:

$$\forall x, y \; FrenchSentence(x) \wedge inSentence(x, y) \rightarrow FrenchWord(y)$$

We could also say that every word has a part of speech by the following axiom:

$$\text{Word} \sqsubseteq \exists\, hasPOS.POS$$

Or equivalently in first-order logic:

$$\forall x\ Word(x) \rightarrow \exists y\ hasPOS(x, y) \wedge POS(y)$$

Similarly, we may also put restrictions on the number of values a property can have, e.g. specifying that a word has exactly one lemma:

$$\text{Word} \equiv\equiv 1\ lemma$$

Axioms as the above that encode specific domain knowledge (e.g. in the domain of French words) can be used to infer new triples or validate existing RDF documents beyond the standard inference rules defined in RDF and RDF Schema, providing a higher level of expressivity to define axioms that should always be enforced.

In many cases, inferences require that we explicitly model the so-called disjointness of classes as per default classes are not disjoint in OWL. For example, the following four axioms state that the classes corresponding to masculine, feminine and neuter nouns are pairwise disjoint:

$$\text{MasculineNoun} \sqcap \text{FeminineNoun} \equiv \bot$$

$$\text{FeminineNoun} \sqcap \text{NeuterNoun} \equiv \bot$$

$$\text{MasculineNoun} \sqcap \text{NeuterNoun} \equiv \bot$$

$$\models\quad \text{FrenchNoun} \sqcap \text{NeuterNoun} \equiv \bot$$

Such disjointness axioms would allow us to deduce that a noun cannot be both a masculine and feminine noun, for instance, and thus help to ensure validity of data.

2.5 The SPARQL Query Language

SPARQL is the de facto standard language for querying RDF data. It allows to define projection, selection, aggregation, etc. operations on RDF graphs. The most recent version is SPARQL 1.1. [15] and allows also to update and delete data by means of the SPARQL Update Language. In this section we introduce SPARQL with a few examples only.

The basic form of a SPARQL query is similar to an SQL query. A SPARQL query consists of a SELECT part selecting variables to be bound in a query result, thus acting as a projection. These query variables are typically marked by a question mark. The body of a query consists of a set of triple patterns that implement a filter

```
1  SELECT ?label WHERE {
2    <http://wordnet-rdf.princeton.edu/rdf/id/06422547-n>
3      <http://www.w3.org/2000/01/rdf-schema#label>
4        ?label .
5  } LIMIT 10
```

Fig. 2.9 A simple example of a SPARQL query for retrieving the label of a given WordNet synset

```
1  PREFIX rdfs: <http://www.w3.org/2000/01/rdf-schema#> .
2  PREFIX wordnet: <http://wordnet-rdf.princeton.edu/rdf/id>
3  SELECT ?x WHERE {
4    ?x a wordnet:Synset .
5    ?x rdfs:label "book" .
6  } LIMIT 10
```

Fig. 2.10 An example of a SPARQL query using prefixes for retrieving all the synsets with the label "book"

```
1  PREFIX rdfs: <http://www.w3.org/2000/01/rdf-schema#> .
2  SELECT ?label WHERE {
3    <http://www.example.org/resource#ex1>
4      rdfs:label ?label .
5    FILTER langMatches(lang(?label), "en")
6  } LIMIT 10
```

Fig. 2.11 An example of a SPARQL query using a filter to retrieve all labels in English

on the data in the sense of specifying substructures that the data needs to match in order to bind elements of the matching structure to query variables. The syntax for these triple patterns is strongly related to Turtle.

For example, we may retrieve all labels for a given resource, i.e. for the synset denoted by the URI http://wordnet-rdf.princeton.edu/rdf/id/06422547-n as in the following SPARQL query in Fig. 2.9 below.

It is possible to limit the number of results using the LIMIT and OFFSET keywords and it is generally recommended that this is done when querying public endpoints. The syntax for declaring prefixes is similar to the syntax used in Turtle. The above query with prefixes would look as shown in Fig. 2.10.

One can add further filters, e.g. requesting only English labels for instance, as shown in the query in Fig. 2.11.

Note that filters may slow queries as the repository generally must first return all matching values and then apply the filter.

In addition to SELECT, there are three further types of queries that are supported by SPARQL:

- **ASK**: Returns true if there are any matches to the pattern, or false otherwise
- **CONSTRUCT**: Builds another RDF graph based on the results of the query
- **DESCRIBE**: Returns all facts about a resource in a given repository

This provides only a very brief overview of the features of SPARQL; for more details, the interested reader is referred to the SPARQL 1.1. overview by Harris et al. [15].

2.5.1 Publishing Data on the Web

Linked data builds on the assumption that resources are available and retrievable by resolving the corresponding URI. For example, information about the resource http://wordnet-rdf.princeton.edu/rdf/id/06422547-n should be retrievable from this very URL. The returned information should consist of triples where this resource is subject, but also triples where the resource in question is in object position. The latter triples are typically called *backlinks*. In addition, further triples relevant for the description of the resource can be returned as well.

When publishing data as linked data, content negotiation should be supported, allowing to retrieve different views of the data. The view that one wants to obtain can be specified as a parameter in a HTTP request. Using the unix tool *cURL*[3] tool, we may resolve a resource and get back information in Turtle by the following command:

```
$ curl -H "Accept: text/turtle"
  http://linguistic.linkeddata.es/data/id/apertium/lexiconAN/
    anejo-adj-an
```

Some resources may use redirects to implement content negotiation, such as done in DBpedia. For example, the following command produces no results:

```
$ curl -H "Accept: text/turtle" \
  http://dbpedia.org/resource/Ireland
```

If we inspect the headers we can see that DBpedia instead redirects us to a single path as in this following simplified example:

```
$ curl -H "Accept: text/turtle" -I \
  http://dbpedia.org/resource/Ireland
Content-Type: text/turtle; qs=0.7
...
Vary: negotiate,accept
Alternates: {"/data/Ireland.atom" ...
Location: http://dbpedia.org/data/Ireland.ttl
```

This informs us about the fact that the data in the requested format is available at http://dbpedia.org/data/Ireland.ttl. In addition, the headers returned give us alternate locations (under `Alternates`) and include the `Vary` header, which informs any web caches that this resource may be different based on the provided `Accept` value.

---

[3]https://curl.haxx.se/.

If we add the -L tag to the cURL command, then both URLs resolve even if they have been redirected, e.g.

```
$ curl -H "Accept: text/turtle" -L \
  http://dbpedia.org/resource/Ireland
```

It is also highly recommended that any linked data returns multiple views in RDF/XML, Turtle, N-Triples and a "human-readable" view in HTML. In order to support the implementation of this functionality by content negotiation, there are a number of tools for hosting data, including Pubby,[4] Yuzu[5] and LODview.[6]

2.6   Summary and Further Reading

This chapter has covered the basics of RDF, RDFS, OWL, SPARQL and linked data publishing. A more comprehensive guide is given by [13], which covers the data models and vocabularies in more detail than it is possible in the scope of this book. The details of the standards covered here are available in the corresponding W3C Recommendations and the reader may refer to these for more details. In particular:

- **RDF:** The RDF Primer gives a good overview of the basic RDF techniques [16].
- **Turtle:** Details of the Turtle format are fully described in the W3C Recommendation [17].
- **SPARQL:** A good introductory tutorial for SPARQL is available from data.world.[7]
- **RDFS/OWL:** The OWL Primer gives a strong overview of reasoning techniques that can be applied to RDF documents [18].
- **JSON-LD:** The JSON-LD Primer [19] gives a good overview of the JSON-LD data model. In addition, the CSV-on-the-Web [20] model allows for tabular data to be understood as RDF using similar principles to the existing model.

References

1. T. Berners-Lee, J. Hendler, O. Lassila et al., The Semantic Web. Sci. Am. **284**(5), 28 (2001)
2. F. Baader, D. Calvanese, D. McGuinness, P. Patel-Schneider, D. Nardi, *The Description Logic Handbook: Theory, Implementation and Applications* (Cambridge University Press, Cambridge, 2003)

---

[4]http://wifo5-03.informatik.uni-mannheim.de/pubby/.

[5]https://github.com/jmccrae/yuzu.

[6]https://github.com/dvcama/LodView.

[7]https://docs.data.world/tutorials/sparql/.

3. R. Cyganiak, Blank nodes considered harmful (2011), http://richard.cyganiak.de/blog/2011/03/blank-nodes-considered-harmful/
4. T. Berners-Lee, R. Fielding, L. Masinter, Uniform Resource Identifier (URI): Generic Syntax. RFC 3986, RFC Editor (2005), https://www.rfc-editor.org/rfc/rfc3986.txt
5. D. Peterson, S. Gao, A. Malhotra, C.M. Sperberg-McQueen, H.S. Thompson, W3C XML Schema Definition Language (XSD) 1.1 Part 2: Datatypes. W3C recommendation, World Wide Web Consortium (2012)
6. P.V. Biron, A. Malhotra, XML Schema part 2: Datatypes, 2nd edn. W3C recommendation, World Wide Web Consortium (2004)
7. I.S. Organization, ISO 639-1:2002 – Codes for the representation of names of languages – Part 1: Alpha-2 code (2002), http://www.iso.org/iso/iso_catalogue/catalogue_tc/catalogue_detail.htm?csnumber=22109
8. A. Phillips, M. Davis, BCP 47 – Tags for Identifying Languages. BCP 47 Standard (2006), http://www.rfc-editor.org/rfc/bcp/bcp47.txt
9. F. Gandon, G. Schreiber, RDF 1.1 XML Syntax. W3C recommendation, World Wide Web Consortium (2014), https://www.w3.org/TR/rdf-syntax-grammar/
10. I. Herman, B. Adida, M. Sporny, M. Birbeck, RDFa 1.1 primer, 3rd edn. W3C working group note, World Wide Web Consortium (2015)
11. M. Sporny, D. Longley, G. Kellogg, M. Lanthaler, N. Lindström, JSON-LD 1.0. W3C recommendation, World Wide Web Consortium (2014)
12. P.J. Hayes, P.F. Patel-Schneider, RDF 1.1 semantics. W3C recommendation, World Wide Web Consortium (2014)
13. D. Allemang, J. Hendler, *Semantic Web for the Working Ontologist: Effective Modeling in RDFS and OWL* (Elsevier, Amsterdam, 2011)
14. M. Horridge, N. Drummond, J. Goodwin, A.L. Rector, R. Stevens, H. Wang, The Manchester OWL syntax, in *Proceedings of the 2nd Workshop on OWL: Experiences and Directions (OWLED 2006)*, Athens (November 2006)
15. S. Harris, A. Seaborne, SPARQL 1.1 query language. W3C recommendation, World Wide Web Consortium (2013)
16. G. Schreiber, Y. Raimond, RDF 1.1 Primer. W3C working group note, World Wide Web Consortium (2014)
17. D. Beckett, T. Berners-Lee, E. Prud'hommeaux, G. Carothers, RDF 1.1 Turtle. W3C recommendation, World Wide Web Consortium (2004)
18. P. Hitzler, M. Krötzsch, B. Parsia, P.F. Patel-Schneider, S. Rudolph, OWL 2 Web Ontology Language Primer (2nd edn.). W3C recommendation, World Wide Web Consortium (2012)
19. D.I. Lehn, JSON-LD Primer: A Context-based JSON Serialization for Linked Data. W3C community group draft report, World Wide Web Consortium (2017), https://json-ld.org/primer/latest/
20. J. Tennison, CSV on the Web: A Primer. W3C working group note, World Wide Web Consortium (2014)

Chapter 3
Linguistic Linked Open Data Cloud

Abstract This chapter introduces the Linguistic Linked Open Data (LLOD) Cloud. In recent years, there has been increasing interest in publishing linguistic datasets following linked data principles. A number of community-driven activities, foremost organized by the Open Linguistics Working Group (OWLG), have fostered and supported the publication of open linguistic datasets and have defined criteria for when a dataset can be regarded as forming part of the so-called LLOD. The LLOD cloud represents an index and temporal snapshot of the linguistic datasets that have been published on the Web following Linked Open Data principles. The LLOD cloud is a result of a coordinated effort of the OWLG, its members and collaborating initiatives, most notably the W3C Ontology-Lexica Community Group (OntoLex), which focuses on modelling lexico-semantic resources as linked data. The LLOD cloud is visualized by means of a cloud diagram that displays all the resources with their relative sizes and their connections. In this chapter we describe the efforts by many community activities and groups that have fostered the creation of the Linguistic Linked Open Data Cloud. We also describe the methodologies and principles that allow anyone to publish a dataset that can be included in the Linguistic Linked Open Data Cloud.

3.1 Background and Motivation

Many fields of linguistics, applied linguistics and computational linguistics, build on empirical methodologies, producing insights by analysing and processing data. Example fields are quantitative typology [1], corpus linguistics [2] and computational lexicography [3]. The empirical grounding of these areas has led to the creation of a large number of linguistic datasets and resources. These resources are not only increasing in number, but are becoming more and more diverse in terms of data formats, metadata and categories. Thus, establishing interoperability between datasets as well as fostering data reuse are becoming increasing challenges.

© Springer Nature Switzerland AG 2020
P. Cimiano et al., *Linguistic Linked Data*,
https://doi.org/10.1007/978-3-030-30225-2_3

Ide and Pustejovsky [4] define interoperability as consisting of two principal aspects:

- **Structural Interoperability:** Structural interoperability is concerned with ensuring that datasets from different origins can be straightforwardly accessed, combined and queried. This requires the standardization of data formats, protocols for obtaining as well as querying and accessing the data.
- **Conceptual Interoperability** Conceptual interoperability requires that metadata and annotations use a common vocabulary in terms of data categories/vocabularies and ontologies used. This would allow, for instance, for automatic integration or reconciliation of different datasets.

In this book, we describe a set of principles that allow to publish linguistic datasets in a way that fosters structural and conceptual interoperability by building on linked data principles. Our focus lies in particular on datasets that fulfil the following requirements:

- **linguistic**: datasets should be useful linguistic sets consisting of annotations or similar that are relevant to researchers in linguistics and NLP.
- **linked**: datasets should include links to third-party category systems to ensure conceptual interoperability in addition to data-level links to other datasets.
- **open**: datasets should be open according to the following definition[1]

    > Open means anyone can freely access, use, modify, and share for any purpose (subject, at most, to requirements that preserve provenance and openness).

In this chapter, we give a brief overview of the linked data principles. Further, we provide an overview over a number of community-driven activities that have fostered the adoption of linked data principles for the publication of language datasets, most importantly the Open Linguistics Working Group. We in particular describe the so-called *Linguistic Linked Open Data Cloud* that represents an index/snapshot of all the language datasets published on the Web following linked data principles.

3.1.1   Linked Data

The Linked Open Data Paradigm is based on four principles for the publication of data on the Web[2]:

1. Use URIs as names for things.
2. Use HTTP URIs so that people can look up those names.

---

[1]Following https://opendefinition.org/.
[2]From https://www.w3.org/DesignIssues/LinkedData.html.

3. When someone looks up a URI, provide useful information, using the standards (RDF*, SPARQL).
4. Include links to other URIs, so that they can discover more things.

These rules facilitate data interoperability in many ways. The use of URIs makes resources and data elements globally uniquely identifiable. If URLs are used in particular, these data elements become also resolvable. Using standards such as RDF and SPARQL ensures structural interoperability as all data sources can be accessed and queried uniformly. Finally, by including links to other datasets, in particular reusing third-party vocabularies and category systems, conceptual interoperability is established. Further, all the datasets published on the Web form a network that can be systematically accessed and browsed, navigating from one resource to a related resource and thus allowing to access all relevant datasets from one entry point.

The Resource Description Framework (RDF) as introduced in Chap. 2 represents the core model for publishing linked data.

The concept of linked data is closely coupled with the idea of **openness** (otherwise, the linking is only partially retrievable) and, in 2010, the original definition of Linked Open Data has been extended with a 5 star rating system for data on the Web.[3] The first star is achieved by publishing data on the Web (in any format) under an open license; the second, third and fourth star require machine-readable data, a non-proprietary format, and using standards like RDF, respectively. The fifth star is achieved by linking the data to other datasets to provide context.

3.1.2 Linked Open Data

Publishing linked data allows resources to be globally and uniquely identified such that they can be retrieved through standard Web protocols. Moreover, resources can be easily linked to one another in a uniform fashion and thus become structurally and conceptually interoperable. Chiarcos et al. [5] identified five main benefits involved in applying the linked data principles to the representation, modelling and publication of linguistic data:

- **Representation and modelling**: Linked data is based on the RDF graph model, which models data as a labelled directed graph. This represents a very versatile data model that can be used to represent stand-off annotations, feature structures, constituent parses, dependency parses, etc. directly without the need for encoding them as tabular structures.
- **Structural Interoperability**: The use of the HTTP protocol to retrieve data without the need for any proprietary protocols or services makes sure that all datasets can be accessed in the same way. The use of RDF eases the integration of datasets coming from different sources, while the use of URIs makes sure that

---

[3] http://www.w3.org/DesignIssues/LinkedData.html, paragraph 'Is your Linked Open Data 5 Star?'

datasets can be uniquely referenced and provenance and governance is associated to the URL behind which data is published.

- **Conceptual Interoperability**: By requiring that datasets are linked, linked data fosters reuse of existing category systems/annotation schemas and thus fosters category reuse and conceptual interoperability. Conceptual interoperability is also fostered by the fact that metadata and functional descriptions can be retrieved by resolving URIs, providing access to definitions, OWL axioms and other constraints that allow to understand how to use the URI as intended by the owner of the corresponding domain.

- **Federation**: Along with HTTP-accessible repositories and resolvable URIs, it is possible to combine information from physically separated repositories in a single query at runtime by federation. Resources can be uniquely identified and easily referenced from any other resource on the Web through URIs. Similar to hyperlinks on the HTML web, the Web of Data created by these links allows to navigate along these connections and to retrieve these related resources. As such, it is not necessary to keep local copies of datasets, but instead data can be accessed remotely by means of APIs, which follow open standards.

- **Dynamicity**: When linguistic resources are interlinked by references to resolvable URIs instead of proprietary IDs (or static copies of parts from another resource), we always provide access to the most recent version of a resource. In community-maintained terminology repositories, new categories, definitions or examples can be introduced occasionally, and this information is available immediately. In order to preserve link consistency among Linguistic Linked Open Data resources, however, it is strongly advised to apply a proper versioning system such that backward-compatibility can be preserved. Adding concepts or examples is unproblematic, but when concepts are deleted or redefined, a new version should be provided.

- **Ecosystem**: RDF as a data model for the Web is maintained by an interdisciplinary, large and active community, and it comes with a mature tool ecosystem that provides APIs, database implementations, technical support and validators for various RDF-based languages, e.g. reasoners for OWL. For developers of linguistic resources, this ecosystem can provide technological support or off-the-shelf implementations for common problems. Further, the distributed approach of the linked data paradigm facilitates the distributed development of web of resources and collaboration between researchers that provide and use this data and that employ a shared set of technologies. One consequence is the emergence of interdisciplinary efforts to create large and interconnected sets of resources in linguistics and beyond.

3.2 Linguistic Linked Open Data

Recent years have seen not only a number of approaches to model linguistic data as linked data, but also the emergence of larger initiatives that aim at interconnecting these resources. The LLOD is part of the LOD Cloud and is made available at the

LOD Cloud website[4] as well as independently on a distinct site for the subcloud.[5] The linguistic subcloud of the Linked Open Data cloud is maintained by the **Open Linguistics Working Group (OWLG)**,[6] an interdisciplinary network open to any individual interested in linguistic resources and/or the publication of these under an open license. The OWLG is a working group of the Open Knowledge Foundation (OKFN),[7] a community-based non-profit organization promoting open knowledge (i.e. data and content that is free to use, re-use and to be distributed without restriction). The group has spearheaded the creation of new data and the republishing of existing linguistic resources as part of an emerging Linked Open Data (sub-) cloud (see below) of linguistic resources. The LLOD cloud is thus a result of a coordinated effort of the OWLG, its members and collaborating initiatives, most notably the W3C Ontology-Lexica Community Group (OntoLex, see below), which focuses on modelling lexico-semantic resources as linked data.

3.2.1   The LLOD Cloud

The Linguistic Linked Open Data Cloud is an index of all linguistic datasets that have been published as LLOD. Furthermore, this is represented by a visualization (see Fig. 3.1), which shows the individual datasets and their connections. The *Linguistic* Linked Open Data is a subset of the larger linked open data cloud, shown in Fig. 3.2, and comprises of any kind of linked open dataset considered relevant for linguistic research or for natural language processing. In the main Linked Open Data Cloud Diagram, the linguistic resources are coloured in green. In March 2015, the OWLG proposed an operational definition to replace the earlier, informal use of the term **linguistically relevant**. In this context, a dataset is linguistically relevant if it provides or describes language data that can be used for the purpose of linguistic research or natural language processing. Besides *linguistic resources in a strict sense*, (1) this includes *other linguistically relevant* resources (2) that can be used for annotating, enriching, retrieving or classifying language resources.

1. **Linguistic resources in a strict sense** are resources which have been intentionally created for the purpose of linguistic research or natural language processing, and which contain linguistic classifications, annotations or analyses or have been used to provide such information about language data.
2. **Other linguistically relevant** resources include all other resources used for linguistic research or natural language processing, but not necessarily created for this purpose, e.g. large collections of texts such as news articles, encyclopedic

---

[4]https://lod-cloud.net.
[5]https://linguistic-lod.org.
[6]http://linguistics.okfn.org.
[7]http://okfn.org/.

Fig. 3.1 The Linguistic Linked Open Data Cloud as of June 2018

or terminological knowledge or general knowledge bases such as DBpedia, or metadata collections, but only if they include incoming or outgoing links with at least one linguistic resource in a strict sense.

This definition is designed to provide clear-cut criteria as to whether a LOD resource can be included in the LLOD diagram, and in condition (2), it is specific to this purpose: Condition (1) can be verified by associated publications at linguistic/NLP conferences, journals or inclusion in metadata collections such as the LRE Map. Condition (2) can be verified by the existence of links between a resource (whose linguistic relevance is to be confirmed) and resources fulfilling condition (1).

A prototypical example for condition (1) would be a linguistics-/NLP-specific vocabulary, a dictionary with rich grammatical information or an annotated corpus.

Fig. 3.2 The Linked Open Data Cloud as of June 2018. The linguistic resources are coloured green

Prototypical examples for condition (2) are resources which are frequently used in NLP and linguistics, but which have neither been created within these communities nor contain specifically linguistic information, e.g. the DBpedia.

It should be noted that condition (1) does not extend to all kinds of language resources, but limits our scope to those with *annotated or analysed data*. A corpus with vast amounts of primary data, even if created for linguistic research, published as such and automatically converted to linked data, e.g. using the NLP Interchange Format is certainly a valuable *language resource*, but does not necessarily constitute a linguistic resource in a strict sense according to condition (1). Nevertheless, it may be a linguistic resource by merits of condition (2).

Linguistic Linked Open Data, then, comprises datasets that are provided under an open license and are published in conformance with the linked data principles as

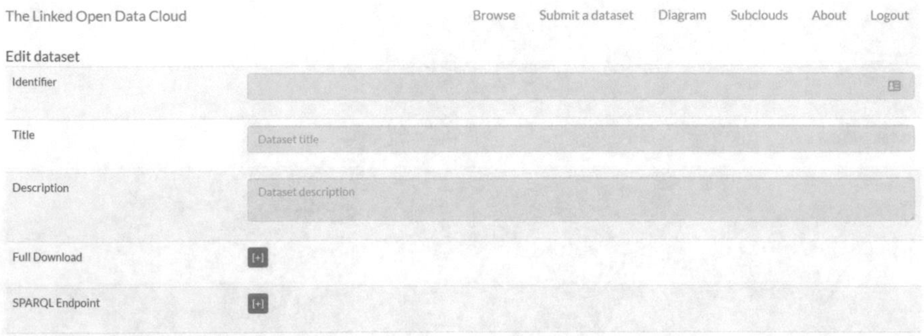

The Linked Open Data Cloud   Browse   Submit a dataset   Diagram   Subclouds   About   Logout

Edit dataset

Identifier   ▣

Title   Dataset title

Description   Dataset description

Full Download   [+]

SPARQL Endpoint   [+]

Fig. 3.3 A screenshot of the LOD Cloud Editor interface

stated above. Typically, these do not represent resources which are RDF-native, but
resources that have been transformed into RDF.

3.2.2 Infrastructure and Metadata

The official LLOD cloud is hosted at http://linguistic-lod.org and is also available
from the main LOD Cloud site at http://lod-cloud.net. The metadata of a LLOD
resource can be updated via the LOD cloud editor interface shown in Fig. 3.3. In
order for the datasets to be included in the LLOD cloud, it is necessary to select
'Linguistics' under the option 'Domain'. In addition, it is recommended that a
keyword be added to describe the dataset type, which should be one of 'corpus',
'lexicon', 'metadata' or 'typology'. These are used to classify LLOD resources into
three broad groups:

Corpora (blue resources in Fig. 3.1) are collections of language data, e.g.
examples, text fragments and entire discourses. It should be noted here that—in
accordance with condition (1)—a 'corpus' is always understood as a linguistically
analysed resource, the defining element are annotations. The notion of 'corpus' thus
extends both to classical RDF-only approaches where annotations *and* primary data
are modelled in RDF [6], as well as to hybrid models where only annotations are
provided as linked data, but the primary data is stored in a conventional format
[7]. According to our definition, it does *not* extend to collections of (unanalysed)
primary data. While it can be seen that corpora are less numerous than in general in
linguistic data, there are still many corpus resources available showing that LLOD
is as suitable for corpus resources as lexical resources.

Lexicons (green resources in Fig. 3.1) focus on the general meaning of words and
the structure of semantic concepts. These represent by far the most established and
flourishing type of linguistic resources in the linked data context. There is a long
tradition and interest in applying Semantic Web data models to modelling lexical
resources, going back to early attempts to integrate WordNet into the Semantic Web

world [8]. In the diagram, we distinguish two types of lexical-conceptual resources, i.e. *lexical resources* which also provide grammatical information (lexicons and dictionaries), and *term bases* which focus on vocabulary rather than linguistics (terminologies, thesauri and knowledge bases such as YAGO and DBpedia) and whose origins lay outside of the stricter boundaries of linguistics or NLP. While the latter do not provide us with grammatical information, they formalize semantic knowledge, and in this respect, they are of immanent relevance for natural language processing tasks such as named entity recognition or anaphora resolution.

Metadata (orange resources in Fig. 3.1) includes resources providing information about language and language resources, i.e. typological databases (collections of features and inventories of individual languages, e.g. from linguistic typology), linguistic terminology repositories (e.g. grammatical categories or language identifiers) and metadata about language resources (linguistic resource metadata repositories, incl. bibliographical data).

Typologies (pink resources in Fig. 3.1) While bibliographical data and terminology management represent classical linked data applications, *typological databases* describe features of individual languages and are a particularly heterogeneous group of linguistic resources as they contain complex and manifold types of information, e.g. feature structures that represent typologically relevant phenomena, along with examples for their illustration and annotations (glosses) and translations applied to these examples (structurally comparable to corpus data) or word lists (structurally comparable to lexical-semantic resources). RDF as a generic representation formalism is thus particularly appealing for this class of resources.

For resources with missing tags, the classification is made in an automatic fashion.

Another type of metadata is concerned with licensing information. Among LLOD data sets, we encourage the use of **open** licenses. As defined by the Open Definition, 'openness' refers to '[any] piece of content or data [that] is open if anyone is free to use, reuse, and redistribute it—subject only, at most, to the requirement to attribute and share-alike.'[8] At the moment, this condition is not yet enforced for the diagram. In fact, of the 86 resources that are declared as linguistic and for which a license is available,[9] all but 4 of these resources (4.7%) are licensed under open licenses, and these 4 are open but for non-commercial restrictions on the re-use of the data. However, legal metadata is also classified and a specific visualization can be generated with the dynamic edition of the diagram.[10] In the longer perspective, we expect a growth of linked data resources, so that our continuous move towards increasingly rigid quality criteria may eventually exclude non-open resources from the LLOD diagram. At the same time, however, we expect a growing number of licensed linked data resources, which may give rise to a 'Licensed Linked Data cloud' diagram which then takes the (pruned) LLOD

---

[8]http://opendefinition.org.

[9]42 resources have no declared license at `lod-cloud.net`.

[10] http://linguistic-lod.org/llod-cloud.

diagram as its core—but extends it to other resources relevant for academic research as well as industry partners.

Furthermore, extensions and limitations of established vocabularies are being noted and an active development cycle has been started, e.g. pertaining possible extensions of lemon (see Chap. 4). It should be noted that such proposals are a sign of maturity and wider adoption, as new use cases and needs are being identified that were not foreseen when the vocabularies where originally developed. As such, NIF (see Chap. 5) was designed as a format for NLP annotations generated on the fly, not linguistic corpora, and lemon was not designed as a generic vocabulary for lexical resources, but for the specific task of adding lexical information to an existing ontology. Recently, however, NIF has been increasingly used to model and represent corpora, while lemon is being more and more used to model non-ontological lexical resources. The extension of vocabularies and the development of downward-compatible extensions will be one of the key issues of the future development of LLOD and the communities behind.

3.3 LLOD Community

The *Open Linguistics Working Group* (OWLG) of the Open Knowledge Foundation has grown steadily since its foundation in October 2010. One of its primary goals is to attain openness in linguistics through:

1. Promoting the idea of open linguistic resources
2. Developing the means for the representation of open data
3. Encouraging the exchange of ideas across different disciplines

The OWLG represents an open forum for interested individuals to address these and related issues. At the time of writing, the group consists of about 150 people from more than 20 different countries. As the group is continuously growing, it also remains heterogeneous, and includes people from library science, typology, historical linguistics, cognitive science, computational linguistics, and information technology. The ground for fruitful interdisciplinary discussions has been laid out. One concrete result emerging out of collaborations between a large number of OWLG members is the LLOD cloud as already sketched above.

The **Ontology-Lexica Community (OntoLex) Group**[11] was founded in September 2011 as a W3C Community and Business Group. As of May 2019, it featured 119 members. It aims to produce specifications for a lexicon-ontology model that can be used to provide rich linguistic grounding for domain ontologies. Rich linguistic grounding includes the representation of morphological and syntactic properties of lexical entries as well as the syntax-semantics interface, i.e., the meaning of these lexical entries with respect to the ontology in question. An

---

[11]http://www.w3.org/community/ontolex.

important issue herein will be to clarify how extant lexical and language resources can be leveraged and reused for this purpose. As a by-product of this work on specifying a lexicon-ontology model, it is hoped that such a model can become the basis for a web of lexical linked data: a network of lexical and terminological resources that are linked according to the Linked Data Principles forming a large network of lexico-syntactic knowledge.

The **Linked Data in Linguistics** (LDL) workshops have been the major focal point for the community and have had successful editions in 2012, 2013,[12] 2014,[13] 2015,[14] 2016[15] and 2018.[16] Here, the community has gathered to discuss and to convert data sets, and the OWLG has continued to refine the classification of language resources and encouraged others to contribute, e.g. by organizing various events on linked data and LLOD. These efforts have met with success such that the number of candidate resources for the cloud has increased substantially. Along with this growth, we continue to enforce increased quality constraints imposed on resources in the cloud diagram. In addition, there have been a number of other workshops on topics related to LLOD, including NLP&DBpedia, the Multilingual Semantic Web (MSW), Multilingual Linked Open Data for Enterprise (MLODE), Knowledge Extraction and Knowledge Integration (KĒKI) and Linked Open Data Resources for Collaborative Data-Intensive Research (LLOD-LSA).

In addition, there have been a number of summer schools and hackathons that support LLOD and encourage people to learn about and adopt these technologies. In particular, the **Summer Datathons on Linguistic Linked Open Data** (SD-LLOD) have been organized in several events and have encouraged a range of participants to make their resources available as linked data. In addition, linguistic linked data has appeared as a topic in a number of other events, including being a theme of the 2014 EUROLAN Summer School and appearing in the program of the 2018 European Summer School on Logic, Language and Information (ESSLLI).

Of particular importance for supporting LLOD is the World Wide Web Consortium (W3C), where a number of groups have been formed for activities in relation to open linguistic resources as well as providing a forum for interested researchers, data providers and user communities from linguistics who would not normally work in the context of the W3C. In addition to the aforementioned Ontolex community group, there has been activity in the **Linked Data For Language Technologies** (LD4LT) and the **Best Practices for Multilingual Linked Open Data** (BPM-LOD) community groups.

---

[12]http://ldl2013.linguistic-lod.org/.

[13]http://ldl2014.linguistic-lod.org/.

[14]http://ldl2015.linguistic-lod.org/.

[15]http://ldl2016.linguistic-lod.org/.

[16]http://ldl2018.linguistic-lod.org/.

3.3.1   Summary and Further Reading

The Linguistic Linked Open Data Cloud is the main visualization to represent the current status of the linguistic datasets that are available as linked data. The steady growth in the size of the cloud clearly corroborates the wider adoption of the linked data principles for the publication of linguistic datasets. Furthermore, this has led to an active community that is continuing to organize events to support the growth of the cloud. The cloud has and will continue to be developed by a principle of slowly increasing requirements to be fulfilled by datasets so that the data is not only increasing in quantity but also increasing in quality.

The main advantages of linguistic linked open data were first described in [5] and then a summary of the developments has been given by McCrae et al. [9]. The LIDER Project[17] has developed many guidelines for publication and linking of linguistic datasets on the Web. A comprehensive review of models, ontologies and their extensions to represent language resources as LLOD, by focusing on the nature of the linguistic content they aim to encode, was developed by Bosque et al. [10].

References

1. J. Greenberg, A quantitative approach to the morphological typology of languages. Int. J. Am. Linguist. **26**, 178 (1960)
2. W.N. Francis, H. Kucera, Brown Corpus manual. Technical Report, Brown University, Providence, Rhode Island (1964). Revised edition 1979
3. W. Morris (ed.), *The American Heritage Dictionary of the English Language* (Houghton Mifflin, New York, 1969)
4. N. Ide, J. Pustejovsky, What does interoperability mean, anyway? Toward an operational definition of interoperability, in *Proceedings of the 2nd International Conference on Global Interoperability for Language Resources (ICGL)*, Hong Kong, 2010
5. C. Chiarcos, J. McCrae, P. Cimiano, C. Fellbaum, Towards open data for linguistics: lexical linked data, in *New Trends of Research in Ontologies and Lexical Resources* (Springer, Berlin, 2013), pp. 7–25
6. A. Burchardt, S. Padó, D. Spohr, A. Frank, U. Heid, Formalising multi-layer corpora in OWL/DL – lexicon modelling, querying and consistency control, in *Proceedings of the 3rd International Joint Conference on NLP (IJCNLP)*, Hyderabad, 2008, pp. 389–396
7. S. Cassidy, An RDF realisation of LAF in the DaDa annotation server, in *Proceedings of the 5th Joint ISO-ACL/SIGSEM Workshop on Interoperable Semantic Annotation (ISA-5)*, Hong Kong, 2010
8. A. Gangemi, R. Navigli, P. Velardi, The OntoWordNet Project: extension and axiomatization of conceptual relations in WordNet, in *On the Move to Meaningful Internet Systems 2003: CoopIS, DOA, and ODBASE* (Springer, Berlin, 2003), pp. 820–838

---

[17]http://lider-project.eu/.

9. J.P. McCrae, C. Chiarcos, F. Bond, P. Cimiano, T. Declerck, G. de Melo, J. Gracia, S. Hellmann, B. Klimek, S. Moran, P. Osenova, A. Pareja-Lora, J. Pool, The Open Linguistics Working Group: developing the Linguistic Linked Open Data cloud, in *Proceedings of the 10th Language Resource and Evaluation Conference (LREC)* (2016)
10. J. Bosque-Gil, J. Gracia, E. Montiel-Ponsoda, A. Gómez-Pérez, Models to represent linguistic linked data. Nat. Lang. Eng. **24**(6) (2018), https://doi.org/10.1017/S1351324918000347

Part II
Modelling

Chapter 4
Modelling Lexical Resources as Linked Data

Abstract This chapter introduces the Lexicon Model for Ontologies (lemon) as defined by the Ontolex W3C community group. The model was originally developed to enrich ontologies with lexical information expressing how the elements of the ontology including classes, properties and individuals are referred to in a given language. In this chapter we cover the core of the Ontolex-lemon model as well as the extra modules developed by the Ontolex group on syntax and semantics, decomposition, variation and translation and metadata. We then briefly describe some applications of the model.

4.1 Introduction

The *Lexicon Model for Ontologies* (lemon) is a model that has been developed to represent rich linguistic information in connection to ontologies. However, the lemon model can not only be used to add linguistic information to an ontology but also as a generic lexicon model. Lemon was first introduced in the context of the Monnet Project [1].[1] Since 2012, the Ontology-Lexicon Community Group has been further developing the model, leading to the release of a new version in May 2015, which we describe in this chapter. The model, which we refer to as the *Ontolex-lemon model*, is divided into five modules, which we cover in this chapter. The *core model* describes the elements that are necessary for the description of the core entities of the model, including lexical entries, forms and senses of a word. The *syntax and semantics module* describes in more detail the interaction of the syntax of words and their interpretation with respect to a given ontology. The *decomposition* module is used to describe the composition of multi-word expressions and compound words. The *variation and translation* module supports the description of relationships between words and senses, including translation and cross-lingual equivalences. Finally, the *metadata module* allows for high-level

---

[1] This first version of the model is still available under the URL http://lemon-model.net/lemon.

© Springer Nature Switzerland AG 2020
P. Cimiano et al., *Linguistic Linked Data*,
https://doi.org/10.1007/978-3-030-30225-2_4

descriptions of a lexicon and the number of links between elements. We conclude
this chapter with an outlook into some of the applications and examples of usage of
the Ontolex-lemon model.

4.2 The Core Model

The primary class in the Ontolex model is the *lexical entry*, which represents a
head word in the lexicon. The lexical entry groups all forms of a word together
into a single element, e.g. including inflected forms for a given part of speech. The
entry for the verb *'(to) lead'* would include inflected forms such as 'lead', 'leads',
'led'. The word *'lead'* as the metal, being of a different part of speech and having
different etymology, would constitute a separate lexical entry. Lexical entries are
further grouped into three classes: (single) words, multiword expressions and affixes
(such as 'anti-'). A lexical entry is composed of a set of lexical forms, each of which
can be represented in different scripts. One of these lexical forms is specified to be
the canonical form (i.e. 'lemma'). Thus a simple form of a lexical entry is as follows:

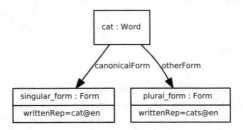

```
1  @prefix ontolex: <http://www.w3.org/ns/lemon/ontolex#> .
2
3  <cat> a ontolex:LexicalEntry, ontolex:Word ;
4  ontolex:canonicalForm <cat#singular_form> ;
5  ontolex:otherForm <cat#plural_form> .
6
7  <cat#singular_form> a ontolex:Form ;
8  ontolex:writtenRep "cat"@en .
9
10 <cat#plural_form> a ontolex:Form ;
11 ontolex:writtenRep "cats"@en .
```

The semantics of a lexical entry can be given by indicating that it *denotes* an
element in the ontology. The element in the ontology can be a class, property or
individual that represents the denotation of the lexical entry in question. In many
cases, this link to the ontology may need to be described in more detail. For this
reason, the model provides the class *lexical sense*, representing the connection
between a single lexical entry and its meaning in the ontology. Most lexicons
require this to represent links between senses or pragmatic information, so that

it is recommended to include a lexical sense for all links between lexical entries and ontology entities. For example, we may model the term *'consumption'* and its meanings as described below, noting that the meaning of *'tuberculosis'* is considered outdated by using vocabulary from the LexInfo ontology [2].

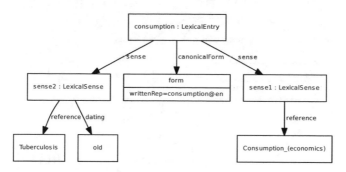

```
1  @prefix ontolex: <http://www.w3.org/ns/lemon/ontolex#> .
2  @prefix lexinfo: <http://www.lexinfo.net/ontology/2.0/lexinfo#
      > .
3
4  <consumption> a ontolex:LexicalEntry, ontolex:Word ;
5    ontolex:canonicalForm <consumption#form> ;
6    ontolex:sense <consumption#sense1>,
7                  <consumption#sense2> .
8
9  <consumption#form> ontolex:writtenRep "consumption"@en .
10
11 <consumption#sense1> a ontolex:LexicalSense ;
12   ontolex:reference <http://dbpedia.org/resource/
        Consumption_(economics)> .
13
14 <consumption#sense2> a ontolex:LexicalSense ;
15   ontolex:reference <http://dbpedia.org/resource/Tuberculosis>
        ;
16   lexinfo:dating lexinfo:old .
```

An alternative to referring to the ontology is to include a conceptual model within the lexicon. For example, Princeton WordNet [3] includes its own conceptual model given by the synsets (see Chap. 12). As an example of this, we consider the verb *'die'*, which may denote a property such as `deathDate` in the ontology. For instance, the meaning of the sentence *'John F. Kennedy died in 1963'* can be captured by the following triple:

```
1  dbpedia:John_F._Kennedy dbp:deathDate "1963"^^^xsd:date
```

However, from a lexical point of view, this is not the meaning of the verb *'die'* and thus the lexical concept evoked by *'die'* is the lexicon concept *'dying'*, which describes the meaning of the verb to *'die'* independent from a given ontology. Such an ontology-independent formalization of the meaning of *'die'*, however, does not support any reasoning as there is no link to an axiomatization of the meaning of the lexical concept. The meaning of the verb *'die'* might then be represented as follows:

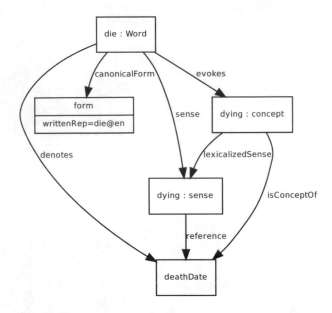

```
1   <die> a ontolex:Word, ontolex:LexicalEntry ;
2     ontolex:canonicalForm <die#form> ;
3     ontolex:sense <die#sense> ;
4     ontolex:evokes <die#concept> ;
5     ontolex:denotes dbp:deathDate .
6
7   <die#form> ontolex:writtenRep "die"@en .
8
9   <die#sense> ontolex:reference dbp:deathDate .
10
11  <die#concept> ontolex:isConceptOf dbp:deathDate ;
12    ontolex:lexicalizedSense <die#sense> .
```

4.3   Syntax and Semantics

The syntax and semantics module describes how a predicate in an ontology can be mapped to the syntactic frame of a lexical entry. In ontology languages such as OWL, there are three kinds of entities:

- **Properties** relate two entities, their *subject* and *object*; logically these can thus be regarded as logical predicates with two arguments.
- **Classes** describe sets of individuals that have properties that define their joint membership to the set.

- **Individuals** correspond logically to constants, that is functions with zero arguments.

Syntactic frames are used to describe the syntactic behaviour of lexical entries. They describe foremost the subcategorization behaviour of a lexical entry by specifying the number and type of arguments a lexical entry requires. Verbs that follow a transitive frame, for example, require a syntactic subject (expressing the semantic agent) and a direct object (expressing the so called patient). We also consider that nouns and adjectives have frames constructed with a copula construction (in English using the verb *'to be'*) and possibly some number of prepositional phrases (or similar), as in *'X is the father of Y'*, which would be considered a frame of the noun *'father'*. It is important to emphasize that the mapping between syntactic arguments can be arbitrary. In particular, it cannot be assumed in general that the syntactic subject realizes the triple's subject position and the syntactic object realizes the triple's object. Consider the predicate daughterOf, which could be lexicalized as *'X is the father of Y'*, where the syntactic subject (X) corresponds to the object of the predicate and the direct object (Y) corresponds to the subject of the predicate.

The syntax and semantics module supports the modelling of the syntactic frame by attaching a frame to the object representing the lexical entry. We give the example of the verb *'(to) know' (someone)* to illustrate this:

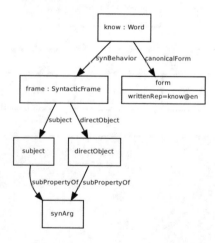

```
1  @prefix lexinfo: <http://www.lexinfo.net/ontology/2.0/lexinfo#
      > .
2
3  <know> a ontolex:Word ;
4    ontolex:canonicalForm <know#form> ;
5    synsem:synBehavior <know#frame> .
6
7  <know#form> ontolex:writtenRep "know"@en .
8
9  <know#frame> a synsem:SyntacticFrame ;
10    lexinfo:subject <know#subject> ;
```

```
11     lexinfo:directObject <know#directObject> .
12
13  lexinfo:subject rdfs:subPropertyOf synsem:synArg .
14  lexinfo:directObject rdfs:subPropertyOf synsem:synArg .
```

In this modelling, we use the LexInfo [2] properties `subject` and `directObject`, which are sub-properties of the generic `synArg` property, which is defined in the LexInfo ontology and is thus not necessary to state in your modelling.

In order to link the meaning of a syntactic frame to a (composed) ontological meaning, the Ontolex-lemon model allows one to express complex meanings (or maps) via multiple senses that each realize a part of the complex ontological meaning. We describe how this is accomplished below, using the example of the verb *'(to) know'*:

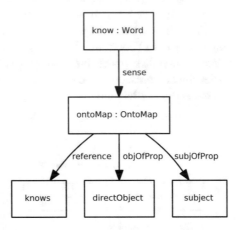

```
1  @prefix foaf: <http://xmlns.com/foaf/0.1/> .
2
3  <know> a ontolex:Word ;
4    ontolex:sense <know#ontoMap> .
5
6  <know#ontoMap> a ontolex:OntoMap, ontolex:LexicalSense ;
7    synsem:subjOfProp <know#subject> ;
8    synsem:objOfProp <know#directObject> ;
9    ontolex:reference foaf:knows .
```

The above example represents the meaning of the transitive verb 'know' following a neo-Davidsonian [4] approach, reifying the property `foaf:knows` and explicitly introducing the subject and object of the property so that they can be referred to by the resources `<know#subject>` and `<know#directObject>` representing the syntactic subject and direct object of the verb, respectively. This move is necessary to represent the meaning of verbs that have more than two arguments and which can therefore not be represented by reference to a single property. The meaning of the verb 'Mary gives Steve a kiss' could be represented following this neo-Davidsonian modelling style as follows in RDF:

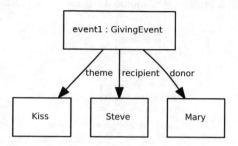

```
1  <event1> a onto:GivingEvent ;
2     onto:donor <Mary> ;
3     onto:recipient <Steve> ;
4     onto:theme <Kiss> .
```

The modelling of the syntactic frame for the verb '(to) give' can be done in lemon as follows:

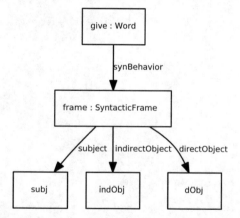

```
1  <give> a ontolex:Word ;
2     synsem:synBehavior <give#frame> .
3
4  <give#frame> a synsem:SyntacticFrame ;
5     lexinfo:subject <give#subj> ;
6     lexinfo:directObject <give#dObj> ;
7     lexinfo:indirectObject <give#indObj> .
```

The connection between the syntactic and a semantic frame is defined by means of an ontology map, but in this case the reference of the verb is an event instead of a single property. Each argument is associated with its own individual ontology map:

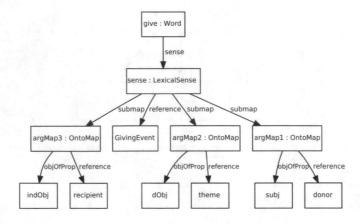

```
1   <give> a ontolex:Word ;
2     ontolex:sense <give#sense> .
3
4   <give#sense> a ontolex:LexicalSense, synsem:OntoMap ;
5     synsem:submap <give#argMap1> ,
6                   <give#argMap2> ,
7                   <give#argMap3> ;
8     ontolex:reference onto:GivingEvent .
9
10  <give#argMap1> a synsem:OntoMap ;
11    synsem:objOfProp <give#subj> ;
12    ontolex:reference onto:donor .
13
14  <give#argMap2> a synsem:OntoMap ;
15    synsem:objOfProp <give#dObj> ;
16    ontolex:reference onto:theme .
17
18  <give#argMap3> a synsem:OntoMap ;
19    synsem:objOfProp <give#indObj> ;
20    ontolex:reference onto:recipient .
```

In the above example, we see that the syntax-semantics mapping for the verb *'give'* is specified via a complex sense consisting of three (sub-)maps. Each of these sub-maps specifies the mapping of arguments for one of the ontological predicates to arguments of the syntactic frame. Thus, each of the three syntactic arguments subj, dObj and indObj are referenced by one of the three ontological maps. A more expanded example of this kind of modelling is covered in the Lemon OILS vocabulary [5].

4.4 Decomposition

The decomposition module has been designed to support the description of the internal structure of multiword expressions like compound nouns in languages such as German. Basically, this is accomplished by linking a lexical entry to the lexical entries it is composed of as subterms, as shown in the following example:

```
1  <AfricanSwineFever> a Ontolex:LexicalEntry ;
2    decomp:subterm <African>;
3    decomp:subterm <SwineFever>.
```

While this modelling is sufficient for many cases, in some cases more detail on the internal structure is needed, indicating the order of words as well as morphological properties of the concrete form that is part of the lexical entry. The decomposition module allows to define a Component, which represents the usage of a single lexical entry within a multiword expression or compound word. For example we may analyse the Spanish term *'comunidad autónoma'*, noting that *'autónoma'* is the feminine form of the adjective 'autónomo', as follows:

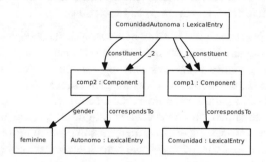

```
1  <ComunidadAutonoma> a ontolex:LexicalEntry ;
2    decomp:constituent <ComunidadAutonoma#comp1> ,
3                       <ComunidadAutonoma#comp2> ;
4    rdf:_1 <ComunidadAutonoma#comp1> ;
5    rdf:_2 <ComunidadAutonoma#comp2> .
6
7  <ComunidadAutonoma#comp1> a decomp:Component ;
8    decomp:correspondsTo <Comunidad> .
9
10 <ComunidadAutonoma#comp2> a decomp:Component ;
11   decomp:correspondsTo <Autonomo> ;
12   lexinfo:gender lexinfo:feminine .
13
14 <Comunidad> a ontolex:LexicalEntry .
15 <Autonomo> a ontolex:LexicalEntry .
```

The order of the constituents is given by considering the lexical entry as a *list* of components as described in the RDF Schema documentation [6], using the RDF properties `rdf:_1`, `rdf:_2`, ... to indicate the order of the elements.

4.5   Variation and Translation

The variation and translation module is concerned with representing relationships between elements of the lexicon. Relations can be defined at three levels:

- *Lexical relations* relate the surface forms of a word, e.g. to represent etymology and derivation.
- *Sense relations* relate the meanings of two words, e.g. to express that two senses are translations, synonyms or antonyms of each other.
- *Conceptual relations* relate concepts regardless of their lexicalization. Examples of such conceptual relations are the hypernymy or meronymy relations.

As an example, consider the case of relating two lexical entries across languages. For this, the module considers three types of relations:

- **Interlingual Synonymy** is a relation between lexical concepts, claiming equivalence in meaning abstracting from the specific lexical meanings involved.
- **Translation** is a relation between senses claiming that a word with a given sense can be translated into another word with a given sense.
- **Translatable As:** At the lexical level, the `translatableAs` property relates two lexical entries that, in some context, might be translated into each other. Specifically, the property says that there is some meaning of the word in the source language that can be translated into some meaning of the word in the source language.

Most of these relations can be described by a simple link between the elements, but in some cases it may be necessary to give additional information about the relationship. In this case a reified relation object as follows might be used:

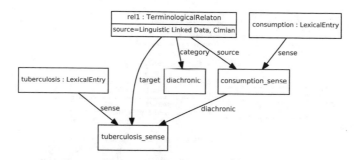

```
1   <tuberculosis> a ontolex:LexicalEntry ;
2     ontolex:sense <tuberculosis_sense> .
3
4   <consumption> a ontolex:LexicalEntry ;
5     ontolex:sense <consumption_sense> .
6
7   # Simple Property
8   <consumption_sense> onto:diachronic
9     <tuberculosis_sense> .
10
11  # Reified relationship
12  <rel1> a vartrans:TerminologicalRelaton ;
13    vartrans:source <consumption_sense> ;
14    vartrans:target <tuberculosis_sense> ;
15    vartrans:category onto:diachronic ;
16    dc:source "Linguistic Linked Data, Cimiano et al. (2017)" .
```

The first modelling is simple but does not allow one to add information about the source or the confidence in the translation relation; the second modelling allows to give such information and is thus more flexible.

4.6 Metadata

Representing information about a dataset, that is metadata, is crucial to index datasets, make them discoverable, provide information about source and/or provenance, etc. The Ontolex model includes a *LInguistic MEtadata (LIME)* module which allows to include elements of description 'about' a lexicon regarding information on how, why, by whom, etc. the elements of the lexicon where created. This is accomplished by representing the whole lexicon as an object to which descriptive elements can be attached. This lexicon object can be included as part of the lexicon (in the same file) or separately, as long as the usual rules about URLs and RDF are followed (see Sect. 2.2). There are also a number of properties provided to describe important information about a resource as follows:

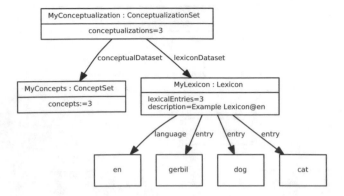

```
1   @prefix iso639: <http://www.lexvo.org/page/iso639-1/> .
2   <MyLexicon> a lime:Lexicon ;
3     # Number of Entries
4     lime:lexicalEntries 3 ;
5     # Each Entry may be linked directly
6     lime:entry <cat>, <dog>, <gerbil> ;
7     # Dublin Core properties may be used
8     dc:language iso639:en ;
9     dc:description "Example Lexicon"@en .
10
11  <MyConcepts> a lime:ConceptSet ;
12    lime:concepts: 3 .
13
14  <MyConceptualization> a lime:ConceptualizationSet ;
15    lime:conceptualDataset <MyConcepts> ;
16    lime:lexiconDataset <MyLexicon> ;
17    lime:conceptualizations 3 .
```

The above example shows how to describe the relationship between (1) a lexicon proper, (2) a conceptualization consisting of sets of concepts and (3) a set of conceptualizations, that is links between lexical entries and concepts. The example describes a lexicon consisting of three lexical entries that are linked to a concept set consisting of three (lexical) concepts. The conceptualization set includes three pairs of lexical entries/concepts.

4.7 Applications

The growth of the linguistic linked open data cloud (see Chap. 3) has led to a growing interest in the publication of dictionaries as linked data. This has two major benefits: firstly, linked data resources are more easily re-used and more visible when they are published on the Web under open licenses. This can be further exploited by linked-data-aware natural language processing tools [7–9]. In addition, as already discussed, linked data is an opportune format for the representation of lexical information [10], allowing dictionaries to move beyond their confines of a fixed set of pages, and instead be more richly linked and connected to other resources, including corpora and other lexico-conceptual resources such as encyclopedias and thesauri.

It is for this reason that linked data has been central in several initiatives in the area of eLexicography, most importantly the ELEXIS[2] project, which aims to build a new infrastructure for lexicography using linked data and Ontolex-lemon as a key building block. Secondly, projects such as LD4HELTA[3] on lexicography for high-end language technology applications and the Linked Open Dictionaries (LiODi)[4] have fostered the development of linked data in language technology and digital humanities.

At the time of writing, Ontolex-lemon can be claimed to be already the most widespread model for representing lexical information on the Web. In fact, a number of dictionaries have already been made available as linked data in the lemon model, including:

- Apertium family of bilingual dictionaries [8]
- The Germ monolingual dictionary in K Dictionary's Series [7]
- Sentiment lexicons from the EuroSentiment project [11]
- The Parole-Simple lexica [12]
- The Pattern Dictionary of English Verbs [13]
- The classical Al-Qamus dictionary [14]
- DBpedia lexicalizations such as DBlexipedia [15]
- Dbnary [16], an RDF version of Wiktionary[5]
- Dictionaries of Austrian dialects [17]
- Etymological dictionaries [18]
- Ancient Greek dictionaries [19]
- Dictionaries of hashtags [20]

As a main benefit of using Ontolex-lemon, dictionaries that have been made available in this format can be easily and quickly integrated.

4.8   Summary and Further Reading

In this chapter we have described the Ontolex-lemon model, which allows dictionaries to be represented as linked data and connected to other resources.

In the context of LLOD, Ontolex-lemon represents the most commonly applied RDF-based standard to represent lexical resources. In particular, this includes uses

---

[2]http://elex.is.

[3]http://www.eurekanetwork.org/project/id/9898.

[4]http://acoli.cs.uni-frankfurt.de/liodi/home.html.

[5]https://en.wiktionary.org.

in computational lexicography beyond its original use case to provide lexicalization information about ontologies. In this area, lemon exists along with other specifications, including the Lexical Markup Framework[6] (LMF) and the dictionary specifications of the Text Encoding Initiative (TEI, see Chap. 13).[7]

We have described the core of the model consisting of lexical entries connected to references in ontologies by means of lexical senses. We have also introduced the four key modules covering: (1) the relationship between the syntax of lexical entries and the semantics represented in the ontology, (2) the decomposition of compound nouns and multiword entries into individual words, (3) the representation of variation and translation between entries and senses and (4) the metadata component allowing to provide descriptive elements 'about' a lexicon seen as an information object. We then described some of the applications of the model. Many of these applications require the conversion of traditional (printed) dictionaries into linked data format to increase connectedness and interoperability as well as re-use of lexical resources. For this reason, several new modules are currently under construction, such as the ones covering morphology and etymology aspects, or have been recently launched such as the module for lexicography.[8]

The lemon model is most thoroughly described in the community report [21] available from the W3C.[9] In addition, the documentation for the previous version, the *lemon Cookbook* [22], is also available. A discussion of the development and applications of the model was also presented recently [23]. The model is still under development and the latest news can be found at the Ontolex Community Group website.[10]

References

1. J. McCrae, G.A. de Cea, P. Buitelaar, P. Cimiano, T. Declerck, A. Gómez-Pérez, J. Gracia, L. Hollink, E. Montiel-Ponsoda, D. Spohr, T. Wunner, Interchanging lexical resources on the Semantic Web. Lang. Resour. Eval. **46**(6), 701 (2012)
2. P. Cimiano, P. Buitelaar, J. McCrae, M. Sintek, LexInfo: a declarative model for the lexicon-ontology interface. Web Semant. Sci. Serv. Agents World Wide Web **9**(1), 29 (2011)
3. C. Fellbaum, Wordnet, in *Theory and Applications of Ontology: Computer Applications* (Springer, Berlin, 2010), pp. 231–243
4. D. Davidson, The logical form of action sentences, in *The Logic of Decision and Action* (University of Pittsburgh Press, Pittsburgh, 1967), pp. 81–95
5. J.P. McCrae, C. Unger, F. Quattri, P. Cimiano, Modelling the semantics of adjectives in the ontology-lexicon interface, in *Proceedings of the 4th Workshop on Cognitive Aspects of the Lexicon* (2014)

---

[6]http://www.lexicalmarkupframework.org/.
[7]http://tei-c.org/, accessed 10-07-2019.
[8]https://www.w3.org/2019/09/lexicog/.
[9]https://www.w3.org/2016/05/Ontolex/.
[10]https://www.w3.org/community/Ontolex/.

6. D. Brickley, R. Gutha, *RDF Schema 1.1. W3C Recommendation* (World Wide Web Consortium, Cambridge, 2014)
7. B. Klimek, M. Brümmer, Enhancing lexicography with semantic language databases. Kernerman Dictionary News **23**, 5 (2015)
8. J. Gracia, M. Villegas, A. Gómez-Pérez, N. Bel, The Apertium bilingual dictionaries on the web of data. Semantic Web J. **9**, 1–10 (2016)
9. H. Ziad, J.P. McCrae, P. Buitelaar, Teanga: a linked data based platform for natural language processing, in *Proceedings of the 11th Language Resource and Evaluation Conference (LREC)* (2018)
10. J. Bosque-Gil, J. Gracia, A. Gómez-Pérez, Linked data in lexicography, Kernerman Dictionary News **24**, 19–24 (2016)
11. G. Vulcu, P. Buitelaar, S. Negi, B. Pereira, M. Arcan, B. Coughlan, J. Sánchez, Fernando, C.A. Iglesias, Generating linked-data based domain-specific sentiment lexicons from legacy language and semantic resources, in *Proceedings of the 5th International Workshop on Emotion, Social Signals, Sentiment and Linked Open Data, co-located with LREC* (2014)
12. M. Villegas, N. Bel, PAROLE/SIMPLE 'lemon' ontology and lexicons. Semantic Web **6**(4), 363 (2015)
13. I. El Maarouf, J. Bradbury, P. Hanks, PDEV-lemon: a linked data implementation of the pattern dictionary of English verbs based on the lemon model, in *Proceedings of the 3rd Workshop on Linked Data in Linguistics (LDL): Multilingual Knowledge Resources and Natural Language Processing at the Ninth International Conference on Language Resources and Evaluation (LREC)* (2014), pp. 88–93
14. M. Khalfi, O. Nahli, A. Zarghili, Classical dictionary Al-Qamus in lemon, in *Proceedings of the 4th IEEE International Colloquium on Information Science and Technology (CiSt)*, ed. by M.E. Mohajir, M. Chahhou, M.A. Achhab, B.E.E. Mohajir (IEEE, Piscataway, 2016), pp. 325–330
15. S. Walter, C. Unger, P. Cimiano, DBlexipedia: a nucleus for a multilingual lexical Semantic Web, in *Proceedings of the 3rd International Workshop on NLP and DBpedia, co-located with the 14th International Semantic Web Conference (ISWC)*, ed. by H. Paulheim, M. van Erp, A. Filipowska, P.N. Mendes, M. Brümmer (2015), pp. 87–92
16. G. Sérasset, DBnary: wiktionary as a lemon-based multilingual lexical resource in RDF, Semantic Web **6**(4), 355 (2015)
17. T. Declerck, K. Mörth, Towards a sense-based access to related online lexical resources, in *Proceedings of the 17th EURALEX International Congress* (Ivane Javakhishvili Tbilisi University Press, Tbilisi, 2016), pp. 660–667
18. F. Abromeit, C. Chiarcos, C. Fath, M. Ionov, Linking the Tower of Babel: modelling a massive set of etymological dictionaries as RDF, in *Proceedings of the 5th Workshop on Linked Data in Linguistics: Managing, Building and Using Linked Language Resources*, Portoroz (2016)
19. F. Khan, J.E. Díaz-Vera, M. Monachini, Representing polysemy and diachronic lexicosemantic data on the Semantic Web, in *Proceedings of the 2nd International Workshop on Semantic Web for Scientific Heritage Co-located with 13th Extended Semantic Web Conference (ESWC 2016)*, vol. 1595, Heraklion, 2016, pp. 37–46
20. T. Declerck, E. Wand-Vogt, K. Mörth, Towards a pan-European lexicography by means of linked (open) data, in *Proceedings of the Biennial Conference on Electronic Lexicography (eLex): Electronic Lexicography in the 21st Century: Linking Lexical Data in the Digital Age* (Trojina, Institute for Applied Slovene Studies/Lexical Computing Ltd., Ljubljana/Brighton, 2015)
21. P. Cimiano, J.P. McCrae, P. Buitelaar, Lexicon model for ontologies: community report, in *W3C Community Group Final Report* (World Wide Web Consortium, Cambridge, 2014)
22. J. McCrae, G.A. de Cea, P. Buitelaar, P. Cimiano, T. Declerck, A.G. Pérez, J. Gracia, L. Hollink, E. Montiel-Ponsoda, D. Spohr, T. Wunner, *The Lemon Cookbook*. Technical Report, The Monnet Project (2012)
23. J.P. McCrae, P. Buitelaar, P. Cimiano, The OntoLex-Lemon Model: development and applications, in *Proceedings of the 5th Biennial Conference on Electronic Lexicography (eLex)* (2017)

Chapter 5
Representing Annotated Texts as RDF

Abstract Text annotation consists in defining markables (elements to be annotated), their features (attributes and values of annotations) and relations between
markables (e.g. syntactic dependencies or semantic links). In this chapter we
describe the principles for annotating text data using RDF-compliant formalisms.
These principles provide the basis for making annotated corporate and text collections accessible from the LLOD ecosystem.

5.1 Introduction

Linguistic analysis of natural language is basically about defining markables
(elements of annotations), their features (attributes and values of annotations) and
relations between markables (e.g. syntactic dependencies or semantic links).

Before discussing RDF-based data models for representing annotations, we discuss state-of-the-art formalisms in NLP and Digital Humanities (DH) to formalize
markables and their annotations, and present possibilities to integrate LLOD-
compliant references to textual and other natural language objects on the web.

5.1.1 Tab-Separated Values: CoNLL TSV

Since 1999, the Conference on Natural Language Learning (CoNLL)[1] established
a highly successful series of shared tasks in NLP. Subsequently, the data formats
employed in these tasks evolved into a widely used community standard for most
forms of linguistic annotations, as illustrated in the following example (1), slightly
simplified from a clause from the OntoNotes corpus [1], file `wsj-0655`:

(1) James Baker ... told reporters Friday: "I have no reason to deny reports that
some Contras ambushed some Sandinista soldiers."

---

[1]http://www.conll.org/, last accessed 09-07-2019.

© Springer Nature Switzerland AG 2020
P. Cimiano et al., *Linguistic Linked Data*,
https://doi.org/10.1007/978-3-030-30225-2_5

```
James      NNP B-PERSON
Baker      NNP E-PERSON
told       VBG O
reporters  NNS O
Friday     NNP S-DATE
:          :   O
...
```

Fig. 5.1 CoNLL sample with WORD, POS and NER columns

```
(TOP (S (NP-SBJ (NNP James)          James      NNP (TOP (S (NP-SBJ *
                (NNP Baker))         Baker      NNP *)
        (VP (VBD told)               told       VBD (VP *
            (NP (NNS reporters))     reporters  NNS (NP *)
            (NP-TMP (NNP Friday))    Friday     NNP (NP-TMP *)
        (: :)                        :          :   *

            (a)                                 (b)
```

Fig. 5.2 Sample of a parsed sentence in original and CoNLL format. (**a**) Original format (**b**) CoNLL conversion

Figure 5.1 illustrates the CoNLL format for the example of parts of speech and named entity annotation. Every word is written in one line, with a series of tab-separated columns holding different annotations; one column contains the surface form of the word. Sentences are separated by an empty line; comments are marked by #. Along with word-level annotations, CoNLL formats support the annotation of spans, illustrated here for named entity annotation using the IOBES scheme, i.e. B-X marking the beginning of the annotation X, E-X its end, I-X intermediate elements, S-X a single-word annotation and O the absence of an annotation.

While word- and span-level annotations can be performed in an intuitive and extensible way with one column per annotation type, the phrase structure syntax can be handled indirectly in CoNLL, only. The original syntax annotation of the OntoNotes uses a bracketing format as illustrated in Fig. 5.2a: Every word is grouped together with its POS tag in a terminal node, e.g. (NNP James). One or more terminal (or nonterminal) nodes may be grouped to a constituent, again marked by parentheses and a label, e.g. (NP ...). The original format is agnostic about line breaks, but for convenience of reading, line breaks may be inserted to put one word (and its annotations) in one single line.

Figure 5.2b shows how this information is split into three different columns for compliance with the CoNLL format: WORD, POS and PARSE, respectively. The column WORD contains the current word form, POS the associated POS tag and PARSE an abbreviated version of the parse structure, where * replaces terminal nodes.

As the phrase structure syntax example in Fig. 5.3 illustrates, some phenomena require special handling in order to be representable in a CoNLL TSV format, but a key advantage is that this representation can be easily extended, and easily merged with additional columns. As an example, the conventional way to represent semantic

```
James       NNP  B-PERSON  (TOP (S (NP-SBJ  *  _                ARG0
Baker       NNP  E-PERSON  *)                  _                ARG0
told        VBD  O         (VP *                 tell.v.01 rel
reporters   NNS  O         (NP *)                _                ARG2
Friday      NNP  S-DATE    (NP-TMP *)            _                ARGM-TMP
:           :    O         *                     _                _
# skipped quote
```

Fig. 5.3 Integrated CoNLL representation of POS, NER, syntax and PropBank annotations

role annotations in CoNLL is to add one column for the predicate as well as another column for every predicate that identifies its arguments. In the fourth column of our example, semantic predicates are identified and marked by a sense identifier. For every predicate instance, its arguments (ARGi with numerical index i for core arguments and ARGM arguments for various modifiers) are represented in a separate column, indicating whether a word occurs in (the span of) a frame argument and in which role. For every predicate in a sentence, an additional column is created.[2]

CoNLL TSV formats are characterized by the use of one word per line, one tab-separated column per annotation layer and an empty line to separate sentences. While CoNLL-based formats are not generic, they are relatively simple and easy to parse (or at least, commonly known), as they have been designed to provide common output specifications for tools participating in these challenges, and with support from many tools—both participating in the original shared tasks but also their successors and competitors—the CoNLL formats ultimately evolved into de facto standards for many types of linguistic annotation. Probably the most influential CoNLL dialect at the moment is CoNLL-U, the format adopted by the Universal Dependency collection of annotated corpora [2].[3] Individual CoNLL dialects, however, differ in the definition, naming and order of columns; their annotations and tools developed on this basis are thus not mutually interoperable.

Aside from interoperability problems, the CoNLL format family suffers from inherent limitations; CoNLL is limited to annotate words and larger units of text, as tokens (words) constitute the minimal unit of analysis (i.e. lines). As a side-effect, CoNLL formats normally lose information about the original layout. In fact, column-based formats do not annotate primary data but rather a segmental annotation of the primary data, in particular, tokens extracted from the primary data, listed one per line. This approach has the disadvantage of imposing one layer of linguistic interpretation (e.g. what constitutes a token, sentence, etc.) that may not be desired by other users. In addition, the 'one token per line' assumption adopted in the CoNLL format can seriously handicap algorithm performance. For example, some

---

[2]While generally accepted, this adds to the complexity of the format: Unlike conventional TSV formats which form fixed-size tables, CoNLL tables have no predictable maximum width and their width may vary from one sentence to the next.

[3]http://universaldependencies.org/, last accessed 09-07-2019.

phenomena (e.g. dots in chemical formulas) need to be split apart for one processing step (e.g. POS tagging), but treated as a unit for others (e.g. syntactic parsing). In many cases, CoNLL-based NLP pipelines thus require transformations between different tokenizations in order to process a sentence. Yet, as CoNLL formats do not systematically preserve whitespace information, such transformations can be lossy. Furthermore, annotations with deviating segmentations cannot be easily aggregated into a single CoNLL file, and neither can reliable references between elements in a CoNLL file be established.[4]

Despite these limitations, TSV formats offer advantages for processing and are thus widely used. Indeed, some of their deficits can be easily compensated if words are complemented with a community-approved way to refer to textual objects on the web or elsewhere. URIs provide such a mechanism, and by adding an additional column that holds a URI that identifies the original string in the original document, it is possible to establish links, to facilitate information integration across different CoNLL dialects (resp., tools that generate or consume these), and with the original document, its metadata and details regarding its layout. Below, URI schemes for this purpose are introduced.

5.1.2   Tree-Based Formats: TEI/XML

In computational philology and parts of the language resource community, XML enjoys a high degree of popularity as a representation formalism, only recently being challenged by JSON. Both formats formalize tree (resp., multi-tree) data structures, so that much of what can be said about the XML-based specifications of the Text Encoding Initiative (TEI) below extends to other approaches to formalize linguistic annotations.

For background, motivations and applications of the Text Encoding Initiative see Chap. 13. Here, we focus solely on the format and its application to the linguistic annotation of texts. The TEI P5 guidelines provide generic datatypes for many forms of linguistic annotation, including elements for orthographic sentences (`<s>`), grammatical words (`<w>`) and grammatical phrases (`<phr>`), as well as attributes for their respective type (`@type`), interpretation (`@ana`) and

---

[4]Strategies employed by different CoNLL Shared Tasks involve ad hoc solutions such as a reference to a word by its number (id) in the sentence (in dependency syntax), explicit ids and co-indexation (for coreference), or off-set based solutions (for Semantic Role Labelling). Neither of these, however, permit *absolute* reference, but they are defined with respect to the current sentence (SRL, dependency syntax), a particular tokenization (dependency syntax) or ad hoc ids (coreference). State of the art are thus more generic data models grounded in labelled directed multigraphs [3].

```
1   <s type="sentence">
2    <cl ana="#S">
3     <phr ana="#NP-SBJ">
4      <w ana="#NNP">James </w>
5      <w ana="#NNP">Baker </w>
6     </phr>
7     <phr ana="#VP">
8      <w ana="#VBD">told </w>
9      <phr ana="#NP">
10      <w ana="#NNS">reporters </w>
11     </phr>
12     <phr ana="#NP-TMP">
13      <w ana="#NNP">Friday </w>
14      <w ana="#colon">: </w>
15      ...
16     </phr>
17    </phr>
18   </cl>
19  </s>
```

Fig. 5.4 POS and syntactic annotation in TEI (inline annotation)

identification (@xml:id).[5] For our example, syntactic annotations are given in
Fig. 5.4, respectively.

The tree structure that both XML and JSON build upon is very convenient to
represent syntactic annotations, as illustrated in Fig. 5.4. The direct annotation of
syntax trees with @ana requires the use of URIs (teidata.pointer) as a reference to
a feature structure <fs> or interpretation <interp> element. References to an
external terminology repository such as OLiA [4] would be syntactically valid as
well.

In comparison with CoNLL, inline XML annotations permit to preserve the
original whitespaces together with the original context of a word, and they provide
a directly processable representation of nested structures. In addition, TEI supports
standoff mechanisms to refer to markables, and thus allows to create directed graph
structures between markables. In the upper part of Fig. 5.5, the @xml:id attribute
introduces a unique identifier (tei.pointer), i.e. (the local name of) a URI within the
current document.

TEI pointers can be used as source and target of interpreted (i.e. typed) links, e.g.
for SRL annotation as in the lower part of Fig. 5.5. In this example, all elements are
URIs, which basically allows to emulate RDF triples.[6] While TEI URI resolution is

---

[5]The original definition and various examples can be found under http://www.tei-c.org/release/
doc/tei-p5-doc/de/html/AI.html#AILA, last accessed 09-07-2019.

[6]Note that, despite interest in Linked Open Data within the TEI, TEI/XML is not a suitable
serialization of RDF in general: On the one hand, it is not sufficiently constrained, *several* different
serializations of RDF triples in TEI have been suggested and no consensus about preferences
among these has been achieved so far (for different approaches, see Sect. 13.3). On the other

```
1  <s>                    <!-- declaration of TEI URIs with @xml:id -->
2  <w xml:id="word-1">James </w>
3  <w xml:id="word-2">Baker </w>
4  <w xml:id="word-3">told </w>
5  <w xml:id="word-4">reporters </w>
6  <w xml:id="word-5">Friday</w>
7  <w xml:id="word-6">: </w>
8  ...
9  </s>
10
11 <linkGrp type="SRL-annotation"> <!-- standoff annotation -->
12 <link source="#word-3" @ana="#ARG0" target="#word-1"/>
13 <link source="#word-3" @ana="#ARG0" target="#word-2"/>
14 <link source="#word-3" @ana="#rel" target="#word-3"/>
15 <link source="#word-3" @ana="#ARG2" target="#word-4"/>
16 <link source="#word-3" @ana="#ARGM-TMP" target="#word-5"/>
17 <!--... -->
18 </linkGrp>
```

Fig. 5.5 Semantic role annotation in TEI (standoff XML)

normally restricted to tei.pointers (i.e. XML elements that are defined with @xml.id within a TEI document), this also provides a suitable device to refer to LLOD URIs in general. In the following sections, we describe two mechanisms to address texts and other natural language entities by means of LLOD formalisms.

5.2   Annotating Web Resources

Documents in the web come in various forms, and, often, it is not possible to embed metadata and annotations directly into them, e.g. because the annotator is not the owner of the document, and distributing a local copy may be restricted. Standoff formalisms support the physical separation of annotated material and annotations. The Open Annotation community and their Web Annotation Data Model provide a RDF-based approach for standoff annotation of web documents, with JSON-LD as its designated serialization. The Web Annotation Data Model provides a flexible means to represent standoff annotations relative to any kind of document on the web. It is being applied to linguistic annotations, primarily in the biomedical domain, although prototypical adaptions in other domains have been described as well, e.g. for NLP [5] or Digital Humanities [6].

---

hand, the TEI constructions used to emulate RDF triples can also have different interpretations— as evident from uses of TEI pointer structures such as <relation>, <link> or <ptr> that pre-date their (ab)use to represent or refer to linked data.

5.2.1   Web Annotation (Open Annotation)

The Web Annotation Data Model [7] provides specifications for the RDF-based annotation of digital resources and the lossless exchange and (re-)usability of such annotations [7]. The Web Annotation Data Model has been developed by the Open Annotation W3C Community Group[7] with precursors in the Annotation Ontology[8] and the Open Annotation Model.[9] The Annotation Ontology [8] was an effort to create an open OWL-DL ontology for the annotation of scientific documents in the web, in particular from the biological domain and BioNLP. In order to bridge the gap between the available array of biomedical ontologies and the linguistic expression of the corresponding concepts in scientific publications, the Annotation Ontology was developed as an open, sharable data structure for integrating documents with terminology resources [8, 9]. It was subsequently aligned with the specifications of the Open Annotation Community project, finally leading to the formation of the W3C Open Annotation Community Group [10].

The Web Annotation data model and vocabulary have been published as W3C recommendations in 2017 [7, 11]. The aim of Web Annotation is to be applicable across different media formats, the most common use case being *"attaching a piece of text to a single web resource"* [7]. However, in a Semantic Web context, annotations can also include structured elements which may provide, for example, machine-readable representations for a particular textual label, e.g. by providing a link with an external ontology. Accordingly, the data model and the vocabulary have been extended to cover a broad band-width of use cases beyond a plain labelling mechanism. Instead, annotations are understood as structured objects. The Web Annotation Model provides fully reified representation of annotated elements and annotations assigned to it. The Web Annotation Data Model follows the following core principles [7]:

- Annotations form a *directed* graph: An annotation consists of a Body (the value of the annotation) that typically expresses information about a Target (the element which is annotated).
- Targets are *external web resources*: Whereas a Body may be embedded in the annotation, a Target may be independently dereferenced.
- Annotations form a *hyper*graph: An annotation can have 0 or more Body elements, and 1 or more Target elements.
- Annotations are *reified*: Body, Target and Annotation are distinct resources, so that they can be further specified with properties and relationships, e.g. a link with a Motivation resource that expresses the intent behind the creation of an annotation.

---

[7]https://www.w3.org/community/openannotation/, last accessed 09-07-2019.
[8]http://code.google.com/p/annotation-ontology/, last accessed 09-07-2019.
[9]http://www.openannotation.org, last accessed 09-07-2019.

Web Annotation is defined by three W3C recommendations:

- The Web Annotation Data Model (https://www.w3.org/TR/annotation-model/, last accessed 09-07-2019) defines the concept and the core vocabulary.
- The Web Annotation Vocabulary (https://www.w3.org/TR/annotation-vocab/, last accessed 09-07-2019) provides the set of RDF classes, predicates and named entities used by the Web Annotation Data Model.
- The Web Annotation Protocol (https://www.w3.org/TR/annotation-protocol/, last accessed 09-07-2019) defines the mechanisms for accessing, creating and managing annotations by means of RESTful web services, also including the recommendation for JSON-LD as serialization.

In addition to these, the Web Annotation Ontology is also provided in a machine-readable view under http://www.w3.org/ns/oa#, and this URL defines the `oa:` namespace prefix. The core data structure of the Web Annotation Data Model is `oa:Annotation` as illustrated in Fig. 5.6: Annotations are required to be declared as instances (`rdf:type`) of `oa:Annotation`. Furthermore, the presence of a `oa:hasTarget` property defining the relationship between annotation and the annotated element is necessary. The target can be an IRI or a selector, i.e. "[a] resource which describes the segment of interest in a representation of a Source resource, indicated with `oa:hasSelector` from the Specific Resource. This class is not used directly in the Annotation model, only its subclasses" [11].

A number of selectors for various source formats and addressing mechanisms are supported, including, for example, the `TextPositionSelector` that identifies text segments based on character offsets, the `TextQuoteSelector` that identifies text segments on grounds of their textual context, and the `XPathSelector` that uses XPaths to identify elements of an XML document. Selectors for other modalities also exist, e.g. the `DataPositionSelector` and the `SvgSelector`; it is thus possible to create annotations across different media

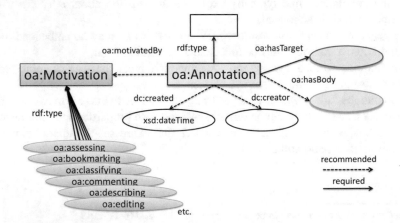

Fig. 5.6 Required and optional features of annotations in the Web Annotation Data Model [7]

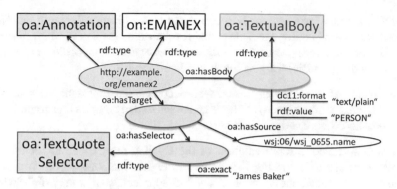

Fig. 5.7 Web Annotation example with named entity annotation, cf. Fig. 5.1

types, and using different reference strategies. Selectors are a highly generic and flexible way to refer to text passages in a text, however, also a comparably verbose one, so that for plain string references in plain text documents, users may want to consider using string URIs (see Sect. 5.3) instead of selectors. Where selectors for other data types exist, these should be preferred.

Additional predicates recommended for annotations are the metadata properties dcterms:creator, dcterms:created and oa:motivatedBy, but most importantly, the property oa:hasBody. The property oa:hasBody is an object property that specifies its object to be the body of the annotation. Different kinds of bodies are supported, e.g. a textual body, as illustrated in Fig. 5.7. As this representation is rather verbose, Web Annotation also provides the datatype property oa:bodyValue, which serves as a short-hand for the property path oa:hasBody/rdf:value.

5.2.2 Annotating Named Entities on the Web

The primary goal of language technology as well as linguistic research has been to analyse, to formalize and eventually to reproduce the function of language as a relation between form (grammar) and function (meaning). Web Annotation allows to formalize references to forms, e.g. linguistic expressions, but in addition, different target selectors also allow to perform a similar functionality across different modalities. In the context of linked data, the annotation of reference covers a particularly important aspect of meaning, as entities in texts refer to the same entity in the world, and are thus pivotal for creating links between texts and external knowledge bases as well as across texts. Named entities have thus long stood in the focus of interest in the Semantic Web and NLP communities. Their analysis in texts involves several aspects, most notably Entity Linking, where an entity mention in a text is assigned an identifier that represents this individual (say, a URI from a knowledge base such as DBpedia), and Named Entity Recognition (NER), where entities are identified and classified for their type (say, general types such as organizations, persons, geopolitical entities, dates, or domain-specific concepts such as genes or drugs in BioNLP), as illustrated in example 2:

(2) Secretary of State James Baker, who accompanied President Bush to Costa Rica, told reporters Friday: "I have no reason to deny reports that some Contras ambushed some Sandinista soldiers. "

A Web Annotation representation of the CoNLL representation for the NER annotation of example 2 in Fig. 5.1 is given in Fig. 5.7. In comparison, Web Annotation is less compact, but it pursues a standoff approach, so that the primary data is left intact. Annotations are physically separated from the annotated document, with annotations preferably serialized in JSON-LD.

For the example, we employ the `oa:TextQuoteSelector` (see Table 5.1), which allows to describe a range of text by means of a literal match with the designated string, but also (optionally) some of the text immediately before (a prefix) and after (a suffix) in order to distinguish multiple copies of the same character sequence. As prefix and suffix are optional, text quote selectors are a very elegant solution to annotate all occurrences of a particular entity in a document with the same entity link. If different entities with the same surface string are to be distinguished (e.g. for pronouns), they can be disambiguated by context information.

Considering the first two named entities in the sentence only, this could be encoded in the Web Annotation fragment shown in Fig. 5.8 (in JSON-LD), resp. Fig. 5.9 (in Turtle).

Table 5.1 Characteristics of text quote selectors according to http://www.w3.org/ns/oa# TextQuoteSelector (accessed 09-07-2019)

Term	Type	Description
Type	Relationship	The class of the selector. Text quote selectors MUST have exactly 1 type and the value MUST be TextQuoteSelector
TextQuoteSelector	Class	The class for a selector that describes a textual segment by means of quoting it, plus passages before or after it. The TextQuoteSelector MUST have this class associated with it
Exact	Property	A copy of the text which is being selected, after normalization. Each TextQuoteSelector MUST have exactly 1 exact property
Prefix	Property	A snippet of text that occurs immediately before the text which is being selected. Each TextQuoteSelector SHOULD have exactly 1 prefix property, and MUST NOT have more than 1
Suffix	Property	The snippet of text that occurs immediately after the text which is being selected. Each TextQuoteSelector SHOULD have exactly 1 suffix property, and MUST NOT have more than 1

```
1   {
2     "@graph": [
3          {
4             "@context": "http://www.w3.org/ns/anno.jsonld",
5             "id": "http://example.org/enamex2",
6             "type": [
7                "Annotation",
8                   "https://catalog.ldc.upenn.edu/docs/LDC2007T21/
                        ontonotes-1.0-documentation.pdf#ENAMEX"
9             ],
10            "body": {
11                 "type" : "TextualBody",
12                 "value" : "PERSON",
13                 "format" : "text/plain"
14            },
15            "target": {
16                 "source": "https://catalog.ldc.upenn.edu/
                        ldc2013t19/data/files/data/english/
                        annotations/nw/wsj/06/wsj_0655.name",
17                 "selector": {
18                    "type": "TextQuoteSelector",
19                    "exact": "James Baker"
20                 } }
21         }
22   ] }
```

Fig. 5.8 Partial named entity annotation with Web Annotation and JSON-LD

```
1    <http://example.org/enamex2>
2      a oa:Annotation, on:ENAMEX ;
3      oa:hasBody [
4        a oa:TextualBody ;
5        dc11:format "text/plain"^^xsd:string ;
6        rdf:value "PERSON"^^xsd:string
7      ] ;
8      oa:hasTarget [
9        oa:hasSelector [
10          a oa:TextQuoteSelector ;
11          oa:exact "James Baker"^^xsd:string
12        ] ;
13        oa:hasSource wsj:06/wsj_0655.name
14      ] .
```

Fig. 5.9 Partial named entity annotation with Web Annotation and Turtle

Similarly, alternative body values are possible, including references to external resources. Web Annotation thus provides an elegant mechanism to represent the output of Entity Linking systems. Using a service such as DBpedia Spotlight [12] (sample output in Fig. 5.10), the textual mention of *James Baker* can now be enriched with the URI dbpedia:James_Baker as annotation body. Note that an annotation can have multiple bodies (and/or targets), with the interpretation

```
1  <?xml version="1.0" encoding="utf-8"?>
2  <Annotation text="Secretary of State James Baker, ..." confidence
      ="0.35" support="0" types="" sparql="" policy="whitelist">
3    <Resources>
4      <Resource URI="http://dbpedia.org/resource/James_Baker"
          support="299" types="DBpedia:Agent,Schema:Person,Http://
          xmlns.com/foaf/0.1/Person,DBpedia:Person,DBpedia:
          OfficeHolder" surfaceForm="James Baker" offset="19"
          similarityScore="0.9999999912981821"
          percentageOfSecondRank="7.541871793467152E-9"/>
5      ...
6    </Resources>
7  </Annotation>
```

Fig. 5.10 Sample output of DBpedia Spotlight

```
1  {
2    "@context": "http://www.w3.org/ns/anno.jsonld",
3    "id": "http://example.org/enamex2",
4    "type": [
5      "Annotation",
6        "Schema:Person",
7        "http://xmlns.com/foaf/0.1/Person",
8        "http://dbpedia.org/ontology/Agent",
9        "http://dbpedia.org/ontology/Person",
10       "http://dbpedia.org/ontology/OfficeHolder",
11       "https://catalog.ldc.upenn.edu/docs/LDC2007T21/ontonotes
            -1.0-documentation.pdf#ENAMEX"
12    ] ,
13    "body": [
14      "http://dbpedia.org/resource/James_Baker",
15      {
16        "type" : "TextualBody",
17        "value" : "PERSON",
18        "format" : "text/plain"
19      } ] ,
20    "target": {
21      "source": "https://catalog.ldc.upenn.edu/ldc2013t19/data/
            files/data/english/annotations/nw/wsj/06/wsj_0655.name",
22      "selector": {
23        "type": "TextQuoteSelector",
24        "exact": "James Baker"
25      } }
26  }
```

Fig. 5.11 Joint named entity and entity linking annotation with Web Annotation and JSON-LD

that every oa:Body is individually and equally related to the respective target(s). This mechanism can be applied to joint named entity and entity linking annotations (Figs. 5.11, resp. 5.12), but it should be noted that this integration of different body elements also means that their respective types are being conflated.

```
1   <http://example.org/enamex2>
2     a oa:Annotation, on:ENAMEX,
3     schema:Person, foaf:Person,
4     dbo:Agent, dbo:Person, dbo:OfficeHolder;
5     oa:hasBody <http://dbpedia.org/resource/James_Baker>, [
6       a oa:TextualBody ;
7       dc11:format "text/plain"^^xsd:string ;
8       rdf:value "PERSON"^^xsd:string
9     ] ;
10    oa:hasTarget [
11      oa:hasSelector [
12        a oa:TextQuoteSelector ;
13        oa:exact "James Baker"^^xsd:string
14      ] ;
15      oa:hasSource wsj:06/wsj_0655.name
16    ] .
```

Fig. 5.12 Joint named entity and entity linking annotation with Web Annotation and Turtle

Likewise, it is now possible to extend this annotation to other modalities. For example, if James Baker is shown on a digitized and web-accessible photograph, an `oa:FragmentSelector` (providing the source image and the relevant coordinates) can be added to the annotation as yet another target.

5.3 Annotating Textual Objects

Whereas Web Annotation covers the full bandwidth of web resources, more specialized and less verbose formalisms for referencing strings and formalizing them as objects of linguistic annotation have been developed. Of particular importance in this context is the NLP Interchange Format [13, NIF]. Building on RFC 5147 specifications for URI Fragment Identifiers for the text/plain media type, NIF provides a URI scheme that allows to directly address strings in web-accessible documents, as well as ontologies formalizing strings and selected aspects of 'typical' annotations in NLP.

A key advantage in comparison to Web Annotation is a more compact representation of string references, whereas Web Annotation provides the verbose selector concepts, selector, reference and source document are identified in a compact fashion in a single URI. While Web Annotation focuses on formalizing annotations, NIF focuses on strings to which annotations may be assigned. RFC 5147 [14] defines an extension of earlier specifications for the text/plain MIME type, i.e. simple, unformatted text 'seen simply as a linear sequence of characters, possibly interrupted by line breaks or page breaks' [15, RFC 2046]. In general, URI fragment identifiers extend document URIs with a local name separated from the document URI using a hash sign (#).

RFC 5147 provides a simple offset mechanism to address strings, i.e. sequences of characters, in a web document as follows:

- **Position**: A character offset starting from the beginning of the document, defining an empty string at a particular position in the document. For the document https://catalog.ldc.upenn.edu/docs/LDC95T7/raw/06/wsj_0655.txt and using the offsets from Fig. 5.10 for *James Baker* from example 2, we arrive at the following position URI:

  https://catalog.ldc.upenn.edu/docs/LDC95T7/raw/06/wsj_0655.txt#char=19

  Note that the initial BOM character does not count, and that line endings (regardless of whether defined as LF, CR or LF+CR) count as one character.
- **Range:** A consecutive sequence of characters with a particular start position and a particular end position, both defined as character offsets:

  https://catalog.ldc.upenn.edu/docs/LDC95T7/raw/06/wsj_0655.txt#char=19, 30

  If the first value of a range is not defined, it defaults to 0, if the second is not defined, it defaults to the end of the document.
- **Character Offsets:** Number of characters before the designated string, i.e. 0 for the first character. This is illustrated in the examples above.
- **Line Offsets:** Analogously to character offsets, a line offset refers to the number of lines (resp., line separators) before the designated position. The following example refers to the first line in the document:

  https://catalog.ldc.upenn.edu/docs/LDC95T7/raw/06/wsj_0655.txt#line=0

  With a range definition and underspecified end, the following URI refers to the *textual content* of the entire document (which can thus be distinguished from the document itself):

  https://catalog.ldc.upenn.edu/docs/LDC95T7/raw/06/wsj_0655.txt#line=0,

The text scheme is optionally followed by an integrity check, i.e. a length specification or an MD5 value:

```
...#char=19,30;length=12
...#char=19,30;md5=67f60186fe687bb898ab7faed17dd96a
```

Furthermore, a character encoding can be defined:

```
...#char=19,30;length=12,UTF-8
...#char=19,30;,UTF-8
```

Originally, RFC 5147 has been developed for highlighting strings in web documents. Aside from this application, its uses seem to be largely limited to language technology, where its URIs can be directly used as targets of web annotations and thus provide a compact alternative to Web Annotation selectors.

It should be noted, however, that RFC 5147 URIs are defined with reference to the text/plain MIME type, and that their application to other kinds of documents on the web (in particular, documents with markup) is somewhat abusive.[10] Nevertheless, RFC 5147 represents the basis for *all* URI schemes for strings, including NIF [13], NAF [17] and LIF [18]—which are designed to address strings in character streams regardless of MIME type declarations.

Another potential issue of RFC 5147 URIs is that they may involve implicit information. Most importantly, string URIs are sensitive to the respective encoding. Defining the character encoding is optional, but without explicit declarations, RFC 5147 defaults to ASCII. However, with today's predominant use of UTF-8, this default can easily lead to unexpected results. Integrity checks help to detect possible errors, but their specification is optional. To explicate such information in RDF has been one motivation for developing the NLP Interchange Format.

5.3.1 The NLP Interchange Format (NIF 2.0)

The NLP Interchange Format (NIF) [19] is an RDF/OWL-based format designed to combine NLP tools in a flexible, light-weight fashion, originally developed in the FP7 LOD2 EU project (2010–2014). NIF aims to complement aggregator infrastructures for NLP such as UiMA [20] or GATE [21] with a representation that excels beyond either exchange format in terms of interoperability. UiMA, for example, builds on proprietary annotation type systems which are often maintained in-house, so that annotations between modules developed for different UiMA pipelines, e.g. by different providers, cannot be easily interchanged—or require writing new adapters, so that NLP modules from one pipeline can be integrated in the other. NIF provides a way to map the annotations of two or more NLP pipelines into a common representation and to integrate them seamlessly.

NIF includes the following core components:

- URI schemes to refer to strings in documents and to add annotations to such URIs
- An OWL-based vocabulary to express relations between String URIs
- Vocabulary extensions to represent frequent types of annotations in common NLP pipelines
- Best practices on how to integrate NLP tools, adapt them to NIF, and expose them as web services
- A reference implementation and a web demo for this functionality

NIF is a community standard developed at the Agile Knowledge Engineering and Semantic Web group at the University of Leipzig, Germany, with various external contributors. Albeit not being W3C-endorsed yet, it enjoys relatively wide adaptation for NLP services in the LLOD ecosystem, and has also been applied

---

[10]Indeed, other recommendations for this purpose have been developed, most notably XPointer [16]. In practical applications, however, XPointer seems to be largely unused.

to represent annotated corpora—although this is not its original focus and imposes limitations on the types of annotations that can be represented. NIF is well-suited for word-based annotations, e.g. for entity linking, but it is not capable of differentiating annotations of the same string on multiple annotation layers.

The core of NIF consists of a vocabulary for addressing arbitrary character sequences by RDF URIs to which linguistic annotations can be attached in a flexible fashion. By reference to a common pool of URIs, resp., by means of a mapping of annotated text data to a NIF representation, annotations from different NLP tools can be aggregated easily (if the same URI scheme is chosen).

For referencing strings, NIF provides two URI schemes [22], roughly corresponding in their function to text position selectors and text quote selectors in Web Annotation:

- **offset-based URIs** define strings by the character positions in the underlying document. They consist of four parts:

  1. the namespace (normally, the URI of the annotated document), followed by # or /,
  2. the scheme identifier offset, followed by _,
  3. start index, followed by _, and
  4. end index

  Indexes start with 0, and the underlying encoding is assumed to be Unicode Normal Form C [23, NFC]. Using the offsets from Fig. 5.10 for *James Baker* from example 2, we arrive at the following URI[11]:

  ```
  https://catalog.ldc.upenn.edu/docs/LDC95T7/raw/06/wsj_0655.txt
                        #offset_19_30
  ```

  In Web Annotation, expressing the same information would require a TextPositionSelector and 5 triples.

- **context-hash URIs** identify strings on grounds of their forms and context. They have been introduced as a means to improve robustness against document changes, but they can also be applied to annotate multiple strings at the same time if these occur in the same contexts. They consist of six parts:

  1. the namespace, followed by # or /
  2. the scheme identifier hash, followed by _
  3. the context length, i.e. number of preceding and following characters considered, followed by _
  4. the length of the string, followed by _
  5. the message digest, a 32-character hexadecimal MD5 hash index generated from preceding context, the string (enclosed in parenthesis) and the following context, followed by _

---

[11]Note that we replaced the URI of the annotated file with the URI of the original text file in the Penn Treebank. As LDC corpora are available for download only, but not for online access, however, neither of these URIs resolve.

6. the first 20 characters of the string itself, in URL encoding

For James Baker and context size 0, this yields the URI

```
https://catalog.ldc.upenn.edu/docs/LDC95T7/raw/06/wsj_0655.txt
#hash_0_11_67f60186fe687bb898ab7faed17dd96a_James%20Baker
```

The information provided by this URI corresponds to five Web Annotation triples in Fig. 5.9.

- **Other String URIs** supported by NIF include RFC 5147 strings, as well as consecutive string instantiations (CStringInst), another schema for offset- and context-based selection introduced in compliance with Apache Stanbol.[12]

In practice, NIF context hash URIs seem to be rarely used, but they are a powerful (albeit potentially dangerous) instrument to annotate all instances of a particular string simultaneously. A disadvantage is that for every context size, the string has a different URI and the relation between these can no longer be treated (nor easily recognized) as owl:sameAs because a URI generated from a long context may be unambiguous, but another URI with a short (or no) context that designates the same string may also identify another string in the same document. In combination with Web Annotation, the NIF URI scheme also provides an elegant alternative to the verbose system of selectors. Because web documents may change, either kind of URIs may resolve to an incorrect string, and to preserve interpretability, it is recommended to include the full text of the annotated document in the NIF RDF data. As shown below, string URIs allow us to elegantly mashup different annotations—a feature which is desirable for NLP pipelines, but which may be problematic for linguistic annotations in general.

In addition to string URIs, NIF allows to define relations between and contexts of strings. As shown in Fig. 5.13, the different URI schemes can be made explicit and their transformation can be tracked, and explicit offset information can be added. The (optional) property nif:anchorOf allows to provide the string value of the annotated element in RDF, a functionality required for querying NIF data. Furthermore, strings can be positioned relatively to each other (before, after), and string embedding can be expressed (subString, etc.)—a feature which can be subsequently used to model parse trees. As mentioned above, it is recommended to complement strings with an explicit representation of their context, i.e. the content of the full document (itself modelled as a nif:String).

Beyond text anchoring, NIF provides a core vocabulary for types of annotations specific for NLP pipelines as shown in Fig. 5.14, covering many practically relevant use cases. The NIF 2.0 Core Ontology [13] provides datastructures for the annotation of words and sentences, (hierarchical—i.e. nif:subString—and) sequential relations between these (nif:nextWord, nif:nextSentence), as well as concepts for groups of words, i.e. (syntactic) phrases, sentences, paragraphs

---

[12]https://stanbol.apache.org/, last access 09-07-2019.

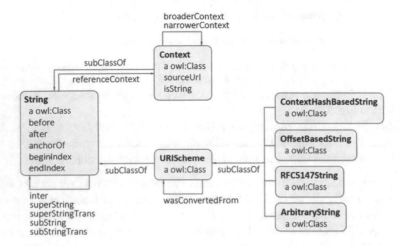

Fig. 5.13 NIF 2.0 Core Ontology, string classes and properties according to [13]

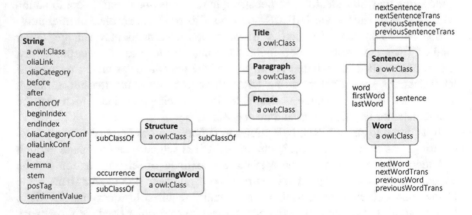

Fig. 5.14 NIF 2.0 Core Ontology, annotation classes and properties according to [13]

and titles. Despite obvious shortcomings, this rudimentary inventory accounts for many applications in NLP.

In addition to this, NIF has been extended for a number of use cases, and nif:Strings can thus be annotated with the corresponding properties for part-of-speech tagging (nif:posTag), morphological base forms (nif:stem, nif:lemma), sentiment (nif:sentimentValue) and (not shown in the diagram) syntactic dependencies (nif:dependency, nif:dependency RelationType). Except for nif:dependency, which points to the URI of the syntactic head, these are data type properties and provide literal values only. However, part-of-speech annotations, syntactic categories and dependency relations can be represented in a machine-readable and formal way by resolving tags to explicit links to the Ontologies of Linguistic Annotation (nif:oliaCategory).

This linking can be performed automatically if tags are compared against the string values or patterns defined in the corresponding OLiA Annotation Models. Further types of linguistic annotation are provided by external, community-maintained vocabularies, e.g. the NERD ontology for entity linking.[13]

The following RDF code represents a sample annotation for tokenization and sentence segmentation with NIF (included in other annotations):

```
1  PREFIX nif: <http://persistence.uni-leipzig.org/nlp2rdf/
       ontologies/nif-core#>
2  PREFIX xsd: <http://www.w3.org/2001/XMLSchema#>
3  PREFIX doc: <https://catalog.ldc.upenn.edu/docs/LDC95T7/raw
       /06/wsj_0655.txt#>
4
5  doc:offset_0_188 a nif:Sentence, nif:Context , nif:
       OffsetBasedString ;
6         nif:isString "Secretary of State James Baker, who
              accompanied President Bush ..." .
7
8  doc:offset_0_9 a nif:Word, nif:OffsetBasedString ;
9         nif:anchorOf "Secretary" ;
10        nif:beginIndex "0" ; nif:endIndex "9" ;
11        nif:nextWord doc:offset_10_12 ;
12        nif:sentence doc:offset_0_188 ;
13        nif:referenceContext doc:offset_0_188 .
14
15 doc:offset_10_12 a nif:Word, nif:OffsetBasedString ;
16        nif:anchorOf "of" ;
17        nif:beginIndex "10" ; nif:endIndex "12" ;
18        nif:nextWord doc:offset_13_18 ;
19        nif:previousWord doc:offset_0_9 ;
20        nif:sentence doc:offset_0_188 ;
21        nif:referenceContext doc:offset_0_188 .
```

A data sample for part-of-speech annotations is provided below:

```
1  PREFIX nif: <http://persistence.uni-leipzig.org/nlp2rdf/
       ontologies/nif-core#>
2  PREFIX xsd: <http://www.w3.org/2001/XMLSchema#>
3  PREFIX doc: <https://catalog.ldc.upenn.edu/docs/LDC95T7/raw
       /06/wsj_0655.txt#>
4
5  doc:offset_0_9 nif:anchorOf "Secretary" ;        # included for
       readability, only
6         nif:posTag "NNP" .
7
8  doc:offset_10_12 nif:anchorOf "of" ;
9         nif:posTag "IN" .
10
11 doc:offset_13_18 nif:anchorOf "State";
12        nif:posTag "NNP" .
```

---

[13] http://nerd.eurecom.fr/ontology, last accessed 09-07-2019.

```
13
14  doc:offset_19_24 nif:anchorOf "James";
15          nif:posTag "NNP" .
16
17  doc:offset_25_30 nif:anchorOf "Baker";
18          nif:posTag "NNP" .
19
20  doc:offset_30_31 nif:anchorOf ",";
21          nif:posTag "," .
22
23  doc:offset_32_35 nif:anchorOf "who";
24          nif:posTag "WP" .
25
26  doc:offset_36_47 nif:anchorOf "accompanied";
27          nif:posTag "VBD" .
28
29  doc:offset_48_57 nif:anchorOf "President";
30          nif:posTag "NNP" .
31
32  doc:offset_58_62 nif:anchorOf "Bush";
33          nif:posTag "NNP" .
```

Named entity categories can be represented analogously in NIF. NIF does not
provide a designated property for the purpose, instead one can apply a property that
points to the original documentation (using the same URI as in Web Annotation, i.e.
on:ENAMEX).

```
1   PREFIX nif: <http://persistence.uni-leipzig.org/nlp2rdf/
        ontologies/nif-core#>
2   PREFIX xsd: <http://www.w3.org/2001/XMLSchema#>
3   PREFIX doc: <https://catalog.ldc.upenn.edu/docs/LDC95T7/raw
        /06/wsj_0655.txt#>
4   PREFIX on: <https://catalog.ldc.upenn.edu/docs/LDC2007T21/
        ontonotes-1.0-documentation.pdf#>
5
6   doc:offset_13_18                        # context information skipped
7           nif:anchorOf "State";   # cf. POS example above
8           nif:beginIndex "13" ; nif:endIndex "18" ;
9           on:ENAMEX "ORG" .
10
11  doc:offset_19_30
12          nif:anchorOf "James Baker";
13          nif:beginIndex "19" ; nif:endIndex "30" ;
14          on:ENAMEX "PERSON" .
15
16  doc:offset_58_62
17          nif:anchorOf "Bush";
18          nif:beginIndex "58" ; nif:endIndex "62" ;
19          nif:posTag "PERSON" .
```

The first annotated `nif:Word` takes a URI that equals that of the POS annotation. Accordingly, both can be trivially merged.

```
1  doc:offset_13_18
2      a nif:Word;                          # tokenization
3          nif:beginIndex "13" ; nif:endIndex "18" ;
4          nif:anchorOf "State";
5          nif:nextWord doc:offset_19_24 ;
6          nif:referenceContext doc:offset_0_188 ;
7          nif:sentence doc:offset_0_188 ; # sentence splitting
8          nif:posTag "NNP" ;               # POS annotation
9          on:ENAMEX "ORG" .                # NER annotation
```

In the example, the IOBES annotation of the original CoNLL annotation (Fig. 5.1) has been expanded to full tokens.[14] However, this leads to a problem in that *James Baker* does not directly correspond to a URI in the POS annotation. Automated merging is thus limited to single-word expressions. With explicit `nif:beginIndex`, and `nif:endIndex`, it is possible to query for word spans containing each other.

Similarly, the entity linking annotation from Fig. 5.10 can be rendered in NIF as follows:

```
1   PREFIX itsrdf: <http://www.w3.org/2005/11/its/rdf#>
2
3   doc:offset_19_30 a nif:Word;
4           nif:anchorOf "James Baker";
5           nif:beginIndex "19" ; nif:endIndex "30" ;
6           itsrdf:taIdentRef  <http://dbpedia.org/resource/
                James_Baker> ;
7           a dbo:Agent, dbo:Person, dbo:OfficeHolder .
8
9   doc:offset_48_62 a nif:Word;
10          nif:anchorOf "President Bush";
11          nif:beginIndex "48" ; nif:endIndex "62" ;
12          itsrdf:taIdentRef  <http://dbpedia.org/resource/
                George_W._Bush> ;
13          a dbo:Agent, dbo:Person, dbo:OfficeHolder .
```

While `doc:offset_19_30` matches the URI generated by NER annotation, we have to observe another mismatch with multi-word expressions: Again, the URI `doc:offset_48_62` can only be indirectly related to the URI `doc:offset_58_62`.

In Natural Language Processing, different annotation tools can produce their annotations independently. If the same tokenization is applied, word URIs generated by different annotators become identical, such that the information from different annotators is seamlessly integrated. This is a particularly useful feature for word-level annotations. At those points where the tokenization differs, the anchoring in

---

[14]As an alternative to multi-word expressions, it is possible, of course, to operate with IOBES-based single-word annotations, thereby facilitating the merging process.

the same context as well as `nif:beginIndex` and `nif:endIndex` allows to infer overlaps and spans. Implicit unification of annotations as illustrated above requires the use of the same URI scheme. If annotators use different NIF URI schemes, an explicit conversion routine is to be applied. If the complete original text is provided as reference context and the URI scheme can be identified, NIF URIs are convertible. URI conversion, however, benefits from explicating offset and context information.

5.3.2 Provenance and Annotation Metadata in NIF

In a typical NIF workflow, a stream of textual data or a single document is consumed and transformed by a web service which returns NIF so that the result can be further enriched by further NIF annotation services. Instead, the output of different NIF annotators can be put into different RDF graphs which then represent the corresponding levels of annotation.

It is somewhat problematic, though, in ensemble combination architectures where different NLP modules generate annotations of the same kind in order to achieve a more robust annotation [24]. Similar problems may arise in multi-layer corpora, where the same document may be annotated for the same phenomenon in independent annotation efforts. In both cases, an explicit representation of documents and annotation layers within a document would be preferred.

Coming back to the example, the file `wsj_0655` has not only been annotated within OntoNotes, but also as part of the Penn Treebank [25] as well as various corpora that build on the Penn Treebank, cf. Sect. 6.3.2. For parts of speech and syntax annotation of most OntoNotes texts, we have at least three versions (with marginal differences in tokenization and annotation) of Penn Treebank annotations, as well as an independent annotation (according to the same scheme, but with adjustments in tokenization and certain design decisions) as part of OntoNotes.

Annotations may differ slightly, and without a versioning system, different annotators may generate different values for the same property, thereby leading to a clash of annotations. A NIF 2.1 solution to provenance is to define companion properties for properties that express linguistic annotations, e.g. `nif:taIdentConf` (confidence) and `nif:taIdentProv` (provenance) for the property `itsrdf:taIdentRef` (entity linking) [26]. However, different entity linking routines can produce alternative linkings, and there is no explicit association between a particular `itsrdf:taIdentRef` and a particular `nif:taIdentProv` property. In the NIF 2.1 draft, `nif:AnnotationUnits` have been introduced to cluster annotations of the same string generated from different annotators. However, this is described as a future extension, and this is not reflected in the persistent NIF documentation. If provenance, confidence or other metadata is to be provided, the interested reader may resort to Web Annotation instead, as their specifications are more stable and more mature than those of NIF 2.1.

For the moment, advanced challenges in NLP (architectures that implement parallel rather than sequential processing, i.e. blackboard or ensemble architectures) and corpus linguistics (redundantly annotated corpora) are beyond the scope of NIF and require a representation that disentangles strings and units of annotations and that provides an explicit organization of units of annotations in annotation layers or tiers. Both aspects will be addressed in Chap. 6.

5.4 Summary and Further Reading

We described two representative corpus formalisms currently used in language technology, resp., computational philology and corpus linguistics, and described how they can be complemented with URI references to LLOD resources and thereby establish bridges between state-of-the-art technology and resources on the one hand and the emerging field of linguistic linked data on the other hand. In CoNLL TSV formats, an additional column may be added that links every word to a URI; for TEI/XML, the current use of TEI-specific URIs can be easily extended to URIs in general.

Existing approaches to refer to textual (and non-textual) objects on the web in a linked-data-compliant fashion are based either on the use of target-specific selectors or compact string URIs:

- Web Annotation represents a promising and widely used approach to address textual and non-textual objects on the web by means of selectors, and by linking them with an annotation. If these annotations define a resolvable URI on their own, these URIs may be referred to from pre-RDF formalisms.
- RFC 5147 is a URI scheme that directly allows to address strings in a web document and represents a more compact alternative to Web Annotation selectors. It is the basis for the development of the NLP Interchange Format that extends the applicability of offset- and context-based URI schemes from plain text to web documents in general.

Note that these strategies and formalisms to refer to and to annotate textual objects on the web are not mutually exclusive. The NIF String ontology allows to describe information that underlies the URI formation process, thereby acting in analogy with Web Annotation selectors. Likewise, Web Annotation can refer to NIF or RFC 5147 URIs as targets of annotations as an alternative instead of declaring selectors.

Beyond merely referencing strings and other web objects as units of annotation, Web Annotation provides the expressive means to represent annotations on their own, in particular for annotations that can be reduced to labelling and identification. It is less clear how complex annotations for, say, syntactic dependencies, phrase structure syntax or semantic roles are to be represented in this context. NIF does provide explicit data structures for selected types of linguistic annotation frequently occurring in NLP pipelines, but it is not exhaustive in this regard.

At the time of writing, Web Annotation and NIF (resp., RFC 5147) are the most popular RDF-based formalisms to refer to natural language objects as units of annotation in the web. Far from being the only proposals, both are representative for JSON/LD and RDF/OWL-based approaches, respectively. In technical contexts, NIF enjoys considerable popularity, and its application to NLP pipelines is described in Chap. 11. Likewise, Web Annotation is an established community standard in BioNLP and Digital Humanities.

Independently from developments in language technology, URI-based methods to address text segments have been developed in computational philology: The Canonical Text Service (CTS, see Sect. 13.2.4) in the CITE architecture defines a URI (URN) scheme to address *canonical* units of texts. One goal of CTS is to facilitate intertextuality and stemmatology; these canonical units are thus *not* defined for an individual text, but rather for a family of texts or fragments of texts that originate from a common source, and thereby explicate corresponding passages. These efforts aim at defining intertextual reference points rather than units of annotation and are thus not directly comparable. In the context of language technology, alternative, application- or system-specific representation formalisms have been developed: For example, TELIX [27] used RDFa to infuse RDF content into an exchange format for an NLP pipeline, with the goal of linking it with lexical entries defined in SKOS XL [28].

In the NewsReader project,[15] the standoff format NAF was employed in NLP pipelines for entity and event extractions for Dutch, English and German [29]. NAF is an XML format that uses standoff mechanisms as described in Sect. 5.1.2, but an RDF conversion along the lines of NIF has been suggested [17].[16] NAF covers several types of NLP annotations relevant for event extraction and entity tracking, but only provides a vocabulary specifically oriented towards the NLP pipeline(s) it was originally designed for.

The LAPPS Interchange Format (LIF) was designed to integrate various NLP tools into the LAPPS Grid [30], a workflow system for multi-step analyses, evaluation tools and facilities for sharing and publishing results. LIF thus serves a similar purpose as NIF and NAF, but it adopts JSON-LD as RDF serialization. A LIF document consists of three sections: `metadata`, `text` and `views`. The metadata section contains optional metadata, the text section contains the text that is originally input to the service and the views section contains the annotations that have been added by the service to the text—together with an `id` and annotation-specific `metadata`. Similar to the `oa:TextPositionSelector` in Web Annotation, explicit attributes encode start and end positions of markables. We discuss LAPPS in more detail in Chap. 11.

Furthermore, a number of application- or tool-specific formats with their own URI schemes can be mentioned, e.g. the MATE parser [31],[17] a system for

---

[15] https://github.com/newsreader/NAF, accessed 09-07-2019.

[16] Also see http://wordpress.let.vupr.nl/naf/, accessed 09-07-2019.

[17] http://barbar.cs.lth.se:8081/, accessed 09-07-2019.

dependency parsing and semantic role labelling, the machine reading system FRED [32][18] or the LODeXporter [33],[19] a component for automatic knowledge base construction integrated in the GATE architecture [21]. In the longer perspective, and with continuing growth of the LLOD cloud and LLOD-aware applications, we expect an increasing degree of convergence in this area, probably based on formats and schemes already popular now.

Promising candidates are NIF and Web Annotation. But also these have been developed from an application perspective in a bottom-up fashion and thus require extensions for unforeseen applications, e.g. the annotation of morphology— currently neither addressed by the Web Annotation community nor by maintainers and users of NIF. Such limits of applicability of NIF and Web Annotation are not evident to most of their users, as they focus on frequently requested functionalities such as handling metadata about web objects, and the output of off-the-shelf NLP and Entity Linking pipelines, respectively. With the continuing growth of LLOD technology, we expect that increased exchange between different groups of users of LLOD technology will eventually lead to more expressive and more robust means to address and to annotate textual objects on the web as well as to the emergence of increasingly mature standards. At the moment, we recommend using Web Annotation for the conjoint handling of textual objects and non-textual objects in the web, and NIF/RFC 5147 for representing the output of NLP pipelines. For the future, we expect increased convergency between these and related representations.

Web Annotation and NIF thus aim to facilitate the transition from pre-RDF representation formalisms for linguistic annotation to LLOD-compliant representations. This aspect is further explored in the following chapter.

References

1. E. Hovy, M. Marcus, M. Palmer, L. Ramshaw, R. Weischedel, OntoNotes: the 90% solution, in *Proceedings of the Conference of the North American Chapter of the Association for Computational Linguistics on Human Language Technology (HLT-NAACL 2006)* (Association for Computational Linguistics, New York, 2006), pp. 57–60
2. J. Nivre, Ž. Agić, L. Ahrenberg, et. al., Universal dependencies 1.4 (2016). http://hdl.handle.net/11234/1-1827
3. N. Ide, C. Chiarcos, M. Stede, S. Cassidy, Designing annotation schemes: from model to representation, in *Handbook of Linguistic Annotation*, ed. by N. Ide, J. Pustejovsky, Text, Speech, and Language Technology (Springer, Berlin, 2017)
4. C. Chiarcos, Ontologies of linguistic annotation: survey and perspectives, in *Proceedings of the 8th International Conference on Language Resources and Evaluation (LREC)*, Istanbul, 2012, pp. 303–310
5. K. Verspoor, K. Livingston, Towards adaptation of linguistic annotations to scholarly annotation formalisms on the Semantic Web, in *Proceedings of the 6th Linguistic Annotation Workshop* (Association for Computational Linguistics, Jeju, 2012), pp. 75–84

---

[18]http://wit.istc.cnr.it/stlab-tools/fred/, accessed 09-07-2019.

[19]https://github.com/SemanticSoftwareLab/TextMining-LODeXporter, accessed 09-07-2019.

6. L. Isaksen, R. Simon, E.T. Barker, P. de Soto Cañamares, Pelagios and the emerging graph of ancient world data, in *Proceedings of the 2014 ACM Conference on Web Science* (ACM, New York, 2014), pp. 197–201

7. R. Sanderson, P. Ciccarese, B. Young, Web Annotation Data Model. Technical Report, W3C Recommendation (2017). https://www.w3.org/TR/annotation-model/

8. P. Ciccarese, M. Ocana, L.J. Garcia Castro, S. Das, T. Clark, An open annotation ontology for science on web 3.0, J. Biomed. Semant. **2**(Suppl. 2), S4 (2011). https://doi.org/10.1186/2041-1480-2-S2-S4, http://www.jbiomedsem.com/content/2/S2/S4/abstract

9. D.C. Comeau, R. Islamaj Doğan, P. Ciccarese, K.B. Cohen, M. Krallinger, F. Leitner, Z. Lu, Y. Peng, F. Rinaldi, M. Torii, et al., BioC: a minimalist approach to interoperability for biomedical text processing, Database **2013**, bat064 (2013)

10. R. Sanderson, P. Ciccarese, H. Van de Sompel, Designing the W3C Open Annotation data model, in *Proceedings of the 5th Annual ACM Web Science Conference, WebSci '13* (ACM, New York, 2013), pp. 366–375. https://doi.org/10.1145/2464464.2464474

11. R. Sanderson, P. Ciccarese, B. Young, Web Annotation vocabulary. Technical Report, W3C Recommendation (2017). https://www.w3.org/TR/annotation-vocab/

12. P. Mendes, M. Jakob, A. García-Silva, C. Bizer, DBpedia Spotlight: shedding light on the web of documents, in *Proceedings of the 7th International Conference on Semantic Systems (I-Semantics 2011)*, Graz, 2011

13. S. Hellmann, NIF 2.0 Core Ontology. Technical Report, AKSW, University Leipzig (2015). http://persistence.uni-leipzig.org/nlp2rdf/ontologies/nif-core.html, version of 08-04-2015. Accessed 9 July 2019

14. E. Wilde, M. Duerst, RFC 5147 – URI fragment identifiers for the text/plain media type. Technical Report, Internet Engineering Task Force (IETF), Network Working Group (2008)

15. N. Freed, N. Borenstein, RFC 2046 – Multipurpose Internet Mail Extensions (MIME) Part Two: Media Types. Technical Report, Internet Engineering Task Force (IETF), Network Working Group (1996)

16. P. Grosso, E. Maler, J. Marsh, N. Walsh, XPointer Framework. W3C Recommendation 25 March 2003. Technical Report, W3C (2003)

17. A. Fokkens, A. Soroa, Z. Beloki, N. Ockeloen, G. Rigau, W.R. van Hage, P. Vossen, NAF and GAF: Linking linguistic annotations, in *Proceedings of the 10th Joint ISO-ACL SIGSEM Workshop on Interoperable Semantic Annotation* (2014), pp. 9–16

18. N. Ide, K. Suderman, E. Nyberg, J. Pustejovsky, M. Verhagen, LAPPS/Galaxy: Current state and next steps, in *Proceedings of the 3rd International Workshop on Worldwide Language Service Infrastructure and 2nd Workshop on Open Infrastructures and Analysis Frameworks for Human Language Technologies (WLSI/OIAF4HLT2016)* (2016), pp. 11–18

19. S. Hellmann, J. Lehmann, S. Auer, M. Brümmer, Integrating NLP using Linked Data, in *Proceedings of the 12th International Semantic Web Conference, 21–25 October 2013*, Sydney, 2013. Also see http://persistence.uni-leipzig.org/nlp2rdf/

20. M. Egner, M. Lorch, E. Biddle, UIMA Grid: Distributed large-scale text analysis, in *Proceedings of the 7th IEEE International Symposium on Cluster Computing and the Grid (CCGRID'07)*, Rio de Janeiro, 2007, pp. 317–326

21. H. Cunningham, GATE, a general architecture for text engineering. Comput. Hum. **36**(2), 223 (2002)

22. S. Hellmann, J. Lehmann, S. Auer, Linked-data aware URI schemes for referencing text fragments, in *Proceedings of the International Conference on Knowledge Engineering and Knowledge Management* (Springer, Berlin, 2012), pp. 175–184

23. M. Davis, K. Whistler, Unicode Standard Annex #15. Unicode Normalization Forms. Technical Report, Unicode, Inc. (2017). Unicode 10.0.0, version of 2017-05-26, revision 45

24. E. Brill, J. Wu, Classifier combination for improved lexical disambiguation, in *Proceedings of the 36th Annual Meeting of the Association for Computational Linguistics and the 17th International Conference on Computational Linguistics (COLING-ACL 1998)*, Montréal, 1998, pp. 191–195

25. M.P. Marcus, B. Santorini, M.A. Marcinkiewicz, Building a large annotated corpus of English: the Penn treebank. Comput. Linguist. **19**, 313 (1993)
26. S. Hellmann, M. Brümmer, M. Ackermann, Provenance and confidence for NIF annotations. Technical Report, AKSW, University of Leipzig, Germany (2016). Version of Oct 17, 2016
27. E. Rubiera, L. Polo, D. Berrueta, A. El Ghali, TELIX: An RDF-based model for linguistic annotation, in *Proceedings of the 9th Extended Semantic Web Conference (ESWC 2012)*, Heraklion, 2012
28. A. Miles, S. Bechhofer, SKOS Simple Knowledge Organization System eXtension for Labels (SKOS-XL). Technical Report, W3C Recommendation (2009)
29. R. Agerri, I. Aldabe, E. Laparra, G. Rigau Claramunt, A. Fokkens, P. Huijgen, R. Izquierdo Beviá, M. van Erp, P. Vossen, A.L. Minard, et al., Multilingual event detection using the NewsReader pipelines, in *Proceedings of the Workshop on Cross-Platform Text Mining and Natural Language Processing Interoperability, collocated with International Conference on Language Resources and Evaluation (LREC)* (2016)
30. M. Verhagen, K. Suderman, D. Wang, N. Ide, C. Shi, J. Wright, J. Pustejovsky, The LAPPS Interchange Format, in *Proceedings of the International Workshop on Worldwide Language Service Infrastructure* (Springer, Berlin, 2015), pp. 33–47
31. B. Bohnet, J. Kuhn, The best of both worlds: a graph-based completion model for transition-based parsers, in *Proceedings of the 13th Conference of the European Chapter of the Association for Computational Linguistics* (Association for Computational Linguistics, Stroudsburg, 2012), pp. 77–87
32. A. Gangemi, V. Presutti, D. Reforgiato Recupero, A.G. Nuzzolese, F. Draicchio, M. Mongiovì, Semantic Web machine reading with FRED Semantic Web **8**(6), 873 (2017)
33. R. Witte, B. Sateli, The LODeXporter: flexible generation of linked open data triples from NLP frameworks for automatic knowledge base construction, in *Proceedings of the 11th International Conference on Language Resources and Evaluation (LREC)* (2018)

Chapter 6
Modelling Linguistic Annotations

Abstract This chapter describes how linguistic annotations can be represented in RDF. Web Annotation and NIF provide the means to reference text segments on the web. Yet, representing linguistic annotations requires appropriate vocabularies. We discuss relevant vocabularies and illustrate how they can be applied to support annotation at different levels.

6.1 Introduction

In the previous chapter, we discussed mechanisms to address text segments using URIs. While mechanisms to address text segments provide the basis for representing annotations in RDF, an important ingredient is still missing: vocabularies that allow to describe the linguistic phenomena annotated. In this chapter, we describe OWL- and RDF-based vocabularies to represent annotations which provide the basis for semantic interoperability.

With the rising importance of linguistic annotations in linguistics and language technology, the band-width and amount of linguistic annotations is continuously increasing in complexity and heterogeneity, and this is directly reflected in the number and diversity of annotation formats [1].

Two relatively widely used corpus formalisms have been introduced in Sect. 5.1, already. They are two representative examples for the variability of representation formalisms available, but suffer either from restrictions in terms of expressivity (CoNLL-TSV, TEI/inline XML) or processability (TEI/standoff XML):

- CoNLL-TSV (Sect. 5.1.1) annotates one word per line; it can neither adequately represent segments smaller than words (as necessary for morphology), nor nested structures (as necessary for phrase structure grammar). Instead, morphological and phrase-structure grammars are reduced to opaque strings whose semantics are not defined by the format, but left to client software.
- Inline XML (e.g. in TEI, Sect. 5.1.2, Fig. 5.4) can represent annotations at arbitrary granularity, but is limited to tree structures.

- Standoff XML (e.g. in TEI, Sect. 5.1.2, Fig. 5.5) can represent arbitrary graph structures (and thus any kind of linguistic annotation). This genericity, however, comes at the price of insufficient readability and limited technological support outside the language resource community.

As a result, interoperability between and across formats becomes a major concern, and has traditionally been addressed by graph-based data models and XML standoff formats. Standoff formats have a longer history in the language resource community, in particular for annotations with overlapping segments. While XML had been considered a solution for language resource interoperability during the late 1990s, such constellations required extensions of the original XML data model, i.e. the support for directed multi-graphs in annotation.[1] Standoff XML has been considered state of the art for multi-layer corpora during the early 2000s. As it forms the basis for the Linguistic Annotation Framework [3, LAF]—i.e. ISO 24612:2012 [4]—and its instantiations in the GrAF format [5], PAULA XML [6] and KAF [7], it is still considered technologically relevant [1], albeit it declined in popularity because of poor support by off-the-shelf XML technology [8] and the rise of JSON.

More recently, standoff XML in human language technology is thus being increasingly replaced by LLOD-compliant representations, often based on JSON-LD, e.g. Web Annotation (Sect. 5.2) or LIF (Sect. 11.4). Like earlier standoff XML formats, RDF implements labelled directed multi-graphs, but does benefit from a richer technological ecosystem and a broader developer community. Burchardt et al. [9] demonstrated that syntactic and semantic annotations can be integrated and jointly queried on grounds of an RDF formalization. Cassidy et al. [10] developed an early RDF serialization of LAF, and the standoff XML format NAF [11] has been explicitly designed with the goal to facilitate its transformation to RDF. Subsequently, various NLP infrastructures have adopted RDF-native exchange formats, including TELIX [12], NIF [13] and LIF [14].

In this chapter, we describe two approaches to represent linguistic annotations in RDF and as linked data: CoNLL-RDF and POWLA. Based on a fragment of NIF, CoNLL-RDF provides a semantically shallow and isomorphic reconstruction of TSV formats in RDF and thus represents a technological bridge between the most popular format family in NLP and LLOD technologies. POWLA is an OWL2/DL vocabulary that defines generic linguistic data structures, which can be used in combination with CoNLL-RDF, Web Annotation or NIF to formalize any kind of linguistic annotation.

---

[1]In the language resource community, it is generally assumed that labelled directed (multi-) graphs can represent *every* kind of linguistic annotation [2].

6.2   Transforming Legacy Annotation Formats into RDF

In NLP and DH, established annotation formats such as CoNLL are still much more prevalent than native RDF-based annotation formats. Even in the case that RDF backends are used for storing or transforming annotations, legacy formats are used as input/output to maintain compatibility with existing NLP pipelines. However, RDF excels at information integration, and where annotations from different sources are to be combined with each other, to be transformed or to be linked with other pieces of information, RDF-native formalisms enjoy increasing popularity (see Chap. 11).

Depending on whether developers see their priority in backward compatibility with legacy formats or in interoperability and re-usability, there are two approaches to transform legacy annotation formats into RDF:

- **Shallow transformation:** In this approach, a direct mapping of the original legacy data source to RDF is created. The mapping is shallow in that it provides a 1:1 mapping of the data elements of the original data source to RDF properties and classes, preserving by and large the original data model. There is thus no semantic integration or interoperability as the resulting vocabulary is proprietary for the source data model. Yet, this allows to transform, query and process annotations with RDF technology and to link them with LOD resources as required. The resulting RDF is specific to a given legacy data format and thus lacks interoperability to other RDF datasets.
- **Alignment with RDF/OWL native annotation vocabularies:** In applications where semantic integration and interoperability is important, an approach should be followed in which the source data model is mapped to an existing OWL vocabulary. This approach requires aligning/lifting the data format of the legacy data source to existing RDF/OWL vocabularies. The advantage of this approach is that by reuse of existing vocabularies in machine-readable formats, interoperability across datasets is ensured.

Here, we illustrate the shallow transformation approach using CoNLL as a popular legacy format for linguistic annotations.

6.2.1   CoNLL-RDF: Shallow Transformation of CoNLL into RDF

In NLP, the CoNLL formats (see Sect. 5.1.1) represent a large and diverse family of formats based on tab-separated values (TSV), and used for a wide range of linguistic phenomena. CoNLL-compatible formats have also been the basis for the development of corpus infrastructures, in particular, the Corpus WorkBench [15] and SketchEngine [16], widely used in corpus linguistics and lexicography, respectively. Individual CoNLL formats ('dialects') posit specific constraints on columns and their content.

```
#ID  WORD      LEMMA     UPOS   POS  FEATS         HEAD  EDGE
1    James     James     PROPN  NNP  Number=Sing   2     name
2    Baker     Baker     PROPN  NNP  Number=Sing   3     nsubj
3    told      tell      VERB   VBD  Mood=Ind|...  0     root
4    reporters reporter  NOUN   NNS  Number=Plur   3     obj
5    Friday    Friday    PROPN  NNP  Number=Sing   3     nmod:tmod
6    :         :         PUNCT  :    _             3     punct
```

Fig. 6.1 CoNLL-U annotation for Fig. 5.1 (p. 62)

CoNLL-RDF [17] is a semantically shallow approach to render CoNLL data structures in a generic way in RDF. Building on a minimal core vocabulary drawn from NIF (Sect. 5.3), it provides a generic mechanism to create user-defined datatype properties in the conll namespace, special handling for HEAD and ARG columns to represent dependency syntax and semantic roles, and a basic infrastructure for parsing, transforming, visualizing and converting CoNLL-RDF. Converting CoNLL-RDF includes import from and export to CoNLL TSV, but also to human-readable and graphical representations, as well as to a canonical serialization in Turtle/RDF.

Figure 6.1 shows a CoNLL fragment in the **CoNLL-U** dialect, the CoNLL format used by the Universal Dependencies (UD) initiative [18][2]: ID is the number of the word in the sentence, WORD is the form of the word,[3] LEMMA its lemma, UPOS its UD part-of speech tag, POS its original part-of-speech tag, FEATS its morphosyntactic features, HEAD the ID of its parent word in dependency annotation (or 0 for the root), and EDGE the label of its dependency relation. The final columns DEPS and MISC are not used for this example.

To provide a generic conversion of CoNLL data, CoNLL-RDF expects column labels to be provided at conversion time. For each column, an RDF property is generated using the user-provided label as local name in the conll namespace. As these properties are provided by the user, they lack any alignment to existing RDF/OWL vocabularies. It is in this sense that CoNLL-RDF is shallow as properties are specific for a certain CoNLL format and lack interoperability with other vocabularies.

---

[2]http://universaldependencies.org/, last accessed 09-07-2019.

[3]In CoNLL-U terminology, the columns WORD and EDGE are termed FORM and DEP, respectively. While CoNLL-RDF does not require to use these labels, it provides specialized visualization for them in a human-readable export. We thus recommend following CoNLL-RDF terminology rather than CoNLL-U terminology. Likewise, the column POS should be XPOS in CoNLL-U, but we follow Fig. 5.1 in using the same column label for the same information.

The following URI schema is used[4]:

- During conversion time, the user provides a base URI, e.g. identifying the corpus or document that the current CoNLL file represents.
- The abstract sentence URI consists of the base URI, followed by #s and the number of the sentence in the corpus, starting with 1.
- The word URI consists of the abstract sentence URI, followed by _ and the number of the word in the sentence, starting with 1. If an explicit ID column is provided, this value is used instead.
- The sentence URI consists of the abstract sentence URI, followed by _0. It is thus the 0th word of the sentence, i.e. its virtual root (following a practice used in CoNLL dependency parsing).

Basic data structures are nif:Sentence and nif:Word. Their respective sequential structure is made explicit by nif:nextSentence and nif:nextWord. CoNLL properties are generated from user-provided column labels for every non-empty cell:

- **Syntactic dependencies:** Column HEAD ⇒ object property conll:HEAD pointing to the URI of the parent word, resp. the sentence. If no HEAD column is provided, conll:HEAD points to the sentence.
- **Semantic roles:** In semantic role annotation, one column per frame in the sentence is created, so that the nth SRL-ARGs column contains the roles of the nth predicate in the sentence (i.e. annotated in the PRED column).[5] For a word annotated with the value, say ARG0 in the third SRL-ARGs column, the predicate is the third word in the sentence that has an annotation for PRED ⇒ object property conll:ARG0 pointing from predicate URI to argument URI.
- **Other:** Other column labels yield datatype properties containing an untyped literal. CoNLL-RDF does not require specific column labels, but it provides enhanced visualizations for the columns WORD and EDGE.

As a result, we obtain a shallow rendering of the original CoNLL data structure in RDF (Fig. 6.2), which can be effectively queried, manipulated and serialized back into CoNLL, using off-the-shelf RDF technology. The conll: namespace used here is not backed by an ontology, but populated by properties as defined by the user (column labels) or in the data (values for X-ARGs columns). One of the

---

[4]CoNLL formats do not preserve the original whitespaces, we thus cannot produce valid NIF URIs for a CoNLL-annotated text. (CoNLL-U does provide mechanisms to express the *absence* of whitespaces after a token, but this does not preserve information about the type of whitespace and is specific to a single dialect.) Instead, CoNLL-RDF follows the naming conventions of [19, 20].

[5]More precisely, this is a pattern for every XARGs column label for which the corresponding X column does exist. For CoNLL-RDF, ARGs column must not be followed by other annotations, and their values (not their labels) must by valid URI characters.

```
1    :sl_1 a nif:Word;
2        conll:ID "1";
3        conll:WORD "James";
4        conll:LEMMA "James";
5        conll:UPOS "PROPN";
6        conll:POS "NNP";
7        conll:FEATS "Number=Sing";
8        conll:HEAD :sl_2;
9        conll:EDGE "name";
10       nif:nextWord :sl_2.
```

Fig. 6.2 Turtle fragment for the first row in Fig. 6.1

design goals of CoNLL-RDF has been seamless round-tripping from CoNLL-TSV to CoNLL-RDF and back to TSV. While TSV export from CoNLL-RDF can be easily accomplished with SPARQL SELECT, such queries only support a fixed number of columns. Export of semantic roles is somewhat more complex, as it involves nested SELECT for every word using GROUP_CONCAT with tabulator as separator.

Beyond format specifications and converters, the CoNLL-RDF library permits the iterative application of sequences of SPARQL updates (resp., files that contain these) to documents or data streams providing CoNLL(-RDF) data. Even though it lacks formal semantics by design, the CoNLL RDF model can thus also serve as a basis to transform CoNLL data into semantically richer formalisms such as the NIF ontology or POWLA (Sect. 6.3). The motivation of CoNLL-RDF as a representation formalism is to facilitate the transformation of annotation graphs *provided in a commonly used format* on the basis of available Semantic Web technologies for its querying, manipulation, storage, etc. in a backward-compatible fashion, such that the results can be serialized back into the original format.

6.2.2 Querying and Manipulating CoNLL-RDF Annotations

Figure 5.3 introduced semantic role annotations for the example given above, replicated in Fig. 6.3, with a CoNLL-RDF rendering in Fig. 6.4. NIF data structures identify words and their structural relations, and user-provided column labels (WORD, POS, NER, SRL) yield the corresponding properties in the conll: namespace. For the label SRL-ARGs we have one column only in the example, corresponding to semantic arguments of the first word with SRL annotations, i.e. :sl_4, and accordingly, the predicate :sl_4 is annotated with properties generated from the annotations in the first SRL-ARGs column.

For named entity types, we see that the CoNLL-RDF preserves the original IOBES annotation, with B-PERSON marking the beginning of a person name, and E-PERSON marking the end of the span annotated with PERSON. With SPARQL

```
# WORD       POS  NER        SRL         SRL-ARGs
James        NNP  B-PERSON    _           ARG0
Baker        NNP  E-PERSON    _           ARG0
told         VBD  O           tell.v.01   rel
reporters    NNS  O           _           ARG2
Friday       NNP  S-DATE      _           ARGM-TMP
:            :    O           _           _
```

Fig. 6.3 POS, NER and PropBank (SRL) annotations (replicated from Fig. 5.3)

```
1   :s1_1 a nif:Word; conll:WORD "James";     conll:POS "NNP";
2                     conll:NER "B-PERSON"; nif:nextWord :s1_2.
3   :s1_2 a nif:Word; conll:WORD "Baker";     conll:POS "NNP";
4                     conll:NER "E-PERSON"; nif:nextWord :s1_3.
5   :s1_3 a nif:Word; conll:WORD "told";      conll:POS "VBD";
6                     conll:SRL "tell.v01"; conll:rel :s1_3;
7                     conll:ARG0 :s1_1, :s1_2; conll:ARG2 :s1_4;
8                     conll:ARG-TMP :s1_5;  nif:nextWord :s1_4.
9   :s1_4 a nif:Word; conll:WORD "reporters"; conll:POS "NNS";
10                    nif:nextWord :s1_5.
11  :s1_5 a nif:Word; conll:WORD "Friday";    conll:POS "NNP";
12                    conll:NER "S-DATE";   nif:nextWord :s1_6.
13  :s1_6 a nif:Word; conll:WORD ":";         conll:POS ":".
```

Fig. 6.4 CoNLL-RDF/Turtle fragment for Fig. 6.3

Update, this can be effectively transformed into a more compact representation. In a first step, we eliminate the IOBES codes from `conll:NER`:

```
1   DELETE {
2     ?w conll:NER ?iobes.
3   } INSERT {
4     ?w conll:NER ?short.
5   } WHERE {
6     ?w conll:NER ?iobes.
7     BIND(replace('^[IOBES]-','') AS ?short)
8   };
```

In a second step, we use the dependency annotation from Fig. 6.2 to restrict the NER annotation to the syntactic head of the corresponding phrase:

```
1   DELETE {
2     ?w conll:NER ?ner.
3   } WHERE {
4     ?w conll:NER ?ner.
5     ?w conll:HEAD/conll:NER ?ner.
6   };
```

This update eliminates all NER annotations if the syntactic head carries the same annotation. In the same way, semantic role annotations (exemplified for the example of ARG0 here) can be reduced to the syntactic head:

```
1   DELETE {
2     ?pred ?role ?arg.
```

```
3  } WHERE {
4    ?pred conll:SRL [].
5    ?pred ?role ?argHead, ?argDep.
6    ?argDep conll:HEAD ?argHead.
7    FILTER(?role in (conll:ARG0,conll:ARG1,conll:ARG2,...))
8  };
```

The result can be rendered in a somewhat simplified CoNLL TSV format using SPARQL SELECT (we leave SRL-ARGs as an exercise):

```
1  SELECT ?word ?pos ?ner ?srl
2  WHERE {
3    ?w conll:WORD ?word; conll:POS ?pos.
4    OPTIONAL { ?w conll:POS ?ner_raw. }
5    OPTIONAL { ?w conll:SRL ?srl_raw. }
6    BIND(IF(BOUND(?ner_raw),?ner_raw,'_') as ?ner)
7    BIND(IF(BOUND(?srl_raw),?srl_raw,'_') as ?srl)
8  }
```

This query is trivial for properties where annotations are obligatory (WORD, POS). For properties where empty annotations are possible, CoNLL compliance requires to insert _. Here, _ is inserted for missing (non-bound) values of optional properties.

From this query, the CoNLL RDF libraries (or any other SPARQL engine) will produce the following table:

```
James      NNP _        _
Baker      NNP PERSON   _
told       VBD _        tell.v.01
reporters  NNS _        _
Friday     NNP DATE     _
:          :   _        _
```

The CoNLL RDF libraries guarantee proper sentence segmentation and word order, but this query can also be run using any general SPARQL engine. Reproducing the original word order requires slight modifications in this case[6]:

```
1  SELECT ?word ?pos ?ner ?srl
2  WHERE {
3    ?w conll:WORD ?word; conll:POS ?pos.
4    OPTIONAL { ?w conll:POS ?ner_raw. }
5    OPTIONAL { ?w conll:SRL ?srl_raw. }
6    BIND(IF(BOUND(?ner_raw),?ner_raw,'_') as ?ner)
7    BIND(IF(BOUND(?srl_raw),?srl_raw,'_') as ?srl)
8    { SELECT ?w (COUNT(DISTINCT ?tmp) AS ?id)
```

---

[6]Sentence-level segmentation is left as an exercise. This requires retrieving the sentence URI for every word (by means of ?w conll:HEAD+ ?s. ?s a nif:Sentence) and GROUP BY (and ORDER BY) sentence URIs before ordering words. If a word has no nif:nextWord predecessor, set the value of the WORD column to concat('\\n',?word) rather than to ?word.

```
 9      WHERE {
10         ?tmp nif:nextWord* ?w
11      } GROUP BY ?w
12   }
13 } ORDER BY ?w
```

This query uses an embedded SELECT statement to count the number of preceding NIF words to create a numerical id (alternatively, the optional conll:ID property can be used) and performs an ordering of words on this basis. The original query can also be extended to include the dependency annotations used for disambiguating the NER annotations:

```
 1 SELECT ?id ?word ?pos ?head ?dep ?ner ?srl
 2 WHERE {
 3    ?w conll:WORD ?word; conll:POS ?pos.
 4    OPTIONAL { ?w conll:POS ?ner_raw. }
 5    BIND(IF(BOUND(?ner_raw),?ner_raw,'_') as ?ner)
 6    OPTIONAL { ?w conll:SRL ?srl_raw. }
 7    BIND(IF(BOUND(?srl_raw),?srl_raw,'_') as ?srl)
 8    BIND(replace(str(?w),'.*_','') AS ?id)
 9    ?w conll:HEAD ?h.
10    BIND(replace(str(?h),'.*_','') AS ?head)
11    ?w conll:EDGE ?dep.
12 };
```

For this query, we rely on the CoNLL-RDF URI scheme introduced above, i.e. the URI ends with the original (or implied) ID value for every word (and its head) is the last, separated with _. However, this information cannot be drawn from a URI directly but must rather be cast as a string (str()), before a replacement can be applied. These examples show how CoNLL-RDF and SPARQL can be effectively used to perform complex transformations of CoNLL data. While export to CoNLL TSV is somewhat more challenging (unless the CoNLL-RDF libraries are used), the transformation itself is simple and straight-forward. In addition, it is possible to consult external knowledge sources as part of the transformation. As an example, consider the LLOD edition of VerbNet [21] provided as part of LemonUby [22]. The semantic role annotations of PropBank are grounded in VerbNet. Having both corpus and dictionary available as RDF, resp. LLOD data, we can now produce an alignment of VerbNet classes and PropBank predicates.

6.3 Top-Down Modelling: Generic Data Structures

Common annotation formats have been designed to either fulfil requirements of a specific task (e.g. as training data for syntactic or semantic parsing), the phenomenon they address (e.g. annotation of words and or trees) or with the goal to adopt existing technical solutions for their processing. By rendering linguistic data structures in directed graphs, RDF provides a means to facilitate syntactic or structural interoperability between such formats (resp., annotations expressed by them), but only in the sense that they can be stored and accessed uniformly. Neither the Web Annotation nor the NLP Interchange Format aim for semantic interoperability of annotations. While NIF provides a vocabulary for annotations, it is specific to the types of annotation currently supported, including parts of speech, lemmatization, phrase structure syntax, entity linking and sentiment analysis. For representing linguistic annotations in a way that semantic interoperability is ensured, the above-mentioned models need to be complemented with an explicit vocabulary that allows to describe annotations at a content level. Here, we describe POWLA [23], a small but generic vocabulary developed to facilitate the exchange and querying of multi-layer corpora with arbitrary annotations. As it aims to support *any* kind of linguistic annotation, POWLA is the most general of the vocabularies suggested so far.

6.3.1   Linguistic Annotations in POWLA

POWLA[7] [24] is a small OWL2/DL-based vocabulary grounded in the Linguistic Annotation Framework [4, LAF] and thus capable of representing *any kind* of text-oriented annotation. This genericity sets it apart from earlier approaches on LOD-based corpus representations in that POWLA is not tied to specific types of annotations, e.g. constituent syntax and frame semantics [9], for syntax [25] or selected NLP tasks [26].

POWLA is an OWL2/DL serialization of PAULA [27, 28], an early implementation of LAF [29] and serialized in a standoff XML format comparable to GrAF [30]. PAULA and PAULA XML have been the basis for developing integrative NLP pipelines [31], a corpus information system for multi-layer corpora [32], and a generic converter suite for linguistic annotations [33]. In these applications, the robustness of the PAULA data model has been demonstrated as well as its capabilities to integrate annotations from different sources. POWLA has been applied to modelling multi-layer corpora, including case studies on the Manually Annotated Sub-Corpus of the American National Corpus [34, MASC], syntactic and coreference-annotated corpora [24] and for high-precision information extraction [35], annotation engineering [36] and syntactic parsing [37].

POWLA aims to formalize linguistic annotations by building on existing standards with respect to their anchoring in the original document. In PAULA XML, XLink/XPointer references served this purpose. POWLA is underspecified with respect to this, but both NIF URIs and Web Annotation selectors can be employed. POWLA thus serves to complement existing NIF, Web Annotation or application-specific RDF renderings of linguistic annotations with interoperable linguistic data structures.

---

[7]http://purl.org/powla/powla.owl.

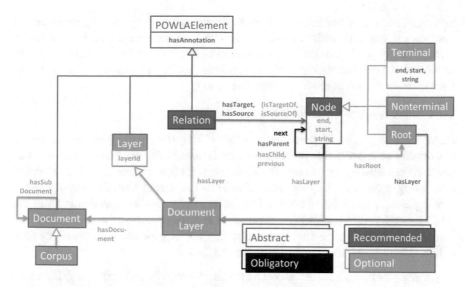

Fig. 6.5 POWLA data model, obligatory, abstract, recommended and optional properties shown in different shades of grey

The POWLA data model is illustrated in Fig. 6.5. It provides a scalable vocabulary in that it defines a minimum core of obligatory and recommended properties and concepts concerned with linguistic annotation, along with a number of optional concepts and properties particularly relevant for corpus organization, or querying.

6.3.1.1   POWLA Nodes

Units of annotation are formalized as `powla:Node`. By means of the property `powla:hasParent` (and its inverse `powla:hasChild`), the hierarchical composition of nodes can be expressed, e.g. for syntax trees or discourse structure. The property `powla:next` (and its inverse `powla:previous`) is used to express the sequential order of two adjacent nodes. It is recommended that `powla:next` is used to link nodes which have the same parent, as this facilitates navigation in tree structures. POWLA does not provide its own mechanism for document linking, but can be applied in combination with NIF or Web Annotation, e.g. a NIF URI (representing, e.g., a `nif:Word`) can be linked via `powla:hasParent` with a `powla:Node` that represents a syntactic phrase. The domain declaration of `powla:hasParent` RDFS entails that the NIF URI represents a `powla:Node`, and thus, `powla:next` transitions can (and should) be created to connect it with adjacent NIF words of the same phrase or, if necessary, with an empty element (represented by a `powla:Node` without an associated NIF URI) to be inserted between string-adjacent NIF words. It is recommended to use `powla:next` transitions for `powla:Nodes` with the same parent not only because this facilitates navigation, but also because it allows to define an order of tree elements that is independent from the order of strings. This may be necessary, e.g., to represent a form of 'deep' or 'canonical' syntax that deviates from the actual strings, e.g. in spoken discourse, but also in complex structures that violate syntactic projectivity. One example here is preposition stranding as in (3):

(3) $[What]_{PP_1}$ are you talking $[about]_{PP_1}$?

Here, *what* is placed in preverbal position ('WH-movement'), but it still forms a syntactic unit with the preposition that remained in its 'base position'. For such constellations, the Penn Treebank uses empty elements and a complex coindexing scheme, but as an alternative POWLA would also allow to specify a direct `powla:next` link between both parts of the PP—independently from the `nif:nextWord` transitions that express the *actual* sequence of words.[8]

POWLA defines three subclasses of nodes, albeit their use is optional, as they can be inferred `powla:hasParent` annotations:

- `powla:Terminal`: A `powla:Node` which is not the object of a `powla:hasParent` property. The notion of 'terminal node' has little practical relevance for modelling and querying corpora in RDF, but a single 'base segmentation', resp., the '(privileged) tokenization layer' have been fundamental concepts in XML standoff formats. We assume that the privileged tokenization layer is the sequence of minimal segments, thereby identifying terminals by the absence of `powla:hasParent` properties. As an alternative to the minimal segmentation principle, explicit `nif:Word` and `nif:nextWord` annotations can be used for querying token sequences, but this is beyond POWLA.
- `powla:Nonterminal`: Every `powla:Node` which is not a terminal.
- `powla:Root`: A root node is a `powla:Node` which is not a subject of a `powla:hasParent` property. For corpus querying and corpus organization, `powla:Root` is an important concept as it provides an 'entry point' into linguistic annotations. In particular, a number of properties that organize linguistic annotations into documents and corpora are based on the notion of root nodes as this limits the number of necessary links between data points and data sets.

---

[8]In fact, we may even express the 'canonical'—albeit in this case, somewhat unnatural—order directly on NIF words. In the absence of any hierarchical annotation, we can specify the following `powla:next` transitions (represented by →):

about → *What* → *are* → *you* → *talking* → *?*

While there are no restrictions regarding the ordering of blank nodes defined as `powla:Nodes`, the antisequential ordering *of externally defined URIs* must be handled with care in order to prevent cycles when combining annotations coming from different sources. It is thus recommended to follow the sequential order and to connect nodes with the same parent via `powla:next` if and only if no sibling does exist that is intermediate in terms of the original string order.

POWLA nodes carry the following object properties:

- `powla:next`: (obligatory) object property (inverse `powla:previous`, optional) used for expressing the sequential order of sibling nodes.
- `powla:hasParent`: (recommended) object property (inverse `powla:has Child`, optional) used for representing hierarchical annotations.

POWLA defines several datatype properties for nodes, including:

- `powla:start`, `powla:end`: (optional, recommended for terminals) specify numerical indices, e.g. an offset (as in NIF) or another, structure-sensitive index [38]. Interpretation is implementation specific, but the end value needs to be greater than the start value.
- `powla:hasAnnotation`: abstract property applying to every POWLA element, should be instantiated with annotation-specific subproperties following the schema hasXY.
- `powla:string`: (optional, recommended for terminals) carries the string value of the tokens to which this annotation unit (node) applies.

6.3.1.2   POWLA Relations

POWLA nodes represent units of annotation and their sequential and hierarchical structure. For representing annotated relations between nodes as labelled edges, POWLA uses a reified representation by means of `powla:Relation`. By means of `powla:hasSource` and `powla:hasTarget` (inverse of `powla:isSourceOf`, resp. `powla:isTargetOf`) POWLA relations are linked with the nodes between which the relation holds.

Note that POWLA relations do not represent whether they encode hierarchical or non-hierarchical relations. Hierarchical (dominance) relations are characterized by coverage inheritance, i.e. the target (parent) node covers the same stretch of terminals as the source (child) nodes. A prototypical example is phrase structure syntax. Non-hierarchical relations do not impose such constrains and hold between nodes independently from their hierarchical structure; prototypical examples are dependency syntax or coreference annotation. In POWLA, this difference is not marked at the relation type, but independently from the reified relation by an accompanying `powla:hasParent` (`powla:hasChild`) property.

In the same way as POWLA nodes, relations can carry `powla:hasAnnotation` subproperties.

6.3.1.3 OLiA Links

The Ontologies of Linguistic Annotation (OLiA, Sect. 8.4.2) provide OWL2/DL formalizations of annotation schemes for a plethora of linguistic annotations and languages. Unlike NIF, POWLA does not provide a specialized property for linking annotations with OLiA concepts. Instead, nodes and relations can be directly assigned an OLiA class (including anonymous classes composed by description-logic operators ⊔, ⊓, ¬ and/or property constraints) as an `rdf:type`. POWLA nodes and POWLA relations can thus be modelled as instances of OLiA concepts or OLiA annotation model concepts.

In fact, this has been a motivating factor in providing a reified representation of linguistic annotations rather than ad hoc properties (as in NIF extensions for dependency syntax). To a certain extent, dependency labels and morphosyntactic annotations overlap,[9] so that an a priori, i.e. tagset-independent, split between relational (property) and non-relational (concept) annotations is not possible. Instead, morphological, syntactic and semantic features are represented in the OLiA Reference Model in terms of a single concept hierarchy. A reified representation of relational annotations avoids type-shifting between annotation properties and OLiA concepts. This is necessary to stay within OWL(2) semantics and thus allows the application of OWL(2) reasoners to OLiA/POWLA data.

Unlike NIF, POWLA does thus not provide a vocabulary for specific linguistic categories. OLiA is indeed the recommended vocabulary to represent specific categories. In this way, POWLA is both more minimalistic than NIF annotation classes and properties, and more expressive, as it relies on a rich background vocabulary.

6.3.1.4 Corpus Organization

Aside from modelling linguistic annotations, annotated corpora may require an explicit representation of the organization of annotations into documents and layers. In principle, RDF graphs can be used for this purpose, but an explicit vocabulary is nevertheless necessary to identify what kind of information a particular RDF graph contains and how this relates to other RDF graphs (e.g. pertaining to the same source document, or representing the same kind of annotation for different source documents).

Beyond formalizing linguistic annotations, POWLA provides such a vocabulary to organize corpora. This includes two orthogonal dimensions:

- **dataset structure**: A corpus is composed of individual *documents* and their associated annotations. Documents can be organized into *collections* (e.g. sub-

---

[9]For example, the Universal Dependencies provide the POS tag DET and the dependency label det, and '[m]ost commonly, a word of POS DET will have the relation det and vice versa.' http://universaldependencies.org/u/dep/all.html#al-u-dep/det, accessed 09-07-2019.

corpora). A corpus is regarded as a special case of a collection. Furthermore, a document may be composed of different *parts*, which may in turn be considered independent documents in their own right (e.g. books in the Bible).

* **annotation structure:** Typically, a corpus features multiple types of annotations, e.g. parts of speech along with dependency syntax. Typically, these are produced by independent annotation efforts or using different annotation tools. Annotations of the same type should be organized into a single annotation layer.

For data set structure, POWLA provides two basic concepts, `powla:Document` and `powla:Corpus`. The POWLA document corresponds to an annotation project in PAULA. An annotation project may contain other annotation projects as sub-documents (`hasSubDocument`). If it does not contain other annotation projects, it represents a collection of documents (e.g., a subcorpus, or a pair of texts in a parallel corpus). Otherwise, it contains the annotations of one particular text. In this case, it aggregates different document layers (see below). A corpus is a document that is not a subdocument of another document.

Annotation structure is rendered by means of `powla:Layer`, which serves to group together annotations of the same kind independently from their document. A `powla:DocumentLayer` is a specific layer *within a document*, as expressed by the property `powla:hasDocument`. `DocumentLayer` is a nexus for linking documents and annotations. Nodes and relations can be assigned a document layer (and thus, a document) via `powla:hasLayer`. The property `powla:hasLayer` is recommended for root nodes. A root may have at most one layer.

POWLA layers and documents can be assigned labels by means of subproperties of `powla:hasAnnotation` that correspond to metadata rather than annotations, e.g. date of creation or name of the annotator.

6.3.2 Complementing NIF with POWLA

We illustrate POWLA with annotations for phrasal syntax (Fig. 6.6), named entities (Fig. 6.7) and semantic relations (Fig. 6.8) for an unabridged fragment of `wsj_0655` and its annotation according to the Penn Treebank [39, phrase structure syntax], PropBank [40, semantic roles], OntoNotes named entity types [41], RST Discourse Treebank [42] and automated annotations with DBpedia Spotlight [43]. For presentational reasons, annotation layers are merged and structural annotations are superimposed over each other (Fig. 6.9). Note that the annotations can still be distinguished by means of `powla:hasAnnotation` subproperties. In addition, external vocabulary can be used to encode additional information, e.g. the ITS vocabulary for entity linking[10] or the NERD ontology for entity types.[11]

---

[10]https://www.w3.org/TR/its20/, last accessed 09-07-2019.

[11]http://nerd.eurecom.fr/ontology, last accessed 09-07-2019.

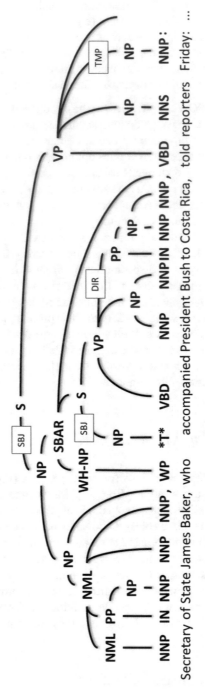

Fig. 6.6 Graph view on syntax annotation of ex. 2 (wsj_0655, OntoNotes **syntax**)

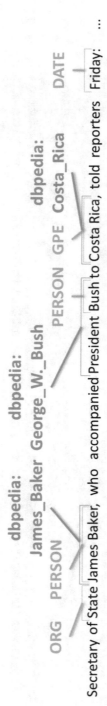

Fig. 6.7 Graph view on named entity annotation of ex. 2 (wsj_0655, manual named entities from OntoNotes and automated [and partially incorrect] entity linking from DBPedia Spotlight)

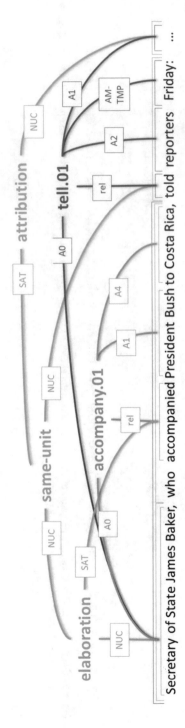

Fig. 6.8 Graph view on selected semantic annotation of ex. 2 (wsj_0655, OntoNotes SRL for **tell.01** and accompany.01, and RST DTB discourse relations)

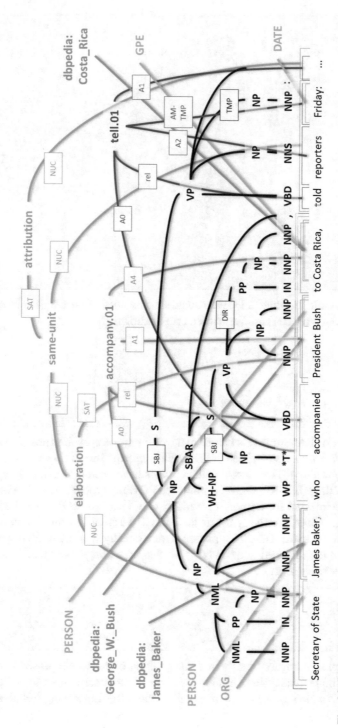

Fig. 6.9 Merged graph from Figs. 6.6, 6.7, and 6.8

```
1    PREFIX nif: <http://persistence.uni-leipzig.org/nlp2rdf/
         ontologies/nif-core#>
2    PREFIX doc: <https://catalog.ldc.upenn.edu/docs/LDC95T7/raw
         /06/wsj_0655.txt#>
3    PREFIX powla: <http://purl.org/powla/powla.owl#>
4    PREFIX itsrdf: <http://www.w3.org/2005/11/its/rdf#>
5    PREFIX : <https://catalog.ldc.upenn.edu/docs/LDC2007T21/
         ontonotes-1.0-documentation.pdf#>
6
7    # user-defined datatypes
8    :hasPOS rdfs:subPropertyOf powla:hasAnnotation. # cf. nif:
         posTag
9    :hasNER rdfs:subPropertyOf powla:hasAnnotation. # cf. on:
         EMANEX
10   :hasCAT rdfs:subPropertyOf powla:hasAnnotation. # phrase
         labels
11   :hasNUC rdfs:subPropertyOf powla:hasAnnotation. # NUC/SAT
         labels
12   :hasSRL rdfs:subPropertyOf powla:hasAnnotation. # semantic
         roles
```

Before providing its data, a POWLA data set may need to introduce user-specific subproperties of powla:hasAnnotation as shown above.

```
13   # data
14   doc:offset_0_9 a powla:Node;
15       powla:string "Secretary" ;
16       :hasPOS "NNP";
17       powla:hasParent _:syntax1;
18       nif:nextWord doc:offset_10_12 .
```

The first POWLA terminal is based on the NIF part-of-speech annotation sample above (Sect. 5.3.1, p. 79)—albeit NIF-specific information (string class, context, offsets) being omitted. The recommended offsets have been omitted as they can be inferred from the NIF URI. The recommended POWLA type powla:Node can in fact be RDFS-inferred from powla:hasParent (etc.) and is thus omitted in the following data points. For the syntactic annotation, we create an anonymous (blank) POWLA node _:syntax1. This phrase covers exactly this token (and would be conflated with the terminal node in NIF), so that no siblings exist which could be linked by powla:next.

```
19   _:syntax1 powla:string "Secretary";
20       :hasCAT "NML";
21       powla:hasParent _:syntax2;
22       powla:next _:syntax3 .
```

The NML phrase covers exactly one token, albeit optional, we provide its string value to facilitate readability. Again, powla:hasParent links to a POWLA nonterminal, but also, powla:next points to the following sibling (relative to the same parent node).

```
24      doc:offset_10_12 powla:string "of" ;
25          :hasPOS "IN";
26          powla:hasParent _:syntax3;
27          nif:nextWord doc:offset_13_18.
28
29      doc:offset_13_18 powla:string "State";
30          :hasPOS "NNP";
31          :hasNER "ORG";
32          powla:hasParent _:syntax4;
33          nif:nextWord doc:offset_19_24.
34
35      _:syntax4 powla:string "State";
36          :hasCAT "NP";
37          powla:hasParent _:syntax3.
```

These nodes illustrate additional annotations for named entities (:hasNER, corresponding to on:ENAMEX above; :hasCAT for phrase labels). It should be noted that the decision whether to create a separate nonterminal for every type of annotation or whether to unify coextensional nonterminals is application specific. Here, we opt for unification as this yields a sparse representation.[12]

```
39      _:syntax3 powla:string "of State";
40          :hasCAT "PP";
41          powla:hasParent _:syntax2;
42          powla:next doc:offset_19_24.
```

This is the first POWLA nonterminal in our data with more than one child node.

```
44      doc:offset_19_24 powla:string "James";
45          :hasPOS "NNP" ;
46          powla:hasParent _:syntax2, _:ner1;
47          nif:nextWord doc:offset_25_30;
48          powla:next doc:offset_25_30.
49
50      doc:offset_25_30 powla:string "Baker";
51          :hasPOS "NNP" ;
52          powla:hasParent _:syntax2, _:ner1;
53          nif:nextWord doc:offset_30_31.
54
55      _:ner1 powla:string "James Baker";
56          :hasNER "PERSON";
57          itsrdf:taIdentRef <http://dbpedia.org/resource/
                James_Baker> ;
58          a dbo:Agent, dbo:Person, dbo:OfficeHolder .
59          # this is a root node not connected to _:syntax2
60
61      _:syntax2 powla:string "Secretary of State James Baker";
```

---

[12]Although not illustrated in the data snippet, coextensional nodes connected by powla:hasParent would not be unified. Only the 'highest' non-branching nonterminals per annotation layer would be unified with each other.

```
62        :hasCAT "NML";
63        powla:isSourceOf         # semantic role annotation,
              pointing to predicate
64                 [ :hasSRL "A0"; powla:hasTarget doc:offset_36_47
                     ];
65        powla:hasParent _:syntax5;
66        powla:next doc:offset_30_31.
```

For the syntactic phrase and the token span annotated for named entities and
entity linking, different nonterminals need to be created as they are not coextensional. In both annotations, however, the sibling structure is identical.

The blank node _:ner1 carries named entity annotations, but also entity linking
(using an external vocabulary in accordance with NIF recommendations). It is
important to note here a semantic difference between POWLA and NIF. In NIF, only
a *string* can be defined as having the type dbo:Agent. This is rather imprecise
as it conflates two levels of abstraction: The textual level and the referential level.
In POWLA, both levels can be more clearly separated, as POWLA nonterminals
are abstract entities (like annotations in Web Annotation), and are thus not a priori
incompatible with referential semantics. It is still semantically weak as it enforces
a reading that dbo:Agent (etc.) is in fact a class of descriptors rather than
entities themselves—an interpretation possibly valid in the context of DBpedia, but
probably counterintuitive.

The nonterminal _:ner1 is a root node; it does not have a following sibling
(as it does not have a parent) and thus remains isolated from _:syntax2.[13]
The blank node _:syntax2 is coextensional with the A0 span of the predicate
accompany.01. This is modelled here as a (non-hierarchical) relation pointing
from _:syntax2 to the verb *accompanied*.

```
68     doc:offset_30_31 powla:string ",";
69          :hasPOS ",";
70          powla:hasParent _:syntax5;
71          nif:nextWord doc:offset_32_35.
72
73     _:syntax5 powla:string "Secretary of State James Baker,";
74          :hasCAT "NP";
75          powla:hasParent _:syntax6;
76          powla:next _:syntax8;    # next relative to syntax parent
77          powla:hasParent _:rst1;
78          powla:isSourceOf              # relation label "NUC"
79                  [ :hasNUC "NUC"; powla:hasTarget _:rst1 ];
80          powla:next _:syntax8.    # next relative to RST parent
```

---

[13] It is possible to infer that _:ner1 is enclosed by _:syntax2 via the following SPARQL
fragment:

```
?ner1 ^powla:hasParent+/powla:hasParent+ ?syntax2.
# at least one descendant of ?ner1 is in ?syntax2
MINUS { ?tmp powla:hasParent+ ?ner1.
MINUS { ?x powla:hasParent ?tmp }
MINUS { ?tmp powla:hasParent+ ?syntax2 }
# there is no terminal descendant of ?ner1 that is not a descendant of ?syntax2
```

This last snippet illustrates a labelled hierarchical relation (i.e. a relation accompanied by `powla:hasParent`). It also shows how the same POWLA node may carry two `powla:hasParent` statements. In principle, a node can also have different `powla:next` statements relative to each parent, illustrated by two `powla:next` triples. In this particular case, the RST sibling and the syntactic sibling are coextensional and have been merged.

6.3.3 Transforming CoNLL-RDF to POWLA

As mentioned above, CoNLL-RDF can be used as an intermediate representation between a specific format and a full-fledged linked data representation. A generic transformation of CoNLL to POWLA can be easily accomplished with CoNLL-RDF and six SPARQL Update rules.

1. Define words and sentences as `powla:Nodes`, but otherwise retain their original annotation.

```
1   INSERT {
2      ?w a powla:Node.
3      ?w powla:hasParent ?s.
4      ?s a powla:Node.
5   } WHERE {
6      ?w a nif:Word.
7      ?w conll:HEAD+ ?s.
8      ?s a nif:Sentence.
9   };
```

As CoNLL(-RDF) is based on word-level annotations, and supports phrase-level annotations only in the form of string fragments, we define the sentence of any particular word as its parent node.

2. Define the sequential order of nodes. As CoNLL does not provide native support for phrase nodes, map `nif:nextWord` and `nif:nextSentence` to `powla:next`:

```
10   INSERT {
11       ?x powla:next ?y
12   } WHERE {
13       ?x ?rel ?y
14       FILTER(?rel in (nif:nextWord,nif:nextSentence))
15   };
```

3. Define string values and offsets for terminal nodes[14]:

```
16  INSERT {
17      ?w powla:string ?word ;
18          powla:start ?start ;
19          powla:end ?end .
20  } WHERE {
21      ?w conll:WORD ?word.
22      { SELECT ?w (COUNT(DISTINCT ?pre) as ?start)
23          WHERE {
24              ?pre nif:nextWord+ ?w
25          } GROUP BY ?w
26      }
27      BIND( (?start + 1) as ?end)
28  };
```

4. Define annotations: Datatype properties from the `conll` namespace are (re)defined as subproperties of `powla:hasAnnotation`. As we cannot directly check for the prefix, we perform a string match on the underlying URI:

```
29  INSERT {
30    ?annotation rdfs:subPropertyOf powla:hasAnnotation
31  } WHERE {
32    ?w ?annotation ?x.
33    FILTER(literal(?x) && strstarts(str(?prop),
34    'http://ufal.mff.cuni.cz/conll2009-st/task-description.html
          #')
35  };
```

5. Create relations for dependency syntax: Dependency annotations in CoNLL-RDF are represented by two properties: the obligatory `conll:HEAD` annotation and the optional `conll:EDGE` annotation. In POWLA, these can be complemented by `powla:Relation`:

```
36  INSERT {
37    ?dependent powla:isSourceOf [
38      rdfs:label ?edge;
39      powla:hasTarget ?head ]
40  } WHERE {
41    ?dependent conll:HEAD ?head.
42    OPTIONAL { ?dependent conll:EDGE ?edge }
43  };
```

---

[14]We follow CoNLL-RDF conventions for naming the column containing the string value WORD. If a different column label is used, the rule needs to be adjusted accordingly. Optionally, the `conll:WORD` property may be deleted to facilitate backward compatibility; we leave it intact here.

Note that POWLA does not define the type of offsets and that we assume the number of preceding tokens. Alternatively, one may use the STRLEN function to get an approximate character offset.

In order to avoid confusion between the original `conll:EDGE` property and the annotation attached to the relation; this is represented here by means of an `rdfs:label`.

6. Create relations for semantic roles: Create a novel annotation property and to map relevant CoNLL properties by means of a `FILTER`:

```
44  INSERT {
45    :hasSRL rdfs:subPropertyOf powla:hasAnnotation.
46    ?arg powla:isSourceOf [
47      :hasSRL ?role;
48      powla:hasTarget ?pred ].
49  } WHERE {
50    ?pred ?srl ?arg.
51    FILTER(?srl in (syn:ARG0,syn:ARG1,syn:ARG2)) # etc
52    BIND(replace(str(?srl),'.*#','') as ?role)
53  };
```

The resulting representation is compliant with POWLA data structures and thus provides the basis for semantic interoperability. POWLA allows to infer recommended and optional properties and classes from obligatory (and recommended) POWLA properties and classes. With this information, the resulting data structure is suitable for effective navigation.

6.4   Querying Annotated Corpora

One motivation for modelling linguistic annotations in RDF is to facilitate accessibility and integration of linguistic annotations from different sources and across processing tools. Other applications include information integration in NLP pipelines (cf. Chap. 11) and enrichment with external knowledge repositories, which may provide annotation terminology (Sect. 8.4.2) or lexical information about a particular domain.

For demonstrating access to and information retrieval from linguistic annotations provided in RDF, we focus on corpus querying using the POWLA vocabulary as a basis. We demonstrate the capability of SPARQL and POWLA for querying corpora by addressing a number of critical problems used to assess the expressivity of corpus query languages. Lai et al. [44] designed seven reference queries to evaluate the extent to which a query language is capable to match and return specific nodes, to navigate trees, sequences and other relations, and their transitive closure, as well as to demonstrate the need for an update mechanism (cf. our solution to Q4 below). We illustrate the application of (expanded) POWLA+NIF and SPARQL for these queries, slightly adapted to match the example data from Sect. 6.3.2, cf. Fig. 6.9 (p. 107) for a visualization of the data.

Q1 Find sentences that include the word *told*.

For identifying sentences, we resort to syntax annotations, i.e., POWLA nodes without parents and with :hasCat "S".[15]

The corresponding SPARQL query would look as follows:

```
1  SELECT ?s
2  WHERE {
3      ?s a powla:Root; :hasCAT "S".
4      ?told powla:string "told"; powla:hasParent+ ?s.
5  }
```

As a result, we return the sentence URI. Resolving this URI should point to the underlying string, using the means of Web Annotation or NIF to address text fragments. However, we can also reconstruct the full string of the sentence from POWLA alone:

```
1   SELECT ?s ?string
2   WHERE {
3       ?s a powla:Root; :hasCAT "S".
4       ?told powla:string "told"; powla:hasParent+ ?s.
5       { SELECT ?s
6         (GROUP_CONCAT(?word; separator=" ") as ?string)
7         WHERE {
8            ?w a powla:Terminal; powla:hasParent+ ?s;
9                powla:start ?start; powla:string ?word.
10       } GROUP BY ?s ORDER BY ?s ?start
11      }
12  }
```

Note that this reconstruction is approximative only as a whitespace is inserted between two tokens whereas the original distribution and number of whitespaces between tokens is unknown (and may already have been lost in the source formats, e.g. if provided in CoNLL TSV).

Q2 Find sentences that do not include the word *told*.

Some corpus query languages do not permit existential negation or universal quantification. In SPARQL this is possible as shown in the following query:

```
1  SELECT ?s
2  WHERE {
3      ?s a powla:Root; :hasCAT "S".
4      MINUS { ?told powla:string "told"; powla:hasParent+ ?s }
5  }
```

Q3 Find noun phrases whose rightmost child is a noun.

This query exploits the fact that powla:next holds between siblings only. However, as siblings are defined only in relation to a particular parent node and

---

[15] Alternatively, one may use NIF data structures and retrieve nif:Sentences.

multiple parent nodes are possible, we need to make sure that the next element is also a child of the same noun phrase. For identifying nouns from Penn Treebank annotations, we need to check against different parts of speech and hence use a corresponding FILTER expression.

```
1  SELECT ?np
2  WHERE {
3    ?np :hasCAT "NP"; powla:hasChild ?noun.
4    ?noun :hasPOS ?pos FILTER(?pos="NNP" || ?pos="NNS").
5    MINUS {
6      ?noun powla:next/powla:hasParent ?np
7    }
8  }
```

Q4 Find verb phrases that contain a verb immediately followed by a noun phrase that is immediately followed by a prepositional phrase.

Verbs are identified by several tags in Penn Treebank annotation, but characterized with a 'V' as a first character. This is used here to define a filter condition. A challenge in this query is that it is not restricted to direct child nodes of verb phrases (between powla:next would hold), but to any descendant. This is solved here by using nif:nextWord (alternatively, start and end indices of terminal nodes may be used). As we compare phrases, we need to rule out that one phrase is contained in another.

```
1   SELECT ?vp
2   WHERE {
3     ?vp :hasCAT "VP"; powla:hasParent+ ?v, ?np, ?pp.
4     ?v  :hasPOS ?pos FILTER(strstarts(?pos,'V')).
5     ?np :hasCAT "NP".
6     ?pp :hasCAT "PP".
7     ?v nif:nextWord/powla:hasParent+ ?np.
8     ?np powla:hasChild+/nif:nextWord/powla:hasParent+ ?pp.
9     MINUS { ?np powla:hasParent* ?pp }
10    MINUS { ?pp powla:hasParent* ?np }
11    MINUS { ?v powla:hasParent+ ?np }
12    MINUS { ?v powla:hasParent+ ?pp }
13  }
```

As an alternative, a SPARQL update may be applied to the data beforehand to assign every nonterminal its left- and right-most token and use this precompiled information to formulate the query in easier terms:

```
1  INSERT {
2      ?node :left ?left; :right ?right.
3  } WHERE {
4      ?node powla:hasChild+ ?left, ?right.
5      ?left a nif:Word. ?right a nif:Word.
6      MINUS { ?node powla:hasChild+/nif:nextWord+ ?left }
7      MINUS { ?right nif:nextWord+/powla:hasParent+ ?node }
8  };
```

Using these task-specific properties, we can simplify the query:

```
1  SELECT ?vp
2  WHERE {
3    ?vp :hasCAT "VP"; powla:hasParent+ ?v, ?np, ?pp.
4    ?v  :hasPOS ?pos FILTER(strstarts(?pos,'V')).
5    ?np :hasCAT "NP".
6    ?pp :hasCAT "PP".
7    ?v nif:nextWord/^:left ?np.
8    ?np :right/nif:nextWord/^:right ?pp.
9  }
```

Q5 Find the first common ancestor of sequences of a noun phrase followed by a verb phrase.

This query requires a result set of all ancestors and its subsequent reduction to the first common ancestor. The variable ?tmp is introduced to eliminate every descendant of a result candidate which is ancestor to *both* the verb phrase and the noun phrase.

```
1   SELECT ?ancestor
2   WHERE {
3     ?np :hasCAT "NP".
4     ?np powla:hasChild+/nif:nextWord/powla:hasParent+ ?vp.
5     MINUS { ?np powla:hasParent* ?vp }
6     MINUS { ?vp powla:hasParent* ?np }
7     ?ancestor powla:hasChild+ ?np, ?vp.
8     MINUS {
9       ?ancestor powla:hasChild+ ?tmp.
10      ?tmp powla:hasChild+ ?np, ?vp
11    }
12  }
```

Q6 Find a clause which dominates a verb phrase, restricted to cases in which this verb phrase is dominated by an RST nucleus.

For this query, we assume an integrated representation of RST and syntax annotations, i.e. that RST segments point to the largest constituents they contain, not directly to strings (cf. lines 73–80 in the listing on p. 110). In Penn Treebank annotation, clauses are identified by category labels starting with S.[16]

```
1  SELECT ?clause
2  WHERE {
3    ?clause :hasCAT ?cat FILTER(strstarts(?cat,'S')).
4    ?clause powla:hasChild ?vp.
5    ?vp :hasCAT "VP".
```

---

[16]Q6 is reformulated from an example in phonology. It is designed to show that queries can be run across different annotation layers. In fact, our version is slightly more complex than Lai et al.'s original as we do not just need to check the annotations of the RST node, but the annotation of its relation.

```
6     ?vp powla:hasParent ?rst.
7     ?rstrel powla:hasSource ?vp;
8             powla:hasTarget ?rst;
9             :hasNUC "NUC".
10  }
```

Q7 Find a noun phrase dominated by a verb phrase. Return the subtree dominated by that noun phrase only.

```
1   SELECT ?np
2   WHERE {
3     ?vp :hasCAT "VP"; powla:hasChild ?np.
4     ?np :hasCAT "NP".
5   }
```

The challenge here is that corpus query languages often do not allow to constrain the returned result, but that they rather return the entire context for a match to the query. Given the expressivity of SPARQL, it should not come as a surprise that each of these seven queries can be expressed in a relatively straightforward fashion, i.e. with a little more complexity than the solutions in existing query languages provided by Lai et al. [44]. Unlike the languages compared by Lai et al., however, *every single* query can be expressed by SPARQL.

A clear benefit of the combined application of SPARQL and LLOD-native vocabularies to represent linguistic data structures in RDF is that queries can be more easily ported over different data sources, and that information conveyed in corpora can be flexibly combined with external knowledge sources.

Beyond expressivity, portability and resource integration, a great benefit in comparison to common corpus query languages is that query fragments can be precompiled in the data (cf. Q4), so that query-specific optimizations can be developed on the fly. Indeed, the direct application of SPARQL (and other RDF query languages) to linguistic corpora has been suggested repeatedly [9, 24, 45, 46].

Yet, SPARQL also has disadvantages in comparison to existing corpus query languages:

- The semantic restrictions of existing corpus language queries are motivated by the need to guarantee adequate response times. With SPARQL being semantically unconstrained, the user is responsible to keep an eye on run time.[17]

---

[17]In fact, advanced users need to acquire some insight into the inner mechanics of SPARQL to optimize queries and to guard themselves against unexpected results. As such, SPARQL is evaluated in a bottom-up fashion: {}-enclosed graph fragments are compiled first, and then joined with the context set. In order to prevent large result sets for optional or alternative statements, users should take care to make the relation between all variables in, say, an OPTIONAL fragment explicit—even if redundant with information expressed before. Moreover, SPARQL engines normally evaluate the query left to right. This means that filters on a variable should only be expressed after this variable is bound, and queries can be optimized by positing the most restrictive conditions first.

- Most RDF databases do not come with graphical visualizations that are appealing to linguists. For this purpose, external tools can be used, but shifting between different applications is relatively inconvenient.
- Many corpus information systems provide user-friendly graphical query builders. It would be possible to develop such a system for SPARQL, but for linguistics-specific visualization, the supported vocabulary needs to be restricted.
- SPARQL has a rather technical appeal in that it is neither developed by nor normally taught to linguists.

Given the state of the art in corpus linguistics, an appealing solution to these problems is to continue to use existing corpus query infrastructures, but to provide SPARQL generators that allow to replicate them against a triple store if data from different sources is to be integrated or a specific problem requires a level of semantic expressivity that the original corpus query does not provide:

- Such a hybrid solution can be used by anyone familiar with existing query languages.
- SPARQL queries generated from semantically constrained corpus query languages lead to more constrained (i.e. more effective) queries.
- If a specific visualization is needed (e.g. to fine-tune query results), the same query can be run against existing infrastructure.

In this way, a linguist can design a query, e.g. to extract features to be fed into an NLP pipeline, and the generated SPARQL query can then be refined if a higher level of expressivity is needed than provided by the original query language. Such reconstructions of corpus query languages in SPARQL have been described by Chiarcos et al. [23] and [46]. Given the increasing shift in the language resource community from XML-based to graph-based corpus infrastructures [47, 48], as well as the growing maturity of RDF-based NLP service architectures (Chap. 11), we expect an increasing interest in this line of research.

6.5   Summary and Further Reading

This chapter has described mechanisms and data models to represent linguistic annotations in RDF, be it for processing and integration with Semantic Web technology and resources or for publication of corpora as Linked Open Data. Both functions overlap, but have very different requirements:

- For applications where backward compatibility with existing community standards is important, a direct reconstruction of the respective format (resp., its semantics) in RDF(S) provides a viable way to facilitate the processing and publication of data. This was illustrated for the CoNLL format and the use of CoNLL-RDF for annotation manipulation. CoNLL-RDF may be serialized back into CoNLL, or, alternatively, transformed into a full-fledged LLOD representation as required by the second use case.

- For applications aiming to facilitate interoperability and resource integration, and for publication of annotated data as LLOD, we recommend the use of generic data models for linguistic data structures. At the time of writing, no widely used community standard for this purpose has emerged yet. We described the POWLA vocabulary which may represent a basis from which such a vocabulary may eventually evolve, and its application for querying linguistic annotations.

In the wider context of LLOD vocabularies, CoNLL-RDF and POWLA complement NIF (resp., Web Annotation) in that they extend them with application-specific, resp., general data structures for representing linguistic annotations. Aside from other applications, it is thus possible to model, to share and to access linguistically annotated corpora on the web of data in an interoperable way. At the time of writing, it is not uncommon to encounter ad hoc formats to model annotations in RDF,[18] or to devise novel, application-specific formats to integrate specific annotations into a coherent representation.[19] In the longer perspective, however, we expect a tendency towards greater harmonization, and ultimately, convergence towards more widely used conventions, most probably based on widely used community standards rather than proprietary or task-specific formats. For open data and data which can be related to LLOD resources, RDF represents a useful publication format, also because it allows to separate the data model from its serialization—be it RDF/Turtle, RDF/XML, JSON-LD, RDF-Thrift or a TSV rendering as produced from CoNLL-RDF. Depending on the respective use case, other serializations can be generated in a lossless fashion.

As for further reading on linguistic annotations, we suggest consulting the *Handbook of Linguistic Annotation* [51] which provides a general overview and a detailed discussion of most representative formats currently being used for linguistic annotation in various modalities. With respect to linguistic annotations in the context of linguistic linked (open) data, it is hard to give a specific recommendation at this time, as the field is evolving at a fast pace. Aside from the present volume, another upcoming publication on the topic includes the book edited by Pareja-Lora et al. [52]. As a general suggestion, the interested reader may want to follow up on proceedings and associated publications of the workshop series on Linked Data in Linguistics (LDL, biannually, since 2012) and the conference series on Language, Data and Knowledge (LDK, biannually, since 2017), as these take the most specific focus on semantic technologies in application to language technology. Beyond this, it is possible to get directly involved, e.g., in the context of the W3C community group on Linked Data for Language Technology Community Group (LD4LT),[20] which provides a mailing list for discussing these issues.

---

[18]For example, the MATE SRL system [49] provides an ad hoc representation in RDF/N3 under http://barbar.cs.lth.se:8081/, accessed 09-07-2019.

[19]For example, the Concrete format [50], designed as an application of Apache Thrift, or JSON-NLP [53], designed as a JSON replacement of earlier generic formats for NLP.

[20]https://www.w3.org/community/ld4lt/, accessed 09-07-2019.

References

1. N. Ide, C. Chiarcos, M. Stede, S. Cassidy, Designing annotation schemes: from model to representation, in *Handbook of Linguistic Annotation*, ed. by N. Ide, J. Pustejovsky. Text, Speech, and Language Technology (Springer, Berlin, 2017)
2. S. Bird, M. Liberman, A formal framework for linguistic annotation. Speech Commun. **33**(1–2), 23 (2001)
3. N. Ide, K. Suderman, The Linguistic Annotation Framework: a standard for annotation interchange and merging. Lang. Resour. Eval. **48**(3), 395 (2014)
4. ISO, ISO 24612:2012. Language resource management—Linguistic Annotation Framework. Technical Report, ISO/TC 37/SC 4, Language resource management (2012). https://www.iso. org/standard/37326.html
5. N. Ide, K. Suderman, GrAF: a graph-based format for linguistic annotations, in *Proceedings of the 1st Linguistic Annotation Workshop (LAW 2007)*, Prague, 2007, pp. 1–8
6. C. Chiarcos, S. Dipper, M. Götze, U. Leser, A. Lüdeling, J. Ritz, M. Stede, A flexible framework for integrating annotations from different tools and tag sets. TAL (Traitement Automatique des Langues) **49**(2), 217 (2008)
7. W. Bosma, P. Vossen, A. Soroa, G. Rigau, M. Tesconi, A. Marchetti, M. Monachini, C. Aliprandi, KAF: a generic semantic annotation format, in *Proceedings of the 5th International Conference on Generative Approaches to the Lexicon GL 2009*, Pisa, 2009
8. R. Eckart, Choosing an XML database for linguistically annotated corpora, in *Sprache und Datenverarbeitung. Proceedings of the KONVENS 2008 Workshop on Datenbanktechnologien für Hypermediale Linguistische Anwendungen*, Berlin, 2008
9. A. Burchardt, S. Padó, D. Spohr, A. Frank, U. Heid, Formalising multi-layer corpora in OWL/DL—Lexicon modelling, querying and consistency control, in *Proceedings of the 3rd International Joint Conference on NLP (IJCNLP)*, Hyderabad, 2008, pp. 389–396
10. S. Cassidy, An RDF realisation of LAF in the DaDa annotation server, in *Proceedings of the 5th Joint ISO-ACL/SIGSEM Workshop on Interoperable Semantic Annotation (ISA-5)*, Hong Kong, 2010
11. A. Fokkens, A. Soroa, Z. Beloki, N. Ockeloen, G. Rigau, W.R. van Hage, P. Vossen, NAF and GAF: linking linguistic annotations, in *Proceedings of the 10th Joint ISO-ACL SIGSEM Workshop on Interoperable Semantic Annotation* (2014), pp. 9–16
12. E. Rubiera, L. Polo, D. Berrueta, A. El Ghali, TELIX: an RDF-based model for linguistic annotation, in *Proceedings of the 9th Extended Semantic Web Conference (ESWC 2012)*, Heraklion, 2012
13. S. Hellmann, J. Lehmann, S. Auer, M. Brümmer, Integrating NLP using linked data, in *Proceedings of the 12th International Semantic Web Conference (ISWC)*. Lecture Notes in Computer Science, vol. 8219 (Springer, Heidelberg, 2013), pp. 98–113
14. N. Ide, K. Suderman, E. Nyberg, J. Pustejovsky, M. Verhagen, LAPPS/Galaxy: current state and next steps, in *Proceedings of the 3rd International Workshop on Worldwide Language Service Infrastructure and 2nd Workshop on Open Infrastructures and Analysis Frameworks for Human Language Technologies (WLSI/OIAF4HLT2016)* (2016), pp. 11–18
15. O. Christ, A modular and flexible architecture for an integrated corpus query system, in *Proceedings of the 3rd Conference on Computational Lexicography and Text Research (COMPLEX'94)*, Budapest, 1994
16. A. Kilgarriff, V. Baisa, J. Bušta, M. Jakubíček, V. Kovář, J. Michelfeit, P. Rychlý, V. Suchomel, The Sketch Engine: ten years on. Lexicography **1**(1), 7 (2014). https://doi.org/10.1007/s40607-014-0009-9
17. C. Chiarcos, C. Fäth, CoNLL-RDF: Linked corpora done in an NLP-friendly way, in *Proceedings of the 1st International Conference on Language, Data, and Knowledge, LDK 2017*, ed. by J. Gracia, F. Bond, J.P. McCrae, P. Buitelaar, C. Chiarcos, S. Hellmann (Springer, Cham, 2017), pp. 74–88. https://doi.org/10.1007/978-3-319-59888-8_6

18. J. Nivre, Ž. Agić, L. Ahrenberg, et al., Universal dependencies 1.4 (2016). http://hdl.handle. net/11234/1-1827
19. S. Brants, S. Hansen, Developments in the TIGER annotation scheme and their realization in the corpus, in *Proceedings of the 3rd International Conference on Language Resources and Evaluation (LREC)*, Las Palmas, 2002, pp. 1643–1649
20. W. Lezius, H. Biesinger, C. Gerstenberger, TigerXML quick reference guide. Technical Report, IMS, University of Stuttgart (2002)
21. K.K. Schuler, VerbNet: a broad-coverage, comprehensive verb lexicon. Ph.D. thesis, University of Pennsylvania, Philadelphia, PA (2005). AAI3179808
22. J. Eckle-Kohler, J. McCrae, C. Chiarcos, *lemonUby*—a large, interlinked, syntactically-rich resource for ontologies. Semantic Web J. **6**(4), 371 (2015)
23. C. Chiarcos, Interoperability of corpora and annotations, in *Linked Data in Linguistics*, ed. by C. Chiarcos, S. Nordhoff, S. Hellmann (Springer, Heidelberg, 2012), pp. 161–179
24. C. Chiarcos, POWLA: modeling linguistic corpora in OWL/DL, in *Proceedings of the 9th Extended Semantic Web Conference (ESWC-2012)*, Heraklion, 2012, pp. 225–239
25. N. Mazziotta, Building the syntactic reference corpus of medieval French using NotaBene RDF annotation tool, in *Proceedings of the 4th Linguistic Annotation Workshop* (Association for Computational Linguistics, Stroudsburg, 2010), pp. 142–146
26. S. Hellmann, J. Lehmann, S. Auer, M. Brümmer, Integrating NLP using linked data, in *Proceedings of the 12th International Semantic Web Conference, 21–25 October 2013*, Sydney, 2013. Also see http://persistence.uni-leipzig.org/nlp2rdf/
27. S. Dipper, M. Götze, Accessing heterogeneous linguistic data—generic XML-based representation and flexible visualization, in *Proceedings of the 2nd Language & Technology Conference 2005*, Poznan, 2005, pp. 23–30
28. M.G. Stefanie Dipper, ANNIS: complex multilevel annotations in a linguistic database, in *Proceedings of the 5th Workshop on NLP and XML (NLPXML-2006): Multi-Dimensional Markup in Natural Language Processing*, Trento, 2006
29. N. Ide, L. Romary, International standard for a Linguistic Annotation Framework. Nat. Lang. Eng. **10**(3–4), 211 (2004)
30. N. Ide, K. Suderman, GrAF: a graph-based format for linguistic annotations, in *Proceedings of the Linguistic Annotation Workshop*. Prague (Association for Computational Linguistics, Stroudsburg, 2007), pp. 1–8
31. M. Stede, H. Bieler, S. Dipper, A. Suriyawongk, Summar: combining linguistics and statistics for text summarization, in *Proceedings of the 17th European Conference on Artificial Intelligence (ECAI)*, Riva del Garda, 2006, pp. 827–828
32. A. Zeldes, J. Ritz, A. Lüdeling, C. Chiarcos, ANNIS: a search tool for multi-layer annotated corpora, in *Corpus Linguistics*, Liverpool, 2009, pp. 20–23
33. F. Zipser, L. Romary, A model oriented approach to the mapping of annotation formats using standards, in *Proceedings of the Workshop on Language Resources and Language Technology Standards, collocated with LREC (LR&LTS 2010)*, Valetta, 2010
34. N. Ide, C.F. Baker, C. Fellbaum, C.J. Fillmore, R. Passonneau, MASC: the manually annotated sub-corpus of American English, in *Proceedings of the 6th International Conference on Language Resources and Evaluation (LREC-2008)*, Marrakech, 2008, pp. 2455–2461
35. D.A. de Araujo, S.J. Rigo, J.L.V. Barbosa, Ontology-based information extraction for juridical events with case studies in Brazilian legal realm. Artif. Intell. Law **25**(4), 379 (2017)
36. C. Chiarcos, C. Fäth, Graph-based annotation engineering: towards a gold corpus for Role and Reference Grammar, in *Proceedings of the 2nd Conference on Language, Data and Knowledge (LDK)*. OpenAccess Series in Informatics (Schloss Dagstuhl, Leibniz-Zentrum fuer Informatik, 2019)
37. C. Chiarcos, B. Kosmehl, C. Fäth, M. Sukhareva, Analyzing Middle High German syntax with RDF and SPARQL, in *Proceedings of the 11th International Conference on Language Resources and Evaluation (LREC)* (Miyazaki, Japan, 2018)
38. T. Krause, U. Leser, A. Lüdeling, graphANNIS: a fast query engine for deeply annotated linguistic corpora. J. Lang. Technol. Comput. Linguist. **31**(1), 1 (2016)

39. M. Marcus, B. Santorini, M.A. Marcinkiewicz, Building a large annotated corpus of English: the Penn Treebank. Comput. Linguist. **19**(2), 313 (1993)
40. P. Kingsbury, M. Palmer, From TreeBank to PropBank, in *Proceedings of the 3rd International Conference on Language Resources and Evaluation (LREC)*, Las Palmas, 2002
41. E. Hovy, M. Marcus, M. Palmer, L. Ramshaw, R. Weischedel, OntoNotes: the 90% solution, in *Proceedings of the Conference of the North American Chapter of the Association for Computational Linguistics on Human Language Technology (HLT-NAACL)* (Association for Computational Linguistics, New York, 2006), pp. 57–60
42. L. Carlson, D. Marcu, M.E. Okurowski, Building a discourse-tagged corpus in the framework of Rhetorical Structure Theory, in *Current and New Directions in Discourse and Dialogue*, ed. by J. van Kuppevelt, R. Smith. Text, Speech, and Language Technology, vol. 22, chap. 5 (Kluwer, Dordrecht, 2003)
43. P. Mendes, M. Jakob, A. García-Silva, C. Bizer, DBpedia SpotLight: shedding light on the web of documents, in *Proceedings of the 7th International Conference on Semantic Systems (I-Semantics 2011)*, Graz, 2011
44. C. Lai, S. Bird, Querying and updating treebanks: a critical survey and requirements analysis, in *Proceedings of the Australasian Language Technology Workshop* (2004), pp. 139–146
45. M. Kouylekov, S. Oepen, Semantic technologies for querying linguistic annotations: an experiment focusing on graph-structured data, in *Proceedings of the 9th International Conference on Language Resources and Evaluation (LREC)* (Reykjavik, Iceland, 2014)
46. A. Frank, C. Ivanovic, Building literary corpora for computational literary analysis—a prototype to bridge the gap between CL and DH, in *Proceedings of the 11th International Conference on Language Resources and Evaluation (LREC)*, Miyazaki, May 7–12, 2018
47. P. Banski, J. Bingel, N. Diewald, E. Frick, M. Hanl, M. Kupietz, P. Pezik, C. Schnober, A. Witt, KorAP: the new corpus analysis platform at IDS Mannheim, in *Proceedings of the 6th Language & Technology Conference on Human Language Technology Challenges for Computer Science and Linguistics*, December 7–9, 2013, Poznan, (2014), pp. 586–587
48. T. Krause, U. Leser, A. Lüdeling, graphANNIS: a fast query engine for deeply annotated linguistic corpora. JLCL **31**(1), 1 (2016)
49. B. Bohnet, J. Kuhn, The best of both worlds: a graph-based completion model for transition-based parsers, in *Proceedings of the 13th Conference of the European Chapter of the Association for Computational Linguistics* (Association for Computational Linguistics, Stroudsburg, 2012), pp. 77–87
50. F. Ferraro, M. Thomas, M.R. Gormley, T. Wolfe, C. Harman, B. Van Durme, Concretely annotated corpora, in *Proceedings of the AKBC Workshop at NIPS* (2014)
51. N. Ide, J. Pustejovsky (eds.), *Designing Annotation Schemes: From Model to Representation*. Text, Speech, and Language Technology (Springer, Berlin, 2017)
52. A. Pareja-Lora, M. Blume, B. Lust, C. Chiarcos (eds.), *Development of Linguistic Linked Open Data Resources for Collaborative Data-Intensive Research in the Language Sciences* (MIT Press, Cambridge, 2019)
53. D. Cavar, O. Baldinger, U.M. Joshua Herring, Y. Zhang, S. Bedekar, S. Panicker, An annotation encoding schema for natural language processing using JSON: NLP JSON schema version 0.1, November 2018. Technical Report, Indiana University (2018)

Chapter 7
Modelling Metadata of Language Resources

Abstract LD technologies allow metadata of datasets to be exposed on the Web in order to improve their automated discovery, sharing and reuse by humans and software agents. In this chapter we deal with the representation of metadata for LRs, with the idea of enabling their cataloguing, discovery and later reuse. We will distinguish two types of metadata: general metadata, i.e. applicable to any type of LD dataset (e.g. author, license, title), and metadata that specifically describes the properties of LRs (e.g. typology, number of languages, number of words). To that end, in this chapter we will review the most commonly used models to document general metadata on the Web of Data, most prominently DCAT and DC-Terms. Then, we will describe Meta-Share.owl, a OWL vocabulary specifically designed for describing metadata of LRs as linked data.

7.1 Introduction

In previous chapters we have reviewed the modelling mechanisms that support the representation of content of language resources (LRs) as linked data on the Web, particularly lexical data (Chap. 4) and corpora (Chap. 5). Beyond the linguistic data itself that LRs contain, the linked data mechanisms also allow the *metadata* of such LRs to be represented, i.e. the data that describe the resources themselves (e.g. typology, languages contained, size of the data, provenance, etc.). Definition of metadata of LRs enables their cataloguing and supports their automated discovery, share and reuse by humans and software agents alike.

In the area of language technologies, there have been several initiatives and coordinated efforts for defining metadata of LRs to support their indexing in digital catalogues, based on pre-linked data techniques. One of the most notable of such initiatives is META-SHARE,[1] an open, integrated, secure and interoperable exchange infrastructure where LRs are uploaded, documented, stored and catalogued, aiming to support their discoverability and reuse [1]. LRs can also

---

[1]http://www.meta-share.eu.

© Springer Nature Switzerland AG 2020   123
P. Cimiano et al., *Linguistic Linked Data*,
https://doi.org/10.1007/978-3-030-30225-2_7

be downloaded, exchanged and discussed in the context of the META-SHARE infrastructure. In order to support such mechanisms, META-SHARE has developed a rich metadata schema [2] that allows to describe aspects of LRs accounting for their whole lifecycle, from their production to their usage. The schema has been implemented as an XML Schema Definition (XSD)[2] and descriptions of specific LRs are available as XML documents.

Besides META-SHARE, other initiatives and organizations dedicated to the promotion and distribution of LRs such as ELRA[3] and LDC,[4] have developed their own catalogues and inventories of LRs. Other infrastructures are the CLARIN Virtual Language Observatory (VLO)[5] [3], the Language Grid[6] and Alveo,[7] the Open Language Archives Community (OLAC),[8] catalogues with crowd-sourced metadata, such as the LRE Map[9] [4], which collects the set of metadata (type, name, use, status and other information) that the authors assign to the language resources they use and/or describe during the submission procedure to CL conferences (the LREC[10] series mostly, but also others like COLING,[11] EMNLP,[12] or RANLP[13]), and repositories coming from various communities (e.g. OpenAire,[14] EUDAT[15]). The metadata schemes of all these sources vary with respect to their coverage and the set of specific metadata captured.

As an evolution of these efforts, there have been initiatives to develop a linked data-based counterpart of some of these models for cataloguing LRs, in order to maximize interoperability and reuse of LR's metadata across different scenarios and infrastructures. For instance, the aforementioned LRE Map has an RDF version of their data [5] and underlying model.[16] A more general effort was carried out in the context of the W3C Linked Data for language Technologies (LD4LT) community group[17] in order to develop an ontology in OWL that allows us to represent the metadata schemes of the aforementioned repositories under an extensible open-world model. The ontology, called *Meta-Share.owl*, builds on the META-SHARE

---

[2]https://github.com/metashare/META-SHARE/tree/master/misc/schema/v3.0.

[3]http://www.elra.info/en.

[4]https://www.ldc.upenn.edu/.

[5]https://vlo.clarin.eu/.

[6]http://langrid.org.

[7]http://alveo.edu.au.

[8]http://www.language-archives.org.

[9]http://www.resourcebook.eu/.

[10]http://www.lrec-conf.org/.

[11]http://www.coling-2010.org/.

[12]http://www.lsi.upc.edu/events/emnlp2010.

[13]http://lml.bas.bg/ranlp2011/start3.php.

[14]https://www.openaire.eu/.

[15]http://eudat.eu.

[16]see http://www.resourcebook.eu/lremap/owl/lremap_resource.owl, last accessed on 17/10/2017.

[17]https://www.w3.org/community/ld4lt/.

XML-based model but it was re-engineered with interoperability in mind and to maximize compatibility with other vocabularies such as DCAT [6] or the most prominent models in the CLARIN VLO data. Meta-Share.owl defines many ontology entities for describing LRs but also reuses a number of entities coming from other vocabularies to account for general metadata.

In the remainder of this chapter, we will review some of the most commonly used models to document general metadata of datasets on the Web of Data (not only LRs but any type of dataset), i.e. DC-Terms and DCAT. Then, we will give an overview of Meta-Share.owl, the most complete vocabulary for describing metadata of LRs as linked data available today.

7.2 Models for General Metadata

When representing metadata of LRs, we will find two types of information: general dataset information (e.g. *title* of the dataset, *date of creation, license, creator*, etc., and information that is characteristic of LRs (e.g. *resource type, modality, number of languages*, etc.). In this section we will focus on the first type of metadata and give an overview of two of the most extensively used vocabularies to represent such general metadata (DC-Terms and DCAT), along with a few examples taken from the language resources domain.

There are other metamodels that we do not discuss in detail here, such as the Vocabulary of Interlinked Datasets (VoID),[18] the Friend of a Friend vocabulary (FOAF),[19] or the PROV ontology (PROV-O),[20] which in most cases can be used in combination with DC-Terms and DCAT. VoID is an RDF Schema vocabulary for expressing metadata about RDF datasets. It is intended as a bridge between the publishers and users of RDF data, with applications ranging from data discovery to cataloguing and archiving of datasets. VoID can be used as an alternative (or complement) to DCAT. The main difference between both approaches is that VoID describes datasets in RDF format only, while DCAT is neutral with regards to format, thus being more appropriate to describe LRs that have no RDF representation. FOAF, on the other hand, is used to document persons, agents, documents, etc. along with their identifying information (webpage, name, nickname, etc.) and the relations among them (e.g. knows). FOAF is frequently used in combination with DCAT, as we will see later in Sect. 7.2.2. Finally, PROV-O, a W3C recommendation since 2013, is intended to provide vocabulary elements to describe the provenance of data. In most cases, the basic mechanisms offered by DC-Terms are enough to cover the needs of provenance representation of LRs. In cases in which such mechanisms

---

[18]https://www.w3.org/TR/void/.

[19]http://www.foaf-project.org/.

[20]https://www.w3.org/TR/prov-o/.

do not suffice, PROV-O offers a more sophisticated and fine-grained description of provenance that can be used in addition to DC-Terms.

7.2.1 DC-Terms

The DCMI Metadata Terms vocabulary[21] (or DC-Terms for short) is a specification of metadata terms maintained by the Dublin Core Metadata Initiative, including properties, vocabulary encoding schemes, syntax encoding schemes, and classes. According to the Linked Open Vocabularies (LOV) catalogue,[22] DC-Terms is the most reused vocabulary on the Web of Data (reused by 508 other vocabularies, at the time of writing). DC-Terms can be expressed in a range of possible syntaxes and formats (text, HTML, XML, etc.) depending on the particular application scenario. DCMI also offers recommendations for the use of DC-Terms in RDF.[23] DC-Terms consist of 34 classes and 55 properties. Out of them, a subset of 15 core properties for representing resources metadata is offered by the 'Dublin Core Metadata Element Set'.[24] Here we list some of the most commonly used properties in DC-Terms (most of them are part of the 'Element Set' as well):

- Title (`dct:title`), or a name given to the resource.
- Subject (`dct:subject`), which, typically, will be represented using keywords, key phrases or classification codes. The use of a controlled vocabulary is recommended here.
- Creator (`dct:creator`), an entity (e.g. a person, an organization or a service) primarily responsible for creating the resource.
- Description (`dct:description`), which may include but is not limited to an abstract, a table of contents, a graphical representation or a free-text account of the resource.
- Source (`dct:source`), a related resource from which the described resource is derived in whole or in part.
- License (`dct:license`), which points to a legal document giving official permission to do something with the resource.
- Publisher (`dct:publisher`), an entity (a person, an organization or a service) responsible for making the resource available.

These properties, along with the rest of the entities provided by DC-Terms, can be used to represent the basic metadata of any resource on the Web, including LRs. In

---

[21] Homepage at http://dublincore.org/documents/dcmi-terms/ and ontology at http://purl.org/dc/terms/.

[22] http://lov.okfn.org/.

[23] http://dublincore.org/documents/dc-rdf/.

[24] http://dublincore.org/documents/dces/.

Sect. 7.2.2 we will describe a particular example of the use of DC-Terms to describe the metadata of a language resource.

7.2.2 DCAT

The Data Catalogue Vocabulary (DCAT)[25] is an RDF vocabulary designed to facilitate interoperability between data catalogues published on the Web [6]. DCAT has the status of W3C Recommendation since January 2014. DCAT is intended to increase discoverability of datasets by enabling applications to consume and combine metadata from multiple catalogues. It also enables decentralized publishing of catalogues as well as federated dataset search across sites. DCAT-based data *catalogues* are organized into *datasets* and *distributions*. A distribution is considered an accessible form of a dataset, for instance a downloadable file, a SPARQL endpoint, an RSS feed or a web service that provides the data. DCAT reuses elements from other vocabularies whenever appropriate, such as `foaf:homepage`, `foaf:Agent`, `dct:title`, etc., and defines their own set of core classes:

- `dcat:Catalog` represents a catalogue, i.e. a collection of datasets.
- `dcat:Dataset` represents a dataset in a catalogue. A dataset is defined as a 'collection of data, published or curated by a single agent, and available for access or download in one or more formats'.
- `dcat:Distribution` represents an accessible form of a dataset (a downloadable file or web service, for instance).
- `dcat:CatalogRecord` represents the record that describes a dataset in the catalogue. It is used to capture provenance information about dataset entries in a catalogue, and its use is considered optional.

Figure 7.1 shows how such entities are related among them and to other external entities. DCAT represents the language by means of the `dct:language` property, and defines the range of the property as follows: (1) use language codes/identifiers defined by the Library of Congress,[26] (2) if an ISO 639-1 (two-letter) code is defined for the language, then its corresponding IRI should be used; (3) if no ISO 639-1 code is defined, then the IRI corresponding to the ISO 639-2 (three-letter) code should be used. The property can be used to indicate the language of the catalogue (language used in the textual metadata describing titles, descriptions, etc.) or the language of the dataset itself. The property can take multiple values if the dataset has several languages. A more detailed discussion of the representation of languages is given in Chap. 8.

We mention also the notion of *DCAT profile*, which is a specification for data catalogues that adds additional constraints to DCAT. Such additional constraints

---

[25]https://www.w3.org/TR/vocab-dcat/.

[26]http://id.loc.gov/vocabulary/iso639-1.html and http://id.loc.gov/vocabulary/iso639-2.html.

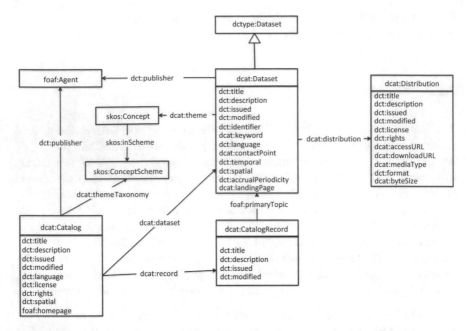

Fig. 7.1 Scheme of the DCAT classes and properties [Copyright ©2014 W3C® (MIT, ERCIM, Keio, Beihang). This picture is taken from the "Data Catalogue Vocabulary (DCAT)" W3C report]

in a profile may include: A minimum set of required metadata fields, classes and properties for additional metadata fields not covered in DCAT, controlled vocabularies or URI sets as acceptable values for properties and requirements for specific access mechanisms (RDF syntaxes, protocols) to the catalogue's RDF description can be specified. An example of a DCAT profile is DCAT-AP[27] (DCAT application profile for portals in Europe), which is intended for describing public sector datasets in Europe.

Example Consider a simplified example of the use of DCAT taken from the metadata of a real LR, the Apertium RDF EN-ES dictionary.[28]

```
1  @prefix dcat: <http://www.w3.org/ns/dcat#> .
2  @prefix owl: <http://www.w3.org/2002/07/owl#> .
3  @prefix dct: <http://purl.org/dc/terms/> .
```

[27] https://joinup.ec.europa.eu/solution/dcat-application-profile-data-portals-europe.

[28] The resource was documented in Datahub at https://datahub.ckan.io/dataset/apertium-rdf-en-es. Datahub created a DCAT file with the basic metadata (see https://datahub.ckan.io/dataset/apertium-rdf-en-es), which was extended by the authors with some additional information (see http://linguistic.linkeddata.es/set/apertium/EN-ES). For convenience, the example shown here is a simplified view with elements taken from such two DCAT records.

```
 4  @prefix rdfs: <http://www.w3.org/2000/01/rdf-schema#> .
 5
 6  <http://linguistic.linkeddata.es/set/apertium/EN-ES>
 7    a dcat:Dataset ;
 8    dct:title "Apertium RDF EN-ES" ;
 9    dct:source <http://hdl.handle.net/10230/17110> ;
10    dct:language <http://id.loc.gov/vocabulary/iso639-1/en> ;
11    dct:language <http://id.loc.gov/vocabulary/iso639-1/es> ;
12    dct:license <http://purl.oclc.org/NET/rdflicense/gpl-3.0> ;
13    dct:publisher <https://datahub.ckan.io/organization/449873a1
         -c92e-4942-9843-b79b1053211b> ;
14    dcat:keyword "llod", "apertium", "lexicon", "bilingual", "
         lemon" ;
15    dcat:distribution <https://datahub.ckan.io/dataset/47e9d8cc
         -5da9-4c02-960e-c00abee2b0d9/resource/4726cf87-200a-41f1
         -8b77-c212aeebb214>.
16
17  <https://datahub.ckan.io/organization/449873a1-c92e-4942-9843-
         b79b1053211b> .
18    a foaf:Organization ;
19    foaf:name "Ontology Engineering Group (UPM)" .
20
21  <https://datahub.ckan.io/dataset/47e9d8cc-5da9-4c02-960e-
         c00abee2b0d9/resource/4726cf87-200a-41f1-8b77-c212aeebb214
         >
22    a dcat:Distribution ;
23    dct:format "SPARQL" ;
24    dct:title "SPARQL endpoint" ;
25    dcat:accessURL <http://linguistic.linkeddata.es/sparql/> .
```

In this example we see how the LR identified with the URI http://linguistic.
linkeddata.es/set/apertium/EN-ES is defined as a *dataset* by declaring it as a
type of dcat:Dataset. Then, properties of the DC-Terms vocabulary (see
Sect. 7.2.1) are used to specifiy basic information such as title (dct:title),
provenance (dct:source), license of the resource (dct:license) and its
languages (dct:language), i.e. English and Spanish. The publisher ('Ontology
Engineering Group') is identified through the dct:publisher property, by
using the URI that Datahub assigned to such an organization (defined as a
foaf:Organization in the code). The DCAT property dcat:keyword is
used to describe some keywords that characterize the resource. Then, the different
distributions available for the resource (i.e. the different means in which data can be
accessed) are described with the use of the dcat:distribution property.

Every particular distribution of the LR is defined as individual of the class
dcat:Distribution. In the example, one distribution has been represented
corresponding to the SPARQL endpoint where the Apertium RDF EN-ES data is
available for querying. The distribution is described with a title (dc:title), format (dc:format) and access URL (dcat:accessURL). Other extra properties
could be used as well, e.g. description (dct:description).

7.3   Modelling Metadata of LRs with Meta-Share.owl

We have introduced models for representing general metadata of LRs (e.g. *title, license, description*), namely DC-Terms and DCAT. In this section, we will focus on Meta-Share.owl, a model aimed at representing information that is characteristic of LRs (e.g. *resource type, modality, number of languages*). The Meta-Share.owl ontology can be found at http://purl.org/net/def/metashare.[29]

The Meta-Share.owl ontology was designed from the META-SHARE XML-based model as a starting point,[30] although it underwent significant re-structuring in order to avoid unnecessary or overly verbose nodes in the produced RDF graph (as described in [7]). The resulting OWL ontology has 192 classes and 358 properties, which enables a very rich and fine-grained description of metadata of LRs. There have been some projects using the ontology, however, which have defined their own 'profile' of the Meta-Share ontology in order to work with a more restricted set of core entities. This is the case, for instance, for the ReTeLe-Share.owl ontology,[31] which re-uses 70 classes and 104 properties of the Meta-Share ontology.

In addition to its own classes, the Meta-Share ontology reuses entities from DC-Terms to represent general information such as language(s) of the resource (`dct:language`), provenance (`dc:source`), creator (`dct:creator`), licence of use (`dct:license`) or a textual description (`dct:description`). Also the FOAF ontology is re-used to represent concepts such as actors (`foaf:Actor`), organizations (`foaf:Organization`) and projects (`foaf:Project`). Additionally, some explicit equivalences have been established between entities of the Meta-Share ontology and DCAT (e.g. between `ms:LanguageResource` and `dcat:Dataset` or between `ms:MetadataInfo` and `dcat:Catalog Record`).

In the following, we review some core classes and properties of Meta-Share.owl, which can be used to describe the most relevant features of a LR. Figure 7.2 gives a simplified view of the core of the ontology.

- `ms:LanguageResource` is the core class in the ontology and represents a language resource and has the following specializations:

  - `ms:Corpus`, which identifies written/text, oral/spoken, multimodal/multimedia corpora in one or several languages.
  - `ms:LexicalConceptualResource`, which represents lexical-conceptual resources, such as terminologies, glossaries, word lists, dictionaries, semantic lexica, ontologies, etc.

---

[29] At the time of writing, a new version of the ontology is being developed. However, such a new version is announced to be backwards compatible with the initial one, so we expect that most of the content of this section will apply to the new version as well. We encourage the reader to check the status of the new version of the ontology at https://github.com/ld4lt/metashare.

[30] http://www.meta-net.eu/meta-share/META-SHARE%20%20documentationUserManual.pdf.

[31] https://w3id.org/def/retele-share.

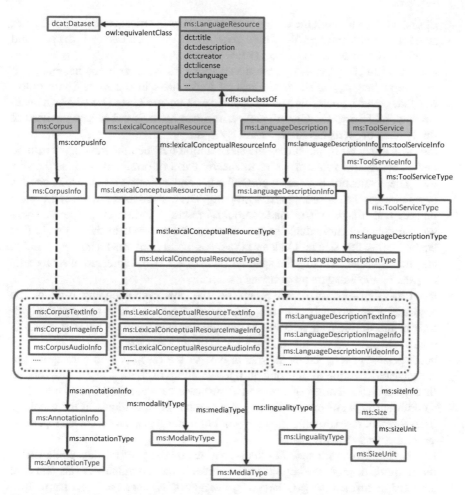

Fig. 7.2 Scheme of some important classes and properties of Meta-Share.owl. The core classes are highlighted in grey. Dashed arrows group a collection of 'info' properties connecting to the different media descriptive properties

- ms:LanguageDescription, which represents resources that describe a language, such as grammars (set of rules that describe a language formally) or language models (containing statistical information).
- ms:ToolService, which represents tools and services for language processing.

• The classes ms:CorpusInfo, ms:LexicalConceptualResource Info, ms:ToolServiceInfo and ms:LanguageDescriptionInfo are used to group together elements required for the description of corpora, lexical-conceptual resources, language description resources and tools and services respectively. Particular language resources can be assigned to individuals of such classes through the corresponding set of properties: ms:corpusInfo, ms:lexicalConceptualResourceInfo, ms:toolServiceInfo and ms:languageDescriptionInfo.

- ms:LingualityType is a class that indicates whether a LR has one, two or several languages. There are several individuals in the Meta-Share ontology that cover its possible values: ms:monolingual, ms:bilingual and ms:multilingual. One of such values can be assigned to a particular LR through the property ms:lingualityType.
- ms:Size is a class that reifies the size relation between the language resource and a certain size value, in order to specify extra information, such as the size unit. The connection between a particular LR and an instance of the Size class is made through the ms:sizeInfo property. The connection between an instance of Size and a size unit is made through the ms:sizeUnit property. There are a number of individuals of the class ms:SizeUnit in the ontology that cover the possible size unit values: ms:bytes, ms:entries, ms:seconds, ms:tokens, etc. Finally, the specific value of the size, expressed in such units, is given by the datatype property ms:size.
- ms:CharacterEncoding represents the character encoding used in the resource or accepted by the tool or service. There are a number of individuals in the ontology that cover its possible values, such as ms:US-ASCII, ms:windows-1250, ms:UTF-8, ms:ISO-2020-JP, etc.
- ms:MediaType specifies the media type of the resource and corresponds to the physical medium of the content representation. Each media type is described through a distinctive set of features. A resource may consist of parts attributed to different types of media. There are a number of individuals in the ontology that represent the particular media types. For instance, ms:audio, ms:image, ms:text, ms:video, etc.
- ms:ModalityType specifies the type of the modality of the data contained in the resource or processed by the tool/service. Some individuals of this class are ms:writtenLanguage, ms:signLanguage, ms:spokenLanguage, etc.

There are also a number of classes and properties that apply only to individuals of a specific subtype of language resource. For instance:

- ms:lexicalConceptualResourceType is a property that indicates the particular type of a lexical conceptual resource. It relates individuals of the class ms:LexicalConceptualResourceInfo to individuals of a class ms:LexicalConceptualResourceType that can take the following values: ms:computationalLexicon, ms:wordnet, ms:machineReadable Dictionary, ms:wordList, among others.
- ms:languageDescriptionType is a property that indicates the particular type of language description resource. It relates individuals of the class ms:LanguageDescriptionInfo to individuals of a class ms:Language DescriptionType, with only two possible values: ms:grammar and ms:other.

- `ms:toolServiceType` is a property that indicates the particular type of tool or service. It relates individuals of the class `ms:ToolServiceInfo` to individuals of a class `ms:ToolServiceType`, with possible values: `ms:platform`, `ms:service`, `ms:infrastructure`, `ms:suiteOf Tools`, etc.
- The way of representing the type of corpus does not follow the same pattern that we have just seen for the other three types of resources. Depending on its media type, several 'info' classes are available, namely `ms:CorpusAudioInfo`, `ms:CorpusImageInfo`, `ms:CorpusTextInfo`, `ms:CorpusTextNgra mInfo`, `ms:CorpusTextNumericalInfo`, and `ms:CorpusVideoInfo`, which groups together the information relevant to every modality (audio, image, text, etc.) that can be present in a corpus.
- Further, a corpus can be characterized (through the properties `ms:annotation Info` and `ms:annotationType`) with instances of the class `ms:Annota tion Type`, e.g.: `ms:discourseAnnotation`, `ms:lemmatization`, `ms:semanticAnnotation-namedEntities`, `ms:stemming`, among many others.

Finally, it is worth mentioning that MetaShare.owl comes with a *licensing module* that allows one to specify clear and concise rights information of the LRs. The module is based on the Open Digital Rights Language (ODRL v2.1),[32] which is a 'policy expression language that provides a flexible and interoperable information model, vocabulary, and encoding mechanisms for representing statements about the usage of content and services'. There exist ODRL-based representations of the most extendedly used licenses, which can be found in the RDF License dataset.[33] Other licenses, more specific to the Meta-Share community of users, have been defined in the Meta-Share licensing module. Such a module can be found either as part of the Meta-Share.owl ontology or separately at http://purl.org/net/ms-rights.

Example Let us illustrate the use of Meta-Share.owl to represent metadata in RDF for a particular language resource, the *Galician LMF Freeling Lexicon*.[34] Such a resource was initially documented in the XML-based representation of the Meta-Share portal, and then converted into RDF and published by the Linghub system (see more details on Linghub in Chap. 14). In the following example, we show an abridged fragment of such RDF representation[35]:

```
1  @prefix dcat: <http://www.w3.org/ns/dcat#> .
2  @prefix owl: <http://www.w3.org/2002/07/owl#> .
3  @prefix dct: <http://purl.org/dc/terms/> .
```

---

[32]https://www.w3.org/TR/odrl-vocab/.

[33]http://purl.org/net/rdflicense.

[34]http://hdl.handle.net/10230/17118.

[35]The whole metadata in RDF of the Galician LMF Freeling Lexicon can be found at https://tinyurl.com/linghub-FreelingLexGL. For simplicity, our example shows a reduced and slightly modified version of the full metadata.

```
4  @prefix rdfs: <http://www.w3.org/2000/01/rdf-schema#> .
5  @prefix ms: <http://purl.org/net/def/metashare> .
6  @prefix : <http://linghub.lider-project.eu/metashare/
   cab54a5692c211e28763000c291ecfc80341c14ddf8f475b8aba7bb70cefde77
   #> .
7
8  :myResource a ms:LexicalConceptualResource ;
9      dc:description "This is the LMF version of the Galician
           Freeling dictionary. FreeLing is a developer-oriented
           library providing language analysis services [...]"@en ;
10     dct:language "gl" ;
11     dct:source    "META-SHARE" ;
12     dct:title     "Galician LMF Freeling Lexicon"@en ;
13     ms:lexicalConceptualResourceInfo :myResourceInfo ;
14     dcat:distribution  :myResourceDistribution .
15
16 :myResourceInfo a ms:LexicalConceptualResourceInfo ;
17     ms:lexicalConceptualResourceType ms:wordList ;
18     ms:lexicalConceptualResourceTextInfo :myResourceTextInfo .
19
20 :myResourceTextInfo a ms:LexicalConceptualResourceTextInfo ;
21     ms:characterEncodingInfo [ ms:characterEncoding   ms:UTF-8 ]
           ;
22     ms:lingualityInfo   [ ms:lingualityType   ms:monolingual ] ;
23     ms:mediaType        ms:text ;
24     ms:sizeInfo         :myResourceSizeInfo .
25
26 :myResourceSizeInfo a ms:SizeInfoType ;
27     ms:size     "49,898" ;
28     ms:sizeUnit  ms:entries .
29
30 :myResourceDistribution a dcat:Distribution ;
31     dct:license <http://www.gnu.org/copyleft/gpl.html> ;
32     dcat:accessURL      <http://hdl.handle.net/10230/17118> .
```

7.4   Summary and Further Reading

In this chapter we reviewed some models for representing metadata of LRs as LD.
The use of such models enables cataloguing, discovery and later reuse of such
LRs. We have distinguished between two types of metadata: (1) general metadata,
i.e. applicable to any type of LD dataset (e.g. author, license, title), for which
we have reviewed the DCAT and DC-Terms vocabularies, and (2) metadata that
specifically describe the properties of LRs (e.g. typology, number of languages,
number of words), as is the case for the Meta-Share.owl ontology, which has been
also described in this chapter. For readers interested in a more detailed description
of the aforementioned models, we refer to their specification documents [6, 8] and
related publications [2, 7]. At the time of writing, a new version of the Meta-
Share.owl ontology is under development. We encourage the interested reader to

check its status at https://github.com/ld4lt/metashare or through the activities of the W3C LD4LT community group at https://www.w3.org/community/ld4lt/.

References

1. S. Piperidis, The META-SHARE language resources sharing infrastructure: principles, challenges, solutions, in *Proceedings of the 8th Conference on International Language Resources and Evaluation (LREC)* (2012), pp. 36–42
2. M. Gavrilidou, P. Labropoulou, E. Desipri, S. Piperidis, H. Papageorgiou, M. Monachini, F. Frontini, T. Declerck, G. Francopoulo, V. Arranz, V. Mapelli, The META-SHARE metadata schema for the description of language resources, in *Proceedings of the 8th International Conference on Language Resources and Evaluation (LREC)* (2012), pp. 1090–1097
3. D. Broeder, M. Kemps-Snijders, D. Van Uytvanck, M. Windhouwer, P. Withers, P. Wittenburg, C. Zinn, A data category registry-and component-based metadata framework, in *Proceedings of the 7th Conference on International Language Resources and Evaluation (LREC)* (2010), pp. 43–47
4. N. Calzolari, R. Del Gratta, G. Francopoulo, J. Mariani, F. Rubino, I. Russo, C. Soria, The LRE map. Harmonising community descriptions of resources, in *Proceedings of the 8th Conference on International Language Resources and Evaluation (LREC)* (2012), pp. 1084–1089
5. R. Del Gratta, G. Pardelli, S. Goggi, The LRE map disclosed, in *Proceedings of the 9th International Conference on Language Resources and Evaluation (LREC)* (2014), pp. 3534–3541
6. F. Maali, J. Erickson, P. Archer, Data catalog vocabulary (DCAT). W3C recommendation. World Wide Web Consortium (2014). https://www.w3.org/TR/vocab-dcat/
7. J.P. McCrae, P. Labropoulou, J. Gracia, M. Villegas, V. Rodriguez-Doncel, P. Cimiano, One ontology to bind them all: the META-SHARE OWL ontology for the interoperability of linguistic datasets on the Web, in *Proceedings of the 12th Extended Semantic Web Conference (ESWC) Satellite Events*, vol. 9341 (Springer, Berlin, 2015), pp. 271–282
8. D.U. board, DCMI Metadata Terms. DCMI recommendation, DCMI (2012). http://purl.org/dc/terms/

Chapter 8
Linguistic Categories

Abstract The (re-)usability of NLP tools and language resources has long been recognized as a key challenge in the language resource and NLP communities. Reuse of resources, however, requires a minimum level of interoperability, and in this chapter, we focus on conceptual interoperability, i.e. harmonization between different annotation schemas by means of terminology repositories. Beyond that, we give special attention to language identifiers, as these can be provided in different ways in an RDF context, either by reference to a concepts in a terminology repository, or by means of language tags.

8.1 Introduction

A significant obstacle to re-usability of language resources and tools is the heterogeneity of data formats, annotation and metadata schemes associated with them. Reuse of resources, however, requires a minimum level of interoperability. NLP tools and language resources (dictionaries, corpora) are *interoperable* if they can be combined with, merged or exchanged for each other so that they can be meaningfully used after the combination or merge. In the preceding chapters of this part, we presented linked-data-based approaches to harmonize data models and metadata schemas by the use of common and generic vocabularies, thereby demonstrating the capabilities of RDF technology to the problems of format variation and re-usable documentation.

This chapter complements these approaches with an account for shared categories in describing linguistic phenomena as annotated in different datasets or by different tools. The use of common terminology for linguistic categories in dictionaries and annotation tools allows to use a dictionary for improving or validating, e.g., morphosyntactic annotations or lemmatization. Furthermore, linking between different dictionaries or between corpora and dictionary data requires shared terminology.

As an example for interoperability between NLP tools, a particular part-of-speech tagger can be combined with a particular parser if they have a shared vocabulary to describe linguistic phenomena. In a corpus or lexical information

© Springer Nature Switzerland AG 2020
P. Cimiano et al., *Linguistic Linked Data*,
https://doi.org/10.1007/978-3-030-30225-2_8

system, resources A and B are interoperable in this sense if the same query can be run on both A and B, thereby leading to comparable results, to a larger result set, and thus to a higher chance for significant results. In the case the same query can be run on both resources, then A and B can be either merged or exchanged for each other.

All of the above-mentioned operations (combine, merge, exchange) require structural and conceptual interoperability. Structural interoperability of linguistic annotations can be achieved with Semantic Web standards as previously described in Chaps. 5 and 6; structural (and conceptual) interoperability of linguistic metadata can be addressed by adherence to commonly used metadata schemata (Chap. 7). Our focus in this chapter is on ensuring conceptual interoperability of linguistic annotations, which is challenging to ensure even for the most basic levels of linguistic annotation such as part-of-speech and morphosyntax. Conceptual interoperability requires that the different components share the same type of annotations in the sense that they re-use the same set of linguistic categories for a very broad range of phenomena, and thus conceptual interoperability of linguistic annotations involves the creation of relatively large terminology repositories which generalize over different theoretical frameworks and extensive and long-standing traditions in the description of various languages.

When language resources for a language (or, likewise, a new domain) are to be developed, different groups, communities or experts may have very different ideas about tagset design [1]. This is an especially disturbing phenomenon for low-resource language as, in these, no community standard has been established before, but the scarce resources that are actually available cannot be easily combined to build state-of-the-art NLP tools or to perform quantitative studies on an amount of data that actually allows to derive statistically significant observations.

The practical challenges arising in ensuring conceptual interoperability are illustrated in Fig. 8.1, comparing POS annotations from the Penn resp. Susanne POS tagsets on the same corpus, i.e. the Brown corpus. The Penn tagset is limited to word classes, it covers no other inflectional features than number and degree. In contrast, the Susanne tagset features semantic, grammatical and lexical distinctions.

The traditional solution to interoperability problems is standardization. The Expert Advisory Group on Language Engineering (EAGLES), e.g. a European standardization project (1993–1996), aimed for standardization of annotation schemas, e.g. for POS tag sets [5], and arrived at common specifications by creating them in a

Fig. 8.1 Fragment of the Brown corpus [2], as annotated in Penn Treebank [3] and the Susanne corpus [4]

	Susanne	Penn
The	AT	DT
Fulton	NP1s	NNP
County	NNL1cb	NNP
Grand	JJ	NNP
Jury	NN1c	NNP
said	VVDv	VBD
Friday	NPD1	NNP

bottom-up manner from existing resources. Without a deep theoretical specification of tags, only commonly used terms have been identified and standardized as annotation features. However, even contemporaries observed that ... *although linguists agree on the general 'common-sense' definitions of categories like proper noun, common noun, etc. our analysis of competing tagsets for English corpora shows that these categories are in fact 'fuzzy', and different corpus tagging projects have adopted subtly but significantly different definitions, probably unaware that their analyses are incompatible with those of other linguists* [6]. Indeed, subsequent and more recent standardization initiatives, e.g. the Universal Dependencies project [7, UD] face similar issues: Kutuzov et al. observed that their approach on predicting parts of speech on UD *'supports the notion of "soft" or "graded" part of speech affiliations'*, and further claims that *'part of speech boundaries are not strict'* [8].[1]

Another problem with the standardization approach is that a standard-conformant tagset *needs to provide certain categories*, even though these may not be relevant to a language. As an example, the Universal Dependencies tagset enforces the use of the tag DET for Slavic attributive pronouns, even though most Slavic languages are lacking a grammaticalized determiner. Similarly, stative verbs in Chinese are considered as 'adjectives', etc. However, the cross-linguistic and general applicability of even more elementary distinctions such as the differentiation between nouns and verbs has been questioned in the literature [9–11].

Many shortcomings of the standardization approach have been addressed by means of more elaborate techniques that *explicate* relations between linguistic tags and categories rather than standardizing them, which ultimately paved the way to apply Semantic Web formalisms for this purpose. By establishing a common level of representation, ISOcat [12] aimed to register and provide annotation inventories for several technology-driven initiatives seeking to establish ISO standards, including the Lexical Markup Framework [13, 14] as well as the Linguistic Annotation Framework [15, 16]. In parallel, but independent from lexicography and natural language processing, the language documentation community developed a similar repository, i.e. the General Ontology of Linguistic Description [17, GOLD]. GOLD has been developed in a top-down fashion on grounds of existing terminology repositories and extended according to the specifics of the language resources it was applied to. This approach has also been followed by domain- or application-specific terminology repositories, such as LexInfo [18] for the lexical domain, and OLiA [19] for NLP tools and annotated corpora.

While widely used terminology repositories represent an appealing solution to most problems in conceptual interoperability for language resources, the handling of language identifiers requires special consideration, as two alternative ways of encoding language information are currently being employed: a URI-based

---

[1]While this may be a controversial opinion, a matter of fact is that the Universal Dependency guidelines often fail to provide language-independent definitions, e.g. *'participles* ... share properties and usage of adjectives and verbs. Depending on language and context, they may be classified as either VERB or ADJ' (https://universaldependencies.org/u/pos/VERB.html, last accessed 08-07-2019).

mechanism that builds on terminology repositories and the use of language tags as a way of typing RDF literals. Before describing terminology repositories, we will thus discuss the relation between both approaches and formulate recommendations for an informed choice between them.

8.2 The Case of Language Identifiers

A fundamental problem for the annotation vocabularies employed by different tools or resources is to *identify* whether these resources or tools actually pertain to the same language variety. As in the case of part-of-speech categories, the standardization approach faces limitations with respect to granularity and interpretability of standardized codes. As a result, hierarchically structured terminology repositories have been developed and have been made available within the LLOD cloud which complement these standards.

General recommendations for language identification are primarily grounded on using standardized language codes as defined in the ISO 639 standard, and this is formulated as part of the RDF specification [20]. Machine-readable identifiers for language varieties are necessary as the same language may be referred to by different names. For example, the Manding language *Bamanakan* (bm) is also known as *Bambara*. In contrast, some language names are used to refer to quite different varieties. For instance, *Saxon* has been the self-designation of Old English (Anglo-Saxon, ang), but also for a number of historical and modern varieties of Low German (Old Saxon, osx; Low Saxon, nds). Further, it continues to denote different dialects of High German (Upper Saxon, sxu; Transylvanian Saxon [no language code]).

This example does not only illustrate how language codes help to differentiate language varieties, but also that language codes may not be sufficient for distinguishing certain variants (e.g. for Transylvanian Saxon). To complement ISO 639 language codes and provide a more fine-grained vocabulary to distinguish between language variants, the use of terminology repositories for language identifiers has been suggested. As a complement to ISO 639 language tags, Glottolog[2] provides greater level of detail and a hierarchical (phylogenetic) structure. We discuss both language tags and URI-based solutions below.

8.2.1   ISO 639 Language Tags

ISO 639 provides language identifiers as standardized by the International Organization for Standardization (ISO), whose standards are most widely used in

---

[2]https://glottolog.org/.

technical applications. The standardization of language identifiers goes back to a standard from 1967. This original standard, still available as ISO 639/R,[3] has been superseded by ISO 639:1988[4], which provided two-letter codes for a substantial set of languages. Unfortunately, combinations of two (ASCII) letters only allow to distinguish up to $26^2 = 676$ language varieties, which covers less than 10% of the languages currently spoken.[5] Accordingly, ISO 639:1988 was withdrawn in 2002 and superseded by the current standards ISO 693-1, ISO 639-2 and ISO 639-3.[6] With this partition, ISO 639 not only extends the earlier two-letter codes, but also integrates other pre-existing standardization efforts, reflected in different profiles.

8.2.1.1 Two-Letter Codes (ISO 639-1)

ISO 639-1 provides two-letter codes for languages. A list (and an alignment with ISO 639-2 codes) is available from the Library of Congress,[7] the ISO 639-2 registration authority. Because of its brevity and wide-spread use in technical applications, ISO 639-1 is recommended to be used *whenever appropriate* [21].

8.2.1.2 Three-Letter Codes from the Librarian Tradition (ISO 639-2)

ISO 639-2 is a standard for three-letter language identifiers, based on the MARC Code List for Languages,[8] a system developed for use in libraries. As the Library of Congress is the maintenance agency for both lists, they are kept compatible in terms of code additions and deletions. However, coming from a librarian tradition, ISO 639-2 is intentionally limited in scope and coverage of language varieties. The original MARC code list aims to "[provide] individual codes for *most of the major languages* of the modern and ancient world, e.g. Arabic, Chinese, English, Hindi, Latin, Tagalog, etc. These are the languages that are *most frequently represented in the total body of the world's literature*." [22, p. 5, our emphasis]. For 22 cases, ISO 639-2 provides two alternative codes, one for terminological (T) use, one for bibliographical (B) use. The T codes are aligned with ISO 639-3, whereas the B

---

[3]http://www.iso.org/iso/iso_catalogue/catalogue_tc/catalogue_detail.htm?csnumber=4765, accessed 10-07-2019.

[4]http://www.iso.org/iso/iso_catalogue/catalogue_ics/catalogue_detail_ics.htm?csnumber=4766, accessed 10-07-2019.

[5]As of July 10, 2019, SIL's Ethnologue lists 7111 languages (http://www.ethnologue.com/statistics), Glottolog lists 8494 language varieties (https://glottolog.org/glottolog/language).

[6]The official ISO 639 standards are available from https://www.iso.org/standard/22109.html, https://www.iso.org/standard/4767.html, and https://www.iso.org/standard/39534.html, respectively (accessed 10-07-2019); in the text below, direct links to their freely accessible versions published by their respective registration authorities are given.

[7]https://www.loc.gov/standards/iso639-2/php/code_list.php, accessed 10-07-2019.

[8]https://www.loc.gov/marc/languages/, accessed 10-07-2019.

codes correspond to deviating MARC codes. For web resources, ISO 639-2/T codes are recommended to be used, but only if no ISO 639-1 code exists [21]. A list (and an alignment with ISO 639-1 codes) is provided by the Library of Congress.[9]

8.2.1.3 Three-Letter Codes for [Almost] All Human Languages (ISO 639-3)

By providing identifiers for about 400 languages only, ISO 639-2 is deliberately limited in its coverage. ISO TC37/SC2 thus invited SIL International[10] to develop a more exhaustive set of language codes known as ISO 639-3. SIL International, originally known as the Summer Institute of Linguistics, is a faith-based (i.e. missionary) organization with a strong profile in linguistics, well-known in academia for Ethnologue,[11] a near-exhaustive database of languages and information about them. Similar to MARC, Ethnologue employed (independently developed) three-letter language identifiers. For ISO 639-3, these were harmonized with ISO 639-2/T and complemented with identifiers for extinct and constructed languages provided by the Linguist List.[12] ISO 639-3 has been designed for compatibility with ISO 639-2: *'At the core of ISO 639-3 are the individual languages already accounted for in ISO 639-2. The large number of ... languages ... beyond those ... was derived primarily from Ethnologue ... [and] from Linguist List'* [23]. Further, *'The alpha-3 codes for ISO 639-2 and ISO 639-3 overlap. In particular, every individual language code element in the terminology code of ISO 639-2 is also included in ISO 639-3 [, and] ... every alpha-3 language identifier has a single denotation across the union of code elements from all parts of ISO 639'* [24].

8.2.2 IETF Language Tags

Language tags are commonly combined with information about the geographical use, script and other information [21]. An IETF language tag[13] is of the following form

```
language(-script)(-region)(-variant)*
  (-extension)*(-x-privateuse)
```

---

[9]https://www.loc.gov/standards/iso639-2/php/code_list.php, accessed 10-07-2019.

[10]http://www.sil.org/, accessed 10-07-2019.

[11]http://ethnologue.com/, accessed 10-07-2019.

[12]http://linguistlist.org/about.cfm, esp. http://linguistlist.org/forms/langs/get-extinct.cfm and http://linguistlist.org/forms/langs/GetListOfConstructedLgs.cfm (accessed 10-07-2019).

[13]IETF language tags are described in a document called Best Common Practices 47 (BCP47) which is also known as RFC 4646. In this book we refer to this standard as 'IETF language tags', but all three acronyms can be encountered in the literature.

These tags are composed from the following elements:

- **Language**: The language as an ISO 639-1 tag if available or otherwise an ISO 639-3 tag, e.g. en for English and ang for Old English.
- **Script** (optional): The ISO 15924 4-letter code for script, e.g. Latn for Latin.
- **Region** (optional): The ISO 3166 2-letter (or UN M.49 3-number) region code, e.g. DE (or 276) for Germany or US (or 840) for the USA
- **Variant**: Zero or more registered variants[14] Of particular interest to linguists are the tags fonipa and fonxsamp used to mark phonetic representations in the International Phonetic Alphabet (IPA) or X-SAMPA (ASCII rendering of IPA), respectively.
- **Extension**: Zero or more extensions in custom schemes
- **Private use** (optional): Used for internal notes about identification within a single application

The text of this chapter can thus be characterized with any of the 12 following language tags:

- en (English)
- en-Latn (English in Latin characters)
- en-Latn-DE (resp. en-Latn-276; English in Latin characters written in Germany)
- en-Latn-GB (resp. en-Latn-826; English in Latin characters compliant with the variety British English as spoken in Great Britain)
- en-Latn-UK (also using en-Latn-826; English in Latin characters compliant with the variety British English as spoken in the United Kingdom)
- en-DE, en-276, en-GB, en-UK, en-826

Language tags are part of the RDF standard (see Chap. 2) and some linked data tools have special tools for handling language tags. In particular, SPARQL has a langMatches function that matches two language tags as long as they match on the same language. Thus, the following SPARQL query

```
1  SELECT ?lab WHERE {
2      example:element rdfs:label ?label .
3      FILTER(langMatches(?label, "en"))
4  }
```

matches any of the following triples:

```
1  example:element rdfs:label "example"@en .
2  example:element rdfs:label "color"@en-US .
3  example:element rdfs:label "kVl.@r\"@en-GB-fonxsamp .
```

---

[14]The current list of registered variants is provided under https://www.iana.org/assignments/language-subtag-registry/language-subtag-registry (accessed 10-07-2019).

8.2.3   URI-Based Language Codes

Tag-based approaches on language classification rely on unstructured lists of strings (tags) as a primary data structure, where relations between different categories are not formally represented. While IETF language tags allow the meaning of language tags to be refined by intersecting these with categories for other levels (language variety, writing system, geographic region), to arrive at a more specific definition, these additional criteria are only indirectly related to linguistic classification, and thus potentially error prone. As an example, region codes are ambiguous in their meaning. By definition, they refer to a geographic region, but they *can* be used to refer to a regional variant. British English written on the isle of Guernsey, e.g., could be either en-GG (for geographical and political reasons, as Guernsey is not part of the United Kingdom), or en-GB (for linguistic reasons). For a deeper discussion of technical and linguistic shortcomings of language tags, see [25].

A second issue is that expanding the IETF, resp. ISO 639 language tags, is a laboursome and formal process. In order to introduce a novel language identifier for ISO 639-3, e.g., a formal proposal needs to be submitted,[15] verified by the ISO 639-3 registrar, and discussed within the community, e.g. on Linguist List[16] and other appropriate discussion lists. Based on its approval, it can be adopted in ISO 639, and subsequently registered at the IANA Language Subtag Registry[17] in order to be fully acknowledged as a IETF language tag.

As an alternative to language tags, we describe two possible sources of URI-based language identifiers. In comparison to language tags, the use of URIs for identifying language varieties facilitates (1) easy, re-usable and distributed extension of the set of language identifiers; (2) the definition of explicit relations between different language varieties, resp., their identifiers; and (3) achieving both extensions with conventional RDF semantics.

8.2.3.1   ISO 639 in RDF

An RDF edition of ISO language codes has been discussed at the World Wide Web Consortium (W3C)[18] already in the mid-2000s, but never evolved into a concrete resource. Only recently, the Library of Congress, the registration authority for ISO 639-1, 639-2 and 639-5, added RDF serializations to their editions[19] whereas SIL,

---

[15] https://iso639-3.sil.org/code_changes/submitting_change_requests, accessed 10-07-2019.

[16] http://linguistlist.org/, accessed 10-07-2019.

[17] https://www.iana.org/assignments/lang-subtags-templates/lang-subtags-templates.xhtml, accessed 10-07-2019.

[18] https://www.w3.org/wiki/Languages_as_RDF_Resources.

[19] http://id.loc.gov/vocabulary/iso639-1, http://id.loc.gov/vocabulary/iso639-2, http://id.loc.gov/vocabulary/iso639-5.

the registration authority for ISO 639-3, only provides TSV data.[20] Accordingly, most LLOD resources point to URIs and RDF data sets provided by third parties instead. A current community practice (also adopted, e.g., by the German National Library[21]) is to refer to lexvo[22] for ISO 639-3 URIs. Accordingly, it is possible to describe the language of this text as one of:

- http://id.loc.gov/vocabulary/iso639-1/en
- http://id.loc.gov/vocabulary/iso639-2/eng
- http://lexvo.org/id/iso639-3/eng

8.2.3.2 Glottolog

ISO 639 has been criticized for not being sufficiently fine-grained for linguistic research and less-resourced languages. To address that gap, Glottolog has been created as an academic repository that provides URIs and machine-readable information for identifying language varieties. It has been collaboratively developed and its languoid (see below) inventory is currently maintained by Martin Haspelmath and colleagues. Glottolog originates out of their efforts to create a unified bibliographical resource for language documentation, but it has found wide reception beyond this original use case.

An important design decision of Glottolog is to avoid the notion of 'language', as it comes with unintended political connotations.[23] Instead, Glottolog uses the more neutral term 'languoid', defined as a language variety about (or in) which written literature does exist. Accordingly, language families, proto-languages, national languages, historical varieties, dialects and sociolects can receive a unified treatment. A Glottolog ID combines a 4-letter alphabetic core with a 4-letter numerical code, e.g. `stan1293` for (Standard) English. These IDs come as a native URI: http://glottolog.org/resource/languoid/id/stan1293, which resolves via content negotiation to an HTML visualization or to RDF data, which then provides further links to ISO 639, lexvo, etc.

In addition to providing mere identifiers, Glottolog also features relations, e.g. phylogenetic relations, between languoids, which are provided in a machine-readable way. For example, English is a subconcept of (`skos:broader`) 'Macro-English' (macr1271, which groups together Modern English with a number of English Pidgins), etc., and it has further subconcepts (`skos:narrower`), such as Indian English (`indi1255`), New Zealand English (`newz1240`), etc. Glottolog is designed to be descriptively adequate, but as being extensible rather than exhaustive.

---

[20] http://www-01.sil.org/iso639-3/download.asp.

[21] https://wiki.dnb.de/pages/viewpage.action?pageId=124132496.

[22] http://www.lexvo.org/.

[23] Remember Max Weinreich's famous observation that 'a language is a dialect with an army and a navy'.

Suggestions about novel or incorrect languoids can be reported via the website and will be addressed by the maintainers. Thus, even where a distinction may be missing, it may be introduced upon request, and if properly justified by the accompanying scientific literature (i.e. bibliographical references), it will be accepted.

As a critical remark, we have to note that Glottolog is biased towards endangered modern languages and thus rather sketchy in its historical dimension. Yet, Glottolog is now widely used beyond the language documentation community, e.g. in Wikipedia, and we expect that with intensified use beyond the academic world, Glottolog codes for historical language varieties may become available—and can be suggested for insertion already now.

The use of URIs for identifying language varieties facilitates (1) extending the set of language identifiers; (2) the definition of explicit relations between different varieties, resp., their identifiers; and (3) achieving both extensions with conventional RDF semantics. In particular, it is possible to define relations between language varieties, and—in case we disagree with a specific design decision in, say, Glottolog—also to provide an independent categorization of languages based on the same URIs.

The downside of URI-based language identifiers is that (1) this can increase overhead and verbosity (one additional triple per typed string) and that (2) a generally agreed-upon object property needs to be found that identifies the language. As for the first aspect, an alternative way to declare language information would be at the level of the resource rather than at the level of the string. However, this solution is restricted to monolingual resources only, and complicates the retrieval of language information in SPARQL. As for the second aspect, we follow DCAT (Sect. 7.2.2) in recommending using dct:language for this purpose, but this is normally used with literal values, whereas URI-based language identification requires an object property. For lexical resources, such a property would be lime:language as defined in the metadata module of Ontolex-lemon (Sect. 4.6).

In summary, we observe that major languages are well covered by conventional RDF technology, and in particular the established IETF language tags. However, when it comes to low resource languages or where scientific or political reasons require to define more fine-grained differentiations, a speaker community, or individuals working on a particular language, may prefer decentralized approaches based on one or multiple repositories of URI-identifiable language identifiers. For the time being, we thus suggest applying IETF language tags wherever appropriate, but to use plain string literals and URI-based language identification where these are not directly applicable or sufficiently clear. As for language tags, we strongly discourage the application of region codes to denote dialectal variants as these are ambiguous between a geographical and a linguistic interpretation.

In the longer perspective, it is possible that the current systems of language tags and URI-based language identification converge, but this requires a change in RDF semantics. This is currently being discussed in an effort to create 'easier RDF' specifications. The interested reader might want to follow the discussion under https://github.com/w3c/EasierRDF/issues/22 (accessed 10-07-2019).

8.3   General Repositories of Linguistic Reference Terminology

An important initiative to standardize linguistic categories is ISOcat [12, 26], whose origins are in the ISO Technical Committee 37 on *Terminology and other language and content resources*, and most terminology repositories in the areas of linguistics, natural language processing and human language technology have been linked, aligned or converged with ISOcat.

8.3.1   Data Category Modelling and Standardization in ISOcat

In the context of the ISO Technical Committee 37 on *Terminology and other language and content resources*, a metadata registry known as the *Data Category Registry (DCR)* was developed along with an associated standard (ISO DIS 12620) for the representation of data categories. The aim of this was to develop a common set of data categories that would provide enough detail such that a domain ontology could be constructed in a 'bottom-up' manner from the set of categories contained within the registry. The TC 37 based this activity on the earlier *Syntax* registry [27], which evolved into *ISOcat* [12, 26].

Data categories were standardized by means of the DCR, an XML schema for the representation of data categories. Each data category record had two main sections: an *administration section*, which contained key information about the category related to its version, origin and most importantly whether it has been accepted, and a *description section* consisting of one or more *language section*s. The description section contains (multilingual) descriptions of the category, including its name, definition, examples and the formal definition of the category. The formal definition divided categories into so-called *simple* and *complex* categories. Simple categories contain no values, and as such can be seen as equivalent to individuals in OWL ontologies. Complex categories in turn are further divided into three categories: *open*, *closed* and *constrained*. Open categories can contain user-defined values and are suitable for extension or for open categories (such as lemmas, glosses). Closed categories can only take a fixed set of values and are intended for Boolean values or for small lists of values. Finally, constrained categories can be limited by, e.g., a regular expression, being suitable for an open set of values that follow a certain pattern, such as language tags.

ISOcat adopted an open approach in that any expert can contribute their own data categories with the result that these can be shared with any other user. The work has been thus structured around the *thematic domain groups* of TC 37, which are shown in Table 8.1. In principle, each of these groups was supposed to manage their individual areas such that when an individual proposes a new category, it would be contributed to one of these TDGs. The approval process was then intended to take a number of steps possibly involving the appointment of extra external experts

Table 8.1 The thematic domain groups of ISO TC 37 involved in ISOcat

TGD 1	Metadata
TGD 2	Morphosyntax
TGD 3	Semantic content representation
TGD 4	Syntax
TGD 6	Language resource ontology
TGD 7	Lexicography
TGD 8	Language codes
TGD 9	Terminology
TGD 11	Multilingual information framework (MLIF)
TGD 12	Lexical resources
TGD 13	Lexical semantics

and either marking it as a duplicate of an existing category, suggesting a hand-off to another TDG, or accepting the category, by which it would be given a unique identifier. The identifier was a number sequentially allocated to each category which could be easily embedded and referenced from an XML or RDF document. For this case the namespace URL http://www.isocat.org/ns/dcr was introduced [28]. The usage of these URLs is not recommended as they do not resolve anymore, as ISOcat is currently undergoing a revision (Sect. 8.3.3).

8.3.2   The General Ontology of Linguistic Description (GOLD)

GOLD is the first ontology being designed specifically for linguistic description on the Semantic Web [17]. It is an OWL ontology for descriptive linguistics, aiming at giving a formalized account of the most basic categories and relations used in the description of human language. The level of description corresponds to the level of knowledge of a well-trained linguistic. GOLD has drawn inspiration from projects that bring together large bodies of language data, including Autotyp [29] as well as WALS [30]. The authors of GOLD see its role as providing a lingua franca as a basis for such annotation projects to map their data categories to in order to foster conceptual interoperability. Furthermore, GOLD also draws inspiration from the development of lexico-conceptual resources, such as WordNet. The categories and relations defined in such lexical resources are linguistically motivated in that they include only those concepts necessary for processing language but partially conform to the organization of knowledge in general.

GOLD followed principles of knowledge engineering, attempting to be maximally explicit in defining domain knowledge by axiomatization in a given knowledge representation language, thus allowing for reasoning on the basis of the encoded knowledge. GOLD represents thus an attempt to merge a rich knowledge of language and language data with the extra-linguistic knowledge already encoded in ontologies, such as in the Suggested Upper Merged Ontology (SUMO) [31].

GOLD aimed at overcoming problems inherent in linguistic typology and language documentation, in particular the lack of interoperability to other projects, and it successfully expanded to other scientific communities.

To facilitate third-party adaptation, GOLD introduced the notion of Community of Practice Extensions [32, COPEs], i.e. independent ontologies that inherit and refine GOLD concepts. For example, OLiA (Sect. 8.4.2) can be considered a GOLD COPE for annotated corpora. Eventually, GOLD and ISOcat began to converge when the 2010 edition of GOLD was mirrored within ISOcat [33]. However, this process, as well as the addition of a large number of tagsets and domain vocabularies, contributed to the emergence of terminological (near-) doublets, and without relational data structures to express identity or near-identity, or an effective community process to eliminate such doublets, ISOcat became increasingly unusable.

8.3.3 Transition to the CLARIN Concept Registry and DatCatInfo

Despite its influence in numerous branches of research, ISOcat failed in general to deliver on its promises and was eventually discontinued in 2014. According to Schuurman et al. [34] the principal issue was that:

> It was very easy to get a login and to get rights to enter new data categories. . . the content of the registry was out of control. People were, for example, urged not to provide entries that were more or less copies of already existing ones, but a) there was no way to prohibit it, and b) people sometimes copied an entry, just in order to make sure the original owner would not change the entry without them knowing it.

In particular, Schuurman et al. [34] claim that two main issues affected ISOcat: firstly the *proliferation* or many duplicate or near-duplicate categories due to too many users having access. This resulted in categories with unclear and unvalidated status that could not be relied upon. Furthermore, they claimed that *complexity* was a significant problem with too many obligatory and overly technical fields. Warburton and Wright elaborate that 'it became clear that although a wide range of linguists were interested in documenting data categories, few supported standardizing them by following a three-stage balloting procedure prescribed by ISO. Consequently, the "Registry" has been rechristened a "Data Category Repository," . . . [and this] shift from standardization to harmonization as a purpose meant that the new DCR was, in effect, no longer an ISO resource. . . . Since the DCR was no longer viewed as an ISO resource, using the existing brand name ISOcat and the URL www.isocat.org was also no longer permitted' [35]. In consequence, ISO 12620:2009 was withdrawn and a new version has been produced for publication in 2019. Since 2014, ISOcat content remains available as a static resource under http://isocat.tbxinfo.net/, and two successor systems are being developed.

As a replacement for ISOcat, Schuurman et al. [34] introduced the CLARIN Concept Registry (CCR),[24] which is based around the OpenSKOS software [36]. They aimed to avoid the issues with ISOcat by allowing only CLARIN National Content coordinators to update the registry, and by requiring a 'good definition' of a concept that is unique, meaningful, reusable and concise. However, this project does not seem to have addressed the issues with ISOcat in a useful manner, and even at the time of writing, basic concepts in the CCR such as 'part of speech' have not reached the 'approved' status.

Simultaneously, ISO TC37 has been developing DatCatInfo as an ISOcat successor registry initially populated with ISOcat concepts [35].[25] DatCatInfo is developed in close connection with the TermBase eXchange format (TBX), cf. Chap. 9. As of early 2019, 2,977 data categories (approximately half the DCs from ISOcat) have been migrated to DatCatInfo, and are currently undergoing continued revision in order to eliminate duplicates and establish a coherent view on the terminology.

Unfortunately, the future division of labour between the CCR and DatCatInfo is not clear, although they clearly diverge, and we may anticipate a specialization of the CCR for applications in language technology and a specialization of DatCatInfo for lexical and terminological resources. In any case, both systems will provide resolvable URIs and, for domain-specific vocabularies, it will be possible to link them to each of them. In fact, the capability to facilitate linking with multiple external reference models has been the motivation for modular ontological architectures such as OLiA (Sect. 8.4.2).

8.4   Application-Specific Terminology Repositories

While general repositories of linguistic reference terminology are still under development, reference vocabularies for specific types of resources have been developed and enjoy considerable popularity. In the context of human language technology, the most important vocabularies are LexInfo (for lexical resources) and OLiA (primarily for linguistic annotations) as presented below. In our concluding remarks in this section, we briefly discuss the extent and limits of axiomatization of application-specific terminology repositories.

8.4.1   LexInfo: Linguistic Categories for Lexical Resources

LexInfo was designed as an ontology for 'associat[ing] linguistic information with respect to any level of linguistic description and expressivity to elements in an

---

[24]https://www.clarin.eu/ccr, accessed 10-07-2019.
[25]http://www.datcatinfo.net, http://demo.termweb.se/termweb/app, accessed 10-07-2019.

ontology' [18]. LexInfo predates the Ontolex-lemon model, but was re-designed in parallel with the definition of Ontolex-lemon to become an ontology of linguistic categories with the goal of making Ontolex-lemon itself agnostic of any linguistic category system to support reuse of different linguistic category systems and ontologies in combination with it. For the first release of the LexInfo ontology, a version of the Lexical Markup Framework [13] in RDF[26] was used. Version 2.0 was updated to use the Ontolex-lemon model, and many of the functions of LexInfo described originally (in Cimiano et al. [18]) are now part of Ontolex-lemon. In terms of its definitions, LexInfo remains to be largely based on LMF, and thus the definitions developed in the context of ISOcat.

By now, LexInfo has been extended with many extra features, leading it to be one of the most widely used vocabularies on the Linguistic Linked Open Data Cloud (see Chap. 3). In particular, LexInfo introduces the following:

- A fixed and axiomatized set of linguistic categories, covering areas such as *part of speech*, *tense*, *number*, *animacy*, *degree*, *mood*, *term types* (e.g. abbreviation), *frequency*, *register*, etc. These categories are partially derived from ISOcat, but with stronger axiomizations (although not as strong as OLiA, covered in the next section).
- Subclasses of Ontolex-lemon's `LexicalEntry` are introduced by part of speech, e.g. `Noun`, `CommonNoun`.
- Syntactic frames that are defined by the arguments they require. These are divided first by part of speech, then by the set of required arguments and finally distinguished by their optional (adjunct) arguments. For example, the `Transitive` class is a subclass of `VerbFrame` and furthermore is required to have exactly one `subject` and exactly one `directObject`. It has a subclass `TransitivePP` that also admits a prepositional phrase as an adjunct, e.g. 'she added salt to the stew'. Note that this is distinct from the `Ditransitive` frame which has a required indirect argument.
- Argument classes and properties are also introduced to enable the axioms for frames to be applied.
- A repertoire to relate senses, lexical entries and forms to each other. For example, `translation` is defined as a relationship between senses, `homonym` is a relationship between two entries. `pastTenseForm` is a relationship between different forms of the same lexical entry.

8.4.2 OLiA: Ontologies of Linguistic Annotation

While the success of LexInfo demonstrated that many concepts in the lexical domain can be standardized against reference terminology provided in a single ontology,

---

[26]This is still available at http://lexinfo.net/lmf.owl, accessed 10-07-2019.

earlier approaches to achieve such a standardization for the more diverse types of information found in linguistic annotation have repeatedly considered to have failed.[27] In response to this situation, the Ontologies of Linguistic Annotation (OLiA) [37, 38] have been designed as a mediator between various terminology repositories on the one hand and linguistically annotated resources, resp., their annotation schemes, on the other hand [39]. OLiA thus applies linked data principles to leverage several distributed terminology repositories. OLiA became subsequently increasingly important as a terminology repository in its own right for both natural language processing and linguistics, and since the conception of the Linguistic Linked Open Data cloud in 2010, it represents a central terminology hub for annotation terminology.

The Ontologies of Linguistic Annotations represent a modular architecture of OWL2/DL ontologies that formalize the mapping between annotations, a 'Reference Model' and existing terminology repositories ('External Reference Models'). The OLiA ontologies are available from http://purl.org/olia under a Creative Commons Attribution license (CC-BY).

The OLiA ontologies were developed as part of an infrastructure for the sustainable maintenance of linguistic resources [39], where their primary fields of application included the formalization of annotation schemes and concept-based querying over heterogeneously annotated corpora [40, 41]. As multiple institutions and manifold resources from several disciplines were involved, no holistic annotation standard could be developed and enforced onto the contributors. Instead, a modular architecture was designed in order to support the integration of annotation terminology from different sources in a lossless and reversible way.

In the OLiA architecture, as illustrated in Fig. 8.2, four different types of ontologies are distinguished (cf. Fig. 8.2 for an example):

- The OLIA REFERENCE MODEL specifies the common terminology that different annotation schemes can refer to. It is based on existing repositories of annotation terminology and extended in accordance with the annotation schemes that it was applied to.
- Multiple OLIA ANNOTATION MODELS formalize annotation schemes and tagsets. Annotation models are based on the original documentation, so that they provide an interpretation-independent representation of the annotation scheme.
- For every annotation model, a LINKING MODEL defines subclass-relationships between concepts/properties in the respective annotation model and the reference model. Linking models are interpretations of annotation model concepts and properties in terms of the reference model.
- Existing terminology repositories can be integrated as EXTERNAL REFERENCE MODELS if they are represented in OWL2/DL. Then, linking models specify

---

[27]See, e.g., the critical remarks by Atwell [1] on EAGLES and non-European tagsets, esp. regarding conceptual mismatches between form-, function- and example-based approaches in the development of tagsets for part-of-speech annotation.

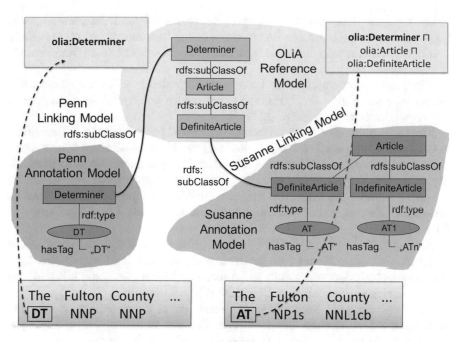

Fig. 8.2 Interpreting divergent annotations in terms of the OLiA Reference Model

subclass-relationships between reference model concepts and external reference model concepts. Important external reference models include ISOcat and GOLD.

The OLiA Reference Model specifies classes for linguistic categories (e.g. olia:Determiner) and grammatical features (e.g. olia:Accusative), as well as properties that define relations between these (e.g. olia:hasCase). Conceptually, annotation models differ from the reference model in that they include not only concepts and properties, but also individuals. Individuals represent concrete tags, while classes represent abstract concepts similar to those of the reference model. Figure 8.2 gives an example for the interpretation of two divergent POS annotations from Fig. 8.1: The word *The* is annotated as AT in the Susanne corpus, but as DT in the Penn Treebank. Using the OLiA Annotation and Linking Models for both tagsets[28] the tags can be matched against the hasTag properties of the respective individuals and we can retrieve the corresponding OLiA classes, either by RDFS inference or with a SPARQL property path such as rdf:type/rdfs:subClassOf+. The resulting descriptions can be compared, and in this case, we find that both agree on olia:Determiner, even though the Susanne annotation is much more fine-grained and gives more information.

---

[28] Available under http://purl.org/olia/susa.owl and http://purl.org/olia/penn.owl, resp. http://purl. org/olia/susa-link.rdf and http://purl.org/olia/penn-link.rdf (accessed 10-07-2019).

Taken together, these allow to interpret the individual (and the part-of-speech tag it represents) as an `olia:Determiner`, and to compare and process these descriptions in a conjoint fashion. In particular, we can losslessly map from Susanne to Penn tags.

The same procedure can then be extended to external reference models, and allows us, e.g., to infer that both tags translate into `gold:Determiner`, resp. http://www.isocat.org/datcat/DC-1272, etc.

The OLiA ontologies cover different grammatical phenomena, including inflectional morphology, word classes, phrase and edge labels of different syntax annotations and extensions for discourse annotations (coreference, discourse relations, discourse structure and information structure). Annotations for lexical semantics are only covered to the extent that they are found in syntactic and morphosyntactic annotation schemes. Other aspects of lexical semantics are beyond the scope of OLiA.

A specific characteristic of OLiA is the relation between tags and instances: In an OLiA Annotation Model for a small-scale tagset, every tag is represented by a single individual, characterized by the Annotation Model concept(s) it is assigned to, by its string representation and, optionally, by a description.

Yet, this 'classical' approach only permits us to cover annotation schemes with up to a few hundred individual tags. For morphologically rich languages, larger part-of-speech tagsets have been designed, which incorporate numerous morphosyntactic features whose combinations generate tagsets with thousands of tags, e.g. MULTEXT-East.[29]

To 'decompose' positional annotation schemes efficiently into morphosyntactic categories, morphological features, etc. OLiA extends the original semantics of individuals to represent groups of tags which share parts of their string representation. For this purpose, the OLiA system sub-ontology[30] provides the properties `hasTagContaining`, `hasTagStartingWith` and `hasTagEndingWith` for matching substrings in a tag, and `hasTagMatching` for full-fledged regular expressions, in addition to `hasTag` for literal matches. Note that this not only permits mapping one individual to a number of tags, but a full $n : m$ mapping where every tag can be assigned multiple individuals. If an actual tag matches multiple individuals, this should be interpreted such that the element to which the tag applies inherits their definitions and falls in the intersection of their respective superclasses.

As some OLiA applications like Apache Stanbol[31] rely on `hasTag` properties alone, it is recommended to compile the `hasTagX` properties into `hasTag` properties: Using an annotated corpus, we bootstrap an exhaustive list of tags and generate `hasTag` properties for all tags matching a particular `hasTag_X` pattern.

---

[29] http://nl.ijs.si/ME/, accessed 10-07-2019.

[30] http://purl.org/olia/system.owl, accessed 10-07-2019.

[31] https://stanbol.apache.org/docs/trunk/components/enhancer/nlp/nlpannotations, accessed 10-07-2019.

Although individuals are thus capable of representing groups of tags, OLiA preserves the instance-based (rather than a class-based) modelling in accordance with the strong typing in OWL2/DL.[32] Still, a class-based model would have the advantage that words or token spans can be directly assigned an annotation as their rdf:type. In fact, we do not exclude this possibility, as users are free to develop annotation models where every individual is defined an instance of a singleton class, so that this single-tag class can be assigned as type.

This discussion touches the core semantics of the OLiA Annotation Model individuals: they do not necessarily provide reference semantics for individual tags, but they act as entry points to OLiA Reference Model concepts. For part-of-speech annotation, individuals may thus represent either of the following:

1. Individual tags (hasTag)
2. Patterns defining a mapping from tags to potentially complex type definitions (hasTagX).

These definitions overlap for the case of singleton classes mentioned above, but they have different implications for possible references to OLiA Annotation Models. Under the first interpretation, it is possible to refer to tags from external resources as target of a designated object property. OLiA does not define such a property, but nif:oliaLink has been designed for this purpose. Under the second interpretation, individuals can be used by a tool developer to aggregate the definition of all matching individuals in a conjunction ($\sqcap$), and then to assign this as a complex type to his (application-specific) unit of analysis using rdf:type.

As a general-purpose repository of linguistic annotation terminology, OLiA stays deliberately agnostic about these interpretations and permits both kinds of references, using nif:oliaLink or direct rdf:type.

As we explicitly permit the second interpretation, it is possible to assign entities of *any* type an OLiA Annotation Model class. OLiA semantics are thus not limited to tag semantics, but cover any entity such annotations can be applied to. OLiA semantics thus refer only to linguistic characteristics of arbitrary entities, but remain *underspecified* with respect to their material manifestation. It is thus equally possible to assign an OLiA class as a type to a word in a text, to an annotation attached to this word, to a lexical entry in a dictionary, to a lexeme in a language, to a term in a grammatical treatise or to a concept in a terminological resource.

8.4.3 Limits of Axiomatization

OWL ontologies support the axiomatization of classes, e.g., to define cardinality constraints for properties and classes. Describing annotation categories in an

---

[32] User-defined properties such as hasTagX should be applied to individuals only, not OWL classes. Otherwise, OWL classes would be re-cast as individuals. While this may be tolerated by reasoners, it represents a design flaw.

OWL ontology naturally calls for a deeper axiomatization of these categories by formalizing dependencies between grammatical features and linguistic categories by subclass axioms, cardinality restrictions as well as domain/range specifications. Rules of this kind are provided, e.g., by MULTEXT/East or the Universal Dependencies.

In contrast, axiomatization in generic and application-specific terminology repositories is limited, as this requires harmonization both across resources and across languages. GOLD, e.g., provides weak axioms only, and the developers of ISOcat did not permit axiomatization in the first place. Most ontologies discussed here are thus relatively weak and often stay within RDFS semantics. OLiA requires OWL2, as it employs disjunction ($\sqcup$), conjunction ($\sqcap$) and negation ($\neg$) for defining relations between Annotation Model concepts and Reference Model concepts.

Taking the OLiA Reference Model as an example, axiomatization is limited, and restricted to properties that hold per definition of the category. For example, a past participle is defined as a participle that has past tense: `PastParticiple` $\equiv$ `Participle` $\sqcap$ $\exists$`hasTense.Past`. Beyond this, the OLiA Reference Model does not provide axioms regarding conventional associations between categories and features, as it will inevitably lead to inconsistencies when directly applied to *existing* corpora, dictionaries and annotations.[33]

This can be illustrated by providing counter-examples to commonly accepted assumptions that represent candidates for axiomatization:

- `Adverb` $\sqsubseteq$ $\nexists$`hasPerson`, i.e. no adverb has a person feature. Indeed, some pronominal adverbs in German do, e.g. *meinetwegen* 'because of me', *deinetwegen* 'because of you (sg.)', *seinet-/ihretwegen* 'because of him/her'.
- `NonFiniteVerb` $\sqsubseteq$ $\nexists$`hasTense`, i.e. non-finite verbs have no tense. Actually, English has past and present participles, which may be modelled as having morphological tense.
- `FiniteVerb` $\sqsubseteq$ $\nexists$`hasGender`, i.e. finite verbs do not have a gender. The simple past in Russian does: *čitat'* 'to read', *on čital* 'he read', but *ona čitala* 'she read'.

Accordingly, OLiA neither restricts the domain of its properties nor provides cardinality axioms requiring or prohibiting the assignment of grammatical features to instances of a particular concept.

For similar reasons, the ontologies described here only provide very few disjointness axioms. In the reality of linguistic annotation, categories may overlap, so that a language-independent and clear-cut differentiation between, say, participles

---

[33] A wider use of cardinality axioms is feasible only for a limited domain, where certain conventions or phenomena can be taken for granted only within a standardization approach that aims at actively transforming existing resources towards common specifications in a labour-intensive process, cf. http://universaldependencies.org/introduction.html (accessed 10-07-2019). In comparison to MULTEXT/East, the terminology repositories discussed here are not restricted to a geographic area. In comparison to Universal Dependencies, Linked-Data-based annotation harmonization is a light-weight approach that does not require data transformation.

in attributive use and deverbal adjectives cannot be taken for granted in resources as currently provided.

General terminology repositories, even if formalized as ontologies, thus stay agnostic about such axioms and expect them to be provided in language-specific or domain-specific sub-models (e.g. MULTEXT/East for Eastern Europe or the Universal Dependencies for their accompanying corpora).

8.5 Summary and Further Reading

In this chapter we have been concerned with the conceptual interoperability of linguistic annotations. Conceptual interoperability ultimately requires the use of shared categories and, practically, the reuse of identifiers from (standardized) category systems.

In an RDF context, such category systems normally take the form of terminology repositories which define categories by means of URIs. Language identification is somewhat more complex because languages are both supported by URI-based references and as primitive types (language tags) directly in the RDF data model. We compared both approaches and formulated the recommendation to apply IETF language tags whenever possible and adequate, but to use standardized properties and repositories such as Glottolog where these are not sufficient. Gillis and Tittel [25] provide a deeper discussion of language tags and their shortcomings. It is possible that in the distant future, IETF language tags and URI-based means of language identification may converge; a recent discussion about such possibilities can be found in the context of the 'EasierRDF' initiative.[34]

For linguistic categories in general, we discussed several terminology repositories, most importantly ISOcat and its successor systems, as well as application-specific terminology repositories, LexInfo for lexical resources and OLiA for linguistic annotations.

As for recent developments on ISOcat, GOLD and other general terminology repositories, we suggest the interested reader to consult the upcoming volume by Pareja-Lora et al. [42], which includes descriptions of the current state of ISOcat migration to DatCatInfo [35], a discussion of CCR and the role of linked data in the CLARIN architecture [43] and an update about the recent development and the current state of the GOLD ontology [44].

The origins of LexInfo are described in the paper by Cimiano et al. [18], but the information there is quite obsolete as the resource has been significantly re-engineered and re-designed since the original publication. The interested reader should directly consult https://lexinfo.net/. For more details on OLiA, the reader is invited to consult the corresponding publications by Chiarcos et al. [19, 37, 38, 45, 46].

---

[34]In particular, https://github.com/w3c/EasierRDF/issues/22, accessed 10-07-2019.

OLiA is also worth mentioning here because of its architecture that may serve as a template for future terminology repositories for linguistic categories: It natively builds on the application of linked data principles in that it features a modular architecture of independent ontologies that permit to leverage both several community-maintained terminology repositories and resource- or language-specific annotation schemes. While we expect that novel terminology repositories will continue to emerge and some terminology repositories will not be indefinitely maintained (as the case for ISOcat at the moment), a clear separation in resource-specific terminologies, general terminologies and a declarative linking between them is probably the most promising way to ensure future interpretability and interoperability of language resources and tools across languages and theoretical frameworks, as formulated in a pregnant fashion in the title of a seminal paper by Dimitriadis et al. [47] for the more specific use case of typological databases: 'How to integrate databases without starting a typology war'.

References

1. E. Atwell, Development of tag sets for part-of-speech tagging, in *Corpus Linguistics: An International Handbook, Volume 1*, ed. by A. Lüdeling, M. Kyto (Walter de Gruyter, New York, 2008), pp. 501–526
2. W.N. Francis, H. Kucera, *Brown Corpus Manual*. Information to accompany a standard corpus of present-day edited American English, for use with digital computers. Providence (1979). http://icame.uib.no/brown/bcm.html. Original edition 1964
3. M.P. Marcus, B. Santorini, M.A. Marcinkiewicz, Building a large annotated corpus of English: the Penn treebank. Comput. Linguist. **19**, 313 (1993)
4. G. Sampson, *English for the Computer: The SUSANNE Corpus and Analytic Scheme* (Oxford University Press, Oxford, 1995)
5. G. Leech, A. Wilson, EAGLES recommendations for the morphosyntactic annotation of corpora (1996), http://www.ilc.cnr.it/EAGLES/annotate/annotate.html. Version of March 1996
6. J. Hughes, D. Souter, E. Atwell, Automatic extraction of tagset mappings from parallel annotated corpora, in *Proceedings of the ACL-SIGDAT Workshop From Text to Tags: Issues in Multilingual Language Analysis* (Association for Computational Linguistics, Stroudsburg, 1995), pp. 10–17
7. J. Nivre, Ž. Agić, L. Ahrenberg, et. al., Universal dependencies 1.4 (2016), http://hdl.handle.net/11234/1-1827
8. A. Kutuzov, E. Velldal, L. Øvrelid, Redefining part-of-speech classes with distributional semantic models, in *Proceedings of the 20th SIGNLL Conference on Computational Natural Language Learning* (Association for Computational Linguistics, Berlin, 2016), pp. 115–125
9. J. Broschart, Why Tongan does it differently: categorial distinctions in a language without nouns and verbs. Linguist. Typol. **1**(2), 123 (1997)
10. N. Evans, T. Osada, Mundari: the myth of a language without word classes. Linguist. Typol. **9**(3), 351–390 (2005)
11. D. Barner, A. Bale, No nouns, no verbs: psycholinguistic arguments in favor of lexical underspecification, in *The Mental Representation of Grammatical Relations*, ed. by J. Bresnan (MIT Press, Cambridge, MA, 2002), pp. 655–726
12. M. Kemps-Snijders, M. Windhouwer, P. Wittenburg, S. Wright, ISOcat: remodelling metadata for language resources. Int. J. Metadata Semant. Ontol. **4**(4), 261 (2009)

13. G. Francopoulo, M. George, N. Calzolari, M. Monachini, N. Bel, M. Pet, C. Soria, et al., Lexical markup framework (LMF), in *Proceedings of the International Conference on Language Resources and Evaluation (LREC)*, vol. 6 (2006)

14. G. Francopoulo, N. Bel, M. George, N. Calzolari, M. Monachini, M. Pet, C. Soria, Multilingual resources for NLP in the Lexical Markup Framework (LMF). Lang. Resour. Eval. **43**, 57 (2009)

15. N. Ide, L. Romary, E. de la Clergerie, International standard for a linguistic annotation framework, in *Proceedings of the HLT-NAACL'03 Workshop on the Software Engineering and Architecture of Language Technology, Edmonton* (2003), pp. 25–30

16. N. Ide, K. Suderman, The Linguistic Annotation Framework: a standard for annotation interchange and merging. Lang. Resour. Eval. **48**(3), 395 (2014)

17. S. Farrar, D.T. Langendoen, An OWL-DL implementation of GOLD: an ontology for the Semantic Web, in *Linguistic Modeling of Information and Markup Languages: Contributions to Language Technology*, ed. by A. Witt, D. Metzing (Springer, Dordrecht, 2010)

18. P. Cimiano, P. Buitelaar, J. McCrae, M. Sintek, LexInfo: a declarative model for the lexicon-ontology interface. Web Semant. Sci. Serv. Agents World Wide Web **9**(1), 29 (2011)

19. C. Chiarcos, M. Sukhareva, OLiA - Ontologies of Linguistic Annotation. Semant. Web J. **518**, 379 (2015)

20. R. Cyganiak, D. Wood, M. Lanthaler, RDF 1.1 concepts and abstract syntax. Technical Report, W3C Recommendation 25 February 2014 (2014)

21. A. Phillips, M. Davis, BCP 47 – tags for identifying languages. BCP 47 Standard (2006), http://www.rfc-editor.org/rfc/bcp/bcp47.txt

22. Library of Congress, MARC code list for languages. Introduction. Technical Report, Library of Congress, Washington, DC (2007). Version of October 2007

23. SIL International, ISO 639-3. Technical Report, SIL International (2015), http://www-01.sil.org/iso639-3/default.asp

24. SIL International, Relationship between ISO 639-3 and the other parts of ISO 639. Technical Report, SIL International (2015), http://www-01.sil.org/iso639-3/relationship.asp

25. F. Gillis-Webber, S. Tittel, The shortcomings of language tags for linked data when modeling lesser-known languages, in *Proceedings of the 2nd Conference on Language, Data and Knowledge (LDK 2019)* OpenAccess Series in Informatics (Schloss Dagstuhl, Leibniz-Zentrum fuer Informatik, 2019), p. 4:1–4:15

26. M. Kemps-Snijders, M. Windhouwer, P. Wittenburg, S.E. Wright, ISOcat: corralling data categories in the wild, in *Proceedings of the 6th International Conference on Language Resources and Evaluation (LREC)* (2008), pp. 887–891

27. N. Ide, L. Romary, A registry of standard data categories for linguistic annotation, in *Proceedings of the 4th International Conference on Language Resources and Evaluation (LREC)* (2004), pp. 135–138

28. M. Windhouwer, S.E. Wright, Linking to linguistic data categories in ISOcat, in *Linked Data in Linguistics* (Springer, Berlin, 2012), pp. 99–107

29. B. Bickel, J. Nichols, The autotyp research program, invited talk at the *Annual Meeting of the Linguistic Typology Resource Center Utrecht* (2002)

30. B. Comrie, Areal typology of mainland southeast Asia: what we learn from the wals maps. Manusya J. Humanit. **10**(3), 18 (2007)

31. I. Niles, A. Pease, Towards a standard upper ontology, in *Proceedings of the 2nd International Conference on Formal Ontology in Information Systems (FOIS), Maine*, ed. by C. Welty, B. Smith (2001)

32. S. Farrar, W.D. Lewis, The GOLD community of practice: an infrastructure for linguistic data on the web. Lang. Resour. Eval. **41**(1), 45 (2007)

33. M. Kemps-Snijders, RELISH: rendering endangered languages lexicons interoperable through standards harmonisation, in *Proceedings of the 7th SaLTMiL Workshop on Creation and Use of Basic Lexical Resources for Less-Resourced Languages* (Valetta, Malta, 2010)

34. I. Schuurman, M. Windhouwer, O. Ohren, D. Zeman, CLARIN concept registry: the new semantic registry, in *CLARIN 2015 Selected Papers* (2015), pp. 62–70
35. K. Warburton, S. Wright, A data category repository for language resources, in *Development of Linguistic Linked Open Data Resources for Collaborative Data-Intensive Research in the Language Sciences*, ed. by A. Pareja-Lora, M. Blume, B. Lust, C. Chiarcos (MIT Press, Cambridge, MA, 2019)
36. H. Brugman, M. Lindeman, Publishing and exploiting vocabularies using the OpenSKOS, in *Proceedings of the Describing Language Resources with Metadata Workshop at LREC 2012* (2012)
37. C. Chiarcos, An ontology of linguistic annotations. LDV Forum **23**(1), 1 (2008)
38. C. Chiarcos, Grounding an ontology of linguistic annotations in the data category registry, in *Proceedings of the LREC 2010 Workshop on Language Resource and Language Technology Standards (LT&LTS). State of the Art, Emerging Needs, and Future Developments, Valetta* (2010), pp. 37–40
39. T. Schmidt, C. Chiarcos, T. Lehmberg, G. Rehm, A. Witt, E. Hinrichs, Avoiding data graveyards: from heterogeneous data collected in multiple research projects to sustainable linguistic resources, in *Proceedings of the E-MELD Workshop on Digital Language Documentation, East Lansing* (2006)
40. G. Rehm, R. Eckart, C. Chiarcos, J. Dellert, Ontology-based XQuery'ing of XML-encoded language resources on multiple annotation layers, in *Proceedings of International Conference on Language Resources and Evaluation (LREC), Marrakech* (2008), 3, pp. 525–532
41. C. Chiarcos, S. Dipper, M. Götze, U. Leser, A. Lüdeling, J. Ritz, M. Stede, A flexible framework for integrating annotations from different tools and tag sets. Traitement automatique des langues **49**(2), 217 (2008)
42. A. Pareja-Lora, M. Blume, B. Lust, C. Chiarcos (eds.), *Development of Linguistic Linked Open Data Resources for Collaborative Data-Intensive Research in the Language Sciences* (MIT Press, Cambridge, MA, 2019)
43. T. Trippel, C. Zinn, Describing research data with CMDI—challenges to establish contact with linked open data, in *Development of Linguistic Linked Open Data Resources for Collaborative Data-Intensive Research in the Language Sciences*, ed. by A. Pareja-Lora, M. Blume, B. Lust, C. Chiarcos (MIT Press, Cambridge, MA, 2019)
44. D. Langendoen, Whither GOLD? in *Development of Linguistic Linked Open Data Resources for Collaborative Data-Intensive Research in the Language Sciences*, ed. by A. Pareja-Lora, M. Blume, B. Lust, C. Chiarcos (MIT Press, Cambridge, MA, 2019)
45. C. Chiarcos, S. Nordhoff, S. Hellmann, Interoperability of Corpora and annotations, in *Linked Data in Linguistics. Representing and Connecting Language Data and Language Metadata*, ed. by C. Chiarcos, S. Nordhoff, S. Hellmann (Springer, Heidelberg, 2012), pp. 161–179
46. C. Chiarcos, J. Ritz, M. Stede, Querying and visualizing coreference annotation in multi-layer corpora, in *Proceedings of the 8th Discourse Anaphora and Anaphor Resolution Colloquium (DAARC 2011), Faro* (2011), pp. 80–92
47. A. Dimitriadis, M. Windhouwer, A. Saulwick, R. Goedemans, T. Bíró, How to integrate databases without starting a typology war: the typological database system, in *The Use of Databases in Cross-Linguistic Studies*, ed. by M. Everaert, S. Musgrave, A. Dimitriadis, Empirical Approaches to Language Typology [EALT] 41 (Walter de Gruyter, Berlin, 2009), pp. 155–208. https://doi.org/10.1515/9783110198744.155

Part III
Generation and Exploitation

Chapter 9
Converting Language Resources into Linked Data

Abstract In previous chapters, we discussed how to model linguistic data sets using the Resource Description Framework as a basis to publish them as linked data on the Web. In this chapter, we describe a methodology that can be followed in the transformation of legacy linguistic datasets into linked data. The methodology comprises of different tasks, including the specification, modelling, generation, linking, publication and exploitation of the data. We will discuss specific guidelines that can be applied in the transformation of particular types of resources, such as bilingual/multilingual dictionaries, WordNets, terminologies and corpora.

9.1 Introduction

A number of general guidelines and methodologies have been proposed in order to guide developers and practitioners in the process of generating and publishing LD on the Web (e.g. [1, 2]). These guidelines identify a set of tasks and best practices to generate LD from existing data sources and to make it available on the Web by following the LD principles. General guidelines for publishing data as linked data have been adapted to the case of publishing multilingual linguistic linked data [3, 4]. In addition, the W3C Best Practices for Multilingual Linked Open Data community group[1] published specific guidelines for generating and publishing linked data for specific types of language resources such as bilingual and multilingual dictionaries, WordNets, terminologies in TermBase eXchange (TBX) format, and corpora.

In Sect. 9.2 we will provide an overview of the general methodology for transforming language resources into RDF and publishing them as linked data. Then, from Sects. 9.3 to 9.8, we will review the different activities of the methodology. Finally, in Sect. 9.9, we will give pointers to more specific guidelines that spell and detail the process for particular types of LRs.

---

[1]http://www.w3.org/community/bpmlod/.

© Springer Nature Switzerland AG 2020
P. Cimiano et al., *Linguistic Linked Data*,
https://doi.org/10.1007/978-3-030-30225-2_9

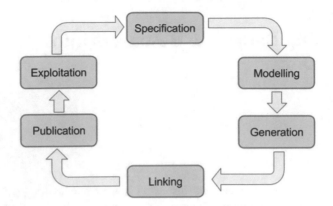

Fig. 9.1 Life cycle of LD, adapted from [1]

9.2   General Methodology for Generating and Publishing LLD

In this section, we review the general methodology for LD publication initially proposed by Villazón-Terrazas et al. [1] in the context of government LD, and later extended by Vila et al. [3] to cover multilingual and linguistic aspects. Such a methodology adopts an iterative incremental approach covering the following activities (see Fig. 9.1): (1) `specification`, to analyse and select data sources; (2) `modelling`, to develop the model that represents the information domain of the data sources; (3) `generation`, to transform the data sources into RDF datasets; (4) `linking`, to create links between different RDF datasets; (5) `publication`, to publish the model, the dataset transformed into RDF, metadata and links to other datasets; and (6) `exploitation`, to develop applications that make use of the published RDF datasets.

Each of the activities of the LD life cycle comprises of several tasks as displayed in Table 9.1. It is important to mention that not all tasks are mandatory, with some of them being optional depending on the specific scenario. For instance, if the exploitation of the data is not directly foreseen, then the exploitation step might be optional. Further, if an existing model is reused, then the modelling activity can be skipped.

In the following sections we give more details on the different activities and their constituent tasks.

9.3   Specification

When building LLD-based applications, a detailed specification of requirements allows to reduce later development efforts, provides a basis for estimating costs and schedules and offers a baseline for validation and verification [1]. A crucial aspect of

Table 9.1 Main activities and tasks in the LLD generation process, adapted from [1, 4]

Activity	Description	Task
1. Specification	Analyzing and describing data characteristics	1.1. Identify and analyse the data sources
		1.2. Design the URIs/IRIs
		1.3. Define license and provenance information
2. Modelling	Creating/selecting ontologies to describe the RDF resources	2.1. Analyse and select existing domain models
		2.2. Develop the model for representing the data
		2.3. Select model(s) for metadata information
3. Generation	Producing RDF datasets from the data sources	3.1. Define mappings between the data source and RDF models
		3.2. Transform the data sources into RDF
		3.3. Validate/clean the generated RDF data
4. Linking	Connecting the generated dataset to other RDF datasets	4.1. Select target datasets
		4.2. Discover and represent links between the RDF data and the target datasets
5. Publication	Making the RDF data and metadata available	5.1. Publish the dataset
		5.2. Publish the metadata
6. Exploitation	Using the dataset	6.1. Develop applications that consume the RDF data

the specification activity is the familiarization with the characteristics of the source dataset, as a basis to formulate a suitable strategy to define a URI schema as well as to define the licensing conditions and provenance information of the resulting dataset.

Identification and Analysis of Data Sources The first task of the specification activity is the identification and selection of relevant language resources to be transformed. Subsequently, all relevant information including documentation of these resources needs to be compiled. Further, the schema of those resources, including the conceptual components and their relationships, have to be identified.

Therefore, we have to consider two layers: the *data model* and the *content* (the data itself). As for the *data model*, this includes vocabularies, standards, terminologies, etc. used for the description of entities, attributes and relationships in the data. As an outcome of this task, all the available information about the data model used in the sources will be compiled, and the natural languages that will be involved in the modelling activity (see Sect. 9.4) will be identified.

Regarding the *content*, this can be language independent or language dependent [3]. Some properties such as identifiers, numbers and some date formats are usually language independent, whereas names, titles, textual descriptions and some date formats are typically language dependent. However, in the source data, language-dependent properties do not always make the language of the content explicit. In this case, it is recommended in this task to specify and classify attributes in the following way: (1) language independent, or language dependent, based on the content they carry, (2) for language-dependent attributes, the language can be explicit (e.g. using a metadata annotation, a pointer to the language description or code, etc.) or unspecified. In the former case (explicit language), the mechanisms that are used to indicate the language should be documented. In the case where the language is underspecified, language identification techniques need to be applied during the generation activity (see Sect. 9.5).

URIs and IRIs Design   The goal of this task is to design the structure of the URIs that will be used to identify RDF resources. As we have seen in Chap. 2, URIs constitute the core mechanism used in LD to identify resources uniquely on the Web. URIs should be designed with simplicity, stability and manageability in mind [5], thinking about them as identifiers rather than as names for Web resources.

A number of guidelines are available that give recommendations on the design of URIs, both at the national level (e.g. the *Designing URI Sets for the UK Public Sector*[2] and the *Technical Interoperability Standard for the Reuse of Information Resources*,[3] targeted at public administrations in UK and Spain respectively) and at the supranational level, such as the *Study on Persistent URIs* [6] developed by the ISA program[4] for the European Commission. For instance, ISA recommends the following pattern to build URIs:

$$\texttt{http://\{domain\}/\{type\}/\{concept\}/\{reference\}}$$

where {`domain`} refers to the host and relevant sector; {`type`} should be one of a small number of possible values that declare the type of resource that is being identified. Typical examples include: 'id' or 'item' for real-world objects; 'doc' for documents that describe those objects; 'def' for concepts; 'set' for datasets; or a string specific to the context, such as 'authority' or 'dcterms'; {`concept`} is something that groups items in a logical set: it might be a collection, the type of real-world object identified or the name of the concept scheme; finally {`reference`} is a specific item, term or concept.

Taking the project for converting the Apertium dictionaries into RDF as example [7], the URL schema to identify an English lexicon would be as follows:

$$\texttt{http://linguistic.linkeddata.es/id/apertium/lexiconEN}$$

---

[2]https://www.gov.uk/government/publications/designing-uri-sets-for-the-uk-public-sector.

[3]http://datos.gob.es/es/documentacion/norma-tecnica-de-interoperabilidad-de-reutilizacion-de-recursos-de-informacion.

[4]http://ec.europa.eu/archives/isa/.

Additionally, ISA recommends following a number of design principles when designing a URI, such as: avoid stating ownership (within the URI), avoid version numbers, re-use existing identifiers, avoid using auto-increment, avoid query strings and avoid file extensions (more details at [6]).

Independently of the chosen pattern, we have two basic options when designing URIs: to use *descriptive* (or *meaningful*) resource identifiers that use natural language descriptions in the local name of URIs or to use *opaque* resource identifiers, i.e. non-human readable local names. One example of a descriptive URI is:

```
http://www.lexinfo.net/ontology/2.0/lexinfo#adjective
```

that corresponds to the URI of the named individual 'adjective' in the LexInfo vocabulary.[5] An example of an opaque URI is:

```
http://www.isocat.org/datcat/DC-1230
```

used to identify 'adjective' in ISOcat. Both approaches have well-known advantages and disadvantages [8, 9]. The main benefit of using meaningful URIs is that they help developers to understand the underlying model faster, are easy to remember and are better displayed by many ontology editing tools. On the other hand, in a Semantic Web context, resource identifiers are intended for machine consumption, so that there is no need for them to be human readable. It is also well accepted that opaque URIs make ontologies more stable, so once the ontology has been published and adopted by a community of users, local names should not change even if the natural language descriptions associated to them are modified (unless the actual meaning of concepts has changed). Opaque URIs may also be a good choice if we want to avoid any language bias.

Technically speaking, several options are available when selecting the strategy for designing URIs for a particular LR [3, 9]:

1. Use of **URIs** in which the local name is in English or any other Latin-based language which makes use of only ASCII characters, e.g.

```
http://www.lexinfo.net/ontology/2.0/lexinfo\#noun.
```

2. Use of **full IRIs** (Internationalized Resource Identifier), created with the aim of allowing the use of Unicode characters for languages that do not follow the Latin alphabet. Full IRIs enable the use of Unicode characters not only for local names but also in the domain part, as in this made-up example IRI:

```
http://www.ejemplo_en_español.org/eñe
```

---

[5]http://www.lexinfo.net/ontology/2.0/lexinfo.

3. Use of **Internationalized Local Names** or path-only IRIs, which are IRIs that restrict their first part (domain) to ASCII characters but allow for Unicode characters in the local name, e.g.

$$\texttt{http://dbpedia.org/resource/Ñ}$$

(which corresponds to the entry in DBpedia that describes the letter Ñ used in Spanish).

The W3C Best Practices for Multilingual Linked Open Data (BPMLOD) community group analysed the arguments in favour and against the different options mentioned above.[6] The use of one or another will largely depend on the legacy data being converted into LD and the type of application. The BPMLOD group has issued the following recommendations in this respect:

1. Agents making use of URIs/IRIs should not attempt to infer language properties or assume linguistic data encoded in the URI itself, and
2. if IRIs are used, it is preferable that an ASCII domain is still used (path-only IRIs).

In the first case, other techniques (e.g. labelling) have to be used to encode linguistic data.

Define License and Provenance Information As a last step in the specification process, it is important to define the license and origin (provenance) of the source data to be converted into linked data.

As reported by some studies, e.g. [10], LD datasets are not always published with a proper license. Sometimes the license is not declared, the license type is not a suitable one (e.g. it is a license for software) or it is not expressed in a standard, machine-readable manner. However, LD resources in general and LRs in particular may be subject to intellectual property and database laws or contain data subject to privacy restrictions. Therefore, a proper declaration of which rights are held, waived or licensed by the resource is necessary during the specification activity. This will allow their representation as LD in a later step (task 2.3 of the 'modelling' activity). In fact, specific data licenses exist and can be identified by their URIs.

The most commonly used data licenses can be classified as follows (see [10]):

1. Public Domain Licenses: They waive all the possible intellectual property and neighbouring rights (database rights) of the dataset and its contents. Examples: the ODC-PDDL (Public Domain Dedication and License) and the CC0 public domain waiver.
2. Attribution Licenses: They waive all the possible rights, requiring only the mere attribution. Example: ODC-By, attribution for data/databases.

---

[6]https://www.w3.org/community/bpmlod/wiki/Best_practises_-_previous_notes#
Patterns_for_Naming.

3. Share-alike Licenses: The rights are also waived requiring that derived or adapted databases keep the same license. Examples: ODC-ODBL (Open Database License) and the UK-OGL (UK Open Government License).

Finally, also the provenance of the source data has to be identified, including aspects such as: who created the original data (persons and/or organizations), who is creating the RDF version, which other data sources are reused, etc. At this specification phase, provenance information has to be recorded and documented to be later represented also as LD, for which some specific vocabularies can be used, as described in Chap. 7.

9.4 Modelling

During the specification activity, relevant linguistic data sources are analysed, and some preliminary design decisions are taken, in particular with respect to URI/IRI design. During the modelling activity, we need to determine the model or models (ontologies, vocabularies, . . .) to be used for transforming the data into RDF/LD.

Analyse and Select Existing Domain Models An important recommendation when building a model for LD is that existing, well-established vocabularies should be reused as much as possible [2], in order to save time during modelling as well as to enhance interoperability with other LD resources. To that end, reuse of existing models and vocabularies has to be considered. We propose, as a starting point, to consider those models already described in previous chapters of this book, such as:

- Ontolex-lemon, to model lexical data
- OLiA, as a hub for annotation terminologies
- LexInfo, as a catalogue of grammatical categories
- NIF, for (sub)string identification and annotation in context

Additionally, some online repositories and catalogues can be used to find other suitable vocabularies. We mention Linked Open Vocabularies (LOV)[7] in the first place because of its suitable support for multilingual information [4]. Moreover, LOV is a well-established framework with long-term support and a clear curation strategy. LOV provides a choice of several hundreds of LD vocabularies, based on quality requirements such as URI stability and availability on the Web, use of standard formats and publication best practices, quality metadata and documentation, identifiable and trustable publication body and proper versioning policy [11]. Other semantic repositories are also available and can help discover vocabularies, such as

---

[7]LOV was originally accessible at http://lov.okfn.org/ but currently is hosted by the Ontology Engineering Group at http://lov.linkeddata.es/.

Swoogle[8] and Watson.[9] Once a suitable model or models have been identified, some checks have to be performed to validate their usefulness [2]:

1. Ensure that they are published by a trusted group or organization.
2. Ensure that they have persistent URIs.
3. Confirm the versioning policy (i.e. the publisher ideally will address compatibility of versions over time, and major changes will be reflected in the documentation).

If after this search and selection process none of the discovered models fully covers the representation needs identified during the specification activity, then an ad hoc extension to one or more such models have to be developed.

Although it is best practice to use or extend an existing vocabulary before creating a new vocabulary, there are cases in which vocabulary reuse is not possible (i.e. our model is not covered by any existing online ontology). In such cases, a domain ontology has to be built from scratch. Explaining the process of ontology building is out of the scope of this book. However, this topic has been sufficiently covered in the literature of ontology engineering, such as in the NeOn methodology [12]. Some considerations on vocabulary creation can also be found in the 'Best Practices for Publishing Linked Data' W3C working group note [2].

Develop the Model for Representing the Data There are several tools that can be used to support the modelling activities, either for extending an existing ontology or building a new one from scratch, such as Protégé[10] or TopBraid Composer.[11]

Even in the case that no further ontology development is needed because the model can be fully supported by existing ontologies, it is still necessary to identify and document which entities of such ontologies will be used to represent the source data, and how the representation scheme of the source will be mapped to the RDF data model.

Consider the example of the conversion of the Apertium English-Spanish bilingual dictionary into RDF.[12] During the modelling activity, Ontolex-lemon and the `vartrans` module in Ontolex-lemon were chosen as domain models to represent the data (English-Spanish translations). Then, it was decided that each dictionary file (in LMF/XML originally) should be converted into three different elements in RDF, namely: (i) source lexicon, (ii) target lexicon and (iii) translation set. This idea is represented in Fig. 9.2.

In terms of the instantiation of the model, Fig. 9.3 illustrates the representation scheme used for a single translation using *lemon* and the translation module. In short, `ontolex:LexicalEntry` and their associated properties are used to

---

[8]http://swoogle.umbc.edu/.

[9]http://watson.kmi.open.ac.uk/.

[10]https://protege.stanford.edu/.

[11]https://www.topquadrant.com/tools/modeling-topbraid-composer-standard-edition/.

[12]https://datahub.io/dataset/apertium-rdf-en-es.

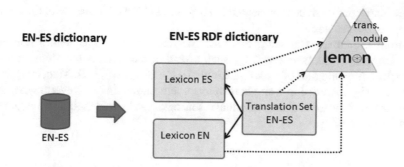

Fig. 9.2 Modelling example: conversion of an Apertium bilingual electronic dictionary into RDF

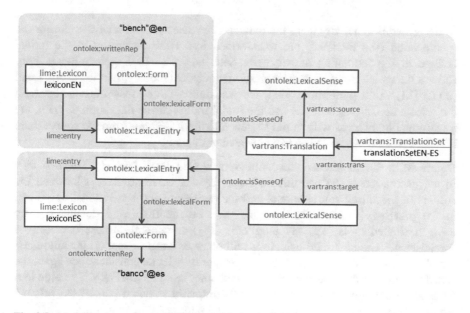

Fig. 9.3 Modelling example: modelling a translation in RDF

account for the lexical information, while the `vartrans:Translation` class puts them in connection through `ontolex:LexicalSense`.

Select Model(s) for Metadata Information During this task of the modelling activity, the information that characterizes the resource, including provenance and licensing information, has to be identified and documented. On this basis, different metadata models have to be reviewed to select a suitable metadata standard that fulfils the information needs best. We refer the reader to Chap. 7 for a more detailed analysis of the metadata models. In short, metadata of LRs comprise two types of information:

1. General information of the dataset, such as *title, date of creation, license*, etc.: documenting general metadata should be mandatory for any type of resource.

Such metadata will be represented in RDF and published jointly with the content data of the resource.

2. Information that is characteristic of LRs, such as *resource type, modality, number of languages*, etc. (see Sect. 7.3): such a kind of metadata is mainly used in the context of catalogues of LRs, e.g. Linghub (see Chap. 10), LRE Map, etc., so not necessarily included in a single resource when publishing it. Nevertheless, their inclusion at the level of an individual resource might benefit their later integration into such catalogues.

9.5   Generation

In the generation activity step, the data sources selected and analysed during the specification (see Sect. 9.3) are transformed into RDF according to the model defined in the modelling activity (see Sect. 9.4). The RDF generation activity follows the typical steps of data integration processes: Extract, Transform and Load (ETL) [13]. As a preliminary step, we will define the correspondences between the selected RDF-based model and the initial model of the data source. Then, the transformation process will be run to generate the RDF data from the source data. Finally, the generated data has to be cleaned/validated.

Define Mappings Between the Data Source and RDF Models The first task in the generation is the definition of mappings or correspondences between the entities of the initial source model and the entities of the RDF model developed in the previous activity. The mappings can be identified and documented by using dedicated tools (e.g. MappingPedia [14]) or general-purpose ones (e.g. a spreadsheet). The identified mappings will serve as basis to support the automatic transformation of the data. In order to illustrate this, let us consider once again the transformation of the Apertium EN-ES dictionary from its LMF/XML version into RDF as an example. The following XML fragment shows a part of the original Apertium data in which an English entry is defined:

```
1   <Lexicon>
2   <feat att="language" val="en"/>
3     ...
4   <LexicalEntry id="bench-n-en">
5   <feat att="partOfSpeech" val="n"/>
6   <Lemma>
7   <feat att="writtenForm" val="bench"/>
8   </Lemma>
9   <Sense id="bench_banco-n-1"/>
10  </LexicalEntry>
11    ...
12  </Lexicon>
```

Table 9.2 Mapping example between some LMF and Ontolex-*lemon*/LexInfo entities

XML tags and attributes	RDF entity	Comments
Lexicon	lime:Lexicon	–
LexicalEntry	ontolex:LexicalEntry	The attribute "id" of the tag lexicalEntry will be used to build the URI
partOfSpeech	lexinfo:partOfSpeech	–
n	lexinfo:noun	–
writtenForm	ontolex:writtenForm	The language tag ('@en' in this case) will be taken from the attribute 'language' of the XML tag 'Lexicon'
...	...	...

Table 9.2 exemplifies a few correspondences identified between the initial XML elements and the entities in the selected RDF model (Ontolex-*lemon* in this case, together with LexInfo).

Transforming the Data Sources into RDF The next task is to actually transform the source data into an RDF representation. There are various tools or technologies that can support this. The choice of a specific technology or tool will ultimately depend on the format of the source data, as well as the personal skills and preferences of the developer. These are some examples[13]:

1. For CSV and spreadsheets: Open Refine[14] with its RDF extension,[15] XLWrap,[16] rdf123.[17]
2. For relational databases: D2RQ,[18] Morph,[19] Virtuoso's RDF Views.[20] Some of these resources support the R2RML[21] W3C Recommendation, a dedicated language to express mappings between relational models and RDF.
3. For XML: Krextor,[22] ReDeFer,[23] Lixr,[24] Open Refine (see above).
4. For Web documents: Apache Any23.[25]

---

[13]For a more complete list see https://www.w3.org/wiki/ConverterToRdf.

[14]http://openrefine.org/.

[15]https://github.com/fadmaa/grefine-rdf-extension/releases.

[16]http://xlwrap.sourceforge.net/.

[17]http://rdf123.umbc.edu/.

[18]http://d2rq.org/.

[19]https://github.com/oeg-upm/morph-rdb.

[20]https://virtuoso.openlinksw.com/whitepapers/relational%20rdf%20views%20mapping.html.

[21]https://www.w3.org/TR/r2rml/.

[22]https://github.com/EIS-Bonn/krextor/wiki.

[23]http://rhizomik.net/html/redefer/.

[24]https://github.com/liderproject/lixr.

[25]http://any23.apache.org/.

5. Other generic frameworks that cover several of the above formats and support other extra features of the ETL process: Unifiedviews,[26] TopBraid composer,[27] Datalift.[28]

Regardless of the approach adopted, the source data can be converted into RDF using any RDF serialization, including RDFa, JSON-LD, Turtle and N-Triples, or RDF/XML (see Chap. 2). A priori, no serialization is to be preferred over another. The particular choice will depend ultimately on the desired balance between simplicity, ease of reading (for a human) and speed of processing [2]. See Chap. 2 for more details about the different RDF serializations.

Validate/Clean the Generated RDF Data Once the RDF data is generated, it has to be validated and explored in order to discover possible mistakes in the RDF conversion process. To that end, some common issues have to be checked [15], grouped in several categories:

- *URI/HTTP: Accessibility and dereferenceability issues:* In a LD context, publishers should be careful to avoid broken links and to make URIs dereferenceable. At this stage, the generated URIs should be revised to check their consistency with the URI strategy defined during the specification activity (Sect. 9.3). The accessibility aspect, though, has to be checked once the publication activity is completed (see Sect. 9.7).
- *Syntax errors.* Suitable validators have to be used to check the syntactic validity of the generated RDF, which will ultimately depend on the chosen RDF serialization. To that end, existing online validation services can be used (such as https://www.w3.org/RDF/Validator/ for RDF/XML documents).
- *Reasoning: noise and inconsistency.* Some errors in RDF only reveal themselves after reasoning (e.g. some unforeseen incorrect inferences occur). According to [15], these are the most typical causes:
  - Atypical use of collections, containers and reification
  - Use of unknown classes and properties (e.g. using `foaf:image` instead of `foaf:img`)
  - Misplaced classes and properties (e.g. a class appears in the predicate position of a triple)
  - Misuse of `owl:DatatypeProperty`/`owl:ObjectProperty`
  - Use of members of deprecated classes/properties
  - Bogus `owl:InverseFunctionalProperty` values
  - Malformed datatype literals (e.g. using non-integer values when `xsd:int` has been specified)
  - Use of literals incompatible with datatype range
  - OWL inconsistencies

---

[26]https://unifiedviews.eu/.

[27]https://www.topquadrant.com/tools/modeling-topbraid-composer/.

[28]https://datalift.org/.

9.6 Linking

The fourth LD principle establishes that links to other datasets should be included, so that extra information from different sources can be navigated to and accessed. To that end, the *linking* activity involves the discovery and representation of relationships between data elements, in particular between the source dataset and other third-party datasets. Such links can be built either manually or with the assistance of (semi)automatic tools. In a multilingual scenario, linked data in one natural language would need to be mapped to equivalent or related information in other languages, thus allowing navigation across multilingual information by software agents. This activity can be carried out in parallel to the *generation* activity.

Several tasks have to be carried out for mono/cross-lingual interlinking: (1) the selection of relevant and authoritative datasets to link, (2) the automatic discovery of equivalent and/or related entities between the dataset and the selected external resources, along with the representation and storage of the discovered links.

Select Target Datasets The goal of this task is to identify other RDF datasets with similar topics that can be potentially used to establish links to entities featuring additional information that complements the information in the given dataset. In the case of LRs, a good starting point is to inspect the LLOD cloud[29] for other LD resources. Typical hubs in the LLOD cloud are DBpedia and BabelNet and can be used to expand the information of the dataset with extra descriptions, translations, images, etc.

Discover and Represent Links Between the RDF Data and the Target Datasets This task involves the automatic discovery of relationships between data items to increase the external connectivity of the RDF dataset. There are many tools and techniques for discovering links between data items of different RDF datasets (see [16] for a survey), although few of them have cross-lingual capabilities. We will discuss specific techniques for link discovery in more detail in Chap. 10.

9.7 Publication

Once the data has been converted into RDF, the next step consists in publishing the data on the Web. This activity is divided in two tasks: (a) dataset publication and (b) metadata publication.

Publish the Dataset Several technical approaches can be used in the publication step, such as having a triple-store to persist and query the data, and setting up a LD front-end as access layer on top of the triple-store. A triple store is a database targeted for the storage and retrieval of triples (usually RDF triples)

---

[29]http://linguistic-lod.org/llod-cloud.

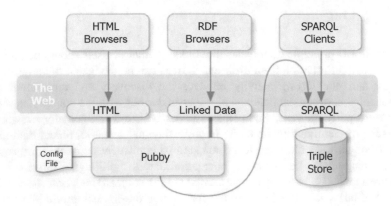

Fig. 9.4 RDF publication architecture based on Pubby [Image by Richard Cyganiak, taken from https://github.com/cygri/pubby/blob/master/doc/images]

through semantic queries (usually SPARQL queries). There are several tools that can serve as triple store with Openlink Virtuoso Universal Server,[30] Apache Jena,[31] AllegroGraph,[32] Blazegraph[33] and GraphDB[34] being the most prominent ones. All of them include a SPARQL endpoint with some of them additionally offering a browsable LD frontend. However, there are other dedicated tools like Pubby[35] that provide the technical means for realizing the LD front-end. The architecture that Pubby and similar systems offer is nicely described in Fig. 9.4. Pubby acts as a proxy in that it handles HTTP requests to resolve URIs by connecting to the SPARQL endpoint, asking it for information about the original URI and passing back the results to the client, properly handling the content negotiation between HTML, RDF/XML and Turtle descriptions of the same resource.

9.8   Exploitation

This last activity involves the development of applications that will consume the linguistic LD of the converted LRs. Such applications can be either generic or domain specific, and cover the needs of different use cases. Typically, applications will access the RDF data through the SPARQL endpoint of the LR for online

---

[30]https://virtuoso.openlinksw.com/.

[31]http://jena.apache.org/.

[32]https://franz.com/agraph/allegrograph/.

[33]https://www.blazegraph.com.

[34]http://graphdb.ontotext.com/.

[35]http://www4.wiwiss.fu-berlin.de/pubby/.

processing, or by pre-fetching a dump with the RDF data for off-line processing. Then, the application can traverse the RDF links and access other external sources, and combine the data with other LD and non-LD resources. We are not entering into the details of concrete applications here, but we will visit several use cases that exploit linguistic linked data in part IV of this book.

9.9 Guidelines for Particular Types of Language Resources

In previous sections, we reviewed the different activities and tasks involved in the conversion of any type of LR into LD. These general guidelines have to be adapted to the particular case of a given LR. In the context of the W3C Best Practices for Multilingual Linked Open Data community group, a number of guidelines have been published describing best practices for the conversion of specific types of LR, in particular bilingual and multilingual dictionaries, multilingual terminologies, WordNets and corpora. These guidelines have been published as W3C community group reports and can be found at https://www.w3.org/community/bpmlod/ and contain advice on vocabulary selection, RDF generation and publication of the results for the different types of LRs:

- **Bilingual dictionaries**[36]: These guidelines document best practices in creating LD versions of bilingual dictionaries building on the Ontolex-lemon model. The guidelines contain advice on vocabulary selection, RDF generation process and publication of the results. In this chapter we have reused a number of examples from these best practice documents, in particular from the conversion of the Apertium dictionaries into RDF.
- **Multilingual dictionaries**[37]: These guidelines describe the process of generating LD from a multilingual lexical resource, in particular BabelNet. The document describes the models used and the design decisions taken during the conversion of BabelNet into a representation based on Ontolex-lemon, along with the common patterns that naturally emerge when converting a multilingual lexical resource into RDF.
- **WordNets**[38]: These guidelines describe best practices for the process of creating a LD version of a wordnet, and may be of interest for other kinds of resources. This document describes the models used and the recommended format (WN-JSON-LD) for transforming wordnets into LD on the basis of the lemon model. The InterLingual Index is also described, which is a common resource for providing interlingual links between wordnets administrated by the Global WordNet Association.

---

[36] http://www.w3.org/2015/09/bpmlod-reports/bilingual-dictionaries/.

[37] http://www.w3.org/2015/09/bpmlod-reports/multilingual-dictionaries/.

[38] http://bpmlod.github.io/report/WordNets/index.html.

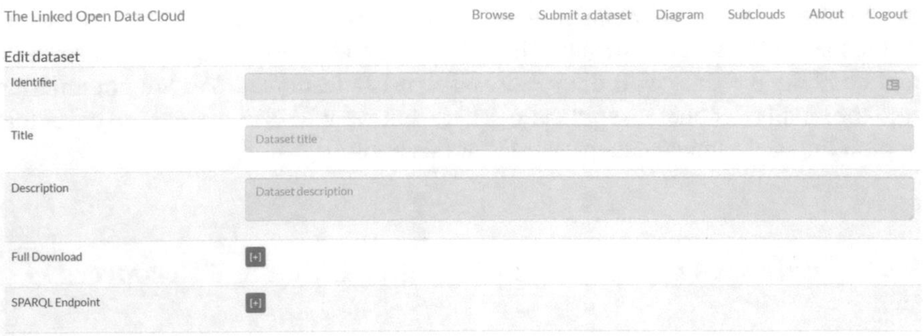

The Linked Open Data Cloud   Browse   Submit a dataset   Diagram   Subclouds   About   Logout

Edit dataset

Identifier

Title
                                                         Dataset title

Description
                                                         Dataset description

Full Download   [+]

SPARQL Endpoint   [+]

Fig. 9.5 The interface for adding LOD datasets to the LOD cloud

- **Terminologies**[39]**:** These guidelines define best practices for transforming multilingual terminologies, particularly those available in TBX format, into a LD version. The process uses the Interactive Terminology for Europe (IATE) as a running example to describe the models and vocabularies to be used.
- **Corpora**[40]**:** This document describes the generation of text corpora as LD using the NLP Interchange Format (NIF). The Brown corpus is used as a running example throughout these guidelines.

9.10   Inclusion into the LLOD Cloud

Providing metadata and adding it to the linked data cloud is achieved by adding the dataset at https://lod-cloud.net, by clicking on the 'Submit a dataset' link, which will bring up a web form as depicted in Fig. 9.5; this is a simple form that involves specifying the following information about the dataset:

- **Identifier:** A unique alphanumeric string that acts as identifier for the dataset.
- **Title:** Full name in English; unlike the identifier there are no limits on the use of special characters or whitespace.
- **Description:** A 2–10 sentence text in English describing what the dataset is about and what its intended usage is.
- **Full Download:** A link to the complete dataset, ideally as compressed N-Triples; this requires specifying a title, description, MIME type and, most importantly URL for the download.
- **SPARQL Endpoint:** If available, the link to the SPARQL endpoint where this data may be queried.

---

[39]http://www.w3.org/2015/09/bpmlod-reports/multilingual-terminologies/.
[40]http://bpmlod.github.io/report/nif-corpus/index.html.

- **Example:** A single resource that resolves; i.e. a URL from the dataset which can be resolved using linked data principles.
- **Other Downloads:** Other formats for download or partial downloads of the dataset.
- **Keywords:** A list of keywords (of any kind) that characterize the dataset; these are used to classify the dataset into colours in the subcloud diagrams, such as the Linguistic Linked Open Data Cloud Diagram (see Chap. 3).
- **Domain:** The primary domain of the dataset, i.e. the main class of the dataset and corresponding colour in the Linked Open Data Cloud Diagram. The options are currently 'Cross Domain', 'Geography', 'Government', 'Life Sciences', 'Linguistics', 'Media', 'Publications', 'Social Networking' and 'User-generated Content'. Most readers of this book should obviously select 'Linguistics'.
- **Website:** The website of the project where people can go to find more information about the dataset.
- **Links:** Number of triples linking to another dataset in the cloud; currently it is only possible to specify links to datasets that are already in the cloud.
- **Size:** Number of triples in this dataset.
- **Namespace, DOI, Image (optional):** This is the namespace (URL prefix) of the dataset, i.e. the Digital Object Identifier if this resource is registered in another website and a link to an image.

Once the form has been submitted, an RDF metadata profile using the VoID vocabulary will be created and be accessible on the LOD Cloud website. Within a short period of time, assuming that the links are valid in the metadata, the dataset will be included in the diagram.

9.11   Summary and Further Reading

The chapter has described the process of publishing a dataset as linked open data as a six-step process that starts with the specification of the dataset and design of the URI schema, followed by the selection of suitable modelling mechanisms and vocabularies. In the generation step, the RDF data is actually generated, while in the linking step the data elements are linked to other datasets. Finally, the dataset should be published and submitted to a relevant repository such as the LOD cloud website to enable the final step which is the exploitation of the data in real-world applications.

For more detail on best practices for the transformation of datasets, we refer the interested reader to the guidelines in the form of reference cards developed by the LIDER project. [41]

---

[41] http://lider-project.eu/lider-project.eu/indexc299.html?q=guidelines.

References

1. B. Villazón-Terrazas, L. Vilches, O. Corcho, A. Gómez-Pérez, Methodological guidelines for publishing government linked data, in *Linking Government Data*, ed. by D. Wood, chap. 2 (Springer, Berlin, 2011)
2. B. Hyland, G. Atemezing, B. Villazón-Terrazas, Best practices for publishing linked data. W3C working group note, World Wide Web Consortium (2014), https://www.w3.org/TR/ld-bp/
3. D. Vila-Suero, A. Gómez-Pérez, E. Montiel-Ponsoda, J. Gracia, G. Aguado-de Cea, Publishing linked data: the multilingual dimension, in *Towards the Multilingual Semantic Web*, ed. by P. Cimiano, P. Buitelaar (Springer, Berlin, 2014), pp. 101–118
4. A. Gómez-Pérez, D. Vila-Suero, E. Montiel-Ponsoda, J. Gracia, G. Aguado-de Cea, Guidelines for multilingual linked data, in *Proceedings of the 3rd International Conference on Web Intelligence, Mining and Semantics (WIMS)* (ACM, New York, 2013)
5. D. Ayers, M. Völkel, Cool URIs for the Semantic Web. W3C interest group note. World Wide Web Consortium (2008), https://www.w3.org/TR/cooluris/
6. P. Archer, S. Goedertier, N. Loutas, Study on persistent URIs. Technical Report, ISA (2012)
7. J. Gracia, M. Villegas, A. Gómez-Pérez, N. Bel, The Apertium bilingual dictionaries on the web of data. Semant. Web J. 9, 231–240 (2018)
8. E. Montiel-Ponsoda, D. Vila-Suero, B. Villazón-Terrazas, G. Dunsire, E. Escolano, A. Gómez-Pérez, Style guidelines for naming and labeling ontologies in the multilingual web, in *Proceedings of the 11th International Conference on Dublin Core and Metadata Applications (DC)* (2011)
9. J.E. Labra Gayo, D. Kontokostas, S. Auer, J.E.L. Gayo, D. Kontokostas, S. Auer, Multilingual linked data patterns, Semant. Web 6(4), 319 (2015)
10. V. Rodríguez-Doncel, A. Gómez-Pérez, N. Mihindukulasooriya, Rights declaration in linked data, in *Proceedings of the 4th International Workshop on Consuming Linked Data (COLD)*, vol. 1034 (CEUR-WS, 2013)
11. P.Y. Vandenbussche, G. Atemezing, M. Poveda, B. Vatant, Linked open vocabularies (LOV): a gateway to reusable semantic vocabularies on the web. Semant. Web J. 8(3), 437 (2017)
12. M.C. Suárez-Figueroa, A. Gómez-Pérez, M. Fernández-López, The NeOn methodology for ontology engineering, in *Ontology Engineering in a Networked World*, ed. by M.C. Suárez-Figueroa, A. Gómez-Pérez, E. Motta, A. Gangemi (Springer, Berlin, 2012), pp. 9–34
13. R. Kimball, J. Caserta, *The Data Warehouse ETL Toolkit: Practical Techniques for Extracting, Cleaning, Conforming and Delivering Data* (Wiley, Hoboken, 2004)
14. F. Priyatna, E. Ruckhaus, N. Mihindukulasooriya, O. Corcho, N. Saturno, Mappingpedia: a collaborative environment for R2RML mappings, in *Proceedings of the 14th Extended Semantic Web Conference (ESWC) Satellite Events* (2017), pp. 114–119
15. A. Hogan, A. Harth, A. Passant, S. Decker, A. Polleres, Weaving the pedantic web, in *Proceedings of Linked Data on the Web Workshop (LDOW), co-located with the 19th International World Wide Web conference (WWW)* (2010)
16. A. Ferrara, A. Nikolov, F. Scharffe, Data linking for the Semantic Web. Int. J. Semant. Web Inf. Syst. 7(3), 46 (2011)

Chapter 10
Link Representation and Discovery

Abstract In this chapter we address the question of how links can be discovered between different datasets published as Linguistic Linked Open Data. We describe common patterns to represent links both between data that are on the same language (monolingual scenario) and between data in different languages (cross-lingual scenario). Further, we describe techniques that can be used to automatically discover links between datasets. As most of these techniques rely on computing similarities between data elements, we briefly review the most common techniques for computing syntactic and semantic similarity. Finally, we provide a brief overview of tools and frameworks that can be used to semi-automatically discover links between language resources.

10.1   Link Representation

Monolingual and cross-lingual links (also referred to as monolingual/cross-lingual mappings) can be established at three different levels according to Gracia et al. [1]:

- At the **conceptual** level, we establish links between *types*, i.e. between classes or concepts as modelled in an ontology or vocabulary.
- At the **instance** level, we establish links between specific individuals/entities.
- At the **linguistic** level, we establish links between the linguistic manifestation of entities.

Other classifications of types of links distinguish only between two levels, conflating the conceptual and instance levels. For the sake of simplicity, we also stick to a two-level classification in the remainder of this section. Further, we consider the case of inducing links between elements of different languages as the more general case, considering the monolingual case as a specialization. We discuss these two classes of links in more detail below.

At the conceptual level, links are created between types described in ontologies that are modelled according to the realities or intuitions of speakers of different languages. Links at the conceptual level can be used to describe taxonomic relations

© Springer Nature Switzerland AG 2020
P. Cimiano et al., *Linguistic Linked Data*,
https://doi.org/10.1007/978-3-030-30225-2_10

specifying that a certain type is a specialization/generalization of a type in another ontology. The RDFS property `rdfs:subClassOf` can be used for this purpose. Further, one can define domain-dependent relations between types/classes from different ontologies. Finally, one can also define that two types in two different ontologies are equivalent, i.e. they describe the same set of individuals. One can use the OWL property `owl:equivalentClass` for this purpose in case of linking two types or classes and `owl:sameAs` in case of linking two individuals that are defined to denote the same entity in the world. Such links allow to establish a correspondence between or among concepts included in different ontologies, and which are described in the same or in a different language. Consider,e.g., the relation between a class 'hospital' (meaning an institution where medical and surgical treatment is given) in an ontology documented in English and the class 'hôpital' in another ontology documented in French. Both labels are referring to the same concept, but they are expressed in different natural languages, thus we could link both classes through an `owl:equivalentClass` relation, for instance.

Another example (already classical in the literature of ontology localization) is the case of the concepts 'fleuve' and 'rivière' in French. A 'fleuve' is a river that flows into the sea, whereas 'rivière' can be defined as a river that flows into the sea or into another stream. Both lexicalized concepts in French do not have an exact equivalence or direct correspondence in English, but its closest concept is described by 'river' in English, which subsumes both concepts. In order to capture such a situation we can use the `rdfs:subClassOf` relation, as Fig. 10.1 illustrates.

At the linguistic (or lexical) level, links are not established between the ontology entities (classes, properties, individuals) themselves but between their associated linguistic forms. The creation of such linguistic mappings requires that the lexical information is reified, i.e. it is represented separately from the ontological entity by a specific individual that becomes a *'first-order citizen'*. There are multiple ways

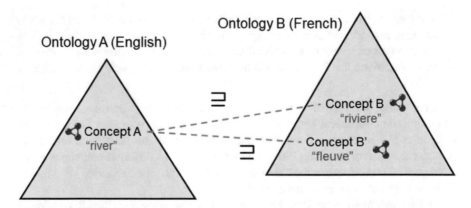

Fig. 10.1 Example of cross-lingual mapping at the conceptual level. The French concepts for the words *'rivière'* and *'fleuve'* are linked to the concept for the word *'river'* in an English ontology, specifying that the French concepts are specializations of the more general English concept [Figure taken from [1]]

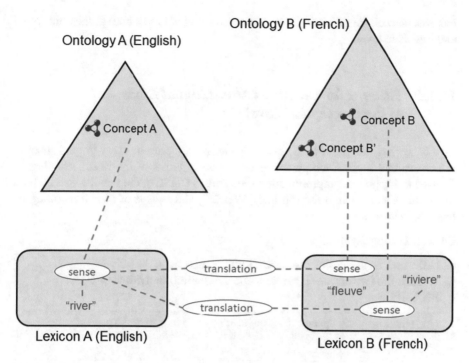

Fig. 10.2 Example of cross-lingual mapping at the linguistic level

to achieve this; the one recommend in this book is the creation of an Ontolex-
lemon lexicon (`lime:Lexicon`) that introduces the lexical entries that denote
a corresponding ontology entity. In this case, in order to allow two ontologies to
interoperate at the linguistic level, mappings would be established between their
respective lexicons and in particular between lexical entries contained in these
lexicons. In addition to introducing links at the conceptual level, some lexico-
semantic relations (typically `vartrans:Translation`) can be established
between the lexical description of such concepts (e.g. between senses, in the case of
translations, i.e. `ontolex:sense`). Figure 10.2 exemplifies such types of links.

In order to provide guidance on how to represent cross-lingual links in Linguistic
Linked Open Data, the W3C BPMLOD community group has proposed a set of
patterns[1] which adapt and extend those defined by Labra et al. [2]. A summary of
these patterns has been published in the form of so-called reference cards in the
context of the Lider project.[2] In the following, we provide a number of recipes or

---

[1]https://www.w3.org/community/bpmlod/wiki/Best_practises_-_previous_notes#Linking.
[2]http://www.lider-project.eu/lider-project.eu/sites/default/files/referencecards/How-to-represent-
crosslingual-links-Reference-Card.pdf.

patterns that can be followed to represent cross-lingual links both at the conceptual and linguistic level.

10.1.1   Patterns for Creating Cross-Lingual Links at the Conceptual Level

In this section, we provide recipes or patterns to represent cross-lingual links at the conceptual level. Each pattern is described in terms of the LD mechanism to be used to support the representation mechanism ('USE'), the conditions in which using such mechanism is appropriate ('WHEN') and a piece of code illustrating its use ('EXAMPLE').

Pattern 1: Identity links

- USE: `owl:sameAs` or `owl:equivalentClass`.
- WHEN: the two entities have the same denotation (individual or class).
- EXAMPLE:

```
1        ontology1:Banco rdfs:label "banco"@es ;
2        ontology2:Bank rdfs:label "bank"@en ;
3        ontology1:Banco owl:equivalentClass ontology2:Bank .
```

Pattern 2: Soft links

- USE: `rdfs:seeAlso, skos:closeMatch, skos:exactMatch, ....`
- WHEN: The linked entities do not denote exactly the same entity or class, but their denotation is 'close enough'. Such links are mainly included for referential purposes. These properties can also be used in case the linked entities are equivalent, but the strong implications of using owl:sameAs are not wanted.
- EXAMPLE:

```
1        ontology1:Banco rdfs:label "banco"@es ;
2        ontology2:Banking rdfs:label "banking"@en ;
3        ontology1:Banco rdfs:seeAlso ontology2:Banking  .
```

Pattern 3: Taxonomical relations

- USE: `rdfs:subClassOf, skos:broader, ....`
- WHEN: Linked entities are a specialization/generalization of each other (see Fig. 10.1).
- EXAMPLE:

```
1        ontology1:Riviere rdfs:label "rivi\'{e}re"@fr .
2        ontology2:River rdfs:label "river"@en .
3        ontology1:Riviere rdfs:subClassOf ontology2:River .
```

Pattern 4: Domain-specific links

- USE: RDF properties defined in specific ontologies.
- WHEN: Individuals need to be linked with relations that are important in a given context or domain and are not covered by standard OWL, RDF or SKOS vocabularies.
- EXAMPLE:

```
1        ontology1:Spain rdfs:label "Spain"@en .
2        ontology2:Madrid rdfs:label "Madrid"@es .
3        ontology1:Spain dbpedia-owl:capital ontology2:Madrid .
```

Pattern 5: Links to domain-independent resources

- USE: Linking ontology entities to entities defined in datasets representing domain-independent background knowledge such as DBpedia, BabelNet, etc. For this purpose, any OWL or SKOS property can be used.
- WHEN: Related ontology entities are linked to a common external ontology, dataset or lexicon for referential or for documentation purposes. In addition, the creation of such links allows to infer new relations between ontology entities by exploiting knowledge in the external resource.
- EXAMPLE:

```
1        :bench-en a ontolex:LexicalEntry ;
2        ontolex:lexicalForm [ontolex:writtenRep "bench"@en] .
3        :bench-en-sense_1 a ontolex:LexicalSense ;
4        ontolex:isSenseOf :bench-en ;
5        ontolex:reference ontology1:bench .
6        :bench-en-sense_2 a ontolex:LexicalSense ;
7        ontolex:isSenseOf :bench-en ;
8        ontolex:reference ontology2:banco.
```

10.1.2   Cross-Lingual Links at the Linguistic Level

Pattern 6: Implicit translations

- USE: Ontolex-lemon, in particular `ontolex:reference`
- WHEN: Two lexical senses in two different languages are specified to have the same ontological reference and a translation can be inferred between them.
- EXAMPLE:

```
1        :lexiconEN lime:entry :bench-en .
2        :bench-en a ontolex:LexicalEntry ;
3        ontlex:lexicalForm [ontolex:writtenRep "bench"@en] .
4        :lexiconES lime:entry :banco-es .
5        :banco-es a ontolex:LexicalEntry ;
6        ontolex:lexicalForm [ontolex:writtenRep "banco"@en] .
```

```
7          :bench-en-sense a ontolex:LexicalSense ;
8          ontolex:isSenseOf :bench-en ;
9          ontolex:reference ontology1:bench .
10         :banco-es-sense a ontolex:LexicalSense ;
11         ontolex:isSenseOf :banco-en ;
12         ontolex:reference ontology1:bench.
```

Pattern 7: Explicit translations

- USE: The variation and translation module (`vartrans`) of Ontolex, in particular the `vartrans:Translation` class.
- WHEN: Lexical information of the ontologies is represented in external lexicons and translation relations need to be reified, e.g. to attach further information such as provenance, confidence degree, etc. (see Fig. 10.2).
- EXAMPLE:

```
1          :bench-en-sense a ontolex:LexicalSense ;
2          ontolex:isSenseOf :bench-en ;
3          ontolex:reference ontology1:bench .
4          :bench-en a ontolex:LexicalEntry ;
5          ontolex:lexicalForm [ontolex:writtenRep "bench"@en] .
6          :banco-es-sense a ontolex:LexicalSense ;
7          ontolex:isSenseOf :banco-es ;
8          ontolex:reference ontology2:banco .
9          :banco-es a ontolex:LexicalEntry ;
10         ontolex:lexicalForm [ontolex:writtenRep "banco"@es] .
11         :bench_banco-trans a vartrans:Translation ;
12         vartrans:source :bench-en-sense ;
13         vartrans:target :banco-es-sense .
```

10.2   Link Discovery

The previous section has provided some patterns to actually represent different types of links across LD datasets, considering the case of representing cross-lingual links in particular.

According to a study conducted in April 2014, only 44% of the datasets in the LOD Cloud were in fact linked [3]. The main reason for this is that linking datasets represents a significant effort in terms of conceptual analysis. As the manual linking of two datasets is time consuming, several authors have investigated how such links can be created automatically. The task of automatically inducing links between datasets has been named *link discovery* (see [4–7]). The task of link discovery has its roots in a related task called 'record linkage' that was first proposed in the 1940s [8]. The goal of this task was to infer equivalence relations between records in a database. Link discovery is a more encompassing task as first of all we consider any dataset on the Web, not only databases, and second we consider inducing not just equivalence relations but also other relations defined in OWL and SKOS, such as the soft links mentioned above. Very related is the task of ontology alignment [9], which is a special case of link discovery in which links between classes of different ontologies need to be induced. Ontology alignment and link discovery, however, have different goals. Link discovery in the context of LLOD is used to establish interoperability between datasets that reuse the same set of categories as well as for referential purposes. In ontology alignment the main use case is the mapping of different data schemas to allow for automatic transformation of a dataset in one schema to a dataset in another schema. Completeness of mappings is thus crucial in the case of ontology alignment. Yet, the techniques used in both cases are very similar. In this section we focus on the task of link discovery and briefly describe the most important frameworks and methods for inducing links.

10.2.1 Problem Statement

Following Nentwig et al. [4], we characterize the link discovery problem as follows: assuming we have two datasets consisting of two sets of entities, S and T and a relation R, the goal is to find all pairs $(s, t) \in S \times T$ such that $R(s, t)$ holds. This result is called a *mapping* $M_{S,T} = \{(s, R, t) \mid s \in S \wedge t \in T\}$. Typically, some constraints are given on R, the most frequent one being the *bipartite assumption*, which states that if $R(s, t)$ holds, then there is no distinct $s' \in S$ or $t' \in T$ such that $R(s, t')$ or $R(s', t)$ holds. Under this assumption, link discovery can be reformulated as the *assignment problem* and can be solved with the Hungarian algorithm [10] in $\mathcal{O}(|S|^2|T|)$ or $\mathcal{O}(|S||T|^2)$ (whichever is least). The bipartite assumption is fulfilled in many cases when inferring `owl:sameAs` links, but inappropriate for other relations such as `rdfs:subclassOf` as well as other taxonomic relations. Most link discovery approaches rely on a similarity measure that can compute the degree of match between pairs in $S \times T$. The quality of the discovered links crucially depends on the similarity function chosen. We will assume that the following information is available to characterize the elements in a dataset, which can be exploited by the different similarity computation techniques:

Label: A label provides a name for the element; in the case of a taxonomic resource, this may identify the topic. For terminological or lexical resources, the label is typically the lemma. For corpus resources, this will generally be the term as it occurs in the data. The resource may have multiple labels in different languages.

Description: A full sentence describing the resource in natural language. Ideally a description should consists of a *genus* indicating what kind of object it is and a *differentia* indicating what separates it from other objects of a similar kind.

Relations: The object should be related to other objects in the same dataset. Such relations can be used to compute structural similarities between elements by considering the context in which they are embedded.

Context: The context comprises of the terms that occur close to the element in question in a resource. In the case of a corpus, word windows around a target word might be considered as context. In a lexico-semantic resource, the hypernyms and hyponyms of a given concept might be considered as context.

10.2.2   Classification of Matching Techniques

The goal of link discovery is to find relations between entities in different datasets or ontologies. As already mentioned, in most cases the degree of similarity with respect to some similarity measure is considered as an indicator of semantic equivalence between entities. A number of basic techniques can be used to compute similarity. Following the classification given in [9],[3] such techniques can be grouped into:

1. **Terminological:** comprising of string-based comparison methods and linguistic methods to compare text. String-based methods regard strings as sequences of characters and rely on language-agnostic similarity measures such as edit distances. Linguistic methods rely on linguistic structure inherent in the compared strings, interpreting them as words, considering their lemmas, etc. as part of the linguistically informed similarity computation.
2. **Structural:** taking into account how the dataset elements are organized and related (e.g. taxonomically, or as a graph) as well as their internal structure (i.e. their attributes).
3. **Extensional:** considering also the so-called extension of classes and types in terms of individuals in the set denoted by a class. For instance, the fact that two classes share common individuals is a good indicator of their similarity.
4. **Semantic:** exploiting the model-theoretic semantics of RDF and OWL and relying on deductive methods as implemented by reasoners to identify links.

In the next sections we will take a closer look at some of the particular techniques contained in the first two groups (terminological and structural) since both types are highly relevant in the context of link discovery for LRs.

10.2.3   Terminological Similarity

The simplest way of computing similarity between two elements in a dataset is by means of string-based techniques, which follow the intuition that the more similar two strings are, the more likely they denote equivalent concepts. A number of string-based techniques have been proposed in the literature (see [11] or [9] for

---

[3]Such a classification was proposed in the context of ontology matching, but we find it equally useful in the context of link discovery among LRs.

a survey). We will mention here one of the most frequently applied ones, which is the *Levenshtein distance* [12]. This is defined as the minimum number of string operations (i.e. insertions, deletions and substitutions) required to transform one string into another. For instance, the Levenshtein distance between 'car' and 'cash' is two, since two operations are needed to convert one into another (one substitution *car* → *cas* and one insertion *cas* → *cash*). Some variations have been proposed in which the costs vary depending on the operation (e.g. giving higher cost to the substitution operation, or to any operation on the first character, for instance.)

Another widely used metric for textual similarity computation is the *Jaccard index*, which considers the input text as a *bag of words*, i.e. the sentence or label is converted into a set of words (without duplicates or frequency counts). A bag-of-words A for input **a** is compared to a bag-of-words B for input **b** by the Jaccard Index as follows:

$$J(A, B) = \frac{|A \cap B|}{|A \cup B|} = \frac{|A \cap B|}{|A| + |B| - |A \cap B|}$$

Other variants have been introduced, including the so-called DICE coefficient and the Containment coefficient:

$$Dice(A, B) = \frac{2|A \cap B|}{|A| + |B|}$$

$$Containment(A, B) = \frac{|A \cap B|}{\min(|A|, |B|)}$$

Recently, a modification of Jaccard to smooth it for short texts has been proposed [13]:

$$J_\alpha(A, B) = \frac{\sigma_\alpha(|A \cap B|)}{\sigma_\alpha(|A|) + \sigma_\alpha(|B|) - \sigma_\alpha(|A \cap B|)}$$

$$\sigma_\alpha(x) = 1 - \exp(-\alpha x)$$

This converges to the standard Jaccard Index as $\alpha \to 0$ and produces generally better results for the link discovery task. A number of other metrics could be of use for estimating textual similarity based on the lemma form of words alone; these include the length of the longest common subsequence, the comparative length of the labels, the average word length as well as the equivalence of certain words such as number words or negation words.

For many datasets, the correct matching entities have distinct labels for which no words match, either due to inflection or more typically due to the use of synonyms in the labels. For this, it is common in link discovery to exploit lexico-semantic resources such as WordNet [14] to find synonyms and discover links. The most simple approach is just to accept any word that is in the same synset. However, this is not generally sufficient as hypernyms may also be used to identify a concept. A number of metrics for estimating the similarity of two senses in a lexico-semantic resource have been proposed including using shortest path [15] and other methods [16–18]. A more complete survey of methods to compute similarity between words exploiting the structure of a lexico-semantic resource is given by Lin and Sandkuhl [15]. While such metrics can estimate the similarity between single words, in many cases ontology labels are multiword labels. Thus, it is necessary to extend the single-word similarity measures to the case of comparing sequences of words and considering synonym or other relations between multiple words.

Recently, new approaches to measure semantic similarity have been proposed by using *word embeddings*, which are vectors that are learned from a text corpus by means of various approaches such as word2vec [19] or GloVe [20]. These approaches assign a vector in $\mathbf{v}_s \in \mathbb{R}^n$ to each word in English (or other language), where n is the dimension of the vector space (typical values range from 100 to 1000). The similarity of two words can be computed by simply computing the cosine similarity between two words.

$$sim(s, t) = \frac{\mathbf{v}_s^{\mathrm{T}} \mathbf{v}_t}{||\mathbf{v}_s|| ||\mathbf{v}_t||}$$

For multi-word labels it is possible to produce vectors for sentences [21]. However, for short labels, results are similar to simply averaging the vectors of all words and calculating the cosine between the averaged vectors. A further option to estimate the similarity of two sequences is to use supervised training data to estimate the similarity of words. For example, in a dataset such as those used for the SemEval Semantic Textual Similarity task [22], a number of sentence pairs are given with human judgements of their similarity on a scale of 1–5. A popular and successful solution is to use *Siamese recurrent neural networks*, which learn to produce a score of the pair of sentences as output [23].

10.2.4   Structural Similarity

In addition to the textual information contained in labels and descriptions, the structure and context of the dataset elements can also be exploited for the purpose of similarity computation. To that end, different features of the ontology context can be compared:

1. **Factoring in equivalent entities:** Ontology entities defined as equivalent by means of properties such as `skos:exactMatch`, `owl:equivalentClass`, `owl:sameAs`, etc. can be used to expand a textual-based comparison between two entities, thus increasing the probabilities of finding a match in case the surface form of both terms differ.
2. **Domain/range comparison:** This involves comparing the property range and domain of two entities. In the case of datatype properties, the datatype can be compared to give a hint about how similar both entities are (e.g. it is expected

that the value of two properties denoting a 'book title' is a string rather than an integer).

3. **Taxonomic structure comparison:** A taxonomy, in a LD context, is essentially described through the use of the `rdfs:subClassOf` relation or other relations such as `skos:broader/skos:narrower`. A hierarchy of properties can be defined as well through the use of the `rdfs:subProperty` relation. The hierarchical information provides excellent structural indicators of the degree of similarity between two entities. For instance, a reasonable hypothesis is that two entities sharing common ancestors and/or descendants denote more similar concepts than two other entities that do not exhibit such commonalities. A number of similarity measures have been proposed in the literature that exploit taxonomical structure, such as the Wu and Palmer similarity [16] or the conceptual distance proposed by Agirre and Rigau [24].

4. **Graph structure comparison:** Comparisons can be made by taking into account the fact that RDF documents form a graph. A basic implementation of a graph-based similarity can be a mere count of the minimum number of edges that link two entities, under the hypothesis that the closer two entities are semantically, the closer they are in the graph. Based on that, more sophisticated graph-based similarities have been proposed in the literature that, for instance, exploit the particular type of relations that can be found between the compared entities (see [9]).

Many systems exploiting context and structural similarity can be found in the ontology matching literature [9]. For illustration, we will mention here two of them[4]:

1. **CIDER-CL** [25] (Cross-lingual CIDER), which is based on the CIDER system (Context and Inference baseD ontology alignER). The system can operate in two modes: (1) as ontology aligner, i.e. taking two OWL ontologies as input and giving their alignment as output in RDF, and (2) as a similarity service, i.e. taking two ontology entities as input and giving the similarity value between them as output. For monolingual comparisons, it uses the SoftTFIDF similarity measure [11], while the computation of cross-lingual similarities relies on the use of Cross-Lingual Explicit Semantic Analysis (CL-ESA) [26] (see Sect. 10.2.5 later). Artificial neural networks are used to combine the elementary similarity computations among the different features extracted from the entities' context. To compute similarities, CIDER-CL first extracts the ontological context of each ontology entity, which is enriched by applying a lightweight semantic reasoning mechanism. Such an enriched context comprises equivalent terms, direct subterms, superterms, properties, domain and range of properties, etc. Then, elementary similarities are computed between different textual features (names, labels, comments, etc.) of the ontological context, by using SoftTFIDF

---

[4]For a more recent account of ontology matching systems, see the participants of the latest editions of the Ontology Alignment Evaluation Initiative (OAEI) at http://oaei.ontologymatching.org/.

and CL-ESA, for monolingual and cross-lingual comparisons, respectively. The different similarities are then combined within artificial neural networks to provide a final similarity degree for each pair of ontology entities.

2. **LogMAP** [27] (Logic-based Matching) provides matching for 'semantically rich ontologies that contain tens (and even hundreds) of thousands of classes'. The system relies on the axiomatization in the ontologies to ensure that the result of adding the induced mappings to the two original ontologies preserves logical consistency. The first step that LogMap performs is *lexical indexation*, in which the labels for every concept are indexed. This is followed by a process of *structural indexation* in which the structural properties of the two datasets are calculated. The string similarity is calculated between the labels using the ISUB metric [28]. The LogMap process then iterates between mapping and repair. In the mapping repair stage, a Horn logic representation of the hierarchy is constructed with all existing mappings to check for inconsistencies. Then, in the mapping discovery step, the contexts of concepts are discovered if their ISUB score exceeds some threshold. Finally, the overlapping sub-ontologies, i.e. the subsections of each dataset that were matched, are computed and output.

10.2.5   Cross-Lingual Linking

A particular case of link discovery, which poses its own specific challenges [29], is the case of cross-lingual linking, whereby we wish to establish links between two ontologies or datasets with labels in different languages. This presents difficulties as the labels in the ontology are not likely to be similar on a string level. A generic approach is the application of machine translation to one of the ontologies to create a translated ontology such as proposed by Fu et al. [30]. It was shown that this approach could be further improved by translating both ontologies into a third pivot language and then applying monolingual matching techniques [31]. An alternative is the use of multilingual string similarity metrics that can be used to match between two strings in different languages. One method, as explored by Gracia et al. [25], consists in the use of Cross-lingual Explicit Semantic Analysis [26]. In this work, a comparable corpus is constructed with documents in multiple languages written in the same language. Such a corpus is readily constructed from Wikipedia by using different language editions of Wikipedia and the cross-lingual links contained in Wikipedia. Then the similarity is computed between the label and the whole article text, using a metric such as TF.IDF (see Sorg and Cimiano [32] for a more detailed evaluation of metric choices). Thus, it is possible for each label to create a vector whose values are the similarity between the input label and the topics in Wikipedia. As these vectors are language independent, it is thus possible to compute the similarity between these vectors using cosine similarity (or, less commonly, Euclidean distance) to provide a cross-linguistic measure of similarity between two strings. It has been shown that this method can under-perform due to the correlation between similar topics in Wikipedia, and decorrelating this can improve performance [33, 34].

10.3 Linking Frameworks

In this section we give a brief overview of two extensively used frameworks for LD interlinking: SILK and LIMES. Both can be used programmatically but also offer user interfaces to facilitate the manipulation of data and links.

- Link Specification (SILK): Silk [35] is a framework for link discovery developed in co-operation between the Freie Universität Berlin and Chemnitz University of Technology and is available for download at http://silkframework.org/. A linking problem is specified by a document specified in the *Link Specification Language* (SILK-SL), which 'provides a flexible declarative language for specifying link conditions' [35], an example of which is given in Fig. 10.3. The elements to be linked are specified via SPARQL queries that identify the subsets to link from a `SourceDataset` and a `TargetDataset` available via SPARQL endpoints. The similarities and thresholds to be used are configured as part of the SILK-SL document. In addition, the output file can be specified.

```
1   <Silk>
2     <DataSource id="dbepdia">
3       <EndpointURI>http://dbpedia.org/sparql</EndpointURI>
4       <Graph>http://dbpedia.org</Graph>
5     </DataSource>
6     <DataSource id="geonames">
7       <EndpointURI>http://localhost:8890/sparql</EndpointURI>
8     </DataSource>
9     <Interlink id="cities">
10      <LinkType>owl:sameAs</LinkType>
11      <SourceDataset dataSource="dbpedia" var="a">
12        <RestrictTo>?a rdf:type dbpedia:City</RestrictTo>
13      </SourceDataset>
14      <TargetDataset dataSource="geonames" var="b">
15        <RestrictTo>?b gn:featureClass gn:P</RestrictTo>
16      </TargetDataset>
17      <LinkCondition>
18        <Compare metric="jaroSimilarity" optional="1">
19          <Param name="str1"
20                 path="?a/rdfs:label[@lang 'en']"/>
21          <Param name="str2"
22                 path="?b/gn:alternateName[@lang 'en']"/>
23        </Compare>
24      </LinkCondition>
25      <Thresholds accept="0.9" verify="0.7"/>
26      <Limit max="1" method="metric_value"/>
27      <Output acceptedLinks="accepted_links.nt"
28              verifyLinks="verified_links.nt"
29              mode="truncate"/>
30    </Interlink>
31  </Silk>
```

Fig. 10.3 A Silk-LSL document linking two datasets, adapted from [35]

- Time-efficient Link Discovery (LIMES): The LIMES framework from the University of Leipzig was introduced to produce a 'lossless and time-efficient approach for the large-scale matching in metric spaces' [36]. As already mentioned, the complexity for matching two sets of instances can be very large and procedures like the lexical indexing require that terms overlap in at least some of the words in order to match, which is often not the case. The LIMES system assumes that the similarity function defines a *metric space*,[5] and in particular that the *triangle inequality* holds. By applying the triangle inequality, it is possible to derive an upper bound on the similarity of two elements and therefore exclude certain candidate pairs as they are similar to examples that have already been rejected. This approach would allow as few as $\mathcal{O}(\min(|S|, |T|))$ pairs evaluated for similarity but in practice more examples need to be found, and the LIMES system is able to do this very efficiently [36].

10.4   Summary and Further Reading

In this chapter we have reviewed the mechanisms to represent monolingual and cross-lingual links in a linked data context. We have provided an overview of techniques for discovering links among different LD datasets, focusing on terminological and structural methods. We have further given a brief overview of some linking frameworks such as SILK and LIMES.

For readers interested in a detailed review of the different patterns for multilingual linked data, see [2], as well as the wiki of the W3C BPMLOD group.[6] Finally, detailed descriptions and comparisons of a number of elementary matching techniques have been provided by Cohen et al. [11] as well as Euzenat et al. [9].

References

1. J. Gracia, E. Montiel-Ponsoda, P. Cimiano, A. Gómez-Pérez, P. Buitelaar, J. McCrae, Challenges for the Multilingual Web of Data. Web Semant. Sci. Serv. Agents World Wide Web **11**, 63 (2012)
2. J.E. Labra Gayo, D. Kontokostas, S. Auer, J.E.L. Gayo, D. Kontokostas, S. Auer, Multilingual linked data patterns. Semantic Web **6**(4), 319 (2015)
3. M. Schmachtenberg, C. Bizer, H. Paulheim, Adoption of the linked data best practices in different topical domains, in *Proceedings of the 13th International Semantic Web Conference (ISWC)* (Springer, Berlin, 2014), pp. 245–260
4. M. Nentwig, M. Hartung, A.C. Ngonga Ngomo, E. Rahm, A survey of current link discovery frameworks. Semantic Web **1**, 419–436 (2017)

---

[5]That is following the definition of Fréchet [37].
[6]https://www.w3.org/community/bpmlod/wiki/Best_practises_-_previous_notes#Linking.

5. A. Ferrara, A. Nikolov, F. Scharffe, Data linking for the Semantic Web. Int. J. Semant. Web Inf. Syst. **7**(3), 46 (2011)
6. S. Wölger, K. Siorpaes, T. Bürger, E. Simperl, S. Thaler, C. Hofer, *A survey on data interlinking methods*. Technical Report, STI Innsbruck (2011)
7. P. Christen, in *Data Matching—Concepts and Techniques for Record Linkage, Entity Resolution and Duplicate Detection*. Data-Centric Systems and Applications (Springer, Berlin, 2012)
8. H.L. Dunn, Record linkage. Am. J. Public Health **36**(12), 1412 (1946)
9. J. Euzenat, P. Shvaiko, *Ontology Matching*, 2nd edn. (Springer, Berlin, 2013)
10. H.W. Kuhn, The Hungarian method for the assignment problem. Nav. Res. Logist. Q. **2**(1–2), 83 (1955)
11. W.W. Cohen, P. Ravikumar, S.E. Fienberg, A comparison of string distance metrics for name-matching tasks, in *Proceedings of the International Conference on Information Integration on the Web* (AAAI Press, Menlo Park, 2003), pp. 73–78
12. V.I. Levenshtein, Binary codes capable of correcting deletions, insertions and reversals. Sov. Phys. Dokl. **10**(8), 707 (1966)
13. J.P. McCrae, P. Buitelaar, Linking datasets using semantic textual similarity. Cybern. Inf Technol. **18**(1), 109 (2018)
14. G.A. Miller, WordNet: a lexical database for English. Commun. Assoc. Comput. Mach. **38**(11), 39 (1995)
15. F. Lin, K. Sandkuhl, A survey of exploiting wordnet in ontology matching, in *Artificial Intelligence in Theory and Practice II* (Springer, Boston, 2008), pp. 341–350
16. Z. Wu, M. Palmer, Verb semantics and lexical selection, in *Proceedings of the 32nd Annual Meeting of the Association for Computational Linguistics (ACL)* (Association for Computational Linguistics, Morristown, 1994), pp. 133–138
17. Y. Li, Z. Bandar, An approach for measuring semantic similarity between words using multiple information sources. Trans. Knowl. Data Eng. **15**(4), 871 (2003)
18. C. Leacock, M. Chodorow, Combining local context and wordnet similarity for word sense identification. WordNet Electron. Lexical database **49**(2), 265 (1998)
19. T. Mikolov, I. Sutskever, K. Chen, G.S. Corrado, J. Dean, Distributed representations of words and phrases and their compositionality, in *Proceedings of Advances in Neural Information Processing Systems (NIPS)* (Curran Associates Inc., Lake Tahoe, 2013), pp. 3111–3119
20. J. Pennington, R. Socher, C. Manning, GloVe: global vectors for word representation, in *Proceedings of the Conference on Empirical Methods in Natural Language Processing (EMNLP)* (Association for Computational Linguistics, Morristown, 2014), pp. 1532–1543
21. Q. Le, T. Mikolov, Distributed representations of sentences and documents, in *Proceedings of the 31st International Conference on Machine Learning (ICML)* (2014), pp. 1188–1196
22. D. Cer, M. Diab, E. Agirre, I. Lopez-Gazpio, L. Specia, Semeval-2017 task 1: semantic textual similarity-multilingual and cross-lingual focused evaluation, in *Proceedings of the 11th International Workshop on Semantic Evaluation (SemEval)* (2017)
23. K.S. Tai, R. Socher, C.D. Manning, Improved semantic representations from tree-structured long short-term memory networks, in *Proceedings of the 53rd Annual Meeting of the Association for Computational Linguistics and the 7th International Joint Conference on Natural Language Processing* (2015), pp. 1556–1566
24. E. Agirre, G. Rigau, Word sense disambiguation using conceptual density, in *Proceedings of the 16th Conference on Computational Linguistics (COLING)* (Association for Computational Linguistics, Morristown, 1996), pp. 16–22
25. J. Gracia, K. Asooja, Monolingual and cross-lingual ontology matching with CIDER-CL: evaluation report for OAEI 2013, in *Proceedings of the 8th International Conference on Ontology Matching*, vol. 1111 (2013), pp. 109–116
26. P. Sorg, P. Cimiano, Cross-lingual information retrieval with explicit semantic analysis, in *Working Notes for the CLEF 2008 Workshop* (GEIE-ERCIM, Sophia Antipolis, 2008)
27. E. Jiménez-Ruiz, B.C. Grau, Logmap: logic-based and scalable ontology matching, in *Proceedings of the 10th International Semantic Web Conference (ISWC)* (Springer, Berlin, 2011), pp. 273–288

28. G. Stoilos, G. Stamou, S. Kollias, A string metric for ontology alignment, in *Proceedings of the 4th International Semantic Web Conference (ISWC)* (Springer, Berlin, 2005), pp. 624–637

29. J. Gracia, E. Montiel-Ponsoda, A. Gómez-Pérez, Cross-lingual linking on the multilingual web of data (position statement), in *Proceedings of the 3rd Workshop on the Multilingual Semantic Web (MSW) at the 11th International Semantic Web Conference (ISWC)*, vol. 936 (CEUR-WS, Aachen, 2012)

30. B. Fu, R. Brennan, D. O'Sullivan, Cross-lingual ontology mapping–an investigation of the impact of machine translation, in *Proceedings of the 4th Asian Semantic Web Conference (ASWC)* (Springer, Berlin, 2009), pp. 1–15

31. D. Spohr, L. Hollink, P. Cimiano, A machine learning approach to multilingual and cross-lingual ontology matching, in *Proceedings of the 10th International Semantic Web Conference (ISWC)* (Springer, Berlin, 2011), pp. 665–680

32. P. Sorg, P. Cimiano, An experimental comparison of explicit semantic analysis implementations for cross-language retrieval, in *Proceedings of the 14th International Conference on Application of Natural Language to Information Systems (NLDB)* (Springer, Berlin, 2009), pp. 36–48

33. N. Aggarwal, K. Asooja, G. Bordea, P. Buitelaar, Non-orthogonal explicit semantic analysis, in *Proceedings of the 4th Joint Conference on Lexical and Computational Semantics* (Association for Computational Linguistics, Stroudsburg, 2015), pp. 92–100

34. J. McCrae, P. Cimiano, R. Klinger, Orthonormal explicit topic analysis for cross-lingual document matching, in *Proceedings of the Conference on Empirical Methods in Natural Language Processing* (Association for Computational Linguistics, Stroudsburg, 2013), pp. 1732–1742

35. J. Volz, C. Bizer, M. Gaedke, G. Kobilarov, Silk-a link discovery framework for the web of data, in *Proceedings of the 2nd Workshop About Linked Data on the Web (LDOW)* (2009)

36. A.C.N. Ngomo, S. Auer, Limes-a time-efficient approach for large-scale link discovery on the web of data, in *Proceedings of the 22nd International Joint Conference on Artificial Intelligence (IJCAI)* (AAAI Press, Menlo Park, 2011)

37. M. Fréchet, Sur quelques points de calcul fonctionnel. Ph.D. thesis, Faculté des sciences de Paris (1906)

Chapter 11
Linked Data-Based NLP Workflows

Abstract In this chapter we describe principles and architectures that support the development of NLP workflows and pipelines based on linked data technology. The benefit of NLP workflows that build on linked data standards is that they build on an open set of data models and Web technologies that can be implemented with standard functionality not requiring additional frameworks and thus avoiding any type of lock-in or dependence on particular frameworks in comparison to using UIMA, GATE or other frameworks. In this chapter we describe, on the one hand, how NLP workflows can be implemented by relying on the Natural Language Processing Interchange Format (NIF). We give examples of how a POS-tagger and a dependency parser can be implemented as NIF-based web services. We then describe Teanga, a recent platform for NLP integration that exploits Docker containers to implement NLP workflows. Finally, we also describe LAPPS Grid, an open-source platform for NLP tools that builds on JSON-LD.

11.1 Introduction

Classical Natural Language Processing (NLP) architectures are characterized by the use of specialized modules for different aspects of analysis, such as tokenization, part-of-speech tagging, lemmatization, named entity recognition, syntactic parsing or semantic annotation, arranged in a particular order and thus forming a pipeline or workflow. One challenge for building such pipelines, especially if they build on external tools that have been developed by third parties, is to develop appropriate interfaces so that the output of one module can be consumed as input for another. Any NLP pipeline is thus based on using common specifications for textual content (cf. Chap. 5), linguistic data structures (Chap. 6), metadata (Chap. 7) and annotation categories (Chap. 8). RDF technologies and linked data resources provide a suitable basis for developing NLP pipelines for a number of reasons. First of all, we have discussed in this book that the RDF model can provide the basis for syntactic interoperability. Second, by vocabulary reuse, semantic interoperability can be

© Springer Nature Switzerland AG 2020
P. Cimiano et al., *Linguistic Linked Data*,
https://doi.org/10.1007/978-3-030-30225-2_11

established. Most importantly, RDF represents an open standard that can be implemented by anyone and there are libraries for most programming languages to process RDF data. Linked data services can be further implemented relying on open web protocols only, e.g. relying on HTTP to implement RESTful services that consume and return open formats.

Service-oriented architectures (SOA) are widespread. A service is a discrete unit of functionality that can be accessed remotely and acted upon and updated independently. A service has the following properties:

- It is implemented in a self-contained operation unit.
- It is a black box for its consumers, who only need to know the interface, not the implementation.
- It may consist of other underlying services.

Every service needs some input and some output. In the case of LD-based services, a service is expected to consume a linked data resource as input and produce a linked data resource as output. Input to NLP services is annotated text. They get annotated text as input and return annotations on text as output, whereby the output ideally should contain additional annotation layers that enrich the input document. For instance, a tokenizer might receive a sentence as input and return a set of token annotations over the sentence as output. A part-of-speech tagger might get a tokenized text as input and add POS annotations over each token. A dependency parser might get a POS-annotated text as input and return a set of dependency relations over these tokens.

A particular important property for NLP services is that they can be chained into more complex workflows where the output of one service can be fed as input into the next service. There are certainly existing frameworks that allow to implement and deploy NLP workflows. Existing examples, such as GATE [1] and UIMA [2], rely on proprietary technology in the sense that they rely on proprietary libraries, datastructures and protocols to glue services together. Instead, linked data-based services rely on open vocabularies and protocols, and thus at the level of chaining do not require any proprietary software frameworks or libraries. Linked data-based services only rely on the HTTP protocol to create workflows of NLP services and thus can be implemented without any lock-in. In this chapter we discuss different technologies that can be used to implement NLP workflows using open and linked data technologies. We discuss in particular how NLP workflows can be implemented using RDF and the HTTP protocol only. Further, we discuss a more recent project, Teanga, that implements an NLP integration platform relying on Docker technology. Finally, we describe the LAPPS Grid open source project that supports workflow composition relying on JSON-LD as the interface format.

Aside from the use of RDF for building integrative web-based architectures for NLP, the output of such systems can also be processed with RDF technology and combined with LOD resources, e.g. for manipulating (or creating) annotations or for transforming annotations from one representation to another.

11.2 Implementing NLP Workflows Using NIF

NIF services should conform to the NIF 2.0 public API specification.[1] The following parameters are supported by a service compliant to the specification. 'Required' parameters need to be specified by the user in order for the service to function. 'Optional' parameters can be omitted, in which case default values are used by the service.

The required parameters for a NIF-based linked data service are the following:

- **Input (i)**: The input to be processed by the service

Optional parameters are the following:

- **Input format (f)**: The format in which the input is given. Supported argument values are text, turtle (default) and json-ld.
- **Input type (t)**: Specifies how the input is retrieved. Supported argument values are direct (default), file and url.
- **Output format (o)**: The format in which the output will be serialized. Supported argument values are turtle (default) and json-ld.
- **URI Scheme (u)**: The URI scheme that the service must use to create new URIs.
- **Prefix (p)**: The service must use this as the prefix part of new URIs. A UUID will be generated if no prefix is specified.

Furthermore, it is recommended to implement an 'info' parameter, which, according to the NIF API specification, can be used to output all implemented parameters if info=true. In addition to that, we recommend to output supported parameters and default values as well.

Further recommended parameters, which are not part of the NIF API specification, are the following:

- **Verbosity (v)**: Accepting two values: true and false. True returns full output in NIF format, while false returns only the triples added to the data.
- **Model (m)**: The path/url of a trained model to be used by the service, a default model should be used if no model is specified.
- **Language (l)**: A parameter specifying the language of the input, default is English.

NIF services should generate log messages in RDF format using the RDF Logging Ontology [3]. An rlog message is of type rlog:entry and should contain the properties rlog:level, rlog:date and rlog:message.

---

[1] https://persistence.uni-leipzig.org/nlp2rdf/specification/api.html.

It is recommended to generate a log entry in the following cases:

- If no input is specified, the log level should be `rlog:FATAL`.
- If the input is given as file or URL but couldn't be retrieved by the service, the log level should be `rlog:FATAL`.
- If a parameter value isn't supported by the service, the log level should be `rlog:FATAL`.
- If an optional parameter is omitted, the log level should be `rlog:WARN`. The message should state the default value being used.

In what follows we describe two example implementations of a LD-based service (singular). The first service is a simple POS tagger that wraps the Stanford POS tagger available at https://nlp.stanford.edu/software/tagger.shtml.

11.2.1   Implementing a NIF-Compliant POS Tagging Service

In this section we give examples for the input and output that a NIF-based service would receive and output. The example assumes that there is a file `example.tll` containing the tokenization of the string *'This is a sample sentence'* that is provided as input with the call to the service. The input to the POS tagging service is shown below; note that the code is shortened, containing the NIF annotations only for the first word *'This'*:

```
1  @prefix nif:     <http://persistence.uni-leipzig.org/nlp2rdf/
        ontologies/nif-core#> .
2  @prefix xsd:     <http://www.w3.org/2001/XMLSchema#> .
3
4  <e899ea51-fb30-4102-8cdd-9d0ec691a0db#char=0,25>
5  a               nif:Context , nif:RFC5147String , nif:Sentence ;
6  nif:isString    "This is a sample sentence"^^xsd:string .
7
8  <e899ea51-fb30-4102-8cdd-9d0ec691a0db#char=0,4>
9  a               nif:RFC5147String , nif:Word ;
10 nif:anchorOf    "This"^^xsd:string ;
11 nif:beginIndex  "0"^^xsd:int ;
12 nif:endIndex    "4"^^xsd:int ;
13 nif:nextWord    <e899ea51-fb30-4102-8cdd-9d0ec691a0db#char
        =5,7> ;
14 nif:sentence    <e899ea51-fb30-4102-8cdd-9d0ec691a0db#char
        =0,25> ;
15 nif:referenceContext
16 <e899ea51-fb30-4102-8cdd-9d0ec691a0db#char=0,25> .
17 ...
```

The NIF-based web service would be called via HTTP, e.g. using the curl command as shown below:

```
1  curl -G \
2    http://sc-lider.techfak.uni-bielefeld.de/
       NifStanfordPOSTaggerWebService/NifStanfordPOSTagger  \
3    -d v=true --data-urlencode i="$(<example.ttl)"
```

The input is expected to be in NIF format and to contain at least one nif:-Context element as well as a set of nif:Word elements. The service reads the nif:anchorOf values of all nif:Words elements belonging to a given nif:Context found in the input and passes them to the Stanford parser. Each word is then annotated by adding a nif:posTag property with the POS tag as a literal value to the nif:Word.

The example output of the service can be found here:

```
1  @prefix xsd:    <http://www.w3.org/2001/XMLSchema#> .
2  @prefix nif:    <http://persistence.uni-leipzig.org/nlp2rdf/
       ontologies/nif-core#> .
3
4  <uuid:e899ea51-fb30-4102-8cdd-9d0ec691a0db#char=0,25>
5  a              nif:Context , nif:RFC5147String , nif:Sentence ;
6  nif:isString   "This is a sample sentence"^^xsd:string .
7
8  <uuid:e899ea51-fb30-4102-8cdd-9d0ec691a0db#char=0,4>
9  a              nif:RFC5147String , nif:Word ;
10 nif:anchorOf   "This"^^xsd:string ;
11 nif:beginIndex "0"^^xsd:int ;
12 nif:endIndex   "4"^^xsd:int ;
13 nif:nextWord   <uuid:e899ea51-fb30-4102-8cdd-9d0ec691a0db#
       char=5,7> ;
14 nif:posTag     "DT"^^xsd:string ;
15 nif:referenceContext
16 <uuid:e899ea51-fb30-4102-8cdd-9d0ec691a0db#char=0,25> ;
17 nif:sentence   <uuid:e899ea51-fb30-4102-8cdd-9d0ec691a0db#
       char=0,25> .
18
19 ...
```

11.2.2 Implementing a NIF-Based Dependency Parsing Web Service

In this section we briefly describe the behaviour of a NIF-based web service that implements a dependency parser. In this case we wrap the Stanford dependency parser available at https://nlp.stanford.edu/software/lex-parser.shtml.

The dependency parsing service can be involved via curl using the following example call where the input is assumed to be given in a Turtle file called `input.ttl`.

```
1  curl -G \
2    http://sc-lider.techfak.uni-bielefeld.de/
        NifStanfordParserWebService/NifStanfordParser  \
3    -d v=true --data-urlencode i="$(<input.ttl)"
```

The service can be used to parse input that is already POS tagged, i.e. it expects the input to be in NIF format and contain at least one `nif:Context` element, one `nif:Word` element for each word in the `nif:isString` property of its context containing a POS annotation in `nif:posTag` and the represented string in `nif:anchorOf`. The words are ordered by context (using `nif:-referenceContext`) and position (using `nif:beginIndex`) in order to reconstruct the original texts. The service then passes the annotated input to the Stanford parser. For each dependency relation of the parse a `nif:dependency` property is added to the relation's head with the URI of the dependent word as object. As a word can only have one head, the type of the relation is annotated in the `nif:dependencyRelationType` property of the dependent word (as a literal).

The following code shows the output of the service:

```
1  @prefix xsd:     <http://www.w3.org/2001/XMLSchema#> .
2  @prefix nif:     <http://persistence.uni-leipzig.org/nlp2rdf/
        ontologies/nif-core#> .
3
4  <uuid:e899ea51-fb30-4102-8cdd-9d0ec691a0db#char=0,4>
5  a                              nif:RFC5147String , nif:Word ;
6  nif:anchorOf                   "This"^^xsd:string ;
7  nif:beginIndex                 "0"^^xsd:int ;
8  nif:dependencyRelationType     "nsubj"^^xsd:string ;
9  nif:endIndex                   "4"^^xsd:int ;
10 nif:nextWord                   <uuid:e899ea51-fb30-4102-8cdd-9
        d0ec691a0db#char=5,7> ;
11 nif:posTag                     "DT"^^xsd:string ;
12 nif:referenceContext           <uuid:e899ea51-fb30-4102-8cdd-9
        d0ec691a0db#char=0,25> ;
13 nif:sentence                   <uuid:e899ea51-fb30-4102-8cdd-9
        d0ec691a0db#char=0,25> .
14
15 <uuid:e899ea51-fb30-4102-8cdd-9d0ec691a0db#char=5,7>
16 a                              nif:Word , nif:RFC5147String ;
17 nif:anchorOf                   "is"^^xsd:string ;
18 nif:beginIndex                 "5"^^xsd:int ;
19 nif:dependencyRelationType     "cop"^^xsd:string ;
20 nif:endIndex                   "7"^^xsd:int ;
21 nif:nextWord                   <uuid:e899ea51-fb30-4102-8cdd-9
        d0ec691a0db#char=8,9> ;
22 nif:posTag                     "VBZ"^^xsd:string ;
```

```
23   nif:previousWord                <uuid:e899ea51-fb30-4102-8cdd-9
         d0ec691a0db#char=0,4> ;
24   nif:referenceContext            <uuid:e899ea51-fb30-4102-8cdd-9
         d0ec691a0db#char=0,25> ;
25   nif:sentence                    <uuid:e899ea51-fb30-4102-8cdd-9
         d0ec691a0db#char=0,25> .

26

27   <uuid:e899ea51-fb30-4102-8cdd-9d0ec691a0db#char=0,25>
28   a               nif:Context , nif:RFC5147String , nif:Sentence ;
29   nif:isString    "This is a sample sentence"^^xsd:string .

30

31   <uuid:e899ea51-fb30-4102-8cdd-9d0ec691a0db#char=10,16>
32   a                               nif:RFC5147String , nif:Word ;
33   nif:anchorOf                    "sample"^^xsd:string ;
34   nif:beginIndex                  "10"^^xsd:int ;
35   nif:dependencyRelationType      "nn"^^xsd:string ;
36   nif:endIndex                    "16"^^xsd:int ;
37   nif:nextWord                    <uuid:e899ea51-fb30-4102-8cdd-9
         d0ec691a0db#char=17,25> ;
38   nif:posTag                      "NN"^^xsd:string ;
39   nif:previousWord                <uuid:e899ea51-fb30-4102-8cdd-9
         d0ec691a0db#char=8,9> ;
40   nif:referenceContext            <uuid:e899ea51-fb30-4102-8cdd-9
         d0ec691a0db#char=0,25> ;
41   nif:sentence                    <uuid:e899ea51-fb30-4102-8cdd-9
         d0ec691a0db#char=0,25> .

42

43   <uuid:e899ea51-fb30-4102-8cdd-9d0ec691a0db#char=8,9>
44   a                               nif:Word , nif:RFC5147String ;
45   nif:anchorOf                    "a"^^xsd:string ;
46   nif:beginIndex                  "8"^^xsd:int ;
47   nif:dependencyRelationType      "det"^^xsd:string ;
48   nif:endIndex                    "9"^^xsd:int ;
49   nif:nextWord                    <uuid:e899ea51-fb30-4102-8cdd-9
         d0ec691a0db#char=10,16> ;
50   nif:posTag                      "DT"^^xsd:string ;
51   nif:previousWord                <uuid:e899ea51-fb30-4102-8cdd-9
         d0ec691a0db#char=5,7> ;
52   nif:referenceContext            <uuid:e899ea51-fb30-4102-8cdd-9
         d0ec691a0db#char=0,25> ;
53   nif:sentence                    <uuid:e899ea51-fb30-4102-8cdd-9
         d0ec691a0db#char=0,25> .

54

55   <uuid:e899ea51-fb30-4102-8cdd-9d0ec691a0db#char=17,25>
56   a                               nif:RFC5147String , nif:Word ;
57   nif:anchorOf                    "sentence"^^xsd:string ;
58   nif:beginIndex                  "17"^^xsd:int ;
59   nif:dependency                  <uuid:e899ea51-fb30-4102-8cdd-9
         d0ec691a0db#char=10,16> ,
60                                   <uuid:e899ea51-fb30-4102-8cdd-9
                                         d0ec691a0db#char=8,9> ,
61                                   <uuid:e899ea51-fb30-4102-8cdd-9
                                         d0ec691a0db#char=0,4> ,
```

```
62                          <uuid:e899ea51-fb30-4102-8cdd-9
                               d0ec691a0db#char=5,7> ;
63  nif:endIndex            "25"^^xsd:int ;
64  nif:posTag              "NN"^^xsd:string ;
65  nif:previousWord        <uuid:e899ea51-fb30-4102-8cdd-9
        d0ec691a0db#char=10,16> ;
66  nif:referenceContext    <uuid:e899ea51-fb30-4102-8cdd-9
        d0ec691a0db#char=0,25> ;
67  nif:sentence            <uuid:e899ea51-fb30-4102-8cdd-9
        d0ec691a0db#char=0,25> .
```

11.2.3 Creating NLP Workflows with NIF-Based Services

As one of the services described above (the tagger) produces output the other one (the parser) relies on, they can be used to demonstrate the integration of NIF-compliant NLP services.

The following nested call combines both calls from the previous two examples. It invokes the tagger which produces the output of Example 1 and passes this POS-annotated NIF data to the parser. The output is the same as in the previous example.

```
1  curl -G \
2    http://sc-lider.techfak.uni-bielefeld.de/
         NifStanfordPOSTaggerWebService/NifStanfordPOSTagger  \
3    -d v=true --data-urlencode i="$(<example.ttl)" | \
4  curl -G \
5    http://sc-lider.techfak.uni-bielefeld.de/
         NifStanfordParserWebService/NifStanfordParser  \
6    -d v=true --data-urlencode i@-
```

This shows that it is very straightforward to chain different services that follow NIF and use the HTTP protocol into more complex workflows.

11.3 Composing NLP Workflows with Teanga

As natural language processing tasks normally consist of many individual components, real-world problems are generally only solvable by the combination of multiple tools into pipelines. This can lead to brittle pipelines that easily break and often requires knowledge of programming languages, such as NLTK [4], which requires knowledge of Python.

In fact, NLP services suffer from the following problems:

- Services are often components of pipelines without clear usage to the end user.

- The technology readiness level of services is often quite low, with little documentation or graphical user interface.
- Services are hard to install, often requiring compiling from source or specialized libraries not found in major software repositories.

In contrast, Web services allow an easy and declarative specification of the functions of a software that allows them to be connected easily. As a solution to this problem, the Teanga[2] Platform [5] has been developed; it allows to combine NLP services by means of JSON-LD as introduced in Chap. 2. The goal of Teanga is to make NLP easy to install and use. For this reason it builds on Docker[3] containerization technology.

11.3.1 Design and Implementation

Teanga reuses existing technologies in order to create its interface; these include:

- Simple, attractive interface using Bootstrap[4] AngularJS[5] and NodeJS[6]
- Simple backend of MongoDB,[7] enabling direct data storage of JSON files
- Docker[8] containerization technology to simplify the running and deployment of services in Teanga

As Teanga is designed to host interoperable NLP services, there is a simple systematic method for allowing service developers to declare the services that are offered in a single docker container. In particular, this allows the input and outputs of the services to be declared so that the user-interface elements can be easily generated. For this, the OpenAPI Specification Language [6] is used, extended with JSON-LD to allow elements to be described semantically.

11.3.2 Services in Teanga

In order to add a service to Teanga, it is necessary to create a Docker container, with the following requirements:

1. The service is available as a Docker container.

---

[2] *'teanga'* [ˈtʲaŋɡə] means 'language' in Irish.
[3] https://docker.io.
[4] http://getbootstrap.com/.
[5] https://angularjs.org/.
[6] https://nodejs.org/.
[7] https://www.mongodb.com.
[8] https://www.docker.com.

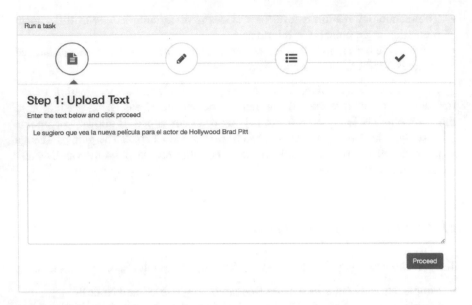

Fig. 11.1 Uploading a text in the Teanga interface

2. The container can be run without networking except to expose a single REST endpoint.
3. There is an OpenAPI description of services in the container accessible at `/services.json`.
4. The OpenAPI services return only JSON objects.
5. There is a JSON-LD context available for each return value, either in the `@context` field in the JSON object or through the HTTP Link Header
6. If the service has a request body, it should be a JSON-LD document.

These requirements ensure that the service is available and can be easily shared to new servers due to it being a Docker container that is not dependent on an external service, that there is a description of the service using the standard of the OpenAPI[9] and that the services take and consume only data that can be captured using JSON-LD [7].

11.3.3   Building Workflows

Workflows in Teanga can be constructed by the interface as shown in Fig. 11.1. The services can be connected by dragging their inputs to their outputs as shown in Fig. 11.2 and then various options, such as the languages for a machine translation service, can be configured as shown in Fig. 11.3.

---

[9]https://swagger.io/specification/.

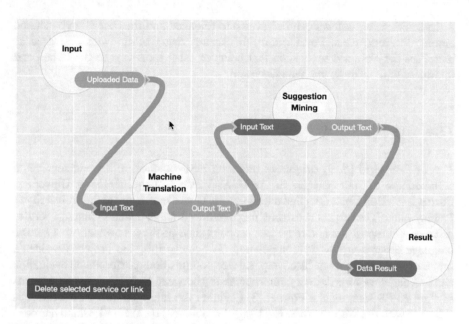

Fig. 11.2 Connecting a workflow graph in Teanga

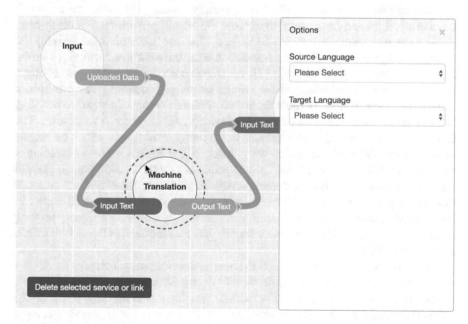

Fig. 11.3 Configuring a service in Teanga

In addition, workflows can be saved and reloaded and thus they can be shared among different users. Furthermore, this means that workflows can be used as templates for standard tools such that complex NLP tools can be developed and interacted with through the Teanga system.

11.4   LAPPS Grid

The LAPPS Grid [8, 9] originates under an NSF-funded project and involves a collaboration of four partners in the USA: Vassar College, Brandeis University, Carnegie-Mellon University and the Linguistic Data Consortium at the University of Pennsylvania. The project is establishing a framework that enables language service discovery, composition and reuse and supports state-of-the-art evaluation of natural language processing (NLP) components. To achieve this, the project provides a range of tools for service discovery, service composition, performance evaluation and language resource delivery. Interoperability between tools is achieved by means of the LAPPS Interchange Format [8, LIF] and the interoperability of services is achieved with the Web Services Exchange Vocabulary [10, WSEV], which has been created from the bottom-up in the context of the LAPPS project.

A further key feature of the LAPPS Grid is the Open Advancement system, a tool that was developed as part of IBM's Jeopardy system [11], which detects weak links in pipelines and can be used to improve the overall performance of the system.

As a key technology, LAPPS Grid also uses Docker to distribute and deploy the complete LAPPS Grid, while the interaction with the platform is provided in the form of the Galaxy pipeline tool [12], which has been developed for life sciences research. The reuse of this tool for natural language processing has provided a synergistic combination of tools from two different areas of research, enabling 'human-in-the-loop' methods of iterative development of research workflows. The Galaxy system supports two methods for creating workflows, either by means of a 'Pipeline Wizard', to guide users through the logical steps in building a workflow, or 'Pipeline-via-Dialog', where users specify the desired goal in English and the workflow is created automatically. In addition, LAPPS Grid supports integration with Jupyter [13], an executable notebook system that is well known in many areas including machine learning. As such, LAPPS Grid is already proving useful in a range of domains, including digital humanities [14] and biomedical applications [15].

The key part of the LAPPS Grid is the interchange format, which uses the JSON-LD model as described in Chap. 2. A LIF document consists of three sections: `metadata`, `text` and `views`. The metadata section describes the type of service and is often omitted, while the text section contains the text that is provided as input to the service. The views section contains the annotations that have been added by the service to the text, and this section has an `id`, as well as a `metadata` section and the actual `annotations`. An example of a simple tokenization result is as follows:

```
1  {
2    "@context": "http://vocab.lappsgrid.org/context-1.0.0.jsonld
       ",
3    "text": { "@value": "Fido barks." },
4    "views": [
5      {
6        "id": "v1",
7        "metadata": {
8          "contains": {
9            "Sentence": {
10             "producer": "edu.brandeis.cs.lappsgrid.opennlp.
                  Splitter:0.0.4",
11             "type": "splitter:opennlp" }}},
12        "annotations": [
13          { "@type": "Sentence", "id": "s0",
14            "start": 0, "end": 11 }
15        ]
16      },
17      {
18        "id": "v2",
19        "metadata": {
20          "contains": {
21            "Token": {
22              "producer": "org.anc.lapps.stanford.SATokenizer
                   :1.4.0",
23              "type": "tokenization:stanford" }}},
24        "annotations": [
25          { "@type": "Token", "id": "tok0",
26            "start": 0, "end": 4 },
27          { "@type": "Token", "id": "tok1",
28            "start": 5, "end": 10 },
29          { "@type": "Token", "id": "tok2",
30            "start": 10, "end": 11 }
31  ]}]}
```

In the example above, we see the original text (in the text element), followed by two annotations, from two sources. Firstly, the OpenNLP splitter has added a sentence annotation between the 0th and 11th character and secondly the Stanford Tokenizer has added three annotations indicating the tokens with a start and an end position.

11.5 Summary and Further Reading

In this chapter we have briefly sketched three different approaches to creating workflows of NLP components using open standards and linked data models and vocabularies. First, we have discussed how to implement NIF-compliant NLP web services that consume NIF-based data as input and produce NIF-based output that adds annotation layers to the original input document. The benefit of this is that

NIF-based tools can be implemented using open standards and web protocols only, without the need for any frameworks or libraries, thus reducing overhead and lock-in effects. We have discussed an example implementation wrapping a POS tagger and dependency parser and shown how they can be composed into a workflow using command lines tools such as curl. We have further described the Teanga platform that builds on virtualization and cloud technology, Docker in particular, to simplify the task of end users for setting up a (hosted) NLP workflow. Finally, we have discussed the LAPPS Grid project that also builds on virtualization technology and introduces its own interchange format based on JSON-LD technology as an interface between the NLP services composed into a workflow. LAPPS Grid provides a lab-like environment that allows rapid prototyping, testing and evaluation of NLP pipelines.

This chapter focuses on uses and tasks within NLP, i.e. LOD-based NLP workflows, but omits any introduction into NLP. Two recent textbooks provide introductions into NLP in a Semantic Web context: Maynard et al. [16] is a general, but concise introduction into NLP, written for a Semantic Web audience. Barrière [17] is somewhat more elaborate, introducing basics of corpus analysis and typical NLP tasks with the ultimate aim of introducing Information Extraction and other problems in Natural Language Understanding.

For general (and deeper) introductions into NLP, we refer to the standard works of Jurafsky and Martin [18] and Manning and Schütze [19] in their respective latest editions.

References

1. H. Cunningham, GATE, a general architecture for text engineering. Comput. Hum. **36**(2), 223 (2002)
2. D. Ferrucci, A. Lally, UIMA: an architectural approach to unstructured information processing in the corporate research environment. Nat. Lang. Eng. **10**(3-4), 327 (2004)
3. S. Hellmann, *RLOG—an RDF Logging Ontology* (AKSW/University Leipzig, Ontology, 2013). http://persistence.uni-leipzig.org/nlp2rdf/ontologies/rlog/rlog.html
4. S. Bird, NLTK: the natural language toolkit, in *Proceedings of the COLING/ACL on Interactive presentation sessions* (Association for Computational Linguistics, Stroudsburg, 2006), pp. 69–72
5. H. Ziad, J.P. McCrae, P. Buitelaar, Teanga: a linked data based platform for natural language processing, in *Proceedings of the 11th Language Resource and Evaluation Conference (LREC)* (2018)
6. F. Haupt, D. Karastoyanova, F. Leymann, B. Schroth, A model-driven approach for REST compliant services, in *Proceedings of the IEEE International Conference on Web Services (ICWS)* (IEEE, Piscataway, 2014), pp. 129–136
7. M. Sporny, D. Longley, G. Kellogg, M. Lanthaler, N. Lindström, JSON-LD 1.0, in *W3C Recommendation* (World Wide Web Consortium, Cambridge, 2014)
8. M. Verhagen, K. Suderman, D. Wang, N. Ide, C. Shi, J. Wright, J. Pustejovsky, The LAPPS interchange format, in *Proceedings of the International Workshop on Worldwide Language Service Infrastructure* (Springer, Berlin, 2015), pp. 33–47

9. N. Ide, K. Suderman, E. Nyberg, J. Pustejovsky, M. Verhagen, LAPPS/Galaxy: current state and next steps, in *Proceedings of the 3rd International Workshop on Worldwide Language Service Infrastructure and 2nd Workshop on Open Infrastructures and Analysis Frameworks for Human Language Technologies (WLSI/OIAF4HLT2016)* (2016), pp. 11–18
10. N. Ide, K. Suderman, M. Verhagen, J. Pustejovsky, The language application grid web service exchange vocabulary, in *Proceedings of the International on Worldwide Language Service Infrastructure* (Springer, Berlin, 2015), pp. 18–32
11. D. Ferrucci, E. Nyberg, J. Allan, K. Barker, E. Brown, J. Chu-Carroll, A. Ciccolo, P. Duboue, J. Fan, D. Gondek, et al., *Towards the Open Advancement of Question Answering Systems* (IBM, Armonk, 2009)
12. J. Goecks, A. Nekrutenko, J. Taylor, Galaxy: a comprehensive approach for supporting accessible, reproducible, and transparent computational research in the life sciences. Genome Biol. **11**(8), R86 (2010)
13. T. Kluyver, B. Ragan-Kelley, F. Pérez, B.E. Granger, M. Bussonnier, J. Frederic, K. Kelley, J.B. Hamrick, J. Grout, S. Corlay, et al., Jupyter notebooks-a publishing format for reproducible computational workflows, in *ELPUB* (IOS Press, Amsterdam, 2016), pp. 87–90
14. N. Ide, K. Suderman, J. Pustejovsky, Demonstration: the language application grid as a platform for digital humanities research, in *Proceedings of the Workshop on Corpora in the Digital Humanities (CDH 2017)*, Bloomington, IN, 19 January 2017. CEUR Workshop Proceedings 1786, CEUR-WS.org 2017, pp. 71–76
15. N. Ide, K. Suderman, J.D. Kim, Mining biomedical publications with the LAPPS grid., in *Proceedings of the 11th Conference on International Language Resources and Evaluation* (2018), pp. 2075–2018
16. D. Maynard, K. Bontcheva, I. Augenstein, *Natural Language Processing for the Semantic Web.* The Semantic Web: Theory and Technology (Morgan & Claypool, San Rafael, 2016)
17. C. Barrière, *Natural Language Understanding in a Semantic Web Context* (Springer, Berlin, 2016)
18. D. Jurafsky, J. Martin, *Speech and Language Processing* (Pearson, Harlow, 2014)
19. C. Manning, H. Schütze, *Foundations of Statistical Natural Language Processing* (MIT Press, Cambridge, 1999)

Part IV
Use Cases

Chapter 12
Applying Linked Data Principles to Linking Multilingual Wordnets

Abstract Wordnets are the most widely used lexical resources in natural language processing (NLP). There exist wordnets in more than 40 languages by now and all of these are connected to the original Princeton WordNet. The origins of linguistic linked data (LD) can thus in some sense be traced to the WordNet project. The implementation of the linking, however, has not relied on stable identifiers and has thus led to technical problems of reference when new versions of a wordnet are released. This chapter describes how linked data principles have been applied in the development of the Global WordNet Grid (GWG), an attempt to form a catalogue of interlingual contexts that extends beyond the Anglo-Saxon roots of the Princeton WordNet. We will describe in particular how LD technologies have been used in realizing a Collaborative Interlingual Index (CILI) that builds on standard LD vocabularies and the resource description framework (RDF) data model. We finally describe a method to link wordnets to external resources such as DBpedia/Wikipedia.

12.1 Princeton WordNet

Princeton WordNet (PWN) first started development under the guidance of George Miller [1] and has since been led by Christiane Fellbaum at Princeton University [2]. The project was one of the first lexical databases of the English language, and is still one of the most widely used resources in natural language processing and computational lexicography. WordNet, in contrast to printed dictionaries, aimed to organize concepts in a manner that could be processed by computers. The most recent version of WordNet, 3.1, released in 2010, consists of 159,015 words organized in 117,791 concepts, and contains 378,203 relations.

Princeton WordNet's approach to lexicography is based on grouping words into sets of words with overlapping meanings called *synonym sets*, or *synsets* in short. Between these synsets, WordNet defines semantic links of different types, most importantly the *hypernym* and *hyponym* links that link a synset that is more specific/narrow (hyponym) to a synset that is more general/broader (hypernym). Other links are meronym/holonym as well as part/whole links. Some relations such

© Springer Nature Switzerland AG 2020
P. Cimiano et al., *Linguistic Linked Data*,
https://doi.org/10.1007/978-3-030-30225-2_12

as the *derivationally related forms* (e.g. relating 'quick', 'quickly' and 'quicken') are relations that relate a synset to a particular word form.

A particular word that is part of a synset is called a *sense* in Princeton WordNet. A sense is uniquely identified by a sense identifier. This inspired the introduction of senses as uniquely identifiable elements in Ontolex-lemon (see Chap. 4). The sense is the key element of WordNet as words are not distinguished beyond lemma and part of speech. In contrast, there is no identifier for synsets in Princeton WordNet. Instead, a synset is identified by the number of bytes in the WordNet file to the start of the corresponding entry. These byte offsets are used as 8-digit codes augmented by the part of speech of the synset, yielding an identifier such as 03196217-n.

Princeton WordNet has established itself as the most widely used resource in natural language processing and it still sees frequent application in a wide variety of tasks. For example, it has been shown that methods such as word embeddings can be improved by taking into account the structure of WordNet [3]. Moreover, WordNet has inspired the creation of a large number of resources that have attempted to deepen the linguistic knowledge, such as VerbNet [4] and FrameNet [5] and other knowledge, such as SentiWordNet [6] and ImageNet [7].

By now, there exist wordnets for over 200 languages. With the exception of the Polish WordNet, plWordNet [8], they are smaller in size than the original Princeton WordNet. The Open Multilingual WordNet project [9] has been collecting these resources into a single central location and providing all resources under a common format. Due to the restrictive licenses that many of the wordnets are released under, the project so far comprises 34 wordnets. Moreover, as the data format of Princeton WordNet is difficult to use, almost all new WordNet projects have created their own format, leading to fragmentation and lack of interoperability between wordnets.

The creation of wordnets for new languages has typically followed one of two approaches: the *expand* or the *merge* approach [10]. The *expand* approach starts from the structure of Princeton WordNet and translates the synsets into the target language, adding additional synsets as required. In contrast, the *merge* approach involves creating a new wordnet from scratch and then linking it with cross-lingual links to the Princeton WordNet. The merge approach involves a significantly higher amount of work and has therefore been adopted only by few WordNet projects.

The largest project for the creation of new wordnets was EuroWordNet [11], which created wordnets for seven European languages: Dutch, Italian, Spanish, German, French, Czech and Estonian. In this project, both models were followed, with five resources being created by the *merge* approach and two resources being created by the *expand* approach. Other later projects have tried to follow the blueprint provided by EuroWordNet and attempted to create wordnets for East European Languages (BalkaNet [12]) as well as for Indian languages (IndoWordNet [13]).

12.1.1 WordNet RDF

As WordNet represents semantic structure as a linked graph of synsets, it lends itself in a straightforward fashion for LD-based modelling. The first RDF version of WordNet was developed by van Assem et al. [14] and was based on WordNet 2.0. McCrae et al. developed an RDF-based version of WordNet 3.0 that was based on Ontolex-lemon [15] (see also Chap. 4). Other resources, including wordnets such as BabelNet [16, 17] and UBY [18, 19], have been published as linked data as well.

Most of the above-mentioned resources are direct conversions of a specific WordNet version and have not been updated with future versions. An exception is the approach of McCrae et al. [20], which has introduced an official version of WordNet at http://wordnet-rdf.princeton.edu that is continually updated and contains links to other resources. More recently, a new open source wordnet for English also provides RDF data [21].

The Ontolex-lemon model is particularly suited for the representation and linking of wordnets. The central elements of WordNet are modelled as follows:

- **Synsets:** Synsets are modelled as *Lexical Concepts*, with a corresponding subclass called *Synset*.
- **Senses:** Senses are modelled as *Lexical Senses*.
- **Words**: Words are modelled as *Lexical Entries*.

As WordNet lacks ontological commitment, the hypernym/hyponym relations between synsets cannot be automatically mapped into subclass relations due to the well-known problem of ISA overloading (see [22]). First, as mentioned above, synsets are not modelled as classes but as (lexical) concepts. The lexical relations were mapped into specific relations that are defined in the WordNet ontology published at https://globalwordnet.github.io/schemas/wn and which are linked to data categories in ISOcat [23] following the guidelines developed by Windhouwer et al. [24].

12.2 Global WordNet Interlingual Index

There are currently 76 wordnets available for 47 languages, including large initiatives such as IndoWordNet [13] and EuroWordNet [11] that cover many languages. While many of these wordnets are not complete or not available under open licenses, the Open Multilingual WordNet project has collected 34 wordnets [9, 25–52], which represent a rich resource for multilingual knowledge. Most of these wordnets have been constructed following the *expand* approaching bootstrapping on Princeton WordNet, translating the exiting synsets and adding new senses if required. A few wordnets have instead used the *merge* approach where equivalence is directly stated between synsets. However, the format and technical implementation of Princeton WordNet has not generally been adopted, especially the use of (byte) offsets to identify synsets. As such, applications that require wordnets are significantly hampered by the wide variation in formats and models. Furthermore, many wordnets have significantly expanded the structure of their wordnet, e.g. by adding novel properties or by introducing new structures such as emotional information [6]. Moreover, the practice of linking all wordnets through English produces a very specific Anglo-Saxon worldview that can cause issues. An example of this is that many languages distinguish gendered role worlds, e.g. 'teacher' has both a male and a female form (German: 'Lehrer'/'Lehrerin', Italian: 'professore'/'professoressa', French: 'professeur'/'professeure'). As Princeton WordNet does not allow synsets without words or multi-word terms that are clearly compositional ('male teacher'), it would be impossible to links these concepts directly through PWN, thus losing information. For these reasons, multilingual wordnets are difficult to apply in many contexts and the use of linked data has been proposed to alleviate this issue in the context of the *Interlingual Index*.

In addition to these conceptual issues, a technical problem is that the different wordnets link to different versions of Princeton WordNet. This leads to the fact that the different wordnets use a different set of identifiers. As result, there is no canonical mapping between synsets of different wordnet versions. Instead, links between synsets can only be inferred based on the sense keys. In addition, the lack of a standardized format for wordnets has led to a proliferation of distinct formats.

As a result, whenever Princeton releases an update of WordNet, it immediately leads to a decrease in the compatibility of wordnets as new synset identifiers are introduced. In this situation, it is impossible to harmonize the different wordnets and create an interoperability layer across wordnets. A principled solution would be the creation of a central multilingual database that all wordnet projects can contribute to. However, a centralized approach to managing all wordnets seems not feasible in practice as this would require one group to maintain all wordnets. Further, many wordnet projects have extended the wordnet model by adding new relations [11], richer domains [53] as well as new parts of speech [54]. It would naturally be very difficult to accommodate all these extensions in a single monolithic project. Instead, a decentralized approach, the Global WordNet Grid, has been proposed that relies on a central index of synsets to which all wordnets can link to.

12.2.1   The Global WordNet Grid

The Global WordNet Association was created by Christiane Fellbaum of Princeton University and Piek Vossen of the Vrije Universiteit in Amsterdam in order to support the development of wordnets across the globe. The organization has recently supported the creation of an interlingual index [55] of terms based on WordNet that can be used to enable wordnets to more easily and consistently map across languages. The first step of this has been to create a standard and non-changing list of identifiers for each synset in the 3.0 version of Princeton WordNet starting from i1 and proceeding sequentially. These are available to access from a linked data interface at http://ili.globalwordnet.com/ili/i1234. However, this index is intended to continually grow on the basis of contributions from other wordnets, introducing new concepts by consensus. As Princeton WordNet does not allow synsets without members, concepts which are not lexicalized in English are not included. In order to create a new concept in the Interlingual Index the following must be provided:

- A definition in English. It is required that the definition is given in English as this generally represents the only common language known to all wordnet developers.
- At least one link to a synset already existing in the interlingual index needs to be provided.
- The synset must appear in an existing wordnet, which should be available in one of the supported Global WordNet (GWN) formats

12.2.2   Collaborative Interlingual Index

In order to manage this proposed multilingual database, a new service was created, called the *Collaborative Interlingual Index* (CILI). [56].[1] This service acts as a central point for contribution of new resources to the Global WordNet Grid. The design principles for this resource were as follows (from [56]):

1. The InterLingual Index (ILI) consists of a flat list of concepts.
2. The semantic and lexical relations should have the same meaning across languages.
3. Concepts should be constructed for salient and frequent lexicalized concepts in all languages.
4. Concepts linked to multiword units (MWUs) in wordnets should be included.
5. A formal ontology separated from the wordnets can be integrated.
6. The license must allow redistribution of the index.
7. ILI IDs should be persistent: they should never be deleted, only *deprecated* or *superceded*; the meaning of a synset should not be changed.
8. Each new ILI concept should have a definition in English, as this is the only way that definitions can be agreed upon and consensus can be established. Definitions should be unique and changes should be moderated.
9. Each new ILI concept should link to a synset in an existing project that is part of the GWG with one of a set of known relations, e.g. *hypernymy, meronomy, antonymy*, ...
10. This synset should link to another synset in an existing project that is part of the GWG and links to an ILI concept.
11. Any project adding new synsets should first check the synset to be added does not already exist. If it does not exist, it should be added to a specific wordnet first and proposed as candidate for addition into the ILI. If no objections to its addition are raised within 3 months, then the synset will be added.

---

[1] Available at http://compling.hss.ntu.edu.sg/iliomw/ili.

These principles have been defined to support the global collaboration across and synchronization of WordNet projects. Firstly, an open license on the resource is a necessary condition so that other collaborators may view and even improve resources in that language. Moreover, this license should not contain restrictions on non-commercial usage so that commercial entities may also be involved in the creation of wordnets.

In order to ensure the persistence of identifiers, they are never deleted so that they can still be resolved and their meaning can be retrieved. In order to foster collaboration across contributing wordnet projects, English was adopted as an intermediate language and all concepts must have a definition in English (even if there are no lemmas for that concept in English). This was inspired by the work on the CIIC project [57] where Thai, Chinese, Japanese, Malay and Indonesian researchers collaborated to develop a lexical resource.

In order to make sure that the resource as a whole represents a consistent semantic network, new concepts/synsets may only be added if they link to a synset in the source WordNet and the synset is properly defined and its provenance is clearly indicated.

12.2.3   ILI Format

To support the linking of wordnets to the Interlingual Index, a common format needed to be defined [58]. Furthermore, this format is intended to be clean, easy to understand and compatible with other existing standards, including the Lexical Markup Framework (LMF) [59] and the Ontolex-lemon model [60, 61] described in Chap. 4.

This has been achieved by making the format available in three serializations[2]: an LMF/XML model, a JSON-LD model and an RDF format. The XML format is based on LMF and in particular the WordNet-LMF (also known as the Kyoto-LMF format [62]). The semantics of the JSON format is provided by a JSON-LD context [63] as described in Chap. 2. Finally, as the JSON-LD format implies an RDF serialization, this is also supported, including serializations to other formats such as Turtle [64] and RDF/XML [65]. We will briefly explain these formats in the remainder of this chapter. The three equivalent forms of the Global WordNet Format are designed such that it should be possible to convert between them with no loss of information. Due to the differences between formats, ensuring this property is a challenge. In particular, XML specifies the relative ordering of elements as well as the use of whitespace in the data model, both of which would be hard to capture in JSON or RDF.

---

[2]Although potentially more as there are multiple serializations of RDF as described in Chap. 2.

12.2.3.1 GWN LMF

The Lexical Markup Framework is an ISO standard (ISO-24613:2008) for the representation of lexical resources. LMF was published as a meta-model with a recommended XML serialization. Several other authors have created distinct XML serializations, including UBY-LMF [66] and RELISH-LMF [67]. The DTD is no longer freely available, so that the GWN proposed the use of a new DTD based on WordNet-LMF [62]. As a drawback, the interoperability with other LMF models is reduced. Further, there is little community and tool support for the WordNet-LMF model so far. The Document Type Definition (DTD) proposed by the Global WordNet Association is freely available at http://globalwordnet.github.io/schemas/WN-LMF-1.0.dtd and is documented on GitHub at https://globalwordnet.github.io/schemas/.

The LMF serialization requires that the entire wordnet be available as a single file, consisting of one or more lexicons (one per language), which are in turn composed of lexical entries and synsets. The DTD provides some validation, including ensuring that all references are valid through the use of IDREFS and that the document is well formed. In Fig. 12.1, a minimal example of a LMF wordnet is given. This defines a single entry for 'wordnet' with a definition and a gloss. In addition, a number of mandatory fields are required to be given in order to process the resource correctly in the CILI, including language, contact email, license, citation, version and the project URL.

```
1   <?xml version="1.0" encoding="UTF-8"?>
2   <!DOCTYPE LexicalResource SYSTEM
3       "http://globalwordnet.github.io/schemas/WN-LMF.dtd">
4   <LexicalResource>
5       <Lexicon id="example"
6       label="Example wordnet (English)"
7       language="en"
8       email="john@mccr.ae"
9       license="https://creativecommons.org/publicdomain/zero/1.0/"
10      version="1.0"
11      citation="Linguistic Linked Data: Representation,... "
12      url="http://www.example.com/wordnet">
13          <LexicalEntry id="w1">
14              <Lemma writtenForm="wordnet" partOfSpeech="n"/>
15              <Sense id="106652077-n-1" synset="106652077-n"/>
16          </LexicalEntry>
17          <Synset id="106652077-n" ili="s35545">
18              <Definition
19                 gloss="any of the..."
20                 iliDef="any of the..."/>
21              <SynsetRelation relType="hypernym"
22                              target="106651393-n"/>
23          </Synset>
24      </Lexicon>
25  </LexicalResource>
```

Fig. 12.1 Example of WordNet entry in WN-LMF

```
1   {
2     "@context": [
3        "http://globalwordnet.github.io/schemas/wn-json-context.
             json",
4        { "@language": "en" } ],
5     "@id": "example",
6     "label": "Example wordnet (English)",
7     "language": "en" ,
8     "email": "john@mccr.ae",
9     "license": "https://creativecommons.org/publicdomain/zero/1.0/"
            ,
10    "version": "1.0",
11    "citation": "Linguistic Linked Data: Representation, ...",
12    "url": "http://www.example.com/wordnet",
13    "entry": [{
14      "@id" : "w1",
15      "lemma": { "writtenForm": "wordnet" },
16      "partOfSpeech": "wn:noun",
17      "sense": [{
18        "@id": "106652077-n-1",
19        "synset": {
20          "@id": "106652077-n",
21          "ili": "s35545",
22          "definition": {
23            "gloss": "any of the..." ,
24            "iliDef": "any of the..."
25          },
26          "hypernym": ["106651393-n"]
27        }
28      }]
29    }]
30  }
```

Fig. 12.2 Example of an entry in WN-JSON

12.2.3.2 GWN JSON

The JSON serialization is based on the LMF format, but uses JSON-LD in order
to ensure that the semantics of the document can be retrieved. In particular, the
properties are defined by a mapping to the Ontolex-lemon model [61]. As Ontolex-
lemon also has its roots in LMF, this mapping is not especially complex; an example
document is given in Fig. 12.2, which follows the previous example in XML.
As JSON-LD only provides the meaning of properties and does not validate the
documents themselves, a JSON schema document is provided,[3] which checks that
all the elements that are necessary actually occur and that the document structure is
sound. As the model is defined using JSON-LD, it is straightforward to extract RDF
(see Chap. 2). As with the previous WordNet RDF model, synsets are mapped to

---

[3]https://raw.githubusercontent.com/globalwordnet/schemas/master/wn-json-schema.json.

lexical concepts, word senses to lexical senses and words to lexical entries. In order to capture the properties of WordNet, the WordNet ontology given above is used. This ontology includes the description of parts of speech and synset relations.

12.2.4 Linking WordNet with Wikipedia

There is a fundamental difference between lexical resources describing how language is used and encyclopedic resources, which focus on the entities that exist in the world. However, there is a significant overlap as Princeton WordNet contains proper nouns corresponding to names of countries, cities, famous people, gods, wars, terrorist groups and books. However, it is not possible for WordNet to cover the wealth of entities in the real world. Other resources such as Wikipedia contain exactly this type of knowledge. To support NLP applications that need both lexical and encyclopedic content, it is necessary to link these two resources. There have been attempts to do this in an automatic manner in projects such as BabelNet [16] and UBY [66]. However, the authors themselves only report about 80–85% accuracy and independent evaluations have suggested that the accuracy may be even lower [68].

A semi-automatic mapping was proposed by McCrae et al. [69], and a set of links for most of the proper nouns was released. This approach relies on finding candidates between categories of Wikipedia articles and hypernyms in a given wordnet. These candidates are found by identifying all the articles the title of which match a word in a synset exactly. For this purpose, the title of Wikipedia articles were normalized by removing all content after the first comma; content in parentheses was removed. In addition to considering the title of a Wikipedia page, all titles of articles redirecting to the article in question were considered. Let a_j denote an article in Wikipedia and $C(a_j)$ its corresponding category. Further, let s_i denote a synset in a wordnet and $H(s_i)$ the set of all hypernyms of s_i. Given a set W of article-synset pairs with a matching title, the set of *category-hypernym mappings* M is defined as:

$$M = \{(h, c) | \exists \{s_i, a_j\} \in W : h \in H(s_i) \wedge c \in C(a_j)\}$$

The above pairs are scored according to a number of criteria to produce a ranked list and filter out candidates that are non-ambiguous in the sense that they are not linked to another article or synset. In a semi-automatic workflow, more than 8,000 new links between Princeton WordNet and Wikipedia could be created (see detailed statistics in Table 12.1).

Table 12.1 Statistics about links semi-automatically induced between Princeton WordNet and Wikipedia

Exact	Broad	Narrow	Related	Unmapped
7582	54	21	30	59

12.3   Summary and Further Reading

This chapter discussed how to apply linked data principles to the representation of wordnets and in particular to the representation of a central interlingual index that all multilingual wordnet projects can link to. Wordnets are one of the most widely used forms of lexical information in natural language processing and the semantic network structure given in wordnets lends itself straightforwardly for linked data-based modelling. In fact, the wordnet community has been one of the first to adopt linked data principles. The Interlingual Index is a clear testimony of this. The chapter has described the transition of wordnet development towards a distributed infrastructure supported by the CILI collaborative tools which will hopefully further encourage research groups to publish their data as RDF and link it to other resources. It is important to note that the community has as a whole still not fully embraced RDF and the use of LMF and XML formats is still preferred by many wordnet creators. However, the appropriate use of linked data technologies has helped this community to solve some of their interoperability issues, demonstrating the value of this technology and the need for more research in this area.

For further reading, we recommend that readers consult the two papers on the definition of the interlingual index [55, 56] as well as the technical definitions of the format at http://globalwordnet.github.io/schemas/. For details on the approach for semi-automatically mapping wordnets to Wikipedia the interested reader is referred to McCrae et al. [69].

References

1. G.A. Miller, WordNet: a lexical database for English. Commun. Assoc. Comput. Mach. **38**(11), 39 (1995)
2. C. Fellbaum, Wordnet, in *Theory and Applications of Ontology: Computer Applications* (Springer, Berlin, 2010), pp. 231–243
3. S. Rothe, H. Schütze, Autoextend: extending word embeddings to embeddings for synsets and lexemes, in *Proceedings of the 53rd Annual Meeting of the Association for Computational Linguistics and the 7th International Joint Conference on Natural Language Processing* (2015), pp. 1793–1803
4. K.K. Schuler, VerbNet: a broad-coverage, comprehensive verb lexicon. Ph.D. thesis (University of Pennsylvania, Pennsylvania, 2005)
5. C.F. Baker, C.J. Fillmore, J.B. Lowe, The Berkeley FrameNet project, in *Proceedings of the 36th Annual Meeting of the Association for Computational Linguistics and 17th International Conference on Computational Linguistics*, vol. 1 (Association for Computational Linguistics, Stroudsburg, 1998), pp. 86–90
6. A. Esuli, F. Sebastiani, SentiWordNet: a high-coverage lexical resource for opinion mining, in *Technical Report ISTI-PP-002/2007, Institute of Information Science and Technologies (ISTI) of the Italian National Research Council (CNR)* (2006). http://tcc.itc.it/projects/ontotext/Publications/sentiWN-TR.pdf
7. J. Deng, W. Dong, R. Socher, L.J. Li, K. Li, F.F. Li, ImageNet: a large-scale hierarchical image database, in *Proceedings of the IEEE Conference on Computer Vision and Pattern Recognition (CVPR)*, 2009, pp. 248–255

8. M. Maziarz, M. Piasecki, E. Rudnicka, S. Szpakowicz, P. Kedzia, plWordNet 3.0—a comprehensive lexical-semantic resource, in *Proceedings of the 26th International Conference on Computational Linguistics (COLING)*, ed. by N. Calzolari, Y. Matsumoto, R. Prasad (ACL, Osaka, 2016), pp. 2259–2268

9. F. Bond, R. Foster, Linking and extending an open multilingual wordnet, in *Proceedings of the 51st Annual Meeting of the Association for Computational Linguistics (ACL)* (The Association for Computer Linguistics, Stroudsburg, 2013), pp. 1352–1362

10. P. Vossen, *EuroWordNet General Document* (University of Amsterdam, The Netherlands, 1999). Technical Report. http://www.illc.uva.nl/EuroWordNet/

11. P. Vossen, Introduction to eurowordnet. Comput. Hum. **32**(2-3), 73 (1998)

12. S. Stamou, K. Oflazer, K. Pala, D. Christoudoulakis, D. Cristea, D. Tufis, S. Koeva, G. Totkov, D. Dutoit, M. Grigoriadou, BalkaNet: a multilingual semantic network for the Balkan languages, in *Proceedings of the International Wordnet Conference, Mysore, India* (2002), pp. 21–25

13. P. Bhattacharyya, IndoWordNet, in *Proceedings of the 7th International Conference on Language Resources and Evaluation (LREC)* (2010)

14. M. Van Assem, A. Gangemi, G. Schreiber, Conversion of WordNet to a standard RDF/OWL representation, in *Proceedings of the 5th International Conference on Language Resources and Evaluation (LREC), Genoa* (2006), pp. 237–242

15. J. McCrae, E. Montiel-Ponsoda, P. Cimiano, Integrating WordNet and Wiktionary with lemon, in *Linked Data in Linguistics* (Springer, Berlin, 2012), pp. 25–34

16. R. Navigli, S.P. Ponzetto, BabelNet: building a very large multilingual semantic network, in *Proceedings of the 48th Annual Meeting of the Association for Computational Linguistics* (2010), pp. 216–225

17. M. Ehrmann, D. Vannela, J.P. McCrae, F. Cecconi, P. Cimiano, R. Navigli, Representing multilingual data as linked data: the case of BabelNet 2.0, in *Proceedings of the 9th International Conference on Language Resources and Evaluation (LREC-14)* (2014)

18. I. Gurevych, J. Eckle-Kohler, S. Hartmann, M. Matuschek, C.M. Meyer, C. Wirth, UBY: A large-scale unified lexical-semantic resource based on LMF, in *Proceedings of the 13th Conference of the European Chapter of the Association for Computational Linguistics* (Association for Computational Linguistics, Stroudsburg, 2012), pp. 580–590

19. J. Eckle-Kohler, J. McCrae, C. Chiarcos, lemonUby-a large, interlinked, syntactically-rich resource for ontologies. Semant. Web **6**(4), 371–378 (2015)

20. J.P. McCrae, C. Fellbaum, P. Cimiano, Publishing and Linking WordNet using lemon and RDF, in *Proceedings of the 3rd Workshop on Linked Data in Linguistics* (2014)

21. J. McCrae, A. Rademaker, F. Bond, E. Rudnicka, C. Fellbaum, English WordNet 2019—an open-source WordNet for english, in *Proceedings of the 10th Global WordNet Conference* (2019)

22. N. Guarino, Some ontological principles for designing upper level lexical resources, in *Proceedings of the 1st International Conference on Language Resources and Evaluation (LREC)*, Granada, 28–30 May 1998

23. M. Kemps-Snijders, M. Windhouwer, P. Wittenburg, S.E. Wright, ISOcat: corralling data categories in the wild, in *Proceedings of the 6th International Conference on Language Resources and Evaluation (LREC)* (2008), pp. 887–891

24. M. Windhouwer, S.E. Wright, Linking to linguistic data categories in ISOcat, in *Linked Data in Linguistics* (Springer, Berlin, 2012), pp. 99–107

25. E. Ruci, On the current state of Albanet and related applications (University of Vlora, University of Vlora, 2008). Technical Report. http://fjalnet.com/technicalreportalbanet.pdf

26. L. Abouenour, K. Bouzoubaa, P. Rosso, On the evaluation and improvement of Arabic wordnet coverage and usability. Lang. Resour. Eval. **47**(3), 891 (2013)

27. S. Elkateb, W. Black, H. Rodríguez, M. Alkhalifa, P. Vossen, A. Pease, C. Fellbaum, Building a wordnet for Arabic, in *Proceedings of the 5th International Conference on Language Resources and Evaluation (LREC)* (2006)

28. K. Simov, P. Osenova, Constructing of an ontology-based lexicon for Bulgarian, in *Proceedings of the 7th International Conference on Language Resources and Evaluation (LREC)*, ed. by N.C.C. Chair, K. Choukri, B. Maegaard, J. Mariani, J. Odijk, S. Piperidis, M. Rosner, D. Tapias (European Language Resources Association (ELRA), Valletta, 2010)

29. S. Wang, F. Bond, Building the Chinese open Wordnet (cow): starting from core synsets, in *Proceedings of the 6th International Joint Conference on Natural Language Processing* (2013), pp. 10–18

30. C.R. Huang, S.K. Hsieh, J.F. Hong, Y.Z. Chen, I.L. Su, Y.X. Chen, S.W. Huang, Chinese wordnet: design and implementation of a cross-lingual knowledge processing infrastructure. J. Chin. Inf. Process. **24**(2), 14 (2010) (in Chinese)

31. B. Pedersen, S. Nimb, J. Asmussen, N. Sørensen, L. Trap-Jensen, H. Lorentzen, DanNet—the challenge of compiling a wordnet for Danish by reusing a monolingual dictionary. Lang. Resour. Eval. **43**(3), 269 (2009)

32. M. Montazery, H. Faili, Automatic Persian wordnet construction, in *Proceedings of the 23rd International Conference on Computational Linguistics (COLING)* (2010), pp. 846–850

33. K. Lindén, L. Carlson., Finnwordnet—wordnet påfinska via översättning. LexicoNordica—Nord. J. Lexicogr. **17**, 119 (2010). In Swedish with an English abstract

34. B. Sagot, D. Fišer, Building a free French wordnet from multilingual resources, in *Proceedings of the 6th International Conference on Language Resources and Evaluation (LREC)*, ed. by E.L.R.A. (ELRA) (Marrakech, Morocco, 2008)

35. N. Ordan, S. Wintner, Hebrew WordNet: a test case of aligning lexical databases across languages. Int. J. Transl. **19**(1), 39 (2007)

36. A. Oliver, K. Šojat, M. Srebačić, Automatic expansion of Croatian wordnet, in *Proceedings of the 29th CALS International Conference on Language "Applied Linguistic Research and Methodology"*, Zadar (2015)

37. I. Raffaelli, B. Bekavac, Agi, M. Tadi, Building croatian wordnet, in *Proceedings of the 4th Global WordNet Conference 2008*, Szeged, ed. by A. Tancs, D. Csendes, V. Vincze, C. Fellbaum, P. Vossen (2008), pp. 349–359

38. E. Pianta, L. Bentivogli, C. Girardi, Multiwordnet: Developing an aligned multilingual database, in *Proceedings of the 1st International Conference on Global WordNet*, Mysore (2002), pp. 293–302

39. A. Toral, S. Bracale, M. Monachini, C. Soria, Rejuvenating the Italian WordNet: upgrading, standardising, extending, in *Proceedings of the 5th International Conference of the Global WordNet Association (GWC)*, Mumbai (2010)

40. H. Isahara, F. Bond, K. Uchimoto, M. Utiyama, K. Kanzaki, Development of the Japanese WordNet, in *Proceedings of the 6th International Conference on Language Resources and Evaluation (LREC)*, Marrakech (2008)

41. A. Gonzalez-Agirre, E. Laparra, G. Rigau, Multilingual central repository version 3.0: upgrading a very large lexical knowledge base, in *Proceedings of the 6th Global WordNet Conference (GWC)*, Matsue (2012)

42. E. Pociello, E. Agirre, I. Aldezabal, Methodology and construction of the Basque wordnet. Lang. Resour. Eval. **45**(2), 121 (2011)

43. N. Mohamed Noor, S. Sapuan, F. Bond, Creating the open Wordnet Bahasa, in *Proceedings of the 25th Pacific Asia Conference on Language, Information and Computation (PACLIC 25)*, Singapore (2011), pp. 258–267

44. M. Postma, E. van Miltenburg, R. Segers, A. Schoen, P. Vossen, Open DutchWordNet, in *Proceedings of the 8th Global Wordnet Conference*, Bucharest (2016)

45. R.V. Fjeld, L. Nygaard, Nornet—a monolingual wordnet of modern Norwegian, in *Proceedings of the NODALIDA 2009 Workshop WordNets and Other Lexical Semantic Resources—Between Lexical Semantics, Lexicography, Terminology and Formal Ontologies*, vol. NEALT Proceedings Series, Vol. 7 (Estonia, 2009), pp. 13–16

46. M. Piasecki, S. Szpakowicz, B. Broda, *A Wordnet from the Ground Up* (Wroclaw University of Technology Press, Wroclaw, 2009). http://www.plwordnet.pwr.wroc.pl/main/content/files/publications/A_Wordnet_from_the_Ground_Up.pdf. ISBN 978-83-7493-476-3

47. D. Tufiş, R. Ion, L. Bozianu, A. Ceauşu, D. Ştefănescu, Romanian wordnet: current state, new applications and prospects, in *Proceedings of the 4th Global WordNet Association Conference*, Szeged (2008), pp. 441–452
48. R. Garabk, I. Pileckyt, From multilingual dictionary to Lithuanian wordnet, in *Natural Language Processing, Corpus Linguistics, E-Learning*, ed. by K. Gajdoov, A. kov (RAM, Ldenscheid, 2013), pp. 74–80
49. D. Fišer, J. Novak, T. Erjavec, sloWNet 3.0: development, extension and cleaning, in *Proceedings of the 6th International Global Wordnet Conference (GWC)* (The Global WordNet Association, Herensingel, 2012), pp. 113–117
50. L. Borin, M. Forsberg, L. Lönngren, Saldo: a touch of yin to wordnet's yang. Lang. Resour. Eval. **47**(4), 1191 (2013)
51. S. Thoongsup, T. Charoenporn, K. Robkop, T. Sinthurahat, C. Mokarat, V. Sornlertlamvanich, H. Isahara, Thai wordnet construction, in *Proceedings of the 7th Workshop on Asian Language Resources (ALR7), co-located with the Joint of the 47th Annual Meeting of the Association for Computational Linguistics (ACL) and the 4th International Joint Conference on Natural Language Processing (IJCNLP)* (Suntec, Singapore, 2009)
52. X.S. Vu, S.B. Park, Construction of Vietnamese SentiWordNet by using Vietnamese dictionary. 40th Conf. Korea Inf. Process. Soc. **21**, 745 (2014)
53. L. Bentivogli, P. Forner, B. Magnini, E. Pianta, Revising wordnet domains hierarchy: semantics, coverage, and balancing, in *Proceedings of the Workshop on Multilingual Linguistic Resources Co-located with COLING*, Geneva (2004), pp. 101–108
54. Y.J. Seah, F. Bond, Annotation of pronouns in a multilingual corpus of Mandarin Chinese, English and Japanese, in *Proceedings of the 10th Joint Annual Meeting of the Association for Computational Linguistics (ACL)—ISO Workshop on Interoperable Semantic Annotation*, Reykjavik (2014)
55. P. Vossen, F. Bond, J.P. McCrae, Toward a truly multilingual Global Wordnet Grid, in *Proceedings of the Global WordNet Conference* (2016)
56. F. Bond, P. Vossen, J.P. McCrae, C. Fellbaum, CILI: the Collaborative Interlingual Index, in *Proceedings of the Global WordNet Conference* (2016)
57. CICC, *Research on Malaysian Dictionary*. Technical Report 6—CICC—MT54 (Center of the International Cooperation for Computerization, Tokyo, 1994)
58. J.P. McCrae, P. Vossen, L.M. da Costa, F. Bond, *The GLobal WOrdNEt ASsociation Schemas*. Linguistic Issues in Language Technology (2018, Under Review)
59. G. Francopoulo, M. George, N. Calzolari, M. Monachini, N. Bel, M. Pet, C. Soria, et al., Lexical markup framework (LMF), in *Proceedings of the International Conference on Language Resources and Evaluation*, vol. 6 (2006)
60. J. McCrae, G.A. de Cea, P. Buitelaar, P. Cimiano, T. Declerck, A. Gómez-Pérez, J. Gracia, L. Hollink, E. Montiel-Ponsoda, D. Spohr, T. Wunner, Interchanging lexical resources on the Semantic Web. Lang. Resour. Eval. **46**(6), 701 (2012)
61. P. Cimiano, J.P. McCrae, P. Buitelaar, Lexicon model for ontologies: community report. *W3C community group final report* (World Wide Web Consortium, Cambridge, 2014)
62. C. Soria, M. Monachini, P. Vossen, Wordnet-LMF: fleshing out a standardized format for wordnet interoperability, in *Proceedings of the International Workshop on Intercultural Collaboration* (ACM, New York, 2009), pp. 139–146
63. M. Sporny, D. Longley, G. Kellogg, M. Lanthaler, N. Lindström, JSON-LD 1.0, in *W3C recommendation* (World Wide Web Consortium, Cambridge, 2014)
64. D. Beckett, T. Berners-Lee, E. Prud'hommeaux, G. Carothers, RDF 1.1 Turtle, in *W3C Recommendation* (World Wide Web Consortium, Cambridge, 2004)
65. D. Beckett, B. McBride, RDF/XML Syntax Specification, in *W3C Recommendation* (World Wide Web Consortium, Cambridge, 2004)
66. J. Eckle-Kohler, I. Gurevych, S. Hartmann, M. Matuschek, C.M. Meyer, UBY-LMF-a uniform model for standardizing heterogeneous lexical-semantic resources in ISO-LMF, in *Proceedings of the 8th International Conference on Language Resources and Evaluation (LREC)* (2012), pp. 275–282

67. M. Windhouwer, J. Petro, S. Shayan, RELISH LMF: unlocking the full power of the Lexical Markup Framework, in *Proceedings of the 9th International Conference on Language Resources and Evaluation (LREC)* (2014), pp. 1032–1037
68. D. Lindemann, F. Kliche, Bilingual Dictionary Drafting: Bootstrapping WordNet and Babel-Net, in *Proceedings of the 5th Biennial Conference on Electronic Lexicography (eLex)* (2017), pp. 23–42
69. J.P. McCrae, P. Buitelaar, Linking datasets using semantic textual similarity. Cybern. Inf. Technol. **18**(1), 109 (2018)

Chapter 13
Linguistic Linked Data in Digital Humanities

Abstract In recent years, Digital Humanities (DH) has become an increasingly flourishing field of research, often posing novel research challenges that require extensions or revisions of existing technologies. One characteristic of this area is the great heterogeneity of scientific disciplines and user communities involved. This leads to heterogeneity of data formats and data sources that represents a technical challenge from the point of view of interoperability. Linked data technology has the potential to facilitate the integration of heterogeneous data formats and distributed data sources. This chapter describes prototypical applications of LLD technologies and LOD resources in Digital Humanities as well as frequently used vocabularies.

13.1 Introduction

While natural sciences focus on developing a better understanding of the fundamentals of our physical universe, humanities owe much of their importance to their contribution to our understanding of the role of culture and society and their development in relation to our individual, historical and national identity in an increasingly globalized world. Digital Humanities (DH) is a set of broader digital scholarship practices in this area, established with pioneering work on Latin philology [1] and English lexicography [2], archaeology [3], history [4], etc. in the 1950s and 1960s.

Despite technological, terminological and methodological traditions developed since then, there is currently no agreed-upon definition for the term. This is due to the fact that, at its core, the term 'digital humanities' refers more to a common methodology rather than to a specific field of study. On the one hand, Digital Humanities thus represents a side qualification of most humanities scholars of our time. Irrespective of whether they identify themselves with this community, they use digital practices and concepts to one degree or another, ranging from digital data management using office software, spreadsheets or off-the-shelf databases, over quantitative analysis using statistics libraries and automatically supported annotation to the development of technical infrastructures for the creation and maintenance of digital editions of historical texts or pieces of art. On the other hand,

© Springer Nature Switzerland AG 2020
P. Cimiano et al., *Linguistic Linked Data*,
https://doi.org/10.1007/978-3-030-30225-2_13

Digital Humanities comes with a set of common techniques and methodologies, such as the increased use of statistical methods, markup languages for textual and non-textual content, and data and metadata management. From this perspective, Digital Humanities qualifies itself as an independent area of research within the broader scope of information science. Increasingly, Linked Open Data is recognized as a component in this pool of technologies and methodologies, and it continues to grow in importance in the participating communities (e.g. there is a TEI Special Interest Group on Ontologies since 2004,[1] and an ADHO Special Interest Group on Linked Open Data since 2014).[2]

Being concerned with *Linguistic* Linked Open Data in this book, we specifically focus on computational philology, i.e. branches of Digital Humanities centred on the analysis of written text and/or natural language. In particular, this includes a traditional focus on XML technologies. Together with the Association for Computational Linguistics (ACL, founded in 1962 as the Association for Machine Translation and Computational Linguistics), the European Association for Digital Humanities (EADH, founded in 1973 as the Association for Literary and Linguistic Computing) and the Association for Computers and the Humanities (ACH, founded in 1978), have been working towards establishing general guidelines for the electronic representation of linguistic and literary resources since the mid-1970s. Following similar events in 1977 in San Diego and 1980 in Pisa [5], a 1987 workshop organized by the ACH and held at Vassar College [6] led to the formulation of the 'Poughkeepsie Principles' and foundation of the Text Encoding Initiative (TEI). Already in 1986, the SGML Markup Language [7, Standard Generalized Markup Language; ISO 8879:1986] had been standardized to facilitate sharing machine-readable documents, albeit with no special emphasis on (or even concern for) linguistically annotated data. Building on the Poughkeepsie Principles, the TEI Guidelines defined a broad range of SGML (resp., since 2002, XML) tags and accompanying DTDs for encoding language data according to the needs in the humanities. The TEI subsequently contributed greatly to the popularization of XML in the language resource community. In its current edition, P5, TEI/XML continues to be the dominating paradigm for the digital edition of textual data in Digital Humanities.

As an XML-based standard, the TEI takes a necessary focus on standardizing the *form* of language resources for the humanities. Semantic Web formalisms allow to complement this 'syntactic approach' with a formal and standardized way to assess the *meaning* of attributes, markup elements and textual elements in text. In the following sections, we thus introduce popular (L)LOD resources and vocabularies developed by the DH community, and then describe strategies for their integration with the TEI.

---

[1]https://tei-c.org/activities/sig/ontologies/, accessed 09-07-2019.
[2]http://digitalhumanities.org/lod/, accessed 09-07-2019.

13.2   Data Models and Vocabularies in DH

In the DH community, the rise of Linked Open Data was initially delayed due to the dominance of XML technologies and of the Text Encoding Initiative (TEI) in particular. However, since 2012, the interest in using LD technologies in Digital Humanities is growing. The popularity and diversity of LOD applications in Digital Humanities can also be seen by collocated events at DH conferences, some examples are given here:

- Two workshops on ontology-based annotation, resp. resource metadata at DH2012
- A workshop on Web Annotation / Open Annotation at DH2013
- The third International Linked Open Data in Libraries, Archives and Museums summit at DH2015
- Two workshops on Linked Geo Data, resp. CIDOC CRM at DH2016
- A workshop on Advancing Linked Open Data in the Humanities at DH2017
- Two workshops on Linked Geo Data, resp., Linked Data at DH2018
- Three technologically oriented workshops at DH2019, on Ontologies for Linked Data in the Humanities, entity linking, extraction of RDF from XML resources, respectively, plus two thematically oriented workshops covering aspects of Linked Open Data in lexicography, resp., intertextuality of historical manuscripts

At the time of writing, important areas of application of LOD resources and methodologies in Digital Humanities include entity linking (geoinformation, prosopography), metadata and terminology (object metadata, text metadata) and resource linking. Beyond DH-specific use cases described below, off-the-shelf linked data resources and Semantic Web technologies are regularly applied in Digital Humanities in the same way as in other areas. This includes their application in APIs [8], NoSQL databases [9], database integration [10] and terminology management [11]. As dictionaries play an important role in the philologies, Ontolex-lemon is increasingly used as vocabulary in this field [12, 13], and also subject to the eLexicography workshop at DH2019.

In the following, we describe the well-known TEI data model prominently used in DH contexts and discuss how it can be made compatible with RDF and linked data approaches. We also introduce relevant vocabularies that have emerged as a result of the linked data movement and are widely adopted in DH: SKOS, CIDOC-DRM and CTS.

13.2.1   The Text Encoding Initiative

The Text Encoding Initiative (TEI), founded in 1987, is the authoritative body that develops and maintains an XML-based interchange format for textual data, in particular for the electronic edition of printed (or printable) publications. Beyond its historical focus on literary science and linguistics, the current edition of the TEI guidelines, P5 (proposal 5), represents a de facto standard for the entire field of Digital Humanities.[3] Reflecting its broad range of applications, TEI provides a very large vocabulary for the semantic and structural markup of electronic text (see Sect. 5.1.2 for its application to representing text corpora).

The TEI defines an XML format that aims to provide a compromise between a formal description of layout elements (e.g. *italics*) and their abstract function (e.g. *emphasis*). Its markup elements are given interpretable names, but the provided definitions are informative only, not normative, as the TEI standardizes only *their form and structure*. Accordingly, the TEI guidelines are traditionally implemented and validated by a set of modular DTDs. For practical applications, the TEI takes a text-driven approach: the form, content and structure of the underlying text is preserved, and are enriched by markup elements. Despite considerable overlap in their intentions (i.e. to facilitate interoperability and make semantics explicit), this is an important difference in comparison with Linguistic Linked Open Data: LLOD pursues a semantics-driven approach to text and linguistic annotations, and—unless explicitly coded in designated RDF properties—the surface characteristics of the text are lost. In particular, this includes sequential order and hierarchical structure of elements in the text, which is obligatory (and implicit) in TEI/XML, but needs to be explicitly asserted in RDF graphs if it is to be preserved.

As it has been extended by necessary modules as they were needed, the TEI today provides a *very rich* vocabulary of markup elements, comprising 569 XML elements and 231 attributes as summarized in Table 13.1. The TEI header structures are of particular importance to the entire field of DH, because they provide a metadata schema almost uniformly used throughout computational philology. Besides its metadata specifications, also the structural TEI vocabulary is extremely rich, and it is often observed in practice that different modelling decisions for the same problem are feasible. In this sense, the TEI does succeed in facilitating interpretability and transformability of philological resources, but it fails to establish interoperability (in the sense that different resources use the same data structures for the same phenomenon). For example, a medieval manuscript of, say, a German-Russian dictionary can be edited either as a diplomatic edition of a manuscript (largely following TEILite), or as a machine-readable dictionary (following tei.dict). While all of these representations would constitute a valid TEI/XML document, only the tei.dict modelling provides interoperability in the sense of language technology. The interoperability problem is partially addressed by the recommended practice to *customize* TEI for the needs of a particular project [14, 15]. By selecting a subset of markup elements before starting an edition project, interoperability between the individual documents of one or several related edition projects can be enforced, but only as long as the same customization (common subset specifications and extensions) are used. Beyond a particular customization, TEI compliance facilitates interpretability and transformability of electronic texts and its annotations, but does not guarantee interoperability.

---

[3]http://www.tei-c.org, accessed 09-07-2019.

Table 13.1 TEI P5 vocabulary statistics

XML elements	XML attributes	TEI modules	Description
Common elements			
82	32	core	Core structures
	107	tei	Common attributes
69	33	header	Metadata
54	78	tagdocs	Documentation of TEI modules
Application-specific extensions			
69	15	msdescription	Manuscript description
52	50	namesdates	Names and dates
35	19	dictionaries	Machine-readable dictionaries
33	4	textstructure	Text structure
29	22	transcr	Transcription of primary sources
28	18	iso-fs	Feature structures
17	8	drama	Performance texts
14	14	textcrit	Critical apparatus
14	11	corpus	Linguistic corpora
14	9	spoken	Transcribed speech
12	33	nets	Graphs, networks, and trees
11	22	linking	Linking, segmentation and alignment
11	9	analysis	Analytic mechanisms
11	2	gaiji	Character and glyph documentation
7	2	figures	Tables, formulas, notated music, and figures
4	9	verse	Verse structures
3	8	certainty	Certainty and uncertainty
Overall counts			
569	505	Total	
569	231	Unique elements	

While the benefits of LOD technologies have long been recognized in the DH community, and led to the formation of a LOD SIG in 2014, there is no agreement on possible technological bridges between TEI/XML and LOD technology. The traditional solution to leverage both technologies follows the technical motivation to use graph databases and RDF technology to process extracted information from and about TEI documents. This line of research required an interpretation of TEI data structures against an ontology, i.e. the creation of project-specific mappings from TEI markup elements to CIDOC CRM [16] (Sect. 13.2.3), the direct formalization of the TEI data model as an ontology [17, 18] or the direct conversion of TEI XML to RDF triples in line with the strategy described in Sect. 6.2 [19].[4] While each of these proposals can be a convenient solution for processing TEI data with

---

[4]Tummarello et al. [19] provide a reconstruction of TEI P4, available under http://rdftef. sourceforge.net/, accessed 10-07-2019. A prototype for the direct conversion of TEI inline XML

RDF-based backend technology, their integration with LOD data requires an explicit conversion, often depending on human interpretation of the specific TEI encoding decisions taken in a particular document.

In particular, TEI is not a suitable publication format for (Linguistic) Linked Open Data,[5] even when linking would be beneficial for using and re-using philological resources, unless proper vocabulary elements for the purpose are being developed. As no such vocabulary elements have been included or properly documented in TEI P5, different research projects have addressed the problem and suggested possible solutions, either by means of *tag abuse* of existing TEI vocabulary (i.e. ad hoc solutions targeting a specific use), or grounded on W3C recommendations to extend XML vocabularies with RDF in attributes (RDFa).

In most cases, these projects are based on extending the definitions of existing TEI vocabulary elements according to their use case, and TEI provides different vocabulary elements that have been exploited for this purpose, e.g. the use of the TEI `<link>` element (introduced for standoff markup in linguistic annotation, cf. Sect. 5.1.2), or of `@ref` (pointer structures originally intended to correspond to, say, the LATEX\ref command), resp., the `<relation>` element (restricted to named entities).

The analogy-driven extension of semantics and syntax of markup elements ('*tag abuse*') is a common strategy to counter the unrestricted growth of the TEI vocabulary. However, it leads to compatibility issues (as the same information can be represented in different ways) and semantic indeterminism (if the same markup is used for two distinct functions, the intended meaning cannot be automatically recovered). In addition to TEI-native strategies to represent RDF and linked data, an alternative approach is possible, i.e. the one of relying on W3C-recommended serializations of RDF, such as RDFa, that can be directly embedded in XML.

13.2.2   Simple Knowledge Organization System (SKOS)

The Simple Knowledge Organization System (SKOS) is an RDF vocabulary for representing semi-formal knowledge organization systems (KOSes), such as thesauri,

---

to RDF can be found under https://github.com/acoli-repo/LLODifier/tree/master/tei, accessed 10-07-2019.

[5]For a generic strategy to publish TEI-based information as LOD, three strategies are imaginable: (1) full (lossless) conversion of TEI to RDF, (2) hybrid TEI+RDF representation with standoff annotation of TEI documents in RDF, or (3) representing RDF triples in TEI/XML. As for (1), the reversible conversion of TEI/XML to RDF requires extremely verbose RDF: Especially information about the sequential structure of documents needs to be made explicit, whereas it is inherent (and implicit) to XML and TEI data structures. As for (2), a hybrid representation of TEI edition data and RDF data describing it would be more efficient. This could be either based on TEI pointer URIs or Web Annotation XPath selectors (Sect. 5.2). The practical problem with such a representation is its maintenance, as updates need to be synchronized in both datasets, and thus this can only be recommended for the annotation of static TEI/XML documents. We thus focus on strategy (3), the integration of LOD references and RDF triples in inline TEI/XML documents.

taxonomies, classification schemes and subject heading lists. It was published as a W3C recommendation in 2009.[6] A fundamental element of the SKOS vocabulary is a `concept`; a concept can be regarded as a unit of thought, as an idea, meaning or category. As such, concepts exist in the mind as abstract entities which are independent of the terms used to label them.

In order to illustrate the SKOS vocabulary, we follow a running example from the SKOS Primer. The following RDF code in Turtle says that the category of animals is a concept and that it is verbalized in natural language via the preferred term *'animals'*:

```
1  ex:animals rdf:type skos:Concept;
2    skos:prefLabel "animals".
```

In addition, we can also add preferred verbalizations for different languages by including language tags:

```
1  ex:animals rdf:type skos:Concept;
2    skos:prefLabel "animals"@en;
3    skos:prefLabel "animaux"@fr.
```

SKOS also allows one to specify semantic relationships between concepts, in particular narrower and broader relationships, e.g. to indicate that the concept *animals* has a more narrower concepts *mammals*. This is described in RDF using the SKOS vocabulary as follows:

```
1  ex:animals rdf:type skos:Concept;
2    skos:prefLabel "animals"@en;
3    skos:narrower ex:mammals.
4  ex:mammals rdf:type skos:Concept;
5    skos:prefLabel "mammals"@en;
6    skos:broader ex:animals.
```

Besides narrower/broader relationships, in SKOS we can also define associative relationships, in order to state that the concept of `birds` is related to the field of `ornithology`. This would be expressed in RDF as follows:

```
1  ex:birds rdf:type skos:Concept;
2    skos:prefLabel 'birds'@en;
3    skos:related ex:ornithology.
4  ex:ornithology rdf:type skos:Concept;
5    skos:prefLabel 'ornithology'@en.
```

This short exposition of SKOS will suffice of the purposes here. For more details, the reader is referred to the SKOS primer as well as to more recent publications [20].

The use of SKOS is not restricted to DH, albeit it builds on a long-standing interest in knowledge organization systems particularly found among digital librarians

---

[6]https://www.w3.org/TR/skos-primer/, accessed 10-07-2019.

[21, 22]. Its continuing popularity in the DH may be partially due to the improved support for multilinguality, which vocabulary elements such as `skos:prefLabel` and the SKOS eXtension for Labels [23] provide. Another important factor may be that it avoids the entry barrier of full-fledged ontology languages such as OWL, as SKOS neither enforces strict types nor supports axiomatization.

Typical examples of SKOS application in DH include terminology integration over distributed data collections, in particular in the infrastructural basis of international and European networks that emerged in the last decades [24, 25]. Beyond that, a large number of individual applications of SKOS can be found, including the application of SKOS to the harmonization of TEI-encoded dictionaries [26], the integration of historical and multimodal data by means of SKOS and semantic technologies [27] and the joint application of SKOS and CIDOC-CRM to the modelling of domain-specific concepts in archaeology [28], etc.

13.2.3   CIDOC Vocabulary for Describing Object Metadata

A prominent metadata vocabulary in the GLAM (galleries, libraries, archives and museums) sector is the CIDOC CRM vocabulary. The International Committee for Documentation (CIDOC, French *Comité International pour la Documentation*)[7] of the International Council of Museums (ICOM)[8] is dedicated to the documentation of museum collections. The committee has been conducting annual conferences since 1991 and brings together curators, librarians, information scientists and scholars interested in digital documentation, registration and collection management. A key result of this work is the CIDOC Conceptual Reference Model (CIDOC CRM), a data model for museum information, originally building on an entity-relationship approach, but subsequently shifting to object-oriented modelling, and since 2012 also towards Linked Open Data and Semantic Web formalisms [29].

CIDOC CRM provides an ontology for concepts and information in the museum domain, in particular. It is an ISO standard for the exchange and integration of heterogeneous scientific documentation relating to museum collections and other cultural heritage information, e.g. from libraries and archives [30]. Work on the CRM began in 1996 under the auspices of the ICOM-CIDOC Documentation Standards Working Group. A designated CIDOC CRM Special Interest Group has been created in 2000. In 2006, the standardization process of CIDOC CRM lead to an ISO standard [30], which was subsequently revised [31]. As of CIDOC CRM 5.0.4 [32], which represents the basis for [31] and is thus the latest 'official' release, the CRM is also published as RDF(S).[9]

---

[7]http://network.icom.museum/cidoc/, accessed 10-07-2019.

[8]http://icom.museum/, accessed 10-07-2019.

[9]http://www.cidoc-crm.org/get-last-official-release, accessed 10-07-2019.

CIDOC CRM is designed as an object-oriented, language-independent data model. Concepts are thus identified by numerical identifiers rather than human-readable labels, and the existing RDF editions combine this pattern with a human-readable English label to form URIs. As such, the top-level concept of CIDOC CRM is E1 CRM Entity, resp., the URI http://www.cidoc-crm.org/cidoc-crm/E1_CRM_Entity, or crm:E1_CRM_Entity.[10]

Selected upper-level classes of the CRM include:

- E2_Temporal_Entity including conditions, states and events ('perdurants'), many of which can be expressed as semantic predicates
- E52_Time_Span to represent the temporal extent (begin, end, duration) of temporal entities
- E53_Place to represent the spatial extent (location) of immobile objects, e.g. settlements, buildings or mountains
- E54_Dimension to represent quantifiable properties in their respective measurements, e.g. colour values in RGB
- E77_Persistent_Item to represent entities with a persistent identity ('endurants'), e.g. people, man-made objects, physical things, but also linguistic objects such as inscriptions

By design, CIDOC CRM is an abstract data model and not tied to a specific serialization. An early RDF/OWL edition going by the name of Erlangen CRM[11] has been developed at the Friedrich-Alexander-University of Erlangen-Nürnberg, Germany, in cooperation with the Germanisches Nationalmuseum at Nürnberg and the Zoologisches Forschungsmuseum Alexander König in Bonn [33], and continues to be used in the WissKi information system [34]. In order to avoid confusion with the official CIDOC CRM edition, the prefix ecrm should be used for the Erlangen CRM namespace under http://erlangen-crm.org/current/, but the prefix crm is exclusively used for http://www.cidoc-crm.org/cidoc-crm/.

More recent applications of CIDOC CRM, however, normally employ the authoritative RDF(S) edition provided by CIDOC that partially superseded Erlangen CRM in 2011. An important difference is that CIDOC CRM provides an RDFS ontology only, whereas Erlangen CRM provides a more rigidly formalized OWL view. For applications that *require* OWL/DL axiomatization, Erlangen CRM continues to be practically relevant, although the current focus of practical application of CIDOC CRM in DH seems to be on linking data and resource integration rather than reasoning. As examples of practical application of CIDOC CRM, consider the

---

[10]Until 1994, CRM classes were defined as 'entities' in the CIDOC Relational Model, hence the initial E. Analogously, properties are prefixed with P.

[11]http://erlangen-crm.org/, accessed 10-07-2019.

SPARQL end points of the Archaeology Data Service (ADS),[12] or the Yale Center for British Art.[13]

Taking the ADS data as an example, the following SPARQL query retrieves the (URIs for the) documentation about archaeological sites within the parish of Amesbury (well-known for the Stonehenge monument):

```
1  PREFIX ecrm: <http://erlangen-crm.org/101001/>
2  PREFIX rdfs: <http://www.w3.org/2000/01/rdf-schema#>
3  SELECT ?siteName ?document
4  WHERE {
5    ?site a ecrm:E53_Place;
6          ecrm:P88i_forms_part_of*/rdfs:label "Amesbury"@en.
7    ?site ecrm:P70i_is_documented_in ?document.
8    ?site ecrm:P87_is_identified_by/rdfs:label ?siteName.
9  }
```

In DH, object metadata can have some overlap with language metadata, text data and annotations, e.g. if texts are considered objects or complemented with information about the medium or artefact they have been conveyed by.

13.2.4   The Canonical Text Service Protocol (CTS)

With its roots in library science, RDF has been applied for bibliography since its very beginnings, and major portals, e.g. the German National Library (*Deutsche Nationalbibliothek*), are providing their data in RDF. However, the needs of digital humanists, and of computational philologists in particular, go beyond the identification of texts, documents and publications in that standardized references to text *passages* are required. One important area of research in computational philology includes the creation of critical editions where multiple witnesses of a text (e.g. manuscripts) are to be aligned with each other. Related research challenges include the study of intertextuality, where the composition of a text is traced back to possible source documents, as well as stemmatology, where a family of manuscripts of a particular text are organized in terms of their mutual dependencies and influences. All of these problems require an alignment of text passages *across multiple documents*. One strategy of doing so is by providing canonical identifiers that provide a unique identifier to corresponding text passages—regardless of the exact formulation of the particular passage in a specific text witness. As an example, consider the following excerpts from different versions of the Bible in English (selected differences highlighted):

---

[12]http://data.archaeologydataservice.ac.uk/query/, accessed 10-07-2019.

[13]https://britishart.yale.edu/collections/using-collections/technology/linked-open-data,   accessed 10-07-2019.

1. *In the beginning God created <u>the</u> heaven<u>s</u> and <u>the</u> earth.* (Darby, American Standard Version, World English Bible, etc.)
2. *In the beginning God created <u>the</u> heaven and <u>the</u> earth.* (Webster, King James Version)
3. *In the beginning God created heaven, and earth.* (Douay Rheims)
4. *In the beginning <u>of</u> God's preparing the heaven<u>s</u> and <u>the</u> earth* (Young's Literal Translation)

Although different in their exact formulation, all of these can be identified by reference to the first verse of the Genesis. Using a reference edition of this text, i.e. its canonical version, as a basis (say, the Greek New Testament or the Latin Vulgate), this reference can be defined in relation to an existing text. Where no such reference edition exists (e.g. if the reference edition is reconstructed from various sources), a canonical text reference can also be defined in an abstract way, i.e. independent from any particular edition. To address such 'scholarly primitives', domain-specific vocabularies have been developed in computational philology— partially overlapping in design and intent with existing URI schemes, but developed and maintained by a different community.

The Canonical Text Service protocol [35, 36] represents a minimal protocol to address and retrieve scholarly primitives by means of the CTS URN scheme. The CTS protocol was originally developed in the context of the Homer Multitext project [37] that aimed to provide an electronic edition of Iliad and Odyssey and their intertextual relations in the historical and literary path of their transmission.

CTS URNs are valid URIs, but not directly resolvable via HTTP. Thus, CTS URNs do not constitute Linked Open Data per se, but they can be re-used in different LOD resources for the humanities, e.g. to identify a particular Bible passage for different resources and studies from areas so diverse as theology, linguistics and literary studies. The CTS protocol aims to be agnostic with respect to the underlying technologies and materials, but also with respect to the internal structures and citation schemes of cited resources. Instead, CTS assumes that texts and text collections involve both a sequential and a hierarchical organization and uses this to address units of text in a scalable and generic fashion at any level. The Ordered Hierarchy of Citation Objects [38] defines citation values as nodes in a hierarchical structure, which can thus be used for navigation.

The CTS provides specifications for resolving CTS URNs using, e.g., the HTTP protocol, and in particular, HTTP-resolvable *CTS request URLs*. This is illustrated here using the Canonical Text Service maintained at the Institute for Computer Science at Leipzig University, Germany,[14] The base name of the CTS service is

```
http://cts.informatik.uni-leipzig.de/pbc/cts/
```

A CTS request includes the URL parameter `request` with one of seven parameters: `GetCapabilities`, `GetValidReff`, `GetFirstUrn`,

---

[14]http://cts.informatik.uni-leipzig.de/Canonical_Text_Service.html, accessed 10-07-2019.

`GetPrevNextUrn`, `GetLabel`, `GetPassage` or `GetPassagePlus`. In combination, these parameters allow for flexible navigation in both collection and document hierarchies:

```
http://cts.informatik.uni-leipzig.de/pbc/cts/?request=
   GetCapabilities
```

This URL provides documentation in XML, including text group URNs. From these, we may pick the King James Version and subsequently explore it, e.g. using the `GetFirstUrn` requests:

```
http://cts.informatik.uni-leipzig.de/pbc/cts/?request=GetFirstUrn
   &urn=urn:cts:pbc:bible.parallel.eng.kingjames:
```

This request yields the URN `urn:cts:pbc:bible.parallel.eng.kingjames:1` (Genesis), and further requests lead to `urn:cts:pbc:bible.parallel.eng.kingjames:1.1` (first chapter) and `urn:cts:pbc:bible.parallel.eng.kingjames:1.1.1` (first verse). A `GetLabel` request can be used to return a human-readable label describing a text or text passage 'semantically comparable to the use of `rdfs:label`' [36]:

```
http://cts.informatik.uni-leipzig.de/pbc/cts/?request=GetLabel&
   urn=urn:cts:pbc:bible.parallel.eng.kingjames:1.1.1
```

This URL returns

```
1  <?xml version="1.0" encoding="UTF-8"?>
2  <GetLabel>
3  <request>...</request>
4  <reply>
5  <label>King James Version of the Christian Bible,
6          book "1", chapter "1", sentence "1"</label>
7  <license>Public Domain</license>
8  <source>Retrieved via Canonical Text Service
9          http://cts.informatik.uni-leipzig.de/pbc/cts/
10         with CTS URN
11         urn:cts:pbc:bible.parallel.eng.kingjames:1.1.1
12 </source>
13 </reply>
14 </GetLabel>
```

An analogous `GetPassage` request retrieves a passage of a text identified by the provided URN:

```
1  <GetPassage>
2  <request>...</request>
3  <reply>
4  <urn>urn:cts:pbc:bible.parallel.eng.kingjames:1.1.1
5  </urn>
6  <passage>In the beginning God created the heaven
```

```
 7          and the earth.</passage>
 8  <license>Public Domain</license>
 9  <source>...</source>
10  </reply>
11  </GetPassage>
```

The CTS has been designed to be agnostic with respect to the underlying database technology. However, it was originally foreseen to be used in the context of TEI documents [35, 39], and thus places focus on XML technologies. For instance, it is required that '[t]he reply to a valid CTS request is always a well-formed XML document with a root element having the same name as the CTS request', and further, that it must be 'validating against one of the schemas identified below', and that 'the XML namespace for all replies is http://chs.harvard.edu/xmlns/cts/' [36]. Thus, CTS URIs are currently not designed to return RDF data. In particular, they are not designed to support RDF/XML. However, adding a content negotiation component and implementing it by means of an XSLT script would be a minor extension to the current architecture and a technologically feasible extension. Nevertheless, CTS URIs can be used as shared identifiers in philological LOD resources and are recommended as such in DH [40].

At the time of writing, a linked data compliant successor specification to CTS is under development, the Distributed Text Services [41, DTS]. The interested reader is strongly encouraged to follow up to the progress of this enterprise, as it is expected to supersede CTS in the immediate future.

13.3 Case Studies and Applications of LLOD in Digital Humanities

Applications of Linked Open Data technologies and resources in Digital Humanities are manifold, and where commonly used LLOD and RDF technology is employed,[15] the scientific challenges involved are comparable to those in other areas of application. A problem specific to Digital Humanities is, however, how these technologies can be related to the current de facto standard for computational philology, the specifications of the TEI. In the remainder of this section, we describe five applications of LLOD in the field of Digital Humanities in more detail, highlighting in particular the benefit of applying LLOD principles. On the one hand, in Sect. 13.3.1 we discuss how LLOD methods and vocabularies can be used in prosopography. In Sect. 13.3.2 we discuss how to use LLOD techniques to reference geographical information, in particular related to ancient locations.

---

[15]This includes, e.g., Web Annotation in Pleiades/Pelagios (Sect. 13.3.2), CoNLL-RDF/NIF for creating and linking linguistically annotated corpora of historical languages [42, 43] (cf. Sect. 6.2.1), POWLA for merging and enriching such corpora [43, 44] (cf. Sect. 6.3) or Ontolex-lemon for digital dictionaries [13, 45], cf. Chap. 4.

In Sects. 13.3.3, 13.3.4 and 13.3.5, we describe three representative projects with philological background, and the strategies they employ to harmonize linked data technology and TEI/XML.

13.3.1 Applying LLOD Methods in Prosopography

Prosopography is the systematic study of a certain group of individuals, their relations with each other, including social or cultural dynamics involved in their interaction, often in historical and sociological, but also theological or cultural, studies. On a methodological level, prosopography touches topics such as network analysis and graph theory, knowledge base creation and maintenance, named entity recognition and entity linking. These are application areas in which LOD formalisms and methods have been intensively used outside of Digital Humanities. A key resource for prosopographical studies is thus a knowledge base with individual, biographical profiles. These can include actual biographical information (if the full biography is known) or references to attestations of an individual (if the biography is still to be reconstructed from, say, textual evidence).

One such example is the *Deutsche Biographie* (NDB, 'German Biography'),[16] a service jointly managed by the Bavarian Academy of Sciences and the Bayerische Staatsbibliothek. As an information system aiming to provide authoritative information about deceased individuals of political, economic, social, scientific or cultural relevance, it provides original contributions (signed by experts by name) along with an access to various bibliographical encyclopedias from the German-speaking world. Covering more than 730,000 biographies,[17] it is considered the single most relevant biographic encyclopedia of the German-speaking area, and represents a fundamental backbone of biographical information for cultural and historical studies in this context. Thus, it provides a reference point for cross-links with resources and databases provided by the German Federal Archives, the German Literature Archive in Marbach, the Germanisches Nationalmuseum (Germanic National Museum), the Bildarchiv Foto Marburg (documentation centre for art history) or the Deutsches Rundfunkarchiv (German Broadcasting Archive, providing broadcasts of the 1920s and 1930s) [46].

Figure 13.1 illustrates the human-readable interface to the Deutsche Biographie for the example of Walther von der Vogelweide, a medieval poet. The RDF link on the left points to an RDF/XML view on the available *structured data* (Fig. 13.2).[18]

The crucial benefit of a LOD representation of the structured data retrievable from the Deutsche Biographie is that globally referenceable URIs are provided (so that external services can refer to this entry), along with (`rdfs:seeAlso`)

---

[16]https://www.deutsche-biographie.de/ueber?language=en, accessed 10-07-2019.

[17]As of November 2016, http://www.ndb.badw-muenchen.de/index_e.htm.

[18]For documentation of the RDF data see http://data.deutsche-biographie.de/about/.

Walther von der Vogelweide

Fig. 13.1 View on Prosopographical data from the Deutsche Biographie; example of Walther von der Vogelweide

```
1   <rdf:RDF
2      xmlns:rdf="http://www.w3.org/1999/02/22-rdf-syntax-ns#"
3      xmlns:rdfs="http://www.w3.org/2000/01/rdf-schema#"
4      xmlns:rdaGr2="http://RDVocab.info/ElementsGr2/"
5      xmlns:gnd="http://d-nb.info/standards/elementset/gnd#"
6      xmlns:ndb="http://data.deutsche-biographie.de/"
7      xmlns:ndbvoc="http://data.deutsche-biographie.de/vocabulary/"
8      xmlns:dc="http://purl.org/dc/elements/1.1/"
9      xml:base="http://data.deutsche-biographie.de/">
10     <rdf:Description rdf:about="http://data.deutsche-biographie.
          de/Person/sfz84442">
11        <rdf:type rdf:resource="http://data.deutsche-biographie.
             de/vocabulary/Person"/>
12        <rdfs:seeAlso rdf:resource="http://d-nb.info/gnd
             /118628976"/>
13        <ndbvoc:page>http://www.deutsche-biographie.de/sfz84442.
             html</ndbvoc:page>
14        <gnd:gender rdf:resource="http://d-nb.info/standards/
             vocab/gnd/Gender#male"/>
15        <ndbvoc:gender rdf:resource="http://data.deutsche-
             biographie.de/vocabulary/Male"/>
16        <rdfs:label>Walther von der Vogelweide</rdfs:label>
17        <gnd:professionOrOccupation>Minnesänger</gnd:
             professionOrOccupation>
18        <rdaGr2:dateOfDeath>1. Hälfte 13. Jahrhundert</rdaGr2:
             dateOfDeath>
19        <dc:creator>Deutsche Biographie</dc:creator>
20        <dc:publisher>Historische Kommission München</dc:
             publisher>
21        <dc:date>2016-12-06</dc:date>
22        <dc:license rdf:resource="http://creativecommons.org/
             licenses/by/4.0/"/>
23     </rdf:Description>
24  </rdf:RDF>
```

Fig. 13.2 Data in RDF/XML from the entry for Walther von der Vogelweide

references to external knowledge bases, e.g. the German National Library in this example. This allows to integrate information from other providers. The link to the German National Library (http://d-nb.info/gnd/118628976) also yields an RDF view on Walther, his compositions, but also provides more precise information on birth and death dates, information about language (Middle High German), etc.

It is now possible to systematically and straightforwardly extract information from one data source to complement another data source. For example, both the German National Library and Deutsche Biographie are providing static RDF access to their data via https://data.dnb.de/opendata/, resp., http://data.deutsche-biographie.de/about/. With a local RDF database in place, data dumps from both sides can be loaded in two different graphs, say, https://data.dnb.de and http://data.deutsche-biographie.de. This can be accomplished by the following nested SPARQL query that allows to integrate information from the German National Library into the Deutsche Biographie dataset by copying dates and language codes:

```
1  PREFIX gndo: <http://d-nb.info/standards/elementset/gnd#>
2  PREFIX rdfs: <http://www.w3.org/2000/01/rdf-schema#>
3
4  INSERT {
5          GRAPH <http://data.deutsche-biographie.de> {
6                  ?a gndo:languageCode ?language.
7                  ?a gndo:dateOfBirth   ?birth.
8                  ?a gndo:dateOfDeath   ?death.
9          }
10 WHERE {
11         GRAPH <http://data.deutsche-biographie.de> {
12                 ?entry rdfs:seeAlso ?a.
13         }
14         GRAPH <https://data.dnb.de>
15                 ?a gndo:languageCode ?language.
16                 OPTIONAL { ?a gndo:dateOfBirth  ?birth. }
17                 OPTIONAL { ?a gndo:dateOfDeath  ?death. }
18         }
19 }
```

The RDF data now can be used, e.g., to retrieve and to visualize relations (i.e. the shortest link) between two people in the dataset. An RDF-based application with this functionality is the RelFinder [47], and a prototype at the Deutsche Biography has been set up under http://data.deutsche-biographie.de/beta/relfinder/RelFinder.swf. An example for NDB connections between Erich Ludendorff, a German WWI general, and Adolf Hitler is given in Fig. 13.3.

13.3.2 Using LLOD Techniques to Reference Geographical Information

Another area with wide application of LOD technologies in DH is Linked Geo Data. In addition to geographical datasets being already available from the LOD

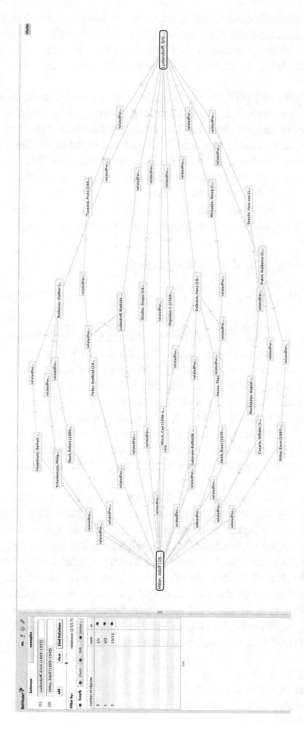

Fig. 13.3 Finding and visualizing relations within the Deutsche Biographie

cloud (e.g. GeoNames[19]), domain-specific gazetteers had to be developed in digital humanities to address the historical depth of place names, but also the special needs of researchers in history or archaeology. Places have been referred to with different names at different times, and many have been abandoned and are thus absent from modern maps.

The Pleiades project [48][20] provides a gazetteer for the ancient world. In its simplest form, a gazetteer is a plain list of place names, nowadays mostly with coordinates and other relevant information, e.g. cross-references to other resources and entities associated with these places. As a hub of Linked Open Geo Data in the DH, Pleiades provides stable URIs and serializations in Atom, HTML, JSON, KML and RDF for currently 35,384 places from the Ancient World, i.e. mostly, Graeco-Roman antiquity. RDF data in Turtle format for all places, errata, authors, place types and time periods is available from https://pleiades.stoa.org/downloads and documented under https://github.com/isawnyu/pleiades-rdf, covering the following types of subjects:

- Ancient World Places (real past world entities)
- Authors
- Places, Names, Locations
- Concepts

As an example, Fig. 13.4 illustrates the Pleiades entry for Uruk/Warka, an ancient Mesopotamian city, see the corresponding RDF document in Fig. 13.5.

The Pleiades gazetteer is widely interlinked with other resources and serves as a point of reference for external datasets. The Pelagios consortium[21] [49] creates annotations of historic documents with references to places building on Pleiades. Pelagios builds on Web Annotation (Sect. 5.2) and Pleiades URIs to link references to ancient places. This permits information integration between resource sets. Pelagios does not provide a centralized infrastructure, but it features tools to create annotations and offers hosting services for datasets, which, by default, should be available under a CC0 license.

One exemplary tool is Recogito [50], a geo-annotation tool for annotating geographic concepts in Web documents. Recogito is an online platform that provides a personal workspace to manage texts and images, and to collaborate in their annotation. As user orientation is essential in Digital Humanities, Recogito does not expose RDF data to its users, but merely requires understanding and appropriate application of URIs to identify place names in the underlying gazetteer. Given a source text or image, the user can highlight a section and assign it a URI—which internally will be wrapped into an Open Annotation declaration, assigned default datatypes, stored as RDF and published as Linked Open Data. Automatizing this process on textual data is technically identical to entity linking.

---

[19]https://www.geonames.org/, accessed 10-07-2019.
[20]http://pleiades.stoa.org, accessed 10-07-2019.
[21]http://pelagios-project.blogspot.co.uk.

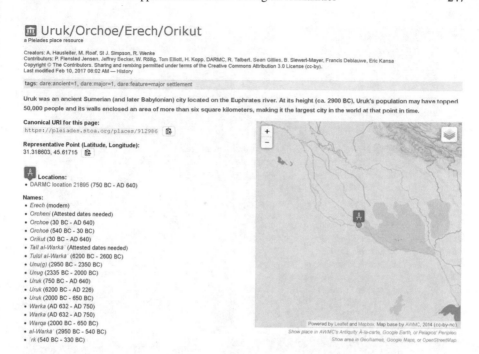

Fig. 13.4 HTML view on Uruk/Warka from the Pleiades project

As of March 2018, Recogito also supports TEI/XML as a format for documents to which Pleiades annotations can be applied, it is thus representative for the combination of Web Annotation and TEI. However, this approach is limited to static TEI documents, i.e. geonames annotations can only be applied to an existing edition, but not created along with the edition itself. At the moment, this functionality can only be achieved with an integrated representation of RDF triples in inline TEI/XML.

13.3.3   Constructing a Database and Dictionary of Maya Hieroglyphic Writing

The project 'Text Database and Dictionary of Classic Mayan' (TWKM, University of Bonn, Germany, 2014–2029) is a long-term project aiming to develop a corpus-based dictionary of Maya hieroglyphic writing. One specific challenge is that Maya writing is not fully deciphered yet, and so different hypotheses for the interpretation of characters need to be represented and re-assessed as part of dictionary development. By developing a near-exhaustive corpus of Maya hieroglyphic writing, the project aims to verify different reading hypotheses on an empirical basis and thus provide a basis for completing the decipherment of Maya writing. The task involves a number of specific challenges:

```
1   PREFIX place: <https://pleiades.stoa.org/places/>
2   PREFIX type: <https://pleiades.stoa.org/vocabularies/place-types/
      >
3   PREFIX time: <https://pleiades.stoa.org/vocabularies/time-periods
      />
4   PREFIX skos: <http://www.w3.org/2004/02/skos/core#>
5   PREFIX vocab: <https://pleiades.stoa.org/places/vocab#>
6   PREFIX author: <https://pleiades.stoa.org/author/>
7
8   places:912986 a skos:Concept, vocab:Place;
9     dcterms:bibliographicCitation "Finkbeiner 1993 ",
10      "Oppenheimer 1983 334-40";
11    dcterms:coverage "Warka IRQ";
12    dcterms:description "Uruk was an ancient Sumerian
13      (and later Babylonian) city located on ...";
14    dcterms:title "Uruk/Orchoe/Erech/Orikut";
15    geo:lat 31.318603; geo:long 45.61715;
16    skos:inScheme <https://pleiades.stoa.org/places>;
17    pleiades:hasFeatureType type:settlement, type:urban;
18    pleiades:hasLocation place:912986/darmc-location-21895;
19    pleiades:hasName place:912986/erech, place:912986/orchoe,
20      place:912986/orikut, place:unug, place:912986/uruk>,
21      place:912986/uruk-1. # etc.
22
23  place:uruk-1 a vocab:Name;
24      dcterms:contributor author:ekansa, author:fdeblauwe;
25      dcterms:description "A place name from the TAVO Index
26        (Vol. 3, p. 1744)";
27      dcterms:title "Uruk";
28      prov:wasDerivedFrom [ rdfs:label "TAVO Index" ];
29      pleiades:during time:early-dynastic-mesopotamia,
30        time:ubaid-early-dynastic-ii-mesopotamia;  # etc.
31      pleiades:end_date 226;
32      pleiades:nameRomanized "Uruk";
33      pleiades:start_date -6200 .
```

Fig. 13.5 RDF excerpt in Turtle syntax for the entry for Uruk/Warka (see Fig. 13.4)

- The same sign may have a great band-width of possible forms, and existing sign catalogues may either group these variants together or distinguish them. The identity of a sign (type) can thus only be defined by reference against a particular catalogue of signs. In order to reflect the state of the art, the project's sign catalogue needs to be linked with other sign catalogues developed in the field.
- The sign catalogue must not be considered as a plain list that provides one or more readings for a particular sign (type). Instead, it must be capable of representing different reading hypotheses—together with their provenance and associated metadata.

Both requirements are addressed by means of a sign catalogue formalized in SKOS/RDF. Based on top-level properties and concepts from CIDOC-CRM and GOLD (Sect. 8.3.2), the project develops a vocabulary for identifying signs, their

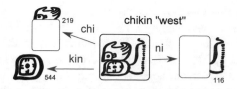

```
1  <ab xml:id="n2" type="glyph-block">
2     <seg xml:id="n2S2" type="glyph-group" rend="left_beside"
          corresp="#n2G3">
3        <g xml:id="n2G1" n="219st" ref="textgrid:30gnx.0" rend="
             above" corresp="#n2G2"/>
4        <g xml:id="n2G2" n="544st" ref="textgrid:2skxk.0" rend="
             beneath" corresp="#n2G1"/>
5     </seg>
6     <g xml:id="n2G3" n="116st" ref="textgrid:34rkg.0" rend="
          right_beside" corresp="#n2S2"/>
7  </ab>
```

Fig. 13.6 Sample glyph and TEI rendering of a glyph block *chikin* taken from [52, p. 269]. Reference images of the glyphs T219, T544 and T116 inspired by the Thompson catalogue [54]

links to different sign catalogues, possible readings, graphical variants, etc. At the time of writing, neither the sign catalogue nor any texts are publicly available; for their description, we follow Diehr et al. [51].

The actual corpus data is provided in TEI/XML, see Fig. 13.6. Maya hieroglyphs are organized in rectangular glyph blocks, illustrated here for the word *chikin* 'west', and represented in TEI as 'anonymous block' (<ab>). The sequence of glyph blocks within a text is normally left-to-right and top-to-bottom, but they can also be organized in columns. The internal organization of glyph blocks, however, is highly complex. Often, a glyph block is organized around a main sign (often an ideogram), and left, above, beneath or right of the main sign, additional signs ('affixes', often logograms) can be placed. In more complicated cases, a sign may be inserted into or visually blended with its main sign rather than affixed. Moreover, a glyph block may also consist of more than one main sign (plus their respective affixes), and, alternatively, the main sign can by itself be composed of logograms.

TWKM thus uses TEI <seg> ('arbitrary segment') to organize individual glyphs (TEI <g>). Within and between segments, the reading order is normally left-to-right and top-to-bottom, and the relative placement to each other is represented by @rend (URI of reference point) and @corresp (placement relation between glyph/segment and reference point). The element @n (TEI 'number or label') is used to provide a human-readable representation of the corresponding entry in the sign catalogue. Here, the glyph block is composed of the sign types 219, 544 and 116 according to [54], and their reference visualization (as upper affix for T219, as right affix for T116 and as main sign for T544) are provided in Fig. 13.6. While this illustrates the entry in the sign catalogue, the actual link to the sign catalogue is represented by a TEI pointer in @ref.[22]

Using @ref (or other TEI pointer structures), it is thus possible to make reference to arbitrary URIs and (L)LOD resources in order to integrate both sources of information in downstream applications, e.g. an application for the integrated browsing of and search over Maya corpus and dictionary. While the target of such a link *must* be represented by a URI, this is optional for its source (@xml:id). A major drawback of this solution is, however, that it is not possible to provide a formal definition of the type of relation.[23] In the context of TWKM, such a feature could be useful for expressing reading (i.e. sign identification) hypotheses for glyphs that have been partially destroyed or whose reading is uncertain for other reasons— and with typed links, they could be represented together with their confidence and provenance. To represent such information (and essentially, full RDF triples) in TEI, other projects make use of TEI elements such as <relation> (Sect. 13.3.4) or <link> (cf. Sect. 5.1.2). All of these can be used to express full triples with native TEI vocabulary, albeit they conflate this functionality with other, unrelated uses and are thus semantically ambiguous.

13.3.4   Facilitating the Study of Ancient Wisdom Literature

The project *Sharing Ancient Wisdoms (SAWS)*[24] (2010–2013) was a joint project at King's College London, UK, the Newman Institute in Uppsala, Sweden, and the University of Vienna, Austria, funded in the context of the Humanities in the European Research Area (HERA) program to facilitate the study and electronic edition of ancient wisdom literature. On the one hand, this task involved the development of electronic editions and edition principles for a wide and rich genre. On the other hand, this genre is characterized by the reflection and philosophical discussion of opinions expressed by earlier authors, so that an additional challenge was to express the links between different texts and their underlying concepts. SAWS combined three existing technologies: TEI and XML for editing the text, Erlangen CRM and OWL for modelling data structures and relations, and CTS-based URLs for expressing cross-references between docu-

---

[22]TWKM builds on the Textgrid Laboratory [53] for data hosting, https://de.dariah.eu/textgridlab, accessed 10-07-2019. With the prefix textgrid and the namespace https://textgridlab.org/1.0/iiif/mirador/?uri=textgrid:, the @ref URIs will resolve as soon as the sign catalogue is being published. The example in Fig. 13.6 thus uses placeholder URIs.

[23]TEI P5 defines g/@ref in a relatively constrained way as an optional TEI pointer/URI that 'points to a description of the character or glyph intended'. The otherwise available @ref attribute defined in TEI att.canonical, is, however, less constrained: a sequence of TEI pointers/URIs that 'provides an explicit means of locating a full definition or identity'. Here, type identity and token identity (as well as other means of providing a definition of an element) are being conflated.

[24]http://www.ancientwisdoms.ac.uk/, accessed 10-07-2019.

ments. The SAWS ontology[25] defines agents, organizations and roles involved
in the creation or transmission of a manuscript. In addition, it defines structural
elements within documents that can be addressed by a CTS URI. As an example,
a `saws:Edition` is thus an `ecrm:E33_Linguistic_Object` that represents edited material, e.g. a specific electronic text, a `saws:ContentItem`
is an `ecrm:F23_Expression_Fragment` that identifies a minimal unit of
interest within the material, corresponding to the TEI `<seg>` element, and a
`saws:Section` is an `ecrm:E33_Linguistic_Object` that serves to group
together content items or more fine-granular sections, e.g. chapters or verses. Within
an edition, the hierarchy of section elements, optionally followed by a content
item, defines CTS URNs. To improve compliance with LOD technology, SAWS
introduced CTS *URLs*. CTS URLs provide HTTP-resolvable URIs by incorporating
the CTS URN directly into the path:

```
1  urn:cts:greekLit:tlg3017.Syno298.sawsGrc01:divedition.
      divsection1.o14.a107
2  http://www.ancientwisdoms.ac.uk/cts/urn:cts:greekLit:tlg3017.
      Syno298.sawsGrc01:divedition.divsection1.o14.a107
```

The URN in line 1 is being transformed into the URL (HTTP URI) in line 2.
Internally, this URL is mapped to a CTS `GetPassage` request which contains
a redirect to an HTML viewer. While SAWS URLs do thus not provide RDF,
they provide unique reference points across different documents. To implement
cross-references between TEI-edited texts, SAWS encodes RDF triples between
CTS URLs and the SAWS ontology by use of TEI `<relation>`:

```
1  <relation
2    ref="http://purl.org/saws/ontology#isVariantOf"
3    active="http://www.ancientwisdoms.ac.uk/cts/urn:cts:greekLit:
        tlg3017.Syno298.sawsGrc01:divedition.divsection1.o14.a107"
4    passive="http://data.perseus.org/citations/urn:cts:greekLit:
        tlg0031.tlg002.perseus-grc1:9.35"/>
```

This fragment is a slightly simplified example taken from the TEI documentation.[26] Currently, this is the recommended way to represent RDF triples and
LOD references in the TEI, where the `@active` attribute represents the RDF
subject(s), the `@passive` attribute represents one or more RDF objects, and the
`@ref` attribute points to the RDF predicate(s). Note that each of the attributes can
contain more than one URI, so that this actually represents a triple set rather than a
triple.

---

[25]Prefix `saws`, namespace http://purl.org/saws/ontology#.

[26]The original example is found under http://www.tei-c.org/release/doc/tei-p5-doc/en/html/ref-
relation.html (accessed 10-07-2019), with the explanation that '[t]his example records a relationship, defined by the SAWS ontology, between a passage of text identified by a CTS URN, and a
variant passage of text in the Perseus Digital Library … (all using resolvable URIs).'

A conventional representation in Turtle would be:

```
1  PREFIX : <http://www.ancientwisdoms.ac.uk/cts/urn:cts:greekLit
       :tlg3017.Syno298.sawsGrc01:>
2  PREFIX saws: <http://purl.org/saws/ontology#>
3  PREFIX greeknt: <http://data.perseus.org/citations/urn:cts:
       greekLit:tlg0031.tlg002.perseus-grc>
4  :divedition.divsection1.o14.a107 saws:isVariantOf greeknt
       :1:9.35.
```

While this approach has the benefit of building on existing TEI vocabulary, as a representation format for RDF triples, it poses a number of challenges:

- The naming conventions of the arguments are semantically intransparent in this use case, and the interpretation of these terms in terms of RDF subject and object is not documented in the TEI documentation (but must be inferred from the examples). This is a likely source of errors.
- All attributes are optional, so that not every relation element can be interpreted as a triple, and even if all three attributes are used, this does not mean that an interpretation as an RDF triple (set) is intended.[27] A possible RDF interpretation of a `relation` with missing @active (or @passive) attribute would be that this resolves to the parent element, but such an interpretation has not been documented.
- RDF triples represented in this way cannot be extracted with off-the-shelf RDF technology, but require relatively complex validation and conversion routines. This is a side-effect of the semantic richness of TEI/XML:

    - All attributes can be iterated. In order to arrive at a more conventional RDF rendering, all possible combinations of @active, @passive and @ref need to be generated.
    - TEI pointers can be abbreviated URIs. This is similar to Turtle, but TEI uses an elaborate and proprietary formalism to define URI prefixes as part of the TEI header: The `<prefixDef>` element allows to use regular expressions and complex string replacement operations as part of the prefix declaration. Likewise, relative URIs are feasible and must be resolved using @xml:base.[28]

In fact, using `<relation>` to represent URIs for entities other than named entities (persons, names, organizations, events, places or relations between such elements) violates TEI syntax.[29] The SAWS use case—even though referred to in

---

[27] According to other examples given for TEI `<relation>`, the original use case seems to have been to represent social networks, with @active and @passive arguments formalizing hierarchical relations, and the attribute @mutual representing symmetric relations.

[28] http://www.tei-c.org/release/doc/tei-p5-doc/de/html/ref-prefixDef.html, accessed 10-07-2019.

[29] TEI P5 restricts the use of `<relation>` to `<listEvent>`, `<listNym>` (canonical names), `<listOrg>`, `<listPerson>`, `<listPlace>`, and `<listRelation>` (relationships identified amongst people, places, and organizations).

the TEI guidelines—required to adjust the schema by extending the list of possible parent nodes of <relation> with <ab> (anonymous block, i.e. any character span) and <seg> (arbitrary segment), thereby enabling the unrestricted use of <relation>.[30] These extensions, even though well motivated by the SAWS use case, have not been taken over into the TEI guidelines, because it would not be clear how other, syntactically valid attributes of <relation> (especially @mutual) should be interpreted, and how the traditional semantics of @active and @passive—motivated from social networks—could be put into relation with RDF subject and RDF object in a more transparent way.

Given the extent and growing importance of LLOD in DH, we tend to discourage this downward-compatible representation, especially for DH projects that aim to provide (rather than to consume) linked data. While it is an effective application of existing vocabulary, an extension of the TEI vocabulary for the sole purpose of representing RDF triples and/or LOD references would be semantically more transparent. Indeed, this can be done on the basis of existing W3C recommendations, i.e. with full technical support by existing RDF technology, by means of RDFa.

13.3.5 Encoding Chauliac's *Grande Chirurgie* with TEI and RDFa

Gui de Chauliac is one of the most widely known physicians and medical authors of the French Middle Ages. His main work, the Latin *Chirurgia magna* from 1363 CE (*Grande Chirurgie* in its French translation), is considered the most profound compendium of the medical knowledge of its day. Within seven treatises, Gui de Chauliac describes the human anatomy, tumours and cancer, wounds and fractures, the plague, eye, ear, and dental pathology, etc. The *Grande Chirurgie* is of particular relevance for the history of the French language as well as for the history both of medicine and mentality. On the one hand, the Grande Chirurgie builds on accepted medical knowledge from the classical antiquity while at the same time attempting to put forth a modern understanding of the body, overcoming outdated explanatory models. As a medical treatise, the edition of the *Grande Chirurgie* requires grounding in a general (or medical) knowledge base. As a philological edition, it must include an interlinked glossary, and as a linguistic resource, its value and usability can be improved if links to a dictionary are added. The electronic edition of the text is thus both particularly challenging, but also particularly promising in a Linked Open Data context, as it can be based on existing resources such as DBpedia (as a preliminary reference for general medical knowledge), and Ontolex-lemon dictionaries such as the *Dictionnaire etymologique*

---

[30]http://www.ancientwisdoms.ac.uk/media/documents/Markup_Guidelines_for_Gnomologia. html#TEI.relation, accessed 10-07-2019.

de l'ancien francais [55, 56, DEAF].[31] In addition, the integrated glossary provides a source of internal links.

At the second Summer Datathon on Linguistic Linked Open Data (SD-LLOD 2017), it was thus chosen as a case study, and subsequently elaborated in collaboration between three projects: the research unit *Dictionnaire etymologique de l'ancien francais* (DEAF) of the Heidelberg Academy of Sciences, the research group *Linked Open Dictionaries* (LiODi, 2015–2020) at Goethe University Frankfurt and the Poetry Standardization and Linked Open Data group (POSTDATA, 2015–2020), an interdisciplinary initiative funded by the European Research Council aiming to create a digital platform for poetry edition based on linked data techniques. In a first step, a fragment of the print edition [57] was transformed into TEI. As very different types of data sources and relations are involved here and the lexical data it provides should be addressable from an electronic dictionary (*ad fontes*), the goal of this conversion was to produce an electronic edition that is compliant with both TEI and off-the-shelf RDF technology in a way that the edition data and its glossary could be directly addressed as Linked Open Data.

As this cannot be accomplished with TEI-specific vocabulary in an inline XML document, Tittel et al. [58] describe the application of RDFa (see Sect. 2.3.4) for this purpose. RDFa is designed to extend HTML and XML markup by including a pre-defined number of attributes into the vocabulary of the host language *within its own namespace.*

As a minimal TEI extension, Tittel et al. [58] added the attributes @about, @property and @resource to the attribute class att.global.linking:[32]

As such, the attribute @about identifies the current markup element as an RDF resource, e.g. the subject of an RDF triple; @property represents the predicate; and @resource the target of an object property, illustrated below for Middle French words, their glosses and their linking to the corresponding DEAF lemma:

```
1  <seg about="http://www.deaf-page.de/guichaul.html/#1"
2      property="rdfs:seeAlso"
3      resource="https://deaf-server.adw.uni-heidelberg.de/lemme
       /nom">
```

In the edition, each analysed segment (seg[@about]) contains an instance of a word with its gloss (<w> and <gloss>). In the listing, a TEI <seg> element (an arbitrary segment) is extended with the simple triple guichaul:1 rdfs:seeAlso deaf:nom. The (most recent) @about attribute also defines the subject for descendant predicates.

```
4  <w property="rdfs:label"
5      lemma="nom" type="m.">nom</w>
```

[31] https://deaf-server.adw.uni-heidelberg.de/, accessed 10-07-2019.

[32] http://www.tei-c.org/release/doc/tei-p5-doc/en/html/ref-att.global.linking.html, accessed 10-07-2019.

If a `@property` is defined without a `@resource`, the CDATA value of the element acts as its object. The result is `guichaul:1 rdfs:label 'nom'`. Analogously, this can be extended to include additional properties, such as `skos:definition`, etc.

```
 6  <gloss property="skos:definition">
 7    mot servant \'{a}  d\'{e}signer les
 8    \^{e}tres, les choses qui
 9    appartiennent \'{a}  une m\^{e}me
10    cat\'{e}gorie logique</gloss>
11  </seg>
```

An inherent limitation to these attributes is that every markup element induces at most one triple.[33] This means that if additional triples are to be expressed, designated markup elements need to be created, e.g. TEI `seg` elements without textual content.

An important difference as compared to transformation-based approaches to generate LOD from TEI documents is that the semantic interpretation of structural elements is directly provided along with the original edition data rather than being hidden in a converter script or an opaque mapping. When generating HTML or ePub from TEI, the RDFa attributes can be directly copied,[34] and provided as a hidden machine-readable layer in human-readable web documents. Tittel et al. [58] have provided their sample data under http://www.deaf-page.de/guichaulmTel/edition. html.

Regardless of whether from the web document or from the original TEI/XML, the RDF data can be retrieved and further processed using off-the-self Semantic Web technology, e.g. using an RDFa parsing service such as https://www.w3.org/ 2012/pyRdfa/. Using other web services, e.g. http://sparql.org/, the triples can be retrieved on the fly and directly queried.

As an example, pyRDFa can be configured with default parameters to process a particular HTML file, say,

```
http://www.deaf-page.de/guichaulmTel/edition.html
```

From the Turtle file obtained in this way, one can inspect its download link to get more insight into the coding of the relevant parameters, and retrieve the following URL[35]:

```
https://www.w3.org/2012/pyRdfa/extract?uri=http://www.deaf-page.
    de/guichaulmTel/edition.html&format=turtle
```

---

[33]With additional vocabulary elements, RDFa can induce up to two triples per XML element, one as described above and an `rdf:type` assessment with the `@typeof` attribute.

[34]In a TEI-native approach, they would have to be generated from TEI-specific data structures. As described above, this can be complex, and it needs to be done redundantly for every target format.

[35]URI encoding may apply, with the source URL escaped like http%3A%2F%2Fwww.deaf-page. de%2F....

This URL may now be used locally with SPARQL Update using the LOAD keyword:

```
1   CREATE SILENT GRAPH
2   <http://www.deaf-page.de/guichaulmTel>;
3
4   LOAD <https://www.w3.org/2012/pyRdfa/extract?uri=http%3A%2F%2
        Fwww.deaf-page.de%2FguichaulmTel%2Fedition.html&format=
        turtle>
5   INTO <http://www.deaf-page.de/guichaulmTel>;
```

Such queries do not necessarily require a local triple store, but web services for querying RDF data *without a data base* can be used, e.g. http://sparql.org/sparql. html. As a result, it is possible to query, e.g., for all attestations of a particular *dictionary* lemma:

```
1   FROM <http://www.deaf-page.de/guichaulmTel>
2   SELECT ?attestation ?form ?dictEntry
3   WHERE {
4     ?attestation rdfs:label ?form.
5     ?attestation rdfs:seeAlso ?dictEntry.
6   }
```

Again, this can be expressed in a single URL:

```
http://sparql.org/sparql?query=PREFIX+rdfs%3A+%3Chttp%3A%2F%2Fwww
    .w3.org%2F2000%2F01%2Frdf-schema%23%3E%0D%0ASELECT+%3
    Fattestation+%3Fform+%3FdictEntry%0D%0AWHERE+%7B%0D%0A++%3
    Fattestation+rdfs%3Alabel+%3Fform.%0D%0A++%3Fattestation+rdfs
    %3AseeAlso+%3FdictEntry.%0D%0A%7D%0D%0A&default-graph-uri=
    https%3A%2F%2Fwww.w3.org%2F2012%2FpyRdfa%2Fextract%3Furi%3
    Dhttp%3A%2F%2Fwww.deaf-page.de%2FguichaulmTel%2Fedition.html
    %26format%3Dturtle&output=xml&stylesheet=%2Fxml-to-html.xsl
```

This URL calls a SPARQL webservice to run the query above against the (dynamically generated) result of the pyRDFa web service on the HTML edition by [58]. Again, this URL can be used in yet another web service or it can be called as a SERVICE from another SPARQL query in order to be integrated with other pieces of information.

13.4   Summary and Further Reading

In the field of Digital Humanities, Linked Open Data is an established technique of continuously growing importance. In order provide an overview, we described representative types of LOD resources (prosopographical databases, gazetteers, citation services) and vocabularies (TEI, CIDOC CRM, SKOS, CTS), as well as a number of case studies. Aside from developing community resources and vocabularies, a specific challenge at the intersection of Linguistic Linked Open Data and Digital Humanities is the interoperability and the integration of the dominant formalisms in either field. We gave a brief introduction into the specifications of the Text Encoding Initiative, and described strategies and use cases that have been pursued in order to address different goals regarding the integration of TEI and LOD technologies, i.e.

- To either use Semantic Web technology as a backend formalism to facilitate the processing and linking of multiple TEI documents by means of graph databases
- To assert RDF statements about TEI/XML documents
- To infuse RDF triples into TEI-compliant inline XML
- To develop TEI/XML (and TEI-generated web documents) into a publication form for (L)LOD

This is an area of on-going research, but these goals entail different preferences regarding the technological choices involved:

- The first goal is usually addressed by means of semi-automated mapping or application-specific conversion tools and this has been the dominating approach on the interface between TEI and LOD [16, 59, 60]. In particular, this does not require the integration of TEI and LOD data, as RDF is derived from the TEI. Section 13.3.3 discusses such an approach from a modelling perspective. A minimal requirement is the use of URIs, i.e. TEI pointers, whereas otherwise the TEI model does not need to be changed.
- The second goal can be achieved by using Web Annotation to express JSON-LD metadata about TEI/XML documents and implemented as such in the tool Recogito (Sect. 13.3.2). At the moment, this approach is the only way to publish data in a way that is compliant with both TEI and LOD technology. This approach is, however, restricted to static TEI documents. Conjoint development of a TEI edition and its linking with LOD resources requires inline XML.[36]
- The third goal can be achieved by (ab)using existing vocabulary elements of the TEI to represent full-fledged RDF triples, illustrated above in Sect. 13.3.4. Various such approaches have been developed, but they suffer from semantic ambiguity (e.g. between the prospographical and the RDF interpretation of <relation>, and a lack of clear definitions for these uses within the TEI guidelines.
- Initial steps towards the third goal have been presented in Sect. 13.3.5 and further elaborated in [62]. These build on the extension of TEI in accordance with RDFa, an extension which is a valid TEI customization, but not officially endorsed by the TEI, yet. At the time of writing, this is the only W3C-standardized vocabulary that allows to convey LOD information directly in TEI documents.

These alternatives have been controversially discussed within the TEI since more than a decade. The interested reader may want to follow the status of two issues

---

[36]Earlier implementations of standoff RDF over TEI/XML built on other formalisms [61], but with the standardization of Web Annotation, these are to be considered deprecated.

in the TEI specification on these topics: https://github.com/TEIC/TEI/issues/311 (on the use of <relation> for encoding RDF triples) and https://github.com/TEIC/TEI/issues/1860 (on a possible extension of TEI with RDFa attributes, both accessed 10-07-2019). For a further reading, we refer the interested reader to [63] for a general overview on Digital Humanities, to [64] for a collection of recent opinion papers on different aspects of data modelling in this context and to [65] for the specific case of linked data for libraries, archives and museums.

At the time of writing, the number of projects and initiatives that adopt linked data for the Humanities is on the rise, and the applications and vocabularies are too manifold and too diverse to be described within the scope of a textbook. Besides domain-specific solutions, however, we also see that DH research adopts and builds on resources and technologies developed in NLP or other fields of Linguistic Linked Open Data. This includes, for example, recent uses of Web Annotation, CoNLL-RDF/NIF or Ontolex-lemon.

Because of its unique challenges, DH will continue to maintain community-specific standards, most importantly the TEI, but in the longer perspective, we expect increasing synergies between general LLOD vocabularies and resources and DH-specific approaches. In parts, we already see that in the development of the Ontolex-lemon vocabulary. Independently from its original use case (ontology lexicalization), it has been gaining wide acceptance in lexicography and philology as an interoperable representation formalism for electronic dictionaries (regardless of whether accompanied with an ontology), and at the time of writing, a designated Ontolex-lemon module for lexicography has been developed and released (see Section 4.8).

References

1. R. Busa, *Sancti Thomae Aquinatis hymnorum ritualium varia specimina concordantiarum.* Archivum Philosophicum Aloisianum, vol. II(7) (Fratelli Bocca, Milan, 1951)
2. W.N. Francis, H. Kucera, Brown Corpus manual. Technical Report, Brown University, Providence, Rhode Island, 1964. Revised edition 1979
3. E. Davis, Three applications of edge-punched cards for recording and analyzing field data. Mem. Soc. Am. Archaeol. **19**, 216 (1965). Contributions of the Wetherill Mesa Archeological Project. http://www.jstor.org/stable/25146687
4. W. Aydelotte, Quantification in history. Am. Hist. Rev. **71**(Apr), 803–825 (1966)
5. N.M. Ide, C.M. Sperberg-McQueen, The TEI: history, goals, and future, in *Text Encoding Initiative: Background and Context*, ed. by N. Ide, J. Véronis (Springer Netherlands, Dordrecht, 1995), pp. 5–15. https://doi.org/10.1007/978-94-011-0325-1_2
6. L. Burnard, Report of workshop on text encoding guidelines. Lit. Linguist. Comput. **3**(2), 131 (1988). https://academic.oup.com/dsh/article-abstract/3/2/131/1020443
7. C.F. Goldfarb, Information processing: text and office systems: Standard Generalized Markup Language (SGML). Technical Report, International Organization for Standardization (ISO), Geneva, Switzerland, 1986
8. B. Albritton, M. Appleby, R. Sanderson, J. Stroop, IIIF Presentation API 2.0. Technical Report, IIIF Consortium, 2017. http://iiif.io/api/presentation/2.0/. Accessed 22.10.2017

9. A. Schreurs, C. Blüm, T. Wübbena, *Sandrart.net: Eine Online-Edition eines Textes des 17. Jahrhunderts* (Universitätsbibliothek Johann Christian Senckenberg, Frankfurt, 2011)
10. E. Gruber, S. Heath, A. Meadows, D. Pett, K. Tolle, D. Wigg-Wolf, Semantic Web technologies applied to numismatic collections, in *Computer Applications and Quantitative Methods in Archaeology (CAA)* (2011)
11. M. Baca, M. Gill, Encoding multilingual knowledge systems in the digital age: the Getty vocabularies, in *Proceedings of the 5th North American Symposium on Knowledge Organization (NASKO)* (Los Angeles, 2015), pp. 41–63
12. F. Khan, F. Boschetti, F. Frontini, Using lemon to model lexical semantic shift in diachronic lexical resources, in *Proceedings of the 3rd Workshop on Linked Data in Linguistics (LDL-2014): Multilingual Knowledge Resources and Natural Language Processing* (Reykjavik, Iceland, 2014), pp. 50–54
13. F. Abromeit, C. Chiarcos, C. Fäth, M. Ionov, Linking the Tower of Babel: modelling a massive set of etymological dictionaries as RDF, in *Proceedings of the 5th Workshop on Linked Data in Linguistics (LDL-2016): Managing, Building and Using Linked Language Resources*, ed. by J. McCrae, C. Chiarcos, E. Montiel Ponsoda, T. Declerck, P. Osenova, S. Hellmann (Portoroz, Slovenia, 2016), pp. 11–19
14. S. Bauman, J. Flanders, ODD customizations, in *Proceedings of Extreme Markup Languages 2004 (EML-2004)* (Montreal, 2004)
15. L. Burnard, C. Sperberg-McQueen, TEI Lite: encoding for interchange: an introduction to the TEI. Technical Report, Text Encoding Initiative, 2012. Final revised edition for TEI P5. www.tei-c.org/release/doc/tei-p5-exemplars/html/tei_lite.doc.html
16. Ø. Eide, A. Felicetti, C. Ore, A. D'Andrea, J. Holmen, Encoding cultural heritage information for the Semantic Web. Procedures for data integration through CIDOC-CRM mapping, in *Proceedings of the EPOCH Conference on Open Digital Cultural Heritage Systems*, ed. by D. Arnold, F. Niccolucci, D. Pletinckx, L. Van Gool (EPOCH/3D-COFORM Publication, Congresso Rospigliosi, Rome, 2008), pp. 47–53
17. F. Ciotti, F. Tomasi, Formal ontologies, linked data and TEI semantics. Journal of the Text Encoding Initiative (9) (2016).
18. F. Ciotti, P. Silvio, T. Francesca, V. Fabio, An OWL 2 formal ontology for the text encoding initiative, in *Digital Humanities 2016: Conference Abstracts* (Jagiellonian University/Pedagogical University, Kraków/Poland, 2016), pp. 151–153
19. G. Tummarello, C. Morbidoni, F. Kepler, F. Piazza, P. Puliti, A novel textual encoding paradigm based on Semantic Web tools and semantics, in *Proceedings of the 5th International Conference on Language Resources and Evaluation* (2006), pp. 247–52
20. T. Baker, S. Bechhofer, A. Isaac, A. Miles, G. Schreiber, E. Summers, Key choices in the design of simple knowledge organization system (SKOS). J. Web Semant. **20**, 35 (2013). https://doi.org/10.1016/j.websem.2013.05.001
21. G. Hodge, Systems of knowledge organization for digital libraries: beyond traditional authority files. Technical Report, Council on Library and Information Resources (2000)
22. T. Baker, E. Bermès, K. Coyle, G. Dunsire, A. Isaac, P. Murray, M. Panzer, J. Schneider, R. Singer, E. Summers, W. Waites, J. Young, M. Zeng, Library Linked Data incubator group final report. Technical Report, W3C Incubator Group Report 25 October 2011 (2011)
23. A. Miles, S. Bechhofer, SKOS Simple Knowledge Organization System eXtension for Labels (SKOS-XL). Technical Report, W3C Recommendation (2009)
24. S. Peroni, F. Tomasi, F. Vitali, Reflecting on the Europeana data model, in *Proceedings of the Italian Research Conference on Digital Libraries* (Springer, Berlin, 2012), pp. 228–240
25. H. Manguinhas, V. Charles, A. Isaac, T. Miles, A. Lima, A. NÃï'roulidis, V. Ginouvès, D. Atsidis, M. Hildebrand, M. Brinkerink, S. Gordea, Linking subject labels in cultural heritage metadata to mimo vocabulary using CultuurLINK, in *Proceedings of the 15th European Workshop on Networked Knowledge Organization Systems (NKOS)* (2016), pp. 32–35
26. T. Declerck, P. Lendvai, K. Mörth, G. Budin, T. Váradi, Towards linked language data for digital humanities, in *Linked Data in Linguistics*, ed. by C. Chiarcos, S. Nordhoff, S. Hellmann (Springer, Heidelberg, 2012), pp. 109–116

27. A. Meroño-Peñuela, Digital humanities on the Semantic Web: accessing historical and musical linked data. J. Catalan Intellect. Hist. **1**(11), 144–149 (2017). https://doi.org/10.1515/jocih-2016-0013. https://www.degruyter.com/view/j/jocih
28. C. Binding, Implementing archaeological time periods using CIDOC CRM and SKOS, in *Proceedings of the Extended Semantic Web Conference*. Lecture Notes in Computer Science, vol. 6088 (Springer, Berlin, 2010), pp. 273–287
29. CIDOC, Statement on linked data identifiers for museum objects, in *Proceedings of the Annual CIDOC General Meeting, 2012-06-13, Helsinki* (2012). http://network.icom.museum/cidoc/resources/cidoc-standards-guidelines/. http://network.icom.museum/fileadmin/user_upload/minisites/cidoc/PDF/StatementOnLinkedDataIdentifiersForMuseumObjects.pdf
30. ISO, ISO 21127:2006 Information and documentation – a reference ontology for the interchange of cultural heritage information. Technical Report, International Standards Organization, 2006. https://www.iso.org/standard/34424.html
31. ISO, ISO 21127:2014 Information and documentation – a reference ontology for the interchange of cultural heritage information. Technical Report, International Standards Organization, 2014. Second edition. https://www.iso.org/standard/57832.html
32. N. Crofts, M. Doerr, T. Gill, S. Stead, M. Stiff, Definition of the CIDOC conceptual reference model, version 5.0.4. Technical Report, ICOM/CIDOC CRM Special Interest Group, 2011. Produced by the ICOM/CIDOC Documentation Standards Group, continued by the CIDOC CRM Special Interest Group. http://new.cidoc-crm.org/get-last-official-release
33. G. Goerz, M. Oischinger, B. Schiemann, An implementation of the CIDOC conceptual reference model (4.2.4) in OWL-DL, in *Proceedings of the Annual Conference of CIDOC-The Digital Curation of Cultural Heritage* (2008)
34. M. Scholz, G. Goerz, WissKI: a virtual research environment for cultural heritage, in *Proceedings of the 20th European Conference on Artificial Intelligence* (IOS Press, Amsterdam, 2012), pp. 1017–1018
35. C. Blackwell, N. Smith, The homer multitext: infrastructure and applications, in *Digital Humanities 2008. Proceedings of the 20th Joint International Conference of the Association for Literary and Linguistic Computing, and the Association for Computers and the Humanities and the 1st Joint International Conference of the Association for Literary and Linguistic Computing, the Association for Computers and the Humanities, and the Society for Digital Humanities Société pour l'étude des médias interactifs* (Oulu, Finland, 2008), pp. 10–11. https://pdfs.semanticscholar.org/fdde/bd4bb4f0e21a803a301361a704572904b0b6.pdf#page=27
36. C. Blackwell, N. Smith, The Canonical text services protocol, version 5.0.rc.2. Technical Report, Center for Hellenic Studies (CHS) Technical Working Group, Harvard University, 2014. http://cite-architecture.github.io/cts_spec/
37. C. Dué, M. Ebbott, A.R. Scaife, W.B. Seales, C. Blackwell, N. Smith, D.C. Porter, R. Baumann, Homer multitext project, in *Digital Humanities 2008. Proceedings of the 20th Joint International Conference of the Association for Literary and Linguistic Computing, and the Association for Computers and the Humanities and the 1st Joint International Conference of the Association for Literary and Linguistic Computing, the Association for Computers and the Humanities, and the Society for Digital Humanities Société pour l'étude des médias interactifs* (Oulu, Finland, 2008), pp. 5–13. https://pdfs.semanticscholar.org/fdde/bd4bb4f0e21a803a301361a704572904b0b6.pdf#page=22
38. D. Smith, G. Weaver, Applying domain knowledge from structured citation formats to text and data mining: examples using the CITE architecture. Technical Report, Dartmouth Computer Science Technical Report TR2009-649, 2009. http://katahdin.cs.dartmouth.edu/reports/TR2009-649.pdf
39. B. Almas, M. Berti, The linked fragment: TEI and the encoding of text re-uses of lost authors, in *TEI Conference 2013* (2013). http://sites.tufts.edu/perseids/files/2013/10/TEI-Meeting-2013.pdf
40. J. Kalvesmaki, Canonical references in electronic texts: rationale and best practices. Digit. Humanit. Q. **8**(2) (2014). http://www.digitalhumanities.org/dhq/vol/8/2/000181/000181.html

41. B. Almas, H. Cayless, T. Clérice, Z. Fletcher, V. Jolivet, P. Liuzzo, E. Morlock, J. Robie, M. Romanello, J. Tauber, J. Witt, Distributed Text Services (DTS). First public working draft. Technical Report, Github (2019). Version of May 23, 2019
42. C. Chiarcos, I. Khait, É. Pagé-Perron, N. Schenk, C. Fäth, J. Steuer, W. Mcgrath, J. Wang, Annotating a low-resource language with LLOD technology: Sumerian morphology and syntax. Information **9**(11), 290 (2018)
43. C. Chiarcos, B. Kosmehl, C. Fäth, M. Sukhareva, Analyzing Middle High German syntax with RDF and SPARQL, in *Proceedings of the 11th International Conference on Language Resources and Evaluation (LREC)*, Miyazaki (2018)
44. C. Chiarcos, K. Donandt, H. Sargsian, M. Ionov, J. Wichers Schreur, Towards LLOD-based language contact studies. A case study in interoperability, in *Proceedings of the 6th Workshop on Linked Data in Linguistics (LDL)*, Miyazaki (May 2018)
45. F. Khan, A. Bellandi, F. Boschetti, M. Monachini, The challenges of converting legacy lexical resources to linked open data using OntoLex-Lemon: the case of the intermediate Lidell-Scott lexicon, in *Proceedings of the LDK Workshops: OntoLex, TIAD and Challenges for Wordnets, Galway, Ireland* (2017), pp. 1–8
46. H. Hockerts, Zertifiziertes biographisches Wissen im Netz. Die "Deutsche Biographie" auf dem Weg zum zentralen historisch-biographischen Informationssystem für den deutschsprachigen Raum. Akademie Aktuell **37**(4), 3–36 (2012)
47. S. Lohmann, P. Heim, T. Stegemann, J. Ziegler, The RelFinder user interface: interactive exploration of relationships between objects of interest, in *Proceedings of the 15th International Conference on Intelligent User Interfaces* (2010), pp. 421–422
48. T. Elliott, S. Gillies, Pleiades: the un-GIS for ancient geography. J. Geogr. Inf. Sci. **22**, 1091 (2008)
49. L. Isaksen, R. Simon, E.T. Barker, P. de Soto Cañamares, Pelagios and the emerging graph of ancient world data, in *Proceedings of the International ACM Conference on Web Science (WebSci)* (ACM, New York, 2014), pp. 197–201
50. R. Simon, E. Barker, L. Isaksen, P. de Soto Cañamares, Linked data annotation without the pointy brackets: introducing Recogito 2. J. Map Geogr. Libr. **13**(1), 111 (2017)
51. F. Diehr, M. Brodhun, S. Gronemeyer, K. Diederichs, C. Prager, E. Wagner, N. Grube, Ein digitaler Zeichenkatalog als Organisationssystem für die noch nicht entzifferte Schrift der Klassischen Maya, in *Proceedings of Wissensorganisation 2017: 15. Tagung der Deutschen Sektion der Internationalen Gesellschaft für Wissensorganisation (ISKO) (WissOrg'17). German Chapter of the ISKO* (Freie Universität Berlin, Berlin, 2018), pp. 37–43. https://doi.org/10.17169/FUDOCS_document_000000028863
52. E. Förstemann, *Commentary on the Maya Manuscripts in the Royal Public Library of Dresden* (The Peabody Museum, Cambridge, 1906)
53. H. Neuroth, F. Lohmeier, K.M. Smith, TextGrid–virtual research environment for the humanities. Int. J. Digit. Curation **6**(2), 222 (2011)
54. J. Thompson, *A Catalog of Maya Hieroglyphs* (University of Oklahoma Press, Norman, 1962)
55. K. Baldinger, *Dictionnaire Étymologique de l'ancien français – DEAF* (Presses de L'Université Laval/Niemeyer/De Gruyter, Québec, Canada/Tübingen/Berlin, Germany, since 1971). Kurt Baldinger (founder), continued by Frankwalt Möhren, published under the direction of Thomas Städtler; electronic version DEAF. https://deaf-server.adw.uni-heidelberg.de. Accessed 24.12.2017
56. S. Tittel, C. Chiarcos, Historical lexicography of old French and linked open data: transforming the resources of the *Dictionnaire Étymologique de l'ancien français* with OntoLex-Lemon, in *Proceedings of the LREC-2018 GLOBALEX Workshop (GLOBALEX-2018)* (Miyazaki, Japan, accepted)
57. S. Tittel, *Die Anathomie in der Grande Chirurgie des Gui de Chauliac: Wort- und sachgeschichtliche Untersuchungen und Edition* (Niemeyer, Tübingen, 2004)
58. S. Tittel, C. Chiarcos, Using RDFa to link text and dictionary data for medieval French, in *Proceedings of the 6th Workshop on Linked Data in Linguistics (LDL): Towards Linguistic Data Science* (European Language Resources Association (ELRA), Paris, 2018)

59. T. Blanke, G. Bodard, M. Bryant, S. Dunn, M. Hedges, M. Jackson, D. Scott, Linked data for humanities research—the SPQR experiment, in *Proceedings of the 6th IEEE International Conference on Digital Ecosystems and Technologies (DEST)* (IEEE, Piscataway, 2012), pp. 1–6
60. J.L. Hardesty, Transitioning from XML to RDF: considerations for an effective move towards linked data and the Semantic Web. Inform. Technol. Libr. **35**(1), 51 (2016)
61. G. Barabucci, A. Di Iorio, S. Peroni, F. Poggi, F. Vitali, Annotations with EARMARK in practice: a fairy tale, in *Proceedings of the 1st International Workshop on Collaborative Annotations in Shared Environment: Metadata, Vocabularies and Techniques in the Digital Humanities* (2013), p. 11
62. P. Ruiz Fabo, H. Bermúdez Sabel, C.I. Martínez Cantón, E. González-Blanco, B. Navarro-Colorado, The diachronic Spanish sonnet corpus (DISCO): TEI and linked open data encoding, data distribution and metrical findings, in *Proceedings of the International Conference on Digital Humanities (DH)* (Ciudad de México, Mexico, 2018), pp. 486–489
63. S. Schreibman, R. Siemens, J. Unsworth (eds.), *A New Companion to Digital Humanities* (Wiley, Chichester, 2016)
64. J. Flanders, F. Jannidis (eds.), *The Shape of Data in Digital Humanities. Modelling Texts and Text-Based Resources*. Digital Research in the Arts and the Humanities (Routledge, Abingdon, New York, 2019)
65. S. Van Hooland, R. Verborgh, *Linked Data for Libraries, Archives and Museums: How to Clean, Link and Publish Your Metadata* (Neal-Shuman/Facet, Chicago, 2014)

Chapter 14
Discovery of Language Resources

Abstract Finding appropriate language resources for a particular research purpose
or task is of crucial importance and represents a significant challenge at the same
time. Currently, there are a number of distributed data repositories which contain
metadata about many language resources. However, the metadata formats and
metadata content is not harmonized across the different repositories, making it
extremely difficult to provide automatic support for the process of searching for
resources across repositories. In this chapter we describe an approach that supports
the harmonization of metadata from a number of relevant repositories. As a proof-
of-concept of this approach, we describe Linghub, a portal that has been developed
to aggregate metadata from a number of repositories to provide a single point of
entry for searching language resources across repositories. We describe the methods
that have been used in the normalization of the data and report on the accuracy of the
methods. The Linghub portal is publicly available and can be used freely to search
for language resources.

14.1 Introduction

As already mentioned in previous chapters of this book, the amount of linguistic
linked data resources published on the Web has been growing significantly in recent
years. The LLOD cloud described in Chap. 3 clearly conveys this trend. Still, finding
relevant language resources for a particular research project, task or purpose still
represents a significant challenge. The main challenge lies in the fact that the
metadata describing language resources is scattered among a number of repositories,
and effective approaches to federated search over repositories are not available.
Second, the different repositories adopt different metadata standards and thus it is
difficult to harmonize the different metadata records to provide a single index or
single point of access for most of the language resources available. In this chapter
we discuss this challenge and propose a first approach that has been implemented to
collect and harmonize the metadata from different repositories. This has culminated
in the implementation of a portal that employs these methods and provides a single
faceted search interface to search for language resources across repositories. The

© Springer Nature Switzerland AG 2020
P. Cimiano et al., *Linguistic Linked Data*,
https://doi.org/10.1007/978-3-030-30225-2_14

Spanish LMF Apertium Dictionary

Instance of: Resource Info

Description	This is the LMF version of the Apertium Spanish dictionary. Monolingual dictionaries for Spanish, Catalan, Gallego and Euskera have been generated from the Apertium expanded lexicons of the es-ca (for both Spanish and Catalan) es-gl (for Galician) and eu-es (for Basque). Apertium is a free/open-source machine translation platform, initially aimed at related-language pairs but recently expanded to deal with more divergent language pairs (such as English-Catalan). The platform provides: a language-independent machine translation engine; tools to manage the linguistic data necessary to build a machine translation system for a given language pair and linguistic data for a growing number of language pairs.
Language	es
Language	Spanish
Rights	GPL
See Also	http://metashare.elda.org/repository/browse/c19c566292c211e28763000c291ecfc80a823eb7acd74cda8594e986e44407eb/

Fig. 14.1 One resource in the Linghub repository

portal, Linghub [1], is freely available at http://Linghub.org, and in this chapter we will briefly describe how the resource was created and how it can be used to find language resources across repositories.

The goal of Linghub is to collect metadata about linguistic resources from different repositories and to provide a single access point to find relevant linguistic resources. Linghub aims to integrate all these data from different sources by means of linked data and thus to create a portal in which all information about language resources can be included and queried using a common interface. The goal of Linghub is thus to enable wider discovery of language resources for researchers in NLP, computational linguistics and linguistics. Figure 14.1 shows an example record from the Linghub repository.

Currently, two approaches to metadata collection for language resources can be distinguished. Firstly, one can distinguish a *curatorial approach* to metadata collection in which a repository of language resource metadata is maintained by a dedicated organization such as META-SHARE or CLARIN project's Virtual Language Observatory (VLO). This approach is characterized by high-quality metadata that is manually entered and edited by experts, at the expense of coverage. A *collaborative approach*, on the other hand, allows anyone to publish language resource metadata. Examples of this are the LRE Map or Datahub. A process for controlling the quality of metadata entered is typically lacking for such collaborative repositories, leading to less qualitative metadata and inhomogeneous metadata resulting from free-text fields, user-provided tags and the lack of controlled vocabularies.

Given the nature of this difference, Linghub has been developed with the goal of overcoming these problems and providing effective harmonization support for metadata records from different repositories. As master data model, Linghub builds on DCAT, as described in Chap. 7. In addition, the RDF version of the META-SHARE model was used to provide for metadata properties that are specific to language data and linguistic research.

In the following section we describe the different repositories from which metadata is harvested by Linghub.

14.2   Data Collection

In order to realize the goal of providing comprehensive metadata about a large number of language resources, it is necessary to collect metadata from a wide range of sources. In particular, four main source repositories were selected, primarily because these resources have been released under an open license. These repositories are:

META-SHARE: META-SHARE is a resource and portal created and maintained by the META-NET project. The portal and data are distributed among a number of sites. The portal provides detailed descriptions of language resources that have been primarily constructed by hand.

CLARIN VLO: The Virtual Language Observatory (VLO) by the CLARIN project represents a collection of resources drawn from a wide variety of institutes participating in the CLARIN project. In general, the data has been manually curated by the individual contributors and only limited integration has been made between the resources. Thus, the metadata descriptions differ in detail and size.

Linked Open Data Cloud/Datahub.io: This portal builds on the CKAN portal software and is primarily used to track open and linked data. As most of the data is not of relevance to language resources, the data was filtered to only consider datasets that actually represent language resources.

LRE Map: The LRE Map has been populated by authors submitting research papers to NLP conferences such as LREC. They could describe and upload datasets used in their papers. Unfortunately, only the data for the 2014 edition of LREC is available under an open license, with the result that only the latter is imported into Linghub.

In addition, there are a number of other sources that that have been considered and imported, but not released as part of Linghub due to licensing restrictions:

LRE Map: Data for several other conferences than LREC 2014 exists in the LRE Map and has been downloaded. As this data is not appropriately licensed, it cannot be released as part of Linghub.

OLAC: The Open Language Archives Community collects a large amount of data, but clearly states that its own data is not 'open'.[1] Fortunately most of the data is also available from CLARIN and other sources.

ELRA/LDA: Data from the catalogue of resources provided by the European Language Resource Association (ELRA) and the Linguistic Data Consortium (LDC) was also imported but not released.

---

[1]From http://www.language-archives.org/documents/faq.html 'Open does not mean that users are free to do whatever they like with the metadata, nor does it mean that the described language resources are openly available'.

Table 14.1 The sizes of the resources in terms of number of metadata records and total data size

Source	Records	Triples	Triples per record
META-SHARE	2442	464,572	190.2
CLARIN	144,570	3,381,736	23.4
Datahub.io	218	10,739	49.3
LRE Map (LREC 2014)	682	10,650	15.6
LRE Map (non-open)	5030	68,926	13.7
OLAC	217,765	2,613,183	12.0
ELRA catalogue	1066	22,580	21.2
LDC catalogue	714	N/a	N/a

In the following sections we describe the format of the resources and the difficulty in mapping them uniformly to the DCAT model. The number of resources per repository is given in Table 14.1. In the following, we provide some more details about the format and extraction procedure that was applied for each resource.

14.2.1 META-SHARE

The META-SHARE repository focuses on curating metadata for multilingual language resources. The metadata is provided primarily in a format described by Gavrilidou et al. [2], which is an XML format that comprises over 150 elements and thus has a significant complexity. A custom invertible framework called LIXR (pronounced 'elixir')[2] [3] was developed, which allows XML data to be easily mapped from META-SHARE to RDF after specifying some transformation rules manually. As many of the elements used in the META-SHARE schema are proprietary, an OWL ontology was developed in cooperation with the META-SHARE project to enhance reuse of these concepts across repositories and thus to enhance interoperability of the META-SHARE data (see [4]). This ontology is used in Linghub.

14.2.2 CLARIN

Similarly to META-SHARE, CLARIN is a large infrastructure that collects metadata from several existing archives and combines them into a single repository called the 'Virtual Language Observatory' [5, VLO]. In this catalogue, the required data can be searched through a search bar in a facetted manner by applying filters. If available, there is a direct download functionality for the data. Although a large

---

[2]http://github.com/liderproject/lixr.

Table 14.2 The relative number of resources in each of the schemas used by CLARIN

Component root tag	Institutes	Frequency
Song	1 (MI)	155,403
Session	1 (MPI)	128,673
OLAC-DcmiTerms	39	95,370
MODS	1 (Utrecht)	64,632
DcmiTerms	2 (BeG,HI)	46,160
SongScan	1 (MI)	28,448
Media-session-profile	1 (Munich)	22,405
SourceScan	1 (MI)	21,256
Source	1 (MI)	16,519
teiHeader	2 (BBAW, Copenhagen)	15,998

number of high-quality linguistic resources are provided and accessible with less effort, it should be noted that the CLARIN VLO does not contain a significant amount of data in linked data formats.

The CLARIN VLO is also released in an XML format and is based on the CMDI metadata infrastructure as defined by Broeder et al. [6]. Within CLARIN VLO there are a number of schemas used that are specific to the data provider. Table 14.2 indicates the number of resources that comply with the ten most frequent schemas. We implemented harvesting and extraction scripts for these ten most frequent schemas.

14.2.3   LRE Map

The LRE Map is an initiative to gather existing and new language resources via the Language Resources and Evaluation Conference (LREC), which is organized biennially by ELRA. Therefore, this language data repository is known to everybody who is familiar with ELRA or belongs to the language technology community. The language resources of LRE Map are the result of the LREC conference survey that asks participants to document their resources. The LRE Map is described by Calzolari et al. [7] and is available partly as RDF. As already mentioned, the data from LREC-2014 is available under an open license. Unfortunately, the integration was not trivial as some of the URI schemes did not resolve and had to be corrected (see [8]).

14.2.4   Linked Open Data Cloud/Datahub.io

Datahub is a platform developed by the Open Knowledge Foundation that enables users to upload, group and search data. Linguistic data could be found by directly searching for a certain dataset or by using the various tags the data providers assign to their data. Given that no regulations on the tagging of linguistic data were offered, some effort has to be invested in order to discover all linguistic datasets from Datahub. Recent changes to the business model of Datahub have caused an abandonment of the use of Datahub in the community, which can be considered a legacy repository. Instead, the Linked Open Data Cloud, which was previously based on the metadata found in Datahub, has stopped using Datahub since the mid-2018, and maintains its own metadata as a distinct repository. This is available and Linghub pulls in the data directly from this source.

14.2.5   Other Repositories

In addition, three other data sources were examined that cannot be included in the public release of Linghub due to the licensing issues. OLAC, for instance, follows CLARIN in using an XML format. Further, there are the catalogues of ELRA and LDC. Custom converters for transforming the XML schema of the ELRA data to RDF were developed. The LDC data was directly crawled from the website.

14.2.5.1   European Language Resources Association (ELRA)

The European Language Resources Association devotes their work to collecting, distributing, standardizing and validating language data for the specific purpose of language engineering. The resources of ELRA are divided into spoken, written and terminological resources, which are mainly corpora and lexicons. Thereby, the main objective is 'to promote language resources for the Human Language Technology (HLT) sector, and to evaluate language engineering technologies'. Because of the many services ELRA offers next to the resource catalogue, it is known to a wide audience. However, for those who do not know of its existence, it is not easy to find on the Web. Even though most of the resources ELRA provides are also interesting to users beyond the HLT sector, the data cannot be used without payment and the data is not in linked data formats.

14.2.5.2   Linguistic Data Consortium (LDC)

Looking for linguistic data on the Web leads quickly to the LDC catalogue of language resources. Being the oldest repository of that kind, it holds a large amount of linguistic datasets of various languages and of high quality. However, it has to be stressed that numerous licenses prohibit the open reuse of the data. What is more, the resources are only available grounded on a LDC membership that is subject to charge. Linked data formats are not promoted by the LDC, which leaves the resources inaccessible for open research reuse and non-interoperable within the growing linked data landscape.

14.2.6 State of Play with Respect to Finding Language Resources on the Web

An overview of the existing repositories shows that more and more language resources are described as part of Web repositories. When searching for linguistic datasets and language resources on the Web, however, information is not easy to find as the metadata is not indexed by search engines. Other repositories expose their metadata so that it can be found on the Web, but the content itself is under prohibitive licenses or requires payment of membership fees to access the data. In our experience, with respect to the provision of access to data, most of the available repositories lack at least one of the following features:

- Provision of domain specific linguistic/language data, which is open for re-use and free of charge
- Search functionality that facilitates finding specific resources
- Possibility to narrow search to open data and to resources in linked data formats as well as to directly download the data.

To conclude, none of the available repositories provides a comprehensive and straightforward approach to search and download the data.

14.3 Modelling

The DCAT vocabulary [9] was used as the basis of the modelling for Linghub, as described in Chap. 7. The DCAT model is centred around the concept of a *dataset*, which has obvious equivalence to many of the elements in the resources. In addition, DCAT models distributions, i.e. downloads and catalogues. Some distinctions made in DCAT, most notably the distinction between access URLs and download URLs, that give the link to the dataset's home page and the direct link to the data, respectively, were not consistently applied in any of the sources considered. This represents a major stumbling block for data access as it does not allow for automatic access of the data by machines. The DCAT model allows for generic descriptions of datasets but does not model the specific characteristics of language resources. Thus, an extension of DCAT based on the META-SHARE model was used, which is called the META-SHARE ontology. This resource is described by McCrae et al. [4] and in Chap. 7, and for the benefit of readers, we briefly recap the model here.

DCAT consists of a *catalogue* composed of *datasets*, with a *catalogue record*, which corresponds to the META-SHARE metadata info element. META-SHARE contains a much richer description of many aspects than DCAT, including contact details, version information, validation and proposed and actual usage of the dataset. These elements, when available, were directly added to the model. In many cases, basic properties in the META-SHARE ontology, such as the language of a resource, were to be found nested under several layers of XML elements. In such cases,

Table 14.3 The distribution
of the ten most used formats
within the analysed sample of
URLs. Note XML is
associated with two MIME
types

Format	Resources	Percentage (%)
HTML	67,419	66.2
RDF/XML	9940	9.8
JPEG image	6599	6.5
XML (application)	5626	5.6
Plain text	4251	4.2
PDF	3641	3.6
XML (text)	3212	3.2
Zip archive	801	0.8
PNG image	207	0.2
gzip Archive	181	0.2

property chain links were added so that they would be more compatible with other resources. For example, the rights statement of a resource could be found only under the headings 'Distribution Info' → 'Licence Info' → 'Licence'. This was reduced to a single property attached to the root data element to comply with DCAT.

META-SHARE further complements DCAT by modelling information that is specific for each type of language resource, where a language resource is a *corpus*, *tool/service*, *language description* or *lexical conceptual resource*. These extra elements include media type (text, audio, video or image) and the encoding of information, formats, classifications, and so forth.

In addition, a number of further minor changes were made, including improving and generalizing names and concepts, grouping similar elements, etc.

14.4   Harmonization

Due to the variety of sources from which metadata were obtained, the metadata records lack a common format and are not aligned from a semantic point of view. Moreover, the quality of description varies greatly across sources. For example, META-SHARE uses ISO 639-3[3] for language codes, but a crowd-sourced resource, such as LRE Map, has a wide variety of representations in free text. In our approach to harmonization, we concentrate on the harmonization/mapping of a set of key data elements and dimensions including availability, licensing information, type of resources and languages covered. For each of these properties, we describe how the data has been normalized to represent it within DCAT (Table 14.3).

---

[3]http://www-01.sil.org/iso639-3/.

14.4.1   Availability

Availability of resources is key to foster reuse. Unfortunately, we realized that in many cases the metadata records contain reference to URLs that do not resolve anymore at the time of writing. In many cases, there is an important distinction that must be made between 'access URLs', which typically resolve to a page containing information and documentation about the resource, and the 'download URL', where the resource can be directly accessed/downloaded. For use cases where software agents can autonomously access resources, the latter type of URL would be necessary. However, unfortunately, at the time of writing, nearly all URLs provided in the metadata records represent 'access URLs'.

We experimentally attempted to resolve 119,920 URLs indicated in the metadata records, finding that about 95% of these resolved successfully (i.e. HTTP Response was 200 OK). We also analysed the content type of the response. Our analysis shows that text formats such as HTML are predominant. We conclude thus that most URLs are actually 'access URLs'. Only a small percentage of the resources, about 14%, are in a data rather than text format. Unexpectedly, a large number of images were also found, which were generally scans of historical documents.

14.4.2   Rights

While accessing the resource itself is one of the main goals of any user of language resources, any responsible user must take into account the license that a resource is released under. Thus, it is a frequent need for users to understand under which license a certain LR is available to check if the resource can be used in the intended way. Each of the different platforms providing access to LRs have different means to select the desired licenses.

- The META-SHARE portal offers faceted browsing functionality where one of the facets is the license declared for the resource. The browsing experience is enhanced by other facets that permit distinguishing resources based on their availability (restricted/unrestricted) or by their restrictions of use (like 'commercial use allowed').
- The CLARIN Virtual Language Observatory[4] also offers faceted browsing, and one of the eight facets is devoted to 'availability'. Many of the resources fall under diffuse categories (such as 'open' or 'free') without referring to the actual licenses. The metadata describing the license is a free text instead of a URI determining the license in use.
- The OLAC Language Resource Catalogue offers text-based search functionality as well as faceted browsing. However, catalogued resources seem to lack this

---

[4]https://vlo.clarin.eu.

information, with only three types of licenses being considered ('CC-BY-ND', 'CC-BY-SA' and 'others'). An additional facet for 'other rights' performs no better due to the opposite reason: there are so many types of 'rights' that it is extremely difficult to find resources following a particular license.

- The LRE Map resource portal[5] permits searching by resource availability. Once a resource is found, the license of a resource is provided by means of a free-text field, which renders machine processing of licensing information difficult.
- Datahub.io permits selecting the license in the faceted browsing they offer. Although nothing prevents dataset creators from declaring their own licenses, they are driven by the user interface to use one of the predetermined license-types. This greatly reduces the license proliferation and makes search for resources with particular license feasible.

The best description of the rights information is given by licenses with a well-defined URI. If this were regularly the case, the *license proliferation* problem would be easily solvable, yet only the META-SHARE portal currently applies this principle.

14.4.3   Usage

The usage of a language resource is an indication of what purpose it was created for. Following the example of META-SHARE a distinction is made between *intended use* and *actual use*, where intended use is the use intended by the creator of the resource and the actual use represents an alternative use of the resource. As the data has very little information on the latter case, the analysis focused primarily on the intended use, which is recorded clearly in two resources: META-SHARE and LRE Map. The taxonomies used in each scheme differ, with META-SHARE defining 83 possible values and LRE Map suggesting 28 values, while actually 3985 values have been used. This is due to the collection method of LRE Map, which has a dropdown list of options; in addition, the user can also enter a custom value.

For the 28 suggested LRE Map values, a manual mapping to the META-SHARE values was performed, and for the rest of the values a mapping algorithm based on using the Snowball stemmer [10] and string inclusion match to detect variants was developed. By manually inspecting a random sample of the automatic mappings for 100 intended use values, we found that 66% represented correct mappings, 16% were empty fields or non-specific terms (e.g. 'various uses') and 16% were overly general (e.g. 'acquisition'). In addition, there was one false negative (due to a typo 'taggin pos' [sic]) and one novel usage that was not in META-SHARE ('semantic system evaluation'). Overall, the sampled evaluation allows to conclude that a level of about 98% accuracy in harmonizing usage information was reached.

---

[5]http://lremap.elra.info/.

Table 14.4 Accuracy of language mappings. Best results are shown in bold font

Resource	Label accuracy (%)	Instance accuracy (%)
SIL dice coefficient	81	99.50
SIL levenshtein	72	99.42
BabelNet dice coefficient	**91**	99.87
BabelNet levenshtein	**89**	99.85
SIL + BabelNet		
Dice coefficient	**91**	99.87
Levenshtein	**89**	99.85

14.4.4 Language

For the case of language codes, we decided to normalize them by mapping them into the ISO 639-3 standard due to its wide adoption and coverage of nearly all human languages. Many of the repositories already used this standard or used the shorter two-letter codes from ISO 639-1 that can be straightforwardly mapped into the ISO 639-3 standard. The challenge lies in mapping string values encoding the language. For this purpose, we relied on the list of language names in the official SIL database[6] as well as from BabelNet [11] to compile a large lexicon of names for languages. We then implemented the mapping by comparing the actual values to the lexicon values using string similarity metrics, i.e. the Dice Coefficient and the Lenvenshtein distance, to map the string to the most similar string and to the corresponding language code.

The accuracy of the harmonization procedure was evaluated by sampling 100 labels and manually mapping them to language codes. Results are reported in terms of total number of labels matched as well as results weighted by frequency of these language labels. The results are given in Table 14.4 for the two different resources and similarity metrics. For both resources, very high accuracy was observed. The labels that were not mapped successfully were mostly labels used very rarely.

When deploying the best-performing approach using a combination of SIL and BabelNet with the Dice Coefficient over all the data harvested by the portal, we noticed a frequent mistake, i.e. the fact that the label 'Greek' was mapped to 'Creek' as there was a label for 'Modern Greek' but not for 'Greek' in our lexicon. A manual mapping rule was implemented to prevent this wrong mapping.

14.4.5 Type

Following the META-SHARE schema, in Linghub we distinguish between four types of resources: 'Corpus', 'Lexical Conceptual Resource', 'Lexical Description'

---

[6]http://www-01.sil.org/iso639-3/download.asp.

Table 14.5 Precision of
matching strategies from a
sample of 100

Duplication	Correct	Unclear	Incorrect
Titles	86	6	8
URLs	95	2	3
Both	99	1	0

and 'Tool/Service'. In order to map values in the data into one of these four categories, we used the Babelfy linking algorithm [12] to identify senses in the values describing the type of resource. On the basis of the output of Babelfy, those senses that correspond to language resources were manually selected, yielding 143 synsets corresponding to types of language resources, including 'Sound', 'Corpus', 'Lexicon', 'Tool' (software), 'Instrumental Music',[7] 'Service', 'Ontology', 'Evaluation', 'Terminology' and 'Translation software'. These senses were manually mapped to the four categories mentioned above.

14.4.6   Duplicate Detection

When harvesting metadata records from different repositories, there is a high likelihood of duplicate entries for the same resource. In order to ensure a consistent experience, however, it is key to merge all the metadata about the same resource. In the following, we distinguish two types of duplicates: *inter-repository duplicates* are those where we have records from different repositories describing the same resource; *intra-repository duplicates* are those resources for which multiple metadata records exist within the same repository. In the case of CLARIN, for instance, it is frequent to see multiple metadata records for the same resource for the different formats in which the resource is available.

As a heuristic, we regard two metadata records as duplicates if they have the same title and the same access URL. In order to evaluate the effectiveness of this matching heuristic, we manually evaluated a sample of 100 matches and decided whether they actually refer to the same resources. The results of this analysis are given in Table 14.5 and the number of duplicates detected in total is given in Table 14.6. These results clearly show that our heuristic is accurate enough to be applied on the data.

The total number of intra-repository duplicates detected is presented in Table 14.7. In the following we discuss the main causes of intra-repository duplicates for each repository:

---

[7]These resources are in fact recordings of singing in under-resourced languages.

Table 14.6 Number of duplicate inter-repository records by type

Resource	Resource	Duplicate titles	Duplicate URLs	Both
CLARIN	CLARIN (other contributing institute)	1202	2884	0
CLARIN	Datahub.io	1	0	0
CLARIN	LRE Map	72	64	0
CLARIN	META-SHARE	1204	1228	28
Datahub.io	LRE Map	59	5	0
Datahub.io	META-SHARE	3	0	0
LRE Map	META-SHARE	91	51	0
All	All	2632	4232	28

Table 14.7 The number of intra-repository duplicate labels and URLs for resources

Resource	Duplicate titles	Duplicate URLs
CLARIN (same contributing institute)	50,589	20
Datahub.io	0	55
META-SHARE	63	967
LRE Map	763	454

META-SHARE: The duplicates found in META-SHARE are due to export errors and could be easily corrected.

CLARIN: In CLARIN, in many cases sequences of resource have multiple metadata records. For example, for the 'Universal Declaration of Human Rights', each language had its own metadata record. We decided to merge all these into one.

Datahub.io: This resource does not allow for duplicate titles, but duplicate URLs are quite common. These duplicate URLs occur as the same backend/SPARQL endpoint is used to host data from different resources.

LRE Map: Duplicates in LRE Map occur due to multiple submissions of the same resource. We merged all these records into one.

14.4.7 Data Completeness and Quality

An important question is what the degree of quality and completeness is for the metadata records in our dataset. To estimate the degree of completeness, we determined for each data element the relative frequency of metadata records that have a value for the given data element. Table 14.8 shows these relative frequencies and reveals significant variation in coverage over the various data elements that can result in unexpected low recall when filtering on facets with low coverage. For instance, 444 Linghub resources containing keywords 'spanish' or 'spain' in their description also carry a corresponding Dublin Core *language* property. On the other hand 493 resources with the aforementioned keywords in the description do

Table 14.8 Portions of
Linghub resources carrying at
least one property value for
the respective required facet

Required facet	Absolute freq	Relative frequency (%)
(None)	688,287	100
Title	331,199	48.12
Description	89,053	12.94
Language	52,392	7.61
Type	62,063	9.02
Rights	36,869	5.36
Creator	244,725	35.56
Subject	72,768	10.57
Contact point	2436	0.35
Access URL	229,020	33.27

not carry a Dublin Core language attribute. Although the mere appearance of the keywords is not conclusively indicative that the resource should be assigned to the corresponding language, the majority of the latter resources appeared to be Spanish or relevant for Spanish when examining a 10% sample.

14.5   Publishing Linghub with Yuzu

In order to make the data collected by Linghub available through an attractive and useful interface, the Yuzu application[8][13] was utilized. This system is intended to support the publishing of data as RDF from source files that can be RDF, but can also be XML, CSV and JSON. Thus, Yuzu keeps the documents in their original formats but supports on-the-fly conversion of data into RDF, thus avoiding the so-called 'RDF tax' [14] found in other databases. These conversions are provided using existing standards, including JSON-LD [15] and CSV-on-the-Web [16, 17].

In order to enable more flexible querying of data using the SPARQL language, while not allowing queries that can easily overload the system, Yuzu employs a query pre-processor that finds the documents (in the case of Linghub that is the resource metadata documents) and creates a mini-dataset on which the query can be executed. By this, the interface becomes more responsive at the expense of not being able to answer queries that do not query for specific data elements/properties.

Proper access to the harmonized data in Linghub requires a human-friendly, usable and functional user interface. Access to the data is provided via the web-hosted data portal (a screen shot is shown in Fig. 14.2)[9] that allows both humans to see the data in the form of HTML pages as well as machines to access that data in the following formats: RDF/XML, Turtle, N-Triple and JSON-LD. Simple templates are used to render the data in HTML so that human users can obtain a consistent

---

[8] Available from http://github.com/jmccrae/yuzu.
[9] http://Linghub.org/.

Spanish LMF Apertium Dictionary

HTML   RDF/XML   N-Triples   Turtle   JSON-LD

Instance of: Resource Info

Description	This is the LMF version of the Apertium Spanish dictionary. Monolingual dictionaries for Spanish, Catalan, Gallego and Euskera have been generated from the Apertium expanded lexicons of the es-ca (for both Spanish and Catalan) es-gl (for Galician) and eu-es (for Basque). Apertium is a free/open-source machine translation platform, initially aimed at related-language pairs but recently expanded to deal with more divergent language pairs (such as English-Catalan). The platform provides: a language-independent machine translation engine; tools to manage the linguistic data necessary to build a machine translation system for a given language pair and linguistic data for a growing number of language pairs.
Language	es
Language	Spanish
Rights	GPL
See Also	http://metashare.elda.org/repository/browse/c19c566292c211e28763000c291ecfc80a823eb7acd74cda8594e986e44407eb/

Fig. 14.2 A screenshot of the Linghub interface

view of the data from all of the repositories included in Linghub. Furthermore, additional mechanisms were provided to support discovery of language resources:

Faceted browsing: Users can choose to slice datasets up by a number of Elements, including language, rights, type, creator, source, contributor and subject. The users can see all relevant datasets and set filters for data elements to view a subset of the data.

Free-text search: This is the most common search method employed on the Web, and it was employed by building a search interface that indexes all the literal values in the data and allows free search over them. In particular, language codes were added in the values of the literals and indexed.

SPARQL search: Finally, SPARQL search was enabled for advanced and API-based access, which improves the ability of clients to find relevant results. For performance reasons, the expressiveness of queries was limited to those that are likely to be easy to compute. The endpoint by default returns results in JSON [18].

14.6   Summary

In this chapter we described the challenges related to the discovery of language resources across repositories. We highlighted, in particular, the difficulties in harmonizing metadata from different repositories as a basis to provide a single point of access to search for relevant language resources across repositories.

We presented an approach to harmonize the metadata and provided a proof-of-concept of this approach via the implementation of Linghub, a portal that collects metadata from a variety of repositories and makes it available and queryable through a single interface. Linghub relies on a number of heuristics to map the values of metadata fields into a harmonized set of values as well as to detect duplicates within and across repositories. We hope that Linghub will become a central point for hosting metadata about language resources as well as a portal for discovering language resources.

References

1. J.P. McCrae, P. Cimiano, Linghub: a linked data based portal supporting the discovery of language resources, in *Proceedings of the 11th International Conference on Semantic Systems* (2015)
2. M. Gavrilidou, P. Labropoulou, E. Desipri, S. Piperidis, H. Papageorgiou, M. Monachini, F. Frontini, T. Declerck, G. Francopoulo, V. Arranz, et al., The META-SHARE metadata schema for the description of language resources, in *Proceedings of the 8th International Conference on Language Resources and Evaluation* (2012), pp. 1090–1097
3. J.P. McCrae, P. Cimiano, LIXR: quick, succinct conversion of XML to RDF, in *Proceedings of the Posters and Demo Track of the International Semantic Web Conference* (2016)
4. J.P. McCrae, P. Labropoulou, J. Gracia, M. Villegas, V. Rodriguez-Doncel, P. Cimiano, One ontology to bind them all: the META-SHARE OWL ontology for the interoperability of linguistic datasets on the web, in *Proceedings of 12th Extended Semantic Web Conference (ESWC) Satellite Events*, vol. 9341 (Springer, Cham, 2015), pp. 271–282
5. D. Van Uytvanck, C. Zinn, D. Broeder, P. Wittenburg, M. Gardelleni, Virtual language observatory: the portal to the language resources and technology universe, in *Proceedings of the 7th Conference on International Language Resources and Evaluation (LREC)* (European Language Resources Association (ELRA), Luxembourg, 2010), pp. 900–903
6. D. Broeder, M. Windhouwer, D. Van Uytvanck, T. Goosen, T. Trippel, CMDI: a component metadata infrastructure, in *Describing LRs with Metadata: Towards Flexibility and Interoperability in the Documentation of LR Workshop Programme* (2012), p. 1
7. N. Calzolari, R. Del Gratta, G. Francopoulo, J. Mariani, F. Rubino, I. Russo, C. Soria, The LRE Map, Harmonising community descriptions of resources, in *Proceedings of the 8th International Conference on Language Resources and Evaluation (LREC)* (2012), pp. 1084–1089
8. R. Del Gratta, G. Pardelli, S. Goggi, The LRE Map disclosed, in *Proceedings of the 9th International Conference on Language Resources and Evaluation (LREC)* (2014), pp. 3534–3541
9. F. Maali, J. Erickson, P. Archer, Data Catalog Vocabulary (DCAT). W3C recommendation (The World Wide Web Consortium, Cambridge, 2014)
10. M.F. Porter, *Snowball: A Language for Stemming Algorithms* (2001), http://snowball.tartarus.org/texts/introduction.html
11. R. Navigli, S.P. Ponzetto, BabelNet: building a very large multilingual semantic network, in *Proceedings of the 48th Annual Meeting of the Association for Computational Linguistics* (2010), pp. 216–225
12. A. Moro, A. Raganato, R. Navigli, Entity linking meets word sense disambiguation: a unified approach. Trans. Assoc. Comput. Linguist. **2**, 231 (2014)
13. J.P. McCrae, Yuzu: publishing any data as linked data, in *Proceedings of the Demo and Posters Track at the International Semantic Web Conference* (2016)
14. P. Boncz, O. Erling, M.D. Pham, Advances in large-scale RDF data management, in *Linked Open Data–Creating Knowledge Out of Interlinked Data* (Springer, Cham, 2014), pp. 21–44
15. M. Sporny, D. Longley, G. Kellogg, M. Lanthaler, N. Lindström, JSON-LD 1.0. W3C recommendation (World Wide Web Consortium, Cambridge, 2014)
16. J. Tennison, CSV on the web: a primer. W3C working group note (World Wide Web Consortium, Cambridge, 2014)

17. J. Tandy, I. Herman, G. Kellogg, Generating RDF from tabular data on the web. W3C recommendation (World Wide Web Consortium, Cambridge, 2015)
18. A. Seaborne, K.G. Clark, L. Feigenbaum, E. Torres, SPARQL 1.1 query results JSON format. W3C recommendation (The World Wide Web Consortium, Cambridge, 2013)

Chapter 15
Conclusion

The Linguistic Linked Data (LLD) paradigm was introduced about 8 years ago by the Open Linguistics Working Group (OWLG). The original mission of this group was to (1) promote the use of open standards in linguistics; (2) act as a central point of reference and provide support for those interested in open linguistic data; (3) develop best practices and use cases concerning the creation, use and distribution of linguistic data; and (4) build and maintain an index of open linguistic data sources. The above-mentioned index has been realized as the Linguistic Linked Open Data (LLOD) cloud that we have mentioned at several places in the book. The LLOD cloud has been steadily growing since 2012 and researchers are increasingly adopting linked data principles and linked data vocabularies when publishing language resources.

This book has provided an overview of the main principles, methods and best practices involved in the application of linked data principles to the modelling and publication of language resources. We have, in particular, discussed modelling principles and presented the most important vocabularies for modelling lexical and lexicographic resources, corpora, linguistic annotations and metadata of language resources. We have proposed best practices for transforming legacy resources into linked data and presented methods to support the linking of resources. We have also described how to apply linked data principles to modelling and representing multilingual wordnets and we have discussed how digital humanities can benefit from linked data.

Publishing data as linguistic linked open data comes at a price. Publishers need to invest in modelling data, finding the appropriate vocabularies and mapping their internal data models to a linked data-based representation. They need to set up an HTTP server that can react to requests for resolving URLs, delivering content for human and machine consumption. They need to invest in linking their resources to other resources. Paying this price comes with an amazing return: an ecosystem of linguistic linked datasets linked to each other and harmonized by using the same vocabularies that allow to query/filter the data for some phenomenon of interest in a straightforward fashion by running a query over all the datasets. Such an ecosystem of linguistic linked data also facilitates the discovery of resources and supports their automatic transformation. All these benefits require normalization at the syntactic and semantic level. Without semantic normalization, none of the above-mentioned benefits is possible. The vocabularies, models and best practices described in this book represent a significant step forward in striving for an ecosystem in which data is semantically interoperable and thus easier to reuse and query across datasets.

We believe that in the data-driven society in which we live, openness and, as a direct consequence, reuse of datasets are key to creating a level playing field in which data is FAIR and can be effectively used by many. The principles described in this book have the potential to represent a game changer in the way we publish and work with data, in particular with language resources.

However, building a linked data-based ecosystem for language resources requires an investment, an investment that we, as a community and society, need to prioritize if we also want to bring about the benefits of a more transparent and simplified access to data. In any case, the techniques are ready.

Appendix A
Selected Prefix Declarations

While not being exhaustive with respect to the namespaces used in this volume, frequently used prefix declarations are summarized in this section. Beyond this, we recommend the service under https://prefix.cc/ for sharing namespace declarations and for resolving unknown or undocumented prefixes, which are sometimes returned by end points or provided in data dumps without the appropriate declaration.

```
1   PREFIX conll:      <http://ufal.mff.cuni.cz/conll2009-st/task-
                       description.html#>
2   PREFIX crm:        <http://www.cidoc-crm.org/cidoc-crm/>
3   PREFIX dbo:        <http://dbpedia.org/ontology/>
4   PREFIX dbpedia:    <http://dbpedia.org/resource/>
5   PREFIX dc:         <http://purl.org/dc/elements/1.1/>
6   PREFIX dct:        <http://purl.org/dc/terms/>
7   PREFIX dcterms:    <http://purl.org/dc/terms/>
8   PREFIX decomp:     <http://www.w3.org/ns/lemon/decomp#>
9   PREFIX ecrm:       <http://erlangen-crm.org/current/>
10  PREFIX gndo:       <http://d-nb.info/standards/elementset/gnd#>
11  PREFIX itsrdf:     <http://www.w3.org/2005/11/its/rdf#>
12  PREFIX lime:       <http://www.w3.org/ns/lemon/lime#>
13  PREFIX ms:         <http://purl.org/net/def/metashare#>
14  PREFIX nerd:       <http://nerd.eurecom.fr/ontology#>
15  PREFIX nif:        <http://persistence.uni-leipzig.org/nlp2rdf/
                       ontologies/nif-core#>
16  PREFIX oa:         <http://www.w3.org/ns/oa#>
17  PREFIX olia:       <http://purl.org/olia/olia.owl#>
18  PREFIX ontolex:    <http://www.w3.org/ns/lemon/ontolex#>
19  PREFIX owl:        <http://www.w3.org/2002/07/owl#>
20  PREFIX powla:      <http://http:/purl.org/powla/powla.owl#>
21  PREFIX rdf:        <http://www.w3.org/1999/02/22-rdf-syntax-ns#>
22  PREFIX rdfs:       <http://www.w3.org/2000/01/rdf-schema#>
23  PREFIX saws:       <http://purl.org/saws/ontology#>
```

© Springer Nature Switzerland AG 2020
P. Cimiano et al., *Linguistic Linked Data*,
https://doi.org/10.1007/978-3-030-30225-2

```
24  PREFIX skos:      <http://www.w3.org/2004/02/skos/core#>
25  PREFIX synsem:    <http://www.w3.org/ns/lemon/synsem#>
26  PREFIX vartrans:  <http://www.w3.org/ns/lemon/vartrans#>
```

Printed in the United States
by Baker & Taylor Publisher Services